GETTYSBURG COLLEGE
LIBRARY

GETTYSBURG, PA

Mikael af Malmborg
NEUTRALITY AND STATE-BUILDING IN SWEDEN

Klaus Gallo
GREAT BRITAIN AND ARGENTINA
From Invasion to Recognition, 1806–26

David Faure and Tao Tao Liu
TOWN AND COUNTRY IN CHINA
Identity and Perception

Peter Mangold
SUCCESS AND FAILURE IN BRITISH FOREIGN POLICY
Evaluating the Record, 1900–2000

Mohamad Tavakoli-Targhi
REFASHIONING IRAN
Orientalism, Occidentalism and Historiography

Louise Haagh
CITIZENSHIP, LABOUR MARKETS AND DEMOCRATIZATION
Chile and the Modern Sequence

Renato Colistete
LABOUR RELATIONS AND INDUSTRIAL PERFORMANCE IN BRAZIL
Greater São Paulo, 1945–60

Peter Lienhardt (*edited by Ahmed Al-Shahi*)
SHAIKHDOMS OF EASTERN ARABIA

John Crabtree and Laurence Whitehead (*editors*)
TOWARDS DEMOCRATIC VIABILITY
The Bolivian Experience

Steve Tsang (*editor*)
JUDICIAL INDEPENDENCE AND THE RULE OF LAW IN HONG KONG

Karen Jochelson
THE COLOUR OF DISEASE
Syphilis and Racism in South Africa, 1880–1950

Julio Crespo MacLennan
SPAIN AND THE PROCESS OF EUROPEAN INTEGRATION, 1957–85

St Antony's Series
Series Standing Order ISBN 0–333–71109–2
(*outside North America only*)

You can receive future titles in this series as they are published by placing a standing order. Please contact your bookseller or, in case of difficulty, write to us at the address below with your name and address, the title of the series and the ISBN quoted above.

Customer Services Department, Macmillan Distribution Ltd, Houndmills, Basingstoke, Hampshire RG21 6XS, England

Social Policy Reform and Market Governance in Latin America

Edited by

Louise Haagh
Department of Politics
University of York

and

Camilla T. Helgø
Oxford Policy Management

palgrave
macmillan

in association with
St Antony's College, Oxford

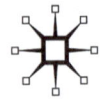

Selection and editorial matter © Louise Haagh and Camilla T. Helgø 2002
Introduction and Chapter 1 © Louise Haagh 2002
Chapter 4 and Conclusion © Camilla T. Helgø 2002
Remaining chapters © Palgrave Macmillan Publishers Ltd 2002

All rights reserved. No reproduction, copy or transmission of this publication may be made without written permission.

No paragraph of this publication may be reproduced, copied or transmitted save with written permission or in accordance with the provisions of the Copyright, Designs and Patents Act 1988, or under the terms of any licence permitting limited copying issued by the Copyright Licensing Agency, 90 Tottenham Court Road, London W1T 4LP.

Any person who does any unauthorised act in relation to this publication may be liable to criminal prosecution and civil claims for damages.

The authors have asserted their rights to be identified as the authors of this work in accordance with the Copyright, Designs and Patents Act 1988.

First published 2002 by
PALGRAVE MACMILLAN
Houndmills, Basingstoke, Hampshire RG21 6XS and
175 Fifth Avenue, New York, N.Y. 10010
Companies and representatives throughout the world

PALGRAVE MACMILLAN is the global academic imprint of the Palgrave Macmillan division of St. Martin's Press, LLC and of Palgrave Macmillan Ltd. Macmillan® is a registered trademark in the United States, United Kingdom and other countries. Palgrave is a registered trademark in the European Union and other countries.

ISBN 0–333–99865–0

This book is printed on paper suitable for recycling and made from fully managed and sustained forest sources.

A catalogue record for this book is available from the British Library.

Library of Congress Cataloging-in-Publication Data
    Social policy reform and market governance in Latin America/edited by Louise Haagh and Camilla T. Helgø.
    p. cm.490 – (St. Antony's series)
    Includes bibliographical references and index.
    ISBN 0–333–99865–0 (cloth)
    1. Latin America – Social policy. 2. Labor market – Latin America. 3. Education and state – Latin America. 4. Public health – Latin America. I. Haagh, Louise, 1967– II. T. Helgø, Camilla, 1973– III. St. Antony's series (Palgrave (Firm))

HN110.5.A8 S629 2002
361.6'1'098–dc21   2002025392

10 9 8 7 6 5 4 3 2 1
11 10 09 08 07 06 05 04 03 02

Printed and bound in Great Britain by
Antony Rowe Ltd, Chippenham and Eastbourne

Contents

Notes on the Contributors	vii
Acknowledgements	ix
List of Tables	x
List of Figures	xii
Glossary	xiii
The Volume in Summary	xix
Introduction: Markets and Rights in the Governance of Welfare – Latin America's Market Reforms *Louise Haagh*	1

Part 1 Labour Market and Social Policies 45

1. Human Resources and Decentralization in Chile 47
   Louise Haagh
2. Gender and Development Policy in Chile: the Aid Programme to Female Heads of Households 77
   Mònica Badia Ibáñez
3. New Labour Market Challenges to Social Policies in Mexico 101
   Maria Cristina Bayon, Bryan Roberts and Georgina Rojas

Part 2 Education and Decentralization Policies 121

4. Market-Oriented Education Reforms and Social Inequalities among the Young Population in Chile 123
   Camilla T. Helgø
5. The Politics of Education Reform in Chile: The *Programa 900 Escuelas* and the MECE-*Básica* 147
   Alan Angell
6. Democratic Decentralization and People's Participation: an Examination of the EDUCO Programme in El Salvador 165
   Suhas D. Parandekar

Part 3 Health Sector Reforms 181

7. Health Insurance Reforms in Latin America: Cream Skimming, Equity and Cost-Containment 183
   Armando Barrientos and Peter Lloyd-Sherlock

vi *Contens*

8 Decentralization, Participation and Inclusion? Reassessing Primary Health Care Delivery in Chile 200
  Jasmine Gideon

Part 4 Social Development Policies **217**

9 The PROGRESA Programme and Social Change in Rural Mexico 219
  Agustín Escobar Latapí
10 Stakeholder Politics in Bolivia: Revisiting Second Generation Reforms 242
  George Gray-Molina

Conclusion: New Approaches to Social Policy Reform in Latin America 261
  Camilla T. Helgø

Index 273

Notes on the Contributors

Alan Angell is University Lecturer in Latin American Politics, Fellow of St Antony's College, University of Oxford. He is the author of many works on aspects of Latin American politics, including studies of the Left, electoral politics in Chile, political decentralization in Chile and Colombia, social policy, and labour unions and political parties in Chile.

Mònica Badia Ibáñez is a PhD candidate at King's College, University of Cambridge and is a member of the Sociological Research Group in the Faculty of Social and Political Sciences. Her research interests include gender and development, the interaction between neo-liberal economic reforms and democratization, and the concept of social citizenship in Latin America. She has written on the family's role as a 'social shock-absorber' in the Southern European Welfare System and on the critical role of the family as a provider of social services.

Armando Barrientos is Lecturer in Public Economics and Development at the Institute for Development Policy and Management at the University of Manchester in the UK. His research focuses on social risk management, and especially the interface between labour markets and social protection programmes. He has written a number of articles and a book on labour markets, pensions, health insurance, and ageing in Latin America and the UK.

Maria Cristina Bayon received her Master's degree at the Latin American Faculty of Social Sciences (FLACSO) in Mexico and is a PhD candidate in Sociology at the University of Texas at Austin. Her research concentrates on economic restructuring and labour markets in Latin America. She has worked on labour union strategies and regional integration in Mexico, the employment structure at the US–Mexican border, and is currently doing research on the contemporary experience of unemployment in Argentina.

Jasmine Gideon is a researcher in the School of Geography, University of Manchester. She has recently completed a doctorate on decentralization and participation in the reform of the Chilean health system. She has also written on the role of NGOs in service provision in Latin America, gender and economic rights, and is looking at economies as gendered structures.

George Gray-Molina is a doctoral candidate in politics at Nuffield College, Oxford. He has written on poverty, decentralization and public policy reform and is currently undertaking research on the politics of pro-poor policies in Latin America. His dissertation focuses on the politics of Popular Participation in Bolivia (1994–99).

Louise Haagh is a former British Academy Post-doctoral Research Fellow at St Antony's College, University of Oxford, where she completed her D.Phil in 1998. She has written comparatively on issues of citizenship, democratization, labour relations and social policy in the contexts of Latin America, East Asia and Europe, and is currently writing a comparative work on the development of occupational citizenship in different national contexts. She is now a permanent lecturer in Politics at the University of York.

Camilla Tveteraas Helgø currently works as an education economist with Oxford Policy Management. She has previously held education positions in UNICEF and the World Bank, where she covered the regions of West and Central Africa and Latin America. She has a PhD from the University of Cambridge and has written on the Chilean education system, education politics in Latin America and inequality of education theory.

Agustín Escobar Latapí is the current director of CIESAS Occidente in Gnadalajara, Mexico. He works mainly on social policy, employment and Mexico–US migration. His work on social policy has dealt mainly with PROGRESA (now called Opportunidades). He also participates in the design and implementation of qualitative evaluations of other social programmes.

Peter Lloyd-Sherlock is Lecturer in Social Development at the School of Development Studies, University of East Anglia. His main research interests are social policy and equity, with special interests in population ageing and Latin America.

Suhas D. Parandekar has a PhD in Economics from Tulane University, New Orleans, USA. His doctoral research dealt with the role of school quality in household educational decisions in developing countries, using case studies from Honduras and Indonesia. Since 1997, Dr Parandekar has been working in the Human Development Division for the Latin American and Caribbean Region of the World Bank. His research interests include decentralization policies, improvement of efficiency and equity in public educational expenditures, and the relation between education and income inequality.

Bryan Roberts is C.B. Smith Sr Centennial Chair in US–Mexico Relations and Professor of Sociology at the University of Texas at Austin. He has written extensively on urbanization and development in Latin America, focusing on labour markets, including the informal economy, and migration. He is currently working on comparative social policy in the Southern Cone, Brazil and Mexico.

Georgina Rojas is a PhD in Sociology candidate at the University of Texas at Austin. She works on the topics of local labour structures and regional inequality in Mexico, industrial flexibility and the quality of employment as well as female labour participation in Mexico.

Acknowledgements

We, the editors, wish to extend a very special thanks to Alan Angell, who, despite his limited time, participated with enthusiasm from an early stage in this project, read several chapters, and provided constant encouragement and support. Anyone who knows Alan will immediately recognize the selflessness and integrity with which he responds to requests from colleagues, students, would-be students, or anyone remotely connected who approaches him for guidance, well aware of his patience and wisdom.

We also wish to extend a special thanks to all the contributors for their commitment to this project; and to Sally Daniell who was an enormous help through the editorial stages.

List of Tables

1.1	Percentage distribution of participants and spending on different SENCE Programmes (selected years)	50
1.2	Percentage distribution of participation of occupational categories through the tax break scheme (selected years)	58
1.3	Union survey: formalization correlated with precarious flexibility	64
1.4	Union survey: labour turnover (#) correlated with level of formalization	65
1.5	Work-force training correlated with indicators of workers' representation	66
1.6	Age of union crossed with labour turnover and training #	67
1.7(a)	Logistic regression to explain high levels of work-force training	68
1.7(b)	Parsimonious model	69
1.7(c)	Significance of the reductions of the original model when progressively controlling for the least significant factors	69
2.1	Distribution of female headed households by activity and range of ages	82
2.2	Average work income by gender of the head of household	83
3.1	Temporary workers by sex and region, 1994–99	107
3.2	Part-time workers by region and sex	108
3.3	Intermittence in the labour force (entries and exits) by sex and region during one year of observation	108
3.4	Economically active female population by household status and region, Mexico, 1987 and 1999	112
4.1	Impact of type of secondary school on generalized inequalities	128
4.2	Impact of type of secondary school on generalized inequalities – controlling for socio-economic background and school resources	129
4.3	The decentralization effect on municipal schools	131
4.4	Academic ranking and monthly fees	136
6.1	Comparison of school directors	169
6.2	Comparison of school infrastructure	170
6.3	Comparison of didactic materials	171
6.4	Comparison of teacher professional development	173
6.5	Comparison of teaching practices	173
6.6	Comparison of absenteeism and repetition	174

6.7	Educational production function (OLS) (dependent variable: language score)	177
7.1	Key features of health care reforms in Chile, Argentina and Colombia	185
8.1	Groups selected for 'Health with the People' programme, May 1995	206
8.2	Potential users and registered users in El Bosque municipal health services	209
10.1	Capitalization programme 1993–97	246

List of Figures

0.1	The decentred development perspective in context	8
0.2	Welfare process in the neo-liberal vision of policy efficiency (education)	15
0.3	Welfare processes in different visions of policy efficiency	15
0.4	Welfare policy cycles	16
3.1	Age-specific rates of female participation in the labour force by region, 1987	111
3.2	Age-specific rates of female participation in the labour force by region, 1999	112
4.1	The 'waste-basket' school	138
6.1	Language test score	176
6.2	Mathematics test score	176

Glossary

ACE	*Asociaciones Comunales para la Educación* (Community Associations for Education)
Administradoras del Régimen Subsidiado	Subsidized Regime Plan Manager
ADN	*Accion Democratica Nacionalista* (National Democratic Action)
AFP	*Administrador de Fondos de Pensiones* (Private Pension Funds)
Aguinaldo	Extra month's salary paid at Christmas to workers on social security
Amistad	Friendship
ASIMET	*Asociación de Industriales Metalúrgicos* (Metallurgical Employers' Association)
ASP	*Asamblea Soberana del Pueblo* (Sovereign People's Assembly)
Ayllu	Bolivian highland indigenous organization
BOLIVIDA	*Bono Vida* (Life Bonus)
BONOSOL	*Bono Solidario* (Solidarity Bonus)
CAJANAL	*Caja Nacional de Previsión Social* (National Social Insurance Fund)
Cajas de Compensación Familiar	Family Compensation Fund
Campesino	Peasant
Canton	Lowest level territorial and administrative unit in Bolivia
CASEN	*Encuesta de Caraterización Socio-económica Nacional* (National Socio-economic Survey)
Centro de salud familiar	Family Health Centre
CINTERFOR	*El Centro Interamericano de Investigación y Documentación sobre Formación Profesional* (Interamerican Centre for Documentation and Research on Professional Training)
Colegio de Profesores	Teachers' Union
Comité Paritario	Health and Safety Committee
CONADI	*Comisión Nacional para la Polación Indigena*
CONAPO	National Population Council

xiv Glossary

Concertación	Governing alliance in Chile
CONDEPA	*Conciencia de Patria* (Conscience of the Fatherland)
Conocimientos	Skills/knowledge
Consejode de Diálogo Social	Council for Social Dialogue
CONSTRAMET	*Confederación de Sindicatos de Trabajadores Metalúrgicos y Metalmecánicos* (Metalmechanic and Metallurgical Workers' Confederation)
Consultorio	Health Centre
COPLAMAR	*Consejo de Planeación para Areas y Regiones Marginadas* (Planning Council for Marginal Areas and Regions)
Cotización	Payroll deduction for health insurance
CPC	*Confederación de la Producción y el Comercio* (Confederation of Production and Commerce)
CSUTB	*Confederacion Sindical Unica de Trabajadores Campesinos de Bolivia* (Confederation of Sindicalized Peasant Workers of Bolivia)
CUT	*Central Unitaria de Trabajadores* (Unitary Workers' Central)
Departamento	Highest level territorial and administrative unit in Bolivia
DIF	*Instituto Nacional del Desarrollo Integral de la Familia* (government agency providing assistance mainly to women and children)
Dirección del Trabajo	The National Labour Inspectorate
EAP	Economically active population
EDUCO	*Educación con Participación de la Comunidad* (Education with the Participation of the Community)
El Enfoque familiar en salud	Family health focus
ENCASEH	*Encuesta sobre las Características Socioeconómicas de los Hogares* (Survey of Socioeconomic Characteristics of Households)
ENDE	*Empresa Nacional de Electificacion* (National Electrification Enterprise)
ENEU	*Encuesta Nacional de Empleo Urbano* (Mexican National Urban Employment Survey)
ENFE	*Empresa Nacional de Ferrocarriles* (National Railways Enterprise)
ENTEL	*Empresa Nacional de Telecomunicaciones* (National Telecommunications Enterprise)
Estatuto Docente	Teachers' Statute

ENCLA	*Encuesta Laboral* (Labour Survey)
EPS	*Entidades de Promoción de Salud* (Health Promotion Enterprises)
FAPEM	*Facturación por Atención Prestada en Establecimientos Municipales* (Reimbursement for service provided in municipal establishments)
FCC	*Fondo Comun de Capitalizacion* (Common Capitalization Fund)
FCI	*Fondo Individual de Capitalizacion* (Individual Capitalization Fund)
FCM	*Fondo Común Municipal* (Shared Municipal Fund)
FHH	*Mujeres jefgas de Hogar* (Female Heads of Household)
Folkeskole	People's school (Denmark)
FONADIS	*Comisión Nacional para los Descapacitados* (National Fund for the Disabled)
FONASA	*Fondo Nacional de Salud* (National Health Fund)
Fondo de Solidaridad y Garantia	Solidarity and Guarantee Fund
Fondo Solidario de Redistribución	Solidarity and Redistribution Fund
Foro del Desarrollo Productivo	Forum for Productive Development
HIPC	Highly indebted poor country
IADB	Inter-American Development Bank
IC	Investment coordination
ICSS	*Instituto Colombiano de Seguros Sociales* (Colombian Social Insurance Institute)
ILO	International Labour Organization
IMSS	*Instituto Mexicano del Seguro Social* (Mexican Social Security Institute)
INACAP	*Instituto Profesional y Centro de Formación Técnica – ex Instituto Nacional de Capacitación Profesional* (Institute for Professional Training and Centre for Technical Education 1976 – ex National Institute of Professional Training 1966–76)
INE	*Instituto Nacional de Estadísticas* (National Institute of Statistics)
INEGI	*Instituto Nacional de Estadísticas, Geografia e Informatica* (National Institute of Statistics, Geography and Informatics)

xvi *Glossary*

INFONAVIT	*Instituto del Fondo Nacional para la Vivienda de los Trabajadores* (government agency providing households for formal workers)
Information	Danish daily newspaper
INJ	*Instituto Nacional de la Juventud* (National Institute of the Youth)
INP	*Instituto Nacional de Prevision* (National Institute of Social Security)
ISAPREs	*Institutos de Salud Previsional* (Health Insurance Institutes)
ISI	Import Substitution Industrialization
ISSSTE	*Instituto de Seguridad y Servicios de los Trabajadores del Estado* (Institute of Security and Social Services for State Employees)
IU	*Izquierda Unida* (United Left)
LAB	*Lloyd Aereo Boliviano* (Bolivian Airways)
Ley Federal del Trabajo	Federal Labour Law of Mexico
maquiladora	In-Bond manufacturing plant in Mexico, usually foreign owned, with licence to import inputs and export products free of custom tariffs
MBL	*Movimento Bolivia Libre* (Free Bolivia Movement)
MECE	MECE-*Básica – Programma de Mejoramiento de la Calidad y Equidad de la Educacion Básica* (Programme for improving the quality and equity of primary education)
MHH	*Jefes de Hogar* (Male Heads of Household)
MIDEPLAN	*Ministerio de Planificación Social* (Ministry of Planning and Development)
MINSAL	*Ministerio de Salud* (Ministry of Health)
MIR	*Movimento de la Izquierda Revolucionaria* (Revolutionary Left Movement)
MIT	Massachusetts Institute of Technology
MNR	*Movimento Nacionalista Revolucionario* (National Revolutionary Movement)
MOE	Ministry of Education (El Salvador)
monitores	Spanish term for persons who perform monitoring functions
Mutuales	Mutual Health Insurance Plans
NAFTA	North American Free Trade Agreement
NFR	*Bueva Fuerza Republicana* (New Republican Force)
NGO	non-government organization
oficinas de colocación	employment relocation offices
OMM	*Oficinas Municipales de la Mujar* (Municipal Women's Bureaux)
OS	*Obras Sociales* (Social Funds)

Glossary xvii

OTB	Territorial base organization (Bolivia)
OTE	*Organismo Técnico de Ejecución* (institutions that offer professional training and bid for public funds)
OTIR	*Organismo Técnico Intermedio* (association of firms formed for the purposes of pooling resources for training)
P900	*Programa de las 900 Esculas* (public programme to improve primary education in Chile)
PAA	*Prueba de Aptitud Académica* (Academic Aptitude Test)
PADEM	*Plan Annual de Desarollo Educativo Municipal* (Annual Municipal Plan of Educational Development)
PAMI	*Programa de Atención Médica Integral* (Integrated Health Care Programme)
Plan de Todos	'The Plan for Everyone', MNR 1993 Campaign Plan
PME	*Proyectos de Mejoramiento Educativo* (Projects of Educational Improvement)
PMJH	*Programa para Mujeres Jefas de Hogar* (Aid Programme to Female Heads of Household)
PNSP	*Plan Nacional de Superación de la Probeza* (National Plan for Alleviating Poverty)
Polla Chilena	Chilean national lottery
POS	*Plan Obligatorio de Salud* (Colombian Basic Health Care Plan)
Pre-pagas	Pre-payment Health Insurance Plans
PRI	*Partido Revolucionario Institucional* (Institutional Revolutionary Party, which has been the governing party in Mexico since its inception, under another name, shortly after the Mexican Revolution)
PROCAMPO	Forms of credit for poor and rural producers
Programa Minimo Obligatorio de Atención Médica	Basic Health Care Plan (Argentina)
PROGRESA	Mexican anti-poverty programme
PRONASOL	*Programa Nacional de Solidaridad* (National Solidarity Programme, an *anti*-poverty programme begun under the presidency of Carlos Salinas de Gortari (1988–94) that targeted poor communities for aid in community development programmes)
Provincia	Third lowest territorial unit in Bolivia, between *seccion* and *departamento*
Seccion de provincia	Second lowest territorial unit, between *canton* and *provincia*
PROTRAC	*Programa de Protección al Trabajador Cesante* (Programme for the Protection of the Unemployed Worker)

xviii *Glossary*

Respeto	Respect
SAPU	Emergency Primary Health Care Unit
SEDESOL	*Secretaría de Desarrollo Social* (Secretariat of Social Development)
SENCE	*Servício Nacional de Capacitación y Empleo* (National Training and Employment Services)
SERCOTEC	*Servicio de Cooperación Técnica* (Technical Cooperation Services – Economy Ministry of Chile)
SERNAM	*Servico Nacional de la Mujer* (National Women's Bureau)
Serivcio Nacional de Salud	National Health Service (Chile)
Sistema de Seguridad Social en Salud	Social Health Insurance System (Colombia)
SIMCE	*Sistema Nacional de la Medición de la Calidad Educativa* (National Measurement System for the Quality of Education)
SNPP	*Secretaria Nacional de Participacion Popular* (National Secretariat of Popular Participation)
Socialforskningsinstitutet	Danish social policy research institute
SOFOFA	*Sociedad de Fomento Fabril* (Industrialists' Association)
SSA	Health Ministry (Mexico)
subvención	education voucher
Superintendencia de ISAPREs	Superintendence of ISAPREs
Superintendencia de Servicios de Salud	Superintendence of Health Services
Superintendencia Nacional de Salud	National Health Superintendence
TBS	Tax Break Scheme
TC	Training Corporation
TD	Task Diversity
Temporeros	Seasonal workers
Tenta	Bolivian lowland indigenous organization
UCS	*Union Civica Solidaridad* (Civic Solidarity Union)
UPC	*Unidad de Pago por Capitación* (Capitation Payment Unit)
YPFB	*Yacimientos Petroliferos Fincales Bolivianos* (Bolivian Fiscal Petroleum Resources)
YTS	*Programa de Jovenes* (Youth Training Scheme)

The Volume in Summary
Louise Haagh

The study of political dimensions in the challenge of welfare reform is only an incipient endeavour in academic inquiry. The chapters in the present collection approach this subject from different angles, using case-study analysis to shed light on the variegated nature of the challenge of reforming states and governing markets in welfare provision. Latin America is a good place to start because the continent has seen the richest and most longstanding experiment in recent market reforms. Most evaluations of the market reforms however have been salutary or based on analysis of individual welfare domains (Introduction). In an effort to begin to construct a more integrated approach to the study of market reforms in welfare, the editors organized a panel at the Annual Conference of the Society for Latin American Studies in 1999, held in Cambridge, to discuss the institutional issues that arise from detailed case studies in different areas of welfare reform. This book contains nine of the 15 papers presented, in addition to a chapter by George Gray-Molina, covering the areas of poverty alleviation and social development, the labour market, training, education, and health, and including case studies from Chile, Mexico, Bolivia, Argentina, Colombia and El Salvador.

Bringing these diverse cases together afforded the editors an opportunity to address central issues of welfare governance, and particularly to break down assumptions that have received too cursory a welcome in the debate, for instance, concerning notions of the relationship of equity to efficiency, and of choice to freedom and, in turn, their conceptual and institutional implications for governance, for instance, the form of welfare decentralization and community participation. The Introduction to the volume sets these in the context of wider debates about economic governance and distributive justice. The body of the book is then divided by policy area into four parts, respectively, the labour market, education, health, and poverty alleviation and social development. The Conclusion to the volume pulls these areas together. The division into policy area allows for greater in-depth analysis and empirical investigation of the issues discussed, and therefore we feel is an essential stepping-stone for further study of the ways problems in social policy are linked across fields. In fact, many of the chapters in the volume point to the problems of institutional coordination between policy areas, which recent deregulatory policies have failed to resolve and, in some ways, have aggravated further. Each section typically contains two kinds of chapters. The first looks at general issues in the design of market reforms in the field (Haagh, Helgø and Barrientos–Lloyd-Sherlock). Generally it is here that broader issues of institutional coordination between welfare domains arise, such as between education and labour markets, or between the latter and the structure of social insurance. Chile is the central case study discussed in these chapters because this country has seen the most consistent and thorough implementation of marketization of welfare. The second kind of chapter (Badia, Bayon *et al.*, Angell, Gideon), on the other hand, looks at more narrowly defined social programmes in the given field, programmes which typically (Badia, Angell and Gideon) seek to address problems in the 'design'. The two chapters in Part 4 stand somewhat apart from this pattern. They discuss two paradigmatic cases in recent development in approaches to poverty alleviation and social development, those of Mexico and Bolivia, where variations in the design of the targeting and decentralization first introduced in Chile have been attempted.

The Introduction to the volume sets the market reforms in Latin America in a general context of welfare analysis, and considers the relationship between welfarist neo-classical economic and Libertarian positions in the debate about the role of markets and states in welfare. It points to contemporary problems of generating mainstreams and integrated services in welfare provision, and critically assesses the core claims underlying the recent wave of marketization in welfare, including claims made in neo-liberal theory as regards the relationship between equity and efficiency, and by Libertarians regarding the trade-off between personal freedoms and distributive justice. The first part of the book on the labour market and social policies is most central to these classical issues of market design, involving problems of market failure and idiosyncratic goods (human resources), and issues of external and internal labour markets and the relationship between production and reproduction. The chapter by Haagh looks at the purest attempt known in recent Latin American history at making social development occur through markets, in the Chilean labour and training reforms of the 1970s on. The examination of the training reforms shows that the identification of consumers and providers in the training market was not impartial. The identification of employers as consumers, for instance, was highly selective, and limited the access of individual workers (the intended targets of social development) to training resources. The effort to establish a multitude of competing training providers, on the other hand, far from improving the availability of information, competition and choice, led to short-sighted behaviour, and the streamlining of course supply towards larger firms by established providers. Thus, at both levels (consumption and service provision), man-made institutions continued to direct investment behaviour although the design of the training market was presented as socially and politically unbiased.

The chapters by Mónica Badia and Maria Cristina Bayon *et al.* are focused on more narrowly targeted policy attempts to help in the insertion of individuals within labour markets. In contrast with the training reforms, these policy attempts imply a recognition that the social integration of individuals needs to be supported by the action of states. However, the 'second-generation'

The Volume in Summary xxi

social programmes suffer from some of the same limitations that charaterized the earlier attempts to lead social care to be guided by markets, namely the assumption that only isolated groups of 'consumers' would need special attention and that these would be able to identify themselves. The programme to support female heads of households (PMJH) initiated in Chile in the early 1990s and discussed by Badia is one of the more innovative attempts to support women in their multiple roles as both producers (in labour markets) and reproducers (in the home). Badia delineates the integrative features of the PMJH, which includes child care, training and help to find jobs. PMJH however does not provide universal access, and Badia shows how already more resourceful women were most likely to gain access to public resources.

Bayon et al. focus on similar loopholes in the relationship women have with liberalized labour markets, namely the access to child care of women who depend on work. The context these authors study is the labour markets in Mexico of the 1980s on, where women came to constitute a growing share of working persons, at the same time as precariousness in working conditions grew and state-provided social welfare contracted. Hence, this case study further supports the argument that the access to participate in markets (the enhanced participation of women) in order to represent a real increase in freedom, needs to be complemented with an increase in social provision (in this case more balanced access to child care). Together with the other chapters on labour markets this undermines the commonplace contrast between social rights and market liberalization. If the end sought is the maximization of agents' positive freedom to develop in labour markets, the relation should be regarded as positive sum.

The question of the relationship between equality of access (social rights) and greater scope for competition and/or diversity also dominates the second section of the book on education reforms.

The chapter by Helgø dissects the three key elements of de-regulation of the educational sector in Chile from the 1970s on, including the introduction of decentralized (municipal) management of educational resources, of a parallel privately-run (publicly-financed) sector, and of a voucher system to increase parental choice. The chapter suggests that 'municipalization' of finance led to greater segmentation in the quality of education (a lowering of the substance of social rights), and also that students from privately-run schools did not perform better. Hence, the private *administration* of a school in itself did not improve school performance, an interesting finding in light of the fact that the greater efficiency of private and smaller units is usually the core justification for privatization reforms. In respect of the voucher system, Helgø's chapter suggests that hierarchy reproduced itself, with the finding that schools selected the students (the better schools screening out those of lesser ability, and less social backing) thus undermining the idea that competition alone would expand the choice and hence the freedom of access to education of the least well-off.

Alan Angell dissects the origins, design and effects of the MECE and P900 programmes begun in the 1990s in Chile and designed to lift the quality of primary education, and particularly improve the infrastructure and results of under-performing schools. He especially focuses on the crucial political aspects of the programmes' design and implementation that made them work. Angell's chapter compared with Helgø's provides greater support for the positive, 'participatory' prospects in decentralizing reforms. But notably the MECE and P900 reforms were centrally financed and coordinated policy efforts, which deliberately put local input first. The contrast between these and the 'design' of the mainstream education reforms (as discussed by Helgø) is therefore great, and highlights the need to analytically differentiate between financial and other forms of decentralization.

Parandekar's chapter further underlines this point. He analyses and compares the performance of schools with greater and lesser autonomy within El Salvador's (rural) primary education sector. He compares the working of so-called EDUCO schools in the decentralizing pilot programme of the same name that was initiated in the 1990s, with that of traditional rural schools administered directly by the Education Ministry. Parandekar highlights the areas where greater local participation improved the quality of education, and where it was a longer history of better infrastructure support from centralized funds that did the trick.

The section on health reforms presents closely related findings. The chapter by Barrientos and Lloyd-Sherlock looks at the general consequences of introducing private insurance markets in health care provision. Barrientos and Lloyd-Sherlock show how strong political backing of insurance markets in Chile led the state to 'take over' services for individuals not in the select age and gender groups where demand for care is low. This was the case even where individuals, such as mothers, could hardly be said to belong to a minority group. As in the case of the other markets in social care studied, there is a tendency for access to and benefits from such markets to be concentrated in the type of consumers that, from a financial point of view, need them least. Life cycle and gender problems are exacerbated by growing segmentation in labour markets, which typically are more likely to exclude women and older workers that return to the labour market from formal sector jobs. In other words, the insurance markets in health, in theory, work for formal sector male workers of particular ages without large health risks, but function poorly for most other citizens. Barrientos and Lloyd-Sherlock also evaluate the evidence from more recent attempts at expanding health insurance markets, in Argentina and Colombia, where the introduction of different mechanisms to stem risk selection (the selection of more healthy consumers) were introduced from the outset. They argue that whereas such measures are essential to avoid pitfalls like those of Chile, it remains unclear whether they are able to overcome the basic problems of insurance markets in unequal societies. Finally, Barrientos and Lloyd-Sherlock evaluate whether the market reforms have led to improvements in cost containment, and that even when judged within the very terms of reference that justified their creation, the performance of private health insurance markets has been disappointing.

The chapter by Jasmine Gideon is also focused on the health sector in Chile, but looks at the effects of decentralization within the public system, and at recent policies to supplement financial decentralization by encouraging the role of participation of voluntary groups. Her findings on decentralization in the finance of health to municipalities are similar to those of Helgø for the educational sector, as concerns geographical inequality in the quality of provision. Meanwhile her description of measures to contain costs and customize service access (by providing a similar package of services for all) raises other concerns about effectiveness, in as much as justifiable health needs could well exceed or fall below the strict minimum (and maximum) defined in this package. In line with our argument in the Introduction, this particular form of cost accounting implies a negative or instrumental (transactional) definition of equality, whereby in principle all receive the same regardless of need, in stark contrast with the holistic and inter-generational notion of social compassion that has traditionally inspired institutions of particularly health care, where needs are closely dependent on the life cycle and therefore on reciprocity between social groups over time. However, the primary concern of Gideon's chapter is with the role of voluntary groups within the decentralized setting of the public health system in Chile. Her chapter helps to demonstrate how voluntary sector involvement that has arisen as a genuine attempt to strengthen community input may be co-opted as a cost savings measure when set in the context of financial decentralization. Together the chapters of both Barrientos–Lloyd-Sherlock and Gideon casts serious doubts on the soundness of the cost savings rationale behind the introduction of markets in health care.

The last two chapters of the book, in the section on social development policies, deal with larger scale reform efforts or social programmes that depend in different ways on local input, and therefore focus our attention on the issue of the relationship between participation and centrally administered welfare provision.

Latapí discusses the nature of the PROGRESA programme of poverty alleviation initiated in Mexico in the mid-1990s. PROGRESA was a targeted programme like those discussed by Badia and Angell in that it sought to cover only individuals that meet certain criteria of social exclusion. Latapí shows how the detailed technical criteria used and nationally consistent and relatively transparent methods of allocating social assistance meant that the programme had some success in reaching its recipients. The programme was very different from the typical format of targeted schemes in Chile, such as for instance PMJH discussed by Badia, where targeting was combined with demand-based approaches that require recipients to compete for scarce resources (therefore, by definition, leaving out some of those targeted) and/or identify themselves as marginal and approach the relevant public authorities. In contrast, PROGRESA aimed to cover all that qualify, hence constituting access as a social right comparable to citizenship. The failings found in the PROGRESA programme by Latapí had more to do with flaws of a technical nature, a particularly crucial one being the failure to identify prospective claimants due, as mentioned, to the use of communities as the basis for seeking out those in need. Nevertheless, the programme constituted a viable starting base for more ambitious initiatives, and provided authorities with a crucial policy resource in the development of a comprehensive register of households in need.

George Gray-Molina discusses the introduction of two alternative approaches to privatizing social security and decentralizing policies to promote social development, as adopted in Bolivia from the mid-1990s on. As Gray-Molina describes, Bolivia has been characterized by a tradition of centralized state initiative and popular mobilization that sets the country somewhat apart in Latin America. The case therefore provides an interesting setting for evaluating some of the general issues concerning privatization and decentralization raised in this book. Gray-Molina first discusses Bolivia's Capitalization and Pension reforms. A system based on individual capitalization, as in Chile, was complemented by a collective fund, paid out in the form of an annuity to citizens over the age of 65. Gray-Molina describes how the establishment of the bonus helped to assemble a register of senior citizens, a tool that could potentially be transferred to other policy areas. This represented a down-scaling of earlier plans to pay a bonus to all adult Bolivians, a process that would have had greater institution-building effects. Gray-Molina's discussion suggests that whilst the bonuses did constitute a tangible benefit, this was in the end rather short-sighted. Gray-Molina's discussion of municipalization provides equally interesting insights into the challenges and dimensions of decentralizing reforms. There is a key difference between the separate introduction of markets into individual areas of social policy (education, training, health, social development programmes, and so on) in the Chilean context, and the massive, integrated fiscal and administrative transfer of resources to municipalities that the Bolivian popular participation programme entailed. Whereas the first reforms sought to introduce cost accounting through separate markets with participation defined as competition for funds by consumers, the political aspect in the Bolivian reforms was deliberate and far more pronounced. Gray-Molina shows how the massive transfer of political power undertaken in the Bolivian case did in a genuine way promote and revitalize community input in the development process, although his description also clearly suggests that this kind of involvement presupposed the prior existence of well-organized, politically motivated and independent civic groups. At the same time the Bolivian case, a best-case scenario for genuine local involvement, sets out the key pitfalls that can occur when provision of social development services comes to *depend* on participation. As the composition, intensity and level of political activism varied from municipality to municipality, as delineated by Gray-Molina, so did the effective access to social services differ.

Together the chapters in this volume show the importance of the unconditional right to social services from both an administration cost and a revised Libertarian welfarist perspective. This includes not letting citizens' access to social services depend on the vagaries of community involvement, or on the working of markets where social needs are reduced to the properties of physical goods. As the Introduction argues, locally responsive public institutions remain essential to social development and citizenship. In this context, and despite its problems, the Mexican PROGRESA stands out because the promotion of mainstream services, through the requirement of association with health clinics and schools, was an in-built feature of social provision within what was, in principle, a universal scheme. The MECE and P900 'second-generation' programmes in Chile similarly sought to combine universal coverage (of under-performing schools) with some measure of community building. In both these cases, efficient and technically sophisticated state bureaucracies were essential to the programmes' design and performance. The attempt at market perfection in the generation of welfare markets in Chile represents the sharpest contrast to these universalizing efforts among the cases discussed. Given the wide acclaim that the marketization has gained, the caution presented about it here represents possibly the core contribution of the present collection. Indeed recent market reforms have not unequivocally advanced the values of autonomy and individual freedom, which at least the libertarian proponents of market reforms in welfare of the Nozickian school have sought to protect. The overwhelming dominance of the financial aspect in decentralization in a case like Chile would in many ways serve to reproduce inequality in social chances and freedoms, thereby also frustrating the independent development of strong community (presupposing a measure of social equality) and of autonomous citizens capable of engaging the state.

Introduction: Markets and Rights in the Governance of Welfare – Latin America's Market Reforms

Louise Haagh

This book evaluates the role of markets and of market governance in welfare provision in Latin America. The decades of the 1970s and 1980s saw a global shift in the relationship between markets and states. States withdrew from a range of economic activities as the postwar boom waned and distributive conflicts could not be resolved.[1] Dispersal of this trend into the welfare domain took its earliest and most systematic form in Latin America. In the effort to streamline public care, state provision was cut, decentralized, infused with competitive forces, or privatized. A central clue to understanding the nature of this response is the common origin of even fairly divergent areas of policy reform in the neo-liberal movement, which has based its policy prescriptions closely on neo-classical economic thought and the libertarian school. Both of these entail a commitment to the maximization of markets, seen as optimizing economic efficiency and individual freedom. This commitment rests on the idea that markets are neutral or natural, separate from the political sphere.[2] Although market neutrality is not the sole inspiration to policy reform, it has tended to dominate at a time when state economic involvement, both for financial (fiscal) and political reasons has been in retreat. At a policy level market neutrality has entailed an attempt to imitate or create perfect markets in as many goods as possible, including welfare. Based on case study detail, this volume offers an assessment of the governance implications that the broad shift from state to market and localized governance of welfare entailed.[3] What are the implications for economic freedoms of the way decision-making about welfare has shifted? In particular, what are the implications for generating more inclusive welfare outcomes, that is, both reaching more people and reaching them in ways that integrate and sustain them into an identifiable mainstream – a state where the ability to enjoy relevant welfare goods between citizens is roughly equal?

This was the broad aim of the postwar expansion of welfare services, that is, progressively to include more people within the mainstream of society through the vehicle of social policy, and in turn make social policy itself a mainstream service, as excluded sectors would cease to exist.[4] This entailed a constitutive or constructive view of welfare production. If mainstreams were explicitly aimed for, they would arise, and be sustained within the mechanisms established through social contract.[5] Thereby it was also implied more generally that welfare production is a systemic or political problem, in contrast with the neo-liberal perspective behind market reforms that we discuss in this chapter, which sees welfare production as individualized and contingent. In this perspective the relationship between welfare process (as markets) and outcome is not explicated or established, but rather assumed. Hence the question arises whether the generation of mainstreams can or should be seen as merely an end goal, or whether it is also part of the process of reproducing the bases of welfare delivery.[6] This in turn points to the importance of the cyclical aspects of welfare production, for instance, of how far the balance between its contingent and its socialized form serve to regenerate the conditions for the future direction of policy, and in turn how far the existence of prior inequalities (in social opportunities, income, or power) affect the impact of policy.

In other words, the central questions in the welfare debate do not so much concern whether a state exists where the ability to enjoy relevant welfare goods between citizens is roughly equal. Rather, the important questions are ones of direction, of how such a state is sustained or deepened. We maintain that the Marshallian question of the balance between the socialized and the market-based generation of welfare remains central to an inquiry into the production and reproduction of mainstreams.[7] This proposition however demands explication. What in fact is implied in generating mainstreams has changed, as labour markets and social stratification have grown more complex. Latin America's radical transition from a relatively inclusive social insurance model based on occupational groups to a residual welfare model where the state protects only the poorest, represents a reversal in historical terms. In practice it entailed a stronger involvement of the state in defining and extending market process in welfare compared with earlier residual or liberal welfare models where the state tended to 'let' private welfare solutions arise rather build them directly.[8]

How exactly social contract has been rewritten, and what this implies for the balance between market and political governance of welfare and, in turn, for welfare outcomes, are central questions we address in this book. The aim of the present chapter is to provide a theoretical introduction to the empirical inquiry contained in individual chapters. We first consider general issues of measurement in the assessment of welfare reforms. We then set the market neutral perspective in the context of the development policy debate broadly conceived, and in a third section we introduce the Latin American policy context. The fourth section evaluates general claims in favour of markets in welfare in neo-liberal economic and libertarian thought. In a fifth section we discuss similar themes more discursively in the context of popular themes in recent welfare reforms.

I. Assessing market reforms in welfare

Because they are the most complete, and have provided a model for other countries, it is convenient to summarize the nature of market reforms in welfare as undertaken in Chile. The first reforms, in the mid-1970s, were tied to the general attempt to expand presentialist contracts in the sphere of production.[9] These ranged from the early most crude but enduring attempt to empower individual employers in labour markets (Chapter 1) to later or 'second-generation' schemes to insert marginal groups (Chapters 1–3 and 9). In the area of training, public institutions were privatized or leased out to the private sector. A new system of tax rebates to firms set up, as a kind of voucher, to support the new market of private providers. Later labour market schemes aimed specifically at vulnerable groups and provided *ad hoc* support towards labour insertion (Chapter 2). A second broad area of marketization comprised the traditional welfare domains of education, health and social insurance. Primary education stands apart given the special justifications that have historically been made in this area for public compulsion.[10] Hence it could be expected that neo-liberal reformers (despite the contradictions this implied with libertarian thought) would not go very far in this field. Instead of overt privatization a system to make public and private schools compete was set up. Administration of publicly managed schools was decentralized to municipalities, and vouchers were introduced as a way to realize the idea of empowering citizens as consumers (Chapters 4 and 5). Vouchers supported both publicly- and privately-run schools, alongside the existing fee-paying schools. A closely related and contemporary set of reforms in Chile covered the areas of pensions and health. As in pensions, market reforms in health aimed to expand consumer choice through the introduction of private, profit-oriented insurance systems that compete with the public domain (Chapter 7). Cost efficiency was sought within the public side of the structure through decentralization of finance and management (Chapter 8).

In summary, market reforms to training, education, and health in Chile all claimed to enhance cost efficiency and consumer choice, through the expansion of local level decisions and markets. Policies to reduce the central role of the state have not all been engineered directly through a neo-liberal programme, in Chile or elsewhere. However, neo-liberal thinking has been prominent in other types of reform, which have tended to emphasize similar claims to the greater efficiency of localized management (such as through increased financial autonomy of regions – Chapter 10) as well as related claims to community participation defined as a replacement for states (Chapters 5 and 8, and section V in this chapter). Hence an assessment of the relationship between market process, on the one hand, and cost efficiency and freedoms, on the other, forms a central part of our analysis in the pages that follow. Independently of market process we also evaluate the claim to greater freedom and enhanced development outcomes through 'participation'. Some such claims are problematic in themselves (section V). However, we also find in this book that modified forms of local involvement, that is, those that do not involve full-scale de-centralization (Chapters 5, 6 and 9), have been more compatible with the generation of mainstreams.

At the heart of the matter in welfare analysis, as we suggested before, is the course of change: Do new forms of welfare governance systemically point towards more inclusive welfare outcomes, and of ways to sustain them? Recent scholarship has provided an overall encouraging response. Positive trends in general economic performance and specific welfare achievements amongst early reformers like Chile have given way to the conclusion that an overall market model of welfare has worked. In academia a prominent tendency nowadays is to depart from this assumption and to concentrate on strategic issues of viability, including how best to address what is perceived as *short-term* (not endemic) equity costs.[11]

Analysts have been quick to present an overall salutary picture of the welfare reforms based on 'new incentives for individual choice',[12] and to suggest how 'the market's magic can finally put public institutions to work for the poor'.[13] In this book we strike a more sceptical note. The relationship between welfare outcomes and governance is complex: the viability of the modern market-oriented model of welfare not easy to measure. There are several reasons for this. The welfare systems that the market reforms sought to improve were themselves fraught with problems, and the goal of tax-based general provision never completed. Hence we cannot easily judge whether their difficulties were inherent or due to their unfinished state. A second problem is the apparent completeness of the neo-liberal response to the failings of postwar social provision (in Latin America), and the lack of an equally complete counterfactual. Outside the Socialist model of Cuba, social democratic tendencies based on universal taxation-based welfare are either limited in terms of historical comparability and focus (in Costa Rica an early unified system centred on health), or limited in coverage (Brazil) due to long-term problems of labour informality and state incapacity.[14] This helped give the market reforms in countries like Chile an appearance of relative coherence, and of inevitability, which may be deceptive.

A third and related difficulty arises in the segmented approach to welfare of the market reforms. These were originally conceived in technical terms within separate policy areas (education, training, the labour market, health, social insurance), and did not represent a holistic vision of social development. The reason was the shift in accent from outcome (general welfare) efficiency to an almost exclusive concern with process (cost) efficiency that motivated this wave of market reforms (section IV.2). Hence both the method (governance) and the goal (welfare) became more fragmented, compared with the previous period, when an integrated citizens' package of welfare was the central aim and the principal navigators in the journey were states. The interdependency between different welfare domains increased in its social salience *as a result* of the market reforms, as the connection became financially individualized through the income nexus. Individuals were no longer entitled to, but had to buy, an increasingly large share of their welfare needs through private insurance.

The implications of this fragmentation for systemic coherence both across welfare areas and over time are difficult to gauge, let alone measure exactly. When mainstream welfare was an institutional aim – through the social contract, not just an expected outcome, policy connections (or lack of them) between welfare domains were easier in principle to perceive and correct. In some ways the analytical task is facilitated by a recent tendency within freedom-oriented welfare analysis to perceive the importance of the interdependency of different welfare domains. Holistic welfare perspectives that place the problem of establishing successful and productive lives at the core of welfare analysis have begun to resurface.[15] These resulted from and entailed further research efforts to establish the connection between components of welfare that are intimately related in the context of individual lives, but which are detached in an administrative sense. In general we can say that specifying the systemic coherence – both spatially and over time – or the network efficiency of welfare models has grown more central to problems of welfare analysis.

Hence, our focus in terms of what is understood as a provided service must also include how far state institutions and social contract respectively guarantee or facilitate the security of welfare transitions. The mainstream generating role of public institutions may be important in deciding the extent to which purchased services can play a role in specific areas without being inequality deepening in a wider sense. For instance, the extent to which welfare is market dependent (purchased as opposed to provided) matters less in societies where incomes are not widely dispersed (through wage minimums, basic minimum income, labour policies that emphasize building tradable skills), and where social contract and policy lessens labour mobility risks (non-compulsory relocation policies, child care, educational services). In other words, the purchase of welfare in itself is not a sufficient indicator of market dependence (or commodification, the degree of freedom from markets, in Esping-Andersen's scheme). Rather, it is mediated in a complex way by other factors such as basic capability equalities (continuous and effective access to choice of occupation), purchasing power security (e.g. unconditional basic income welfare services) and network efficiency. In this sense our emphasis on network efficiency is analogous to Sen's critique of Rawls. According to Sen it is not enough to have access to certain specified (welfare) 'primary goods' (as specified by Rawls). It also matters whether individuals are able to translate these into effective freedoms, and this depends on what we could call general life conditions (functionings, and their sum: capabilities).[16] Sen uses the example of a disabled person who is not able to 'convert' a particular primary good.

The further point we make is that the ability to convert individual primary goods or even functionings into a more complex 'freedom to achieve various life styles' (the ultimate end of Sen's capability freedom[17]) rests additionally on a more general membership of the economic public domain, i.e. on individual potential forming in some way part of the general economic currency, allowing individuals to establish greater control over life trajectories, particularly in the occupational realm. In summary, the pertinent question in the welfare debate today is whether welfare markets produce these kinds of integration effects. This includes to what extent mainstreams need to be aimed for *ex ante*, through the establishment of relevant social rights. Is the existence of mainstreams just a desirable end goal, or also an efficiency function?

Answering such questions in pertinent detail is not an easy endeavour. Methods and statistics relevant in assessing the integration between welfare domains and hence the degree of network efficiency, are rarely available. We hardly know in the context of individual schemes what the possible costs of their decentralized or private management may be, say for nation-wide equity in coverage and the quality of provision, and we are even further from understanding the dynamic interaction effects (negative or positive) between developments in health, education, labour services, and so on, in an overall counterfactual sense, i.e. what such interaction effects might be for the generation of mainstreams in a market model as compared with an alternative rights-based model, *over time*.

The case of Chile – the country in which neo-liberal reforms have been the most conclusive – illustrates many of these related issues of governance and measurement. The evidence from this best-possible-setting has so far been mixed. It has been debated, for instance, whether Chile's most immediate welfare success, the sharp reduction in infant mortality, was mainly the result of a long-term trend, coupled with a general state effectiveness from which the neo-liberal reformers merely drew the advantage. Equally, it is not clear how far the reduction in poverty and unemployment since the mid-1980s was the result of resumed growth, following the 1980s crisis, or of superior market-based institutions of welfare, and hence whether these achievements are indicative of sustainable improvements in social development. As of 2002, income inequality in Chile had barely improved. Welfare institutions had been incapable of containing the fall-out of the 1997 East Asian crisis, with unemployment staying at close to 10 per cent for several years. The generation of quality jobs still remained an unfulfilled challenge.[18]

If we look at the interconnectedness (network efficiency) of welfare domains the evidence also appears disappointing. Social insurance coverage rates had fallen notably by the early 2000s.[19] The explanation is that effective coverage rates are related to labour markets' capacity to generate greater inclusion and income equality. How are we to categorize problems like these? Can we identify general stratification effects from the introduction of market process in welfare across countries and areas of welfare that contribute or detract from network efficiency and the building of welfare mainstreams? In assessing the impact of neo-liberal reforms in welfare, this book pursues two kinds of inquiry. At a general level the present chapter seeks to identify the particular conception of markets and market reforms of the late 1970s onwards and its implications for governance. Meanwhile our second line of inquiry concerns specific and detailed effects on the ground of recent market designs. The case studies contained in the book show the complexity of the negative effects on the generation of mainstream welfare results and institutions of the attempt to introduce market process into welfare delivery. At the same time they bring out what appears to be two central commonalities across diverse policy cases within the welfare field: the universal tendency towards greater segmentation in welfare outcomes and welfare institutions of neo-liberal reforms, and the relevance of rights-based and universal approaches in the attempt to promote greater cohesion in welfare outcomes, and respond to the problems of network efficiency. However, before we enter a more narrow debate of terms, we need first to address the notion of governance itself, and place our usage of the term in the context of Latin America's welfare economy.

II. Decentred versus centralized development governance

(i) The decentred consensus

The contemporary welfare debate is shaped by an implicit disagreement as to how far governance is a political matter. The legal expansion of presentialist contracts since the 1970s, and the resulting extension of instrumental rationality in economic life has given credence to the proposition that markets are self-sustaining governance constructs with which we should trust major areas of human affairs, including the generation of welfare. We wish to distinguish the classical and our own understanding of governance as a political matter from this market neutral approach and to highlight the role of the national political arena in shaping the systemic governance of welfare. The tendency to de-emphasize the national political arena is not unique to the neo-liberal school. Three trends untied the governance term from the liaison with the state, which was the tradition prior to the 1980s. These included the de-legitimation of the state by a diverse set of actors, ranging from the NGO movement to market reformers; second, the withdrawal of the state, both in the formulation of purpose and in practice, from development problems; and, as a corollary of the first two, academia's focus on new centres of power.[20] This new trend divides again into two: the normative, which identifies with the anti-state movement (centres of power 'ought' to lie outside the state), and the analytical-sceptical, which seeks to understand and describe the shift that has occurred between states and markets. Among these the former highly hybrid position, henceforth the 'decentred perspective', is dominant. This perspective covers both the broad postmodernist trend in development and the neo-liberal movement as well as the key international development institutions like the IMF and World Bank (Figure 0.1).[21]

The decentred perspective appears to advocate greater inclusiveness in the development process, but what is meant here is not generally clear. For instance, is inclusiveness as process conceived or valued mainly as (a) decentred political participation (as in 5, but also, if weakly, in 3 – Figure 0.1), or market process (as in 1 to 3), or perhaps as yet other processes not captured in the central discourse?[22] If the focus is decentred political participation, is this through (i) democratized local state bodies, or (ii) more loosely defined communities? In either case, is the notion of process inclusiveness attached to expected outcomes? The sources of confusion lie in the conflicting theoretical traditions (1 and 6, Figure 0.1) that traverse the decentred consensus. In the non-liberal postmodernist development discourse, process inclusiveness refers mainly to (a) (and it seems to a(i)), and it is implicitly assumed that this process will tend to generate more inclusive development (welfare and, in turn, process) outcomes, through local-level delivery and formulation of needs. For the neo-liberal movement, process inclusiveness refers essentially to the expansion of market process. Meanwhile second-generation neo-liberal reformers, as well as the World Bank, have also adopted the claim to participation from below (a(ii)), seen as a strategic alternative to state intervention.[23] Despite their distinct origins, the two traditions have overlapped. Conceptually both detract from the substantive role of the state and of social contract in welfare production, and both can claim some

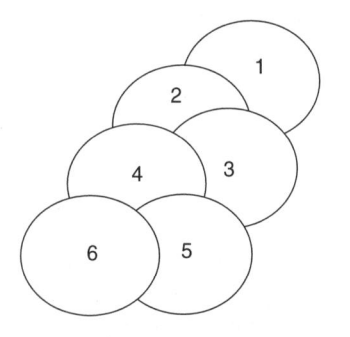

1. Neo-classical economics and neo-libertarianism
2. Neo-liberal movement
3. World Bank (and IMF)
4. Decentred perspective
5. NGO movement
6. Postmodernist development critique

Figure 0.1 The decentred development perspective in context

practical stake in the devolution process since the 1980s whereby central authority over (shrinking) fiscal resources has dropped.

(ii) Welfare systems and political choice

We feel it is important to reiterate an emphasis on the national framework of political governance, for two reasons as stressed above: first to highlight the (still important) systemic properties of welfare production, and within this context, to specify the continuous element of political choice. The Scandinavian example is a useful illustration of both these effects. The craft tradition and the cooperative movement in this case lay the foundation for the development of recognized currencies in skills (a flexible labour market), whereas national wage accords (in Denmark dating to 1899), promoted a lower wage spread and eased later support for this trend through (low-conditionality) social assistance.[24] Such developments allowed the provided and not the purchased service to become the welfare norm, and soiled the ground for later ideas of meaningful work and job market membership. But the survival of the universal model's capacity to generate mainstreams also depended on political choice. For example, it depended on the re-extension of the inclusiveness principle when fundamental tensions began to emerge between those who could afford the better quality services offered by emergent insurance markets or private schools, and those who could not; in other words when the Marshallian balance came into contention.[25] Efforts in the 1990s to boost adult learning parallel with social assistance reform represented an attempt to align cost adjustments with the regeneration of mainstreams.[26]

Whilst the Scandinavian example thus readily brings out the (in this case positive) interaction effects between welfare domains, the case is more complex for Latin America. The scale of interaction effects is relatively easy to pinpoint in welfare systems that are centrally governed. Discerning system effects in atomized systems, which characterize most Latin American settings, that is, in highly informal and marketized economies, is a more difficult task. This contrast between atomized and centralized systems captures the challenge involved in the kind of research presented in the present collection. Various chapters point to the existence of negative interaction effects that affect mainstream welfare. These include interaction effects between labour institutions and training (Chapter 1); between labour markets and households (Chapters 2 and 3); between social stratification and, respectively, decentralized education (Chapter 4) and insurance markets (Chapters 7 and 8); and, finally, between state decentralization and social development (Chapter 10). On the other hand, Chapters 5, 6 and 9, on centralized targeted schemes, point to the prospects for initiating positive cycles into the creation of mainstream provision.

In summary, these research efforts together represent a revisionist movement *vis-à-vis* the more widespread tendency to take the decentring of welfare governance, through marketization and the new interest in participation, at face value; that is, taking these to mean that welfare production *is* in fact localized or that market governance *is* in fact neutral. As we saw, the postmodern critique is concerned with decentred political choices, whereas the dominant neo-liberal paradigm entails a more fundamental rejection of the idea that welfare systems can sensibly be the object of political choice.[27] The World Bank, as a fairly plural institution, evinces the amalgamation of the two debates. The Bank's adoption of the governance term (as '[the way] power is exercised in the management of a country's ... resources'[28]) reflects the Bank's sensitivity to the postmodern critique. The vagueness of the definition, on the other hand, conceals a more narrow understanding of what governance is that coincides broadly with the policy areas where fundamental coherence of purpose between the Bank and the neo-liberal movement exists.[29] The Bank's more value-laden term, 'good governance' reflects this consensus. This notion appears to be neutrally concerned with fair procedure (elections, absence of corruption), but in practice prescribes the remits of what states can and should do, much in the same way the Bank in the 1990s conceded to the key role of the state in East Asia, and then proceeded to limit this to a 'market enhancing' function.[30] In other words, the World Bank appeared to have accepted a comprehensive definition of development problems in the 1990s, only to see the terms of its solution restricted in the re-emphasis on neutral (market) procedure.[31] Participation was advanced as an attendant feature at the point of delivery in parallel with a general weakening of the public sphere as financier and as organizer of welfare. This trade-off was clearly expressed in Chile, where governments of the 1990s, simultaneously expanded anti-poverty projects based on participation, and maintained an ultra-liberal framework of labour rights.[32]

The conceptual fuzziness in development discourse makes it imperative to distinguish precisely where a conception of governance that recognizes political choice differs from market neutrality. In the first, policy combinations (e.g. the use of universal entitlement and competitive pressures) are seen as objects of political choice, and adjustable. Procedural priority is given to expected outcomes in choosing the method of distribution of welfare. Political governance thus understood is not necessarily democratic,[33] even if democratic forms of governance in principle accord more space for open debate as in the well-known tendency for states (like the Scandinavian) that involve economic actors in public debate to produce better welfare statistics. Our choice to use the broader term political governance (as opposed to democratic governance, which is but a variant) is in order that we may distinguish governance from the tendency in the minimalist regulation approach to confine public action to an ostensibly neutral role, like the enforcement of basic contracts and the prevention of oligopolies in service provision. In this approach distributional fairness is seen as *inherent* in classical markets. Classical markets are given procedural priority both as a means of cost containment and relative to principles of distributional and outcome fairness (section IV). This limited informational basis in our argument trivializes governance problems.[34] In order to trace the influence that such principles have come to attain in Latin America we briefly set out the historical backdrop to the marketization process.

III. The background to welfare reforms in Latin America

There are many reasons for the more radical response to the 1970s downturn in Latin America. Some reasons are of an immediate economic nature. The import-substitution industrialization policies the region had followed since the 1920s and 1930s had come unstuck by the late 1950s, and political leaders desperately sought to find solutions to the balance-of-payments problems, inflation and fiscal deficits that had plagued most Latin American countries since then. These were vulnerable emergent economies. Despite the advancement of some countries – Chile and Argentina, as well as Uruguay and Brazil, had adopted pension and compensation schemes before the US – and despite the goal of universal welfare, the vicissitudes of the world economy affected these countries more.[35]

Political developments complicated attempts to solve Latin America's economic problems. The 1960s was also a period of political radicalization, following revolution in Cuba, the expansion of electorates in many countries, and the formation of new political actors who clamoured to be included in emergent safety nets. In the mid-1970s, military rule of a new and more long-term form, pledged to radical economic reforms, had emerged in a series of countries. As if to illustrate the region's dilemma, welfare reforms came first in countries that had advanced the most in key areas of welfare development, such as in the provision of national health care, like Chile. The sense of political and distributive conflict contributed to the radical nature of the reforms in this country.[36] This explains the emergence of a conception of market reforms that was 'anti-political'. Although the approach to marketization in other countries was less ideological, and varied in technical detail in significant ways, the Chilean experience, and its later adoption as a model by the IMF and World Bank, increased the uniformity of purpose of Latin America's welfare reforms, much in the same ways as ISI had spread four decades before.

How far was there a welfare crisis of a magnitude that justified the radical introduction of markets in social provision? That particular insurance funds were in a state of financial crisis, facing demographic change and administrative deadlock, there is no doubt. Poor tax structures and the broader fiscal crises of Latin American states, which intensified from the late 1950s, also put pressure on public resources, and made it clear that political solutions had to be found to distributive problems if any kind of welfare state was to advance at all. At the same time, few Latin American countries had anything that approached integrated systems of social insurance. Even 'pioneer' countries like Chile, Argentina and Uruguay had achieved near-on universality only in health and primary education, and had barely begun extending and coordinating the complex market of occupational pensions. As Tamburi points out, the idea of universal social security was mainly that, an idea and a goal.[37]

Hence, there was ample room both for advancement and change, which any kind of concerted reform, of a radical market kind or not, would have to fill and exploit. An example was the manifest need for administrative unity. The radical market reformers in Chile, for example, were able to take credit for introducing obvious progressive reforms in the way in which labour markets were tied to welfare. Occupational distinctions between white- and blue-collar workers were abolished and, from the mid 1970s, a fiscal surplus was built up, so as to facilitate the administrative simplification of the system which privatization entailed. We could call the method of reforming obvious weaknesses in the old model in particular ways and calling such ways the only alternative, the 'inevitable choice' convention.[38] The inevitable choice convention was used to defend radical market reforms in virtually all areas of welfare, especially in Chile. A possible alternative and logical step following the occupational unification of pensions would have been a system based on universal as opposed to occupational rights (the step envisaged in corporatist states in Europe, and previously, in Latin America). It is characteristic of the mood of this period that such steps were never seriously studied.[39]

But the durability of Latin America's market reforms is also explained in the way new sets of political elites adapted to them. By the 1990s a simple equation between military rule and a narrowing of welfare rights could no longer be made. After this time market reforms in welfare were imposed by democratic rulers top-down. Some of the most thoroughgoing liberalization programmes since the mid-1980s have been initiated by former leaders of nationalist revolutions (like Bolivia's Paz Estenssoro) or by democratic governments led by parties close to the union movement (Menem's Argentina) or which are, in rhetoric at least, on the centre-left of the political spectrum (Cardoso's Brazil). This style of governance reflected the growing influence of market neutrality. During the 1980s, a parallel political transition occurred whereby many of the earlier welfare reforms (especially Chile's) became an accepted part of multilateral development thinking, even of conditionality, as one Latin American country after another had to submit to structural adjustment schemes. For example, a model became common whereby countries would reduce spending on universal welfare as well as curb real wage growth, but would spend either a reduced amount of public resources, or the aid from donors (or both), on selected vulnerable groups.[40] This was how a residual welfare model was reintroduced within Latin America. In Chile, this kind of partial welfare policy emerged in two forms, as permanent targeting of certain sectors, like infants, schoolchildren in poor areas or expectant mothers, and in the form of 'emergency measures', such as public works programmes or the alleviation of poverty in defined communities, to deal with the temporary effects of adjustment. By the late 1990s, the hybrid decentred consensus that characterizes World Bank discourse, as described, had taken root. The claim for economic participation made by proponents of the neo-classical model had merged in the discourse with the claim advanced historically by NGOs and social reformers for *social* participation and a greater say *vis-à-vis* the state by territorial units (Figure 0.1, section II). Former 'emergency measures' had become part of a permanent model of social policy, and several units (local schools, poor communities, marginal youth, pension contributors, and so on) were accepted as consumers in what, by the 2000s, had come to be seen as an overall decentralized model of welfare provision. In this new scenario, military rule seemed a distant past, and goals of political and social inclusion appeared to have been given a space that the new economic model lacked at the outset. As noted, the relationship between markets and governance is not so straightforward. Another shared feature of the more thorough reforms by democratic governments in the region was their autocratic design. This suggests that we need to break down the concept of decentralization itself, and particularly to focus on the dominance of the economic component relative to the social element attached to it in the literature under the heading of participation.[41]

IV. Equity and efficiency

Decentralizing reforms in welfare in Latin America are characterized by great variation. But the tendency across the areas of reform we consider is for the economic, or henceforth the financial component, to dominate. The theory is that enhancing individual choice (by decentralizing administration, leasing out, and introducing vouchers) will produce a higher quality and better priced service. The new model is presented as putting efficiency first, as it is argued that the old concern for equity had placed efficiency last. However, is the juxtaposition of equity and efficiency in welfare markets appropriate? In order to answer that question we need to ascertain the origins of this alleged trade-off in the conception of efficiency characteristic of neo-liberal theory. This conception derives from the cost effectiveness believed to inhere in classical markets, and hence the granting of a prior status to markets as neutral governance structures. As a development vision it represents a level of abstraction not necessarily found in classical liberalism. Both Mill and the utilitarian critique of state intervention rested on a justification of markets in terms of *outcomes* (utilities).[42] Adam Smith's critique of mercantilism and his support of free trade originated historically from his practical concern for immediate issues of outcome fairness.[43] Equally, it is difficult to dissociate

14 *Social Policy Reform and Market Governance in Latin America*

Smith's concern for equality of opportunity in education (the importance of standards) from expected more equal outcomes and freedoms, and even to discern quite how far in other historical circumstances he may have gone to advocate state intervention for the common good.[44] However, if Smith thus promoted both (a) markets (the market mechanism) and (b) state intervention (as in schooling and the regulation of speculative capital) in relation to expectations of specific outcomes, the neo-classical economics tradition – particularly the dominant policy strand associated with Friedman – elevated price mechanisms (a) to an absolute state, in which the relationship between price and the general good was assumed to hold true in a much wider and more abstract sense.[45] The Friedmanite position emanated from a basic distrust, and a basic belief: distrust that no possible political form of governance can be just, or as just as pure markets, and the belief that markets are natural or neutral, or can be made so by removing politics from them as far as possible.[46] The neo-liberal aversion to centralized governance and socialization of funds also included state education, which Friedman saw as a regrettable 'island of socialism'.[47] A corollary of the neo-liberal position was (i) a clear separation of process (markets) from outcome,[48] and (ii) an *a priori* rejection of other institutional means of cost containment than presentialist contracts. These represent two fundamental ways that the neo-liberal paradigm separates efficiency from equity, which we consider in turn below. In a later section we then point to a basic contradiction within neo-liberalism, which suggests that broad equity considerations ultimately cannot after all be dismissed, even by adherents to the neo-liberal school.

IV.1 Market neutrality entails a conception of efficiency that includes only process costs as measured in short-run financial terms, thus in practice excluding outcome gains in the calculation of efficiency

Market neutrality entails a representation of welfare policies as a series of unconnected linear processes, hence giving welfare outcomes a finality that is unrepresentative of the rising mutual dependency between welfare domains (section I). We can identify three related dimensions in the integrated and temporal nature of welfare production.

(i) Interaction effects between process and outcome within single policy areas

Figure 0.2 illustrates how the neo-classical vision of policy efficiency conceives of welfare processes, using the simple example of education, indicating how both cost and outcome efficiency are conceived of as given through the maximization of market process. Each separate process is in principle considered as finite or given, even if the separation itself between primary and secondary schooling is hardly 'natural'. Figure 0.3, takes the case of education through to the job market, including in the illustration the succession of challenges associated with occupational life, and contrasts it with

```
                    Cost efficiency              Outcome efficiency
                    (market process)             (given by market process)

    Pupils          ─────────────▶               (primary education)    ─────────▶
    Pupils          ─────────────▶               (secondary education)  ─────────▶
```

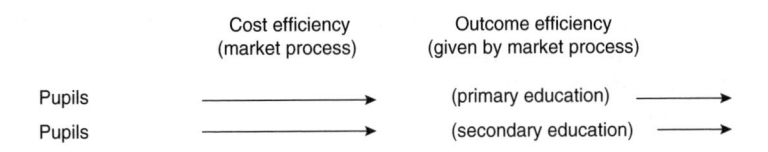

Figure 0.2 Welfare process in the neo-liberal vision of policy efficiency (education)

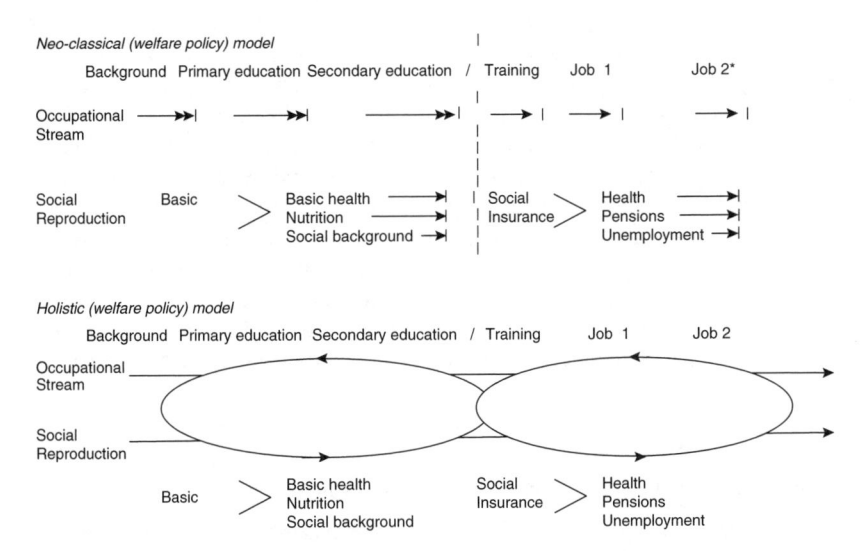

```
Neo-classical (welfare policy) model                    |
          Background  Primary education  Secondary education  /  Training     Job 1           Job 2*
                                                                |
Occupational  ──▶▶|         ──▶▶|              ──▶▶|           ──▶|        ──▶|              ──▶|
Stream                                                          |
                                                                |
Social         Basic          Basic health  ──▶|          | Social      Health       ──▶|
Reproduction              ▷   Nutrition     ──▶|          | Insurance ▷ Pensions     ──▶|
                              Social background ──▶|      |             Unemployment ──▶|

Holistic (welfare policy) model
          Background  Primary education  Secondary education  /  Training     Job 1           Job 2
Occupational _____▶
Stream                    ◀──────────────────────────▶       ◀──────────────────────▶

Social       _____▶
Reproduction                ───────────────▶                        ───────────────▶
                   Basic      Basic health                Social           Health
                          ▷   Nutrition               ▷   Insurance   ▷    Pensions
                              Social background                           Unemployment
```

Note: *'Job' here may also cover work experiences not strictly related to waged labour.
Figure 0.3 Welfare processes in different visions of policy efficiency

a simple holistic conception, in which the occupational stream is understood essentially as a continuous process, in which institutional breaks (from primary to secondary school, from schooling to work etc.) are seen as transitions that have to be managed.[49] Chapters 2 and 4 discuss the problem of inadequate institutional links between primary and secondary schooling, and between schooling and/or training in the context of the neo-liberal policies in the labour market and education implemented in Chile.

(ii) Spatial interaction effects between welfare domains
A second dimension of the integrated nature of welfare production is the inter-dependency effects between welfare domains spatially, for instance interaction effects between education and health, or, in a more extended sense (as illustrated in simple form in Figure 0.3) between social reproduction and the occupational stream. In an applied neo-classical model there is essentially no connection between the two. This is in contrast with a

16 *Social Policy Reform and Market Governance in Latin America*

holistic conception of welfare, which recognizes the cyclical nature of reproduction processes and their interaction effects with the occupational realm. Such interaction effects become instrumental in the case of major life-cycle events (section IV.2.ia).

(iii) The regeneration of welfare policy cycles
A third dimension in the integrated nature of welfare production refers to the regeneration over time of aggregate welfare outcomes and systems (Figure 0.4). Row (a) gives a basic representation of the conception of the relationship between social policy and society in the neo-classical paradigm in contrast with a holistic model. In the first the two (process and outcome) are seen as self-contained and separate. The relationship is unidirectional (from process to outcome). Social policy throws separate inputs into society. In the second the two are seen as overlapping and fluid. Row (b) in turn is a simple illustration of welfare cycles, that is, of the self-reinforcing relationships between welfare policy and society. In the institutional matrix characteristic of the neo-liberal model, a dual welfare policy set-up (market-process based welfare institutions combined with limited state assistance for those left out) reproduces a dual society. Entry inequalities (of income, ability, health etc.) are regenerated through the occupational realm. In turn, the

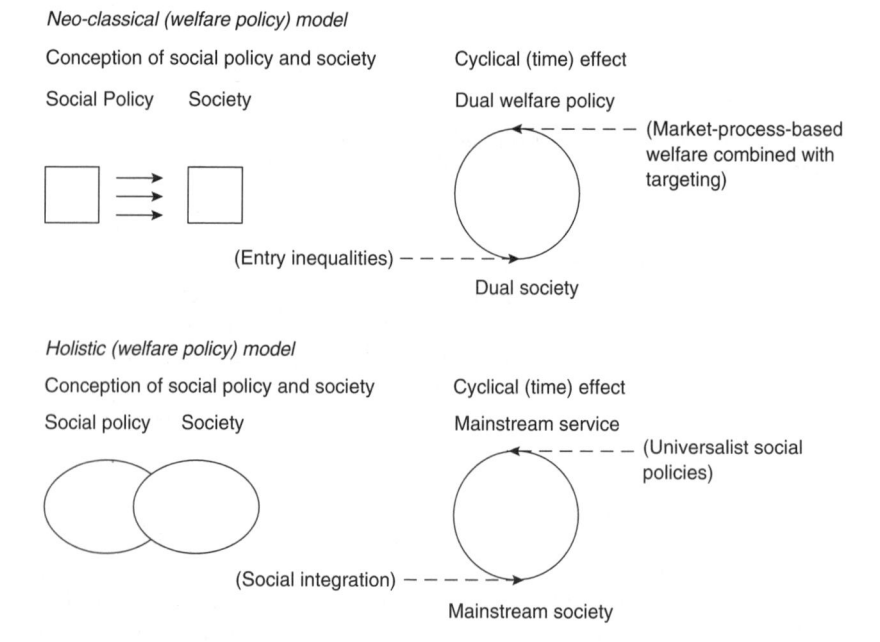

Figure 0.4 Welfare policy cycles

regeneration of social inequalities reinforces the dual policy framework. This is contrasted with a holistic conception of welfare (row (b)). Here we must hasten to add that conceptual and policy models are not the same. In some ways even basic or 'residual' welfare is a deviation from the conceptual model, and hence its contradictions (section IV.3). This book however shows that the practical attempt – or the nature of its direction – to approximate classical markets in practice tends to break up the areas of welfare production. Similarly, a holistic conception of welfare production (and our own only captures basic interaction effects) does not have a perfect policy match. However, rights-based models generally, and those that emphasize truly universal (as opposed to occupation-specific) rights, particularly, have a greater propensity in principle to take the integrated nature of welfare production into account, as the very specification of a right tends to 'spill over' into other domains (say, specifying what health requirements enter into successful schooling, or what educational requirements are entailed in the idea of a meaningful occupational life). The separation of process and outcome in neo-liberal theory is discernible in the way this perspective conceives of and presents the problem of welfare cost. We turn to this next.

IV.2 The prior claim to a concern with cost effectiveness systematically excludes other welfare model alternatives from view

The granting of procedural priority to markets has been given a range of justifications, implicit or explicit, in neo-liberal theory. A strand associated with neo-libertarianism asserts the primacy of antecedent rights as the primary justification. Free markets in this view do not interfere with these (section IV.3).[50] But there is also a strand that reinterprets the classical concern with utility (markets optimize utility), but sees utility narrowly as cost efficiency arising from markets.[51] The supposition that competitive *ad hoc* contracting offers the cheapest given service in a strict sense is true (see note 73). But, in order to arrive at this outcome in welfare, it is necessary as we saw to assume that individual domains can be isolated both spatially and over time. In this case pursuing presentialist contracts at the individual level in a metaphor breaks up the welfare consumer herself into all the wholes into which the service has been divided. Each individual is not 'a' welfare consumer, but a multiple set of consumers. The implication of this view of market neutrality as cost neutrality hides the possibly long-term nature of economic contracting in welfare from view, and entails an *ex ante* dismissal of other forms of governance on the grounds of lack of financial prudence.

(i) Contingency contracting in the welfare domain

Neo-liberal theory does not clearly distinguish its defence of presentialist contracts on efficiency grounds from its defence of such contracts on freedom grounds, and hence does not invite a reasoned debate on cost efficiency.

Market neutrality can be posed as a relevant cost efficiency argument by neo-liberal theorists only because this school applies a presentialist contract model even to welfare markets. In this, however, it folds with libertarian *moral* claims to presentialist contracts. In Nozick's view, for instance, concerns about systemic aspects of welfare production are immoral or unjustified because they imply redistributive measures that violate antecedent rights and liberties.[52] It is implied that anything but *ad hoc* transactions are problematic because they are beyond our individual control and hence incompatible with the primacy of individual freedom.[53] Hence it is difficult in neo-liberal theory to separate the position that cost efficiency is 'naturally' associated with presentialist contracting (pure markets as far as possible) from the defence of presentialist contracting on freedom grounds.[54]

The neo-liberal policy school associated with Friedman focused primarily on *ad hoc* exchange (and costs and price), seeing that these constitute 'markets', and justified markets such conceived in cost process utilitarian terms, i.e. a determined outcome for the lowest cost. This justification represented an adjustment to two contemporary demands: the demand to work with less (fiscal) resources, and the demand to produce socially acceptable results (with available resources). Hence Friedman implicitly accepts a kind of outcome fairness. For instance, he does not deny the good of general education. However, he is unable to evaluate alternative means of cost efficiency because he is wedded *ex ante* to presentialist contracts on freedom grounds. Thus, he only accepts general education *if* this service is delivered (as far as possible) by presentialist contract arguing that only these represent cost effectiveness (the defence of *ad hoc* contracts on freedom grounds is in this case not explicated). Accordingly, in his (highly discursive) calculations, he focuses only on education's most immediate costs and benefits. In calculating the cost of private in relation to public schooling, he considers the per unit cost of an isolated aspect of welfare production (hence excluding the possible systemic and temporal benefits of public provision, such as through the provision of standards and network efficiency). Private schooling in this case is advocated not (mainly it seems) because it enhances choice (which is equated with freedom, an argument also sometimes used), but because it is allegedly cheaper, following the short-term cost accountancy model.[55] This example shows the limits of neo-liberalism as an analytical and policy tool because it (implicitly) selects only the kind of economic processes as relevant for efficiency analysis, which it can accept on narrow and weakly defined (section IV.3) freedom grounds.

For a time, the formal exclusion of complex contracting from neo-classical economics made the association between the libertarian and cost efficiency claims to the superiority of presentialist contracts in neo-liberal theory appear to concur. However, the presentialist view of contracting has been seriously dented by reformed neo-classicist economic analysis, and hence its relevance, at least for efficiency analysis, is called into question. Reformist neo-classical scholars like Solow recognized that labour markets are 'social'. In addition, property rights economics has shown the limits of pure presentialist contracts due to bounded rationality which makes it impossible to anticipate all possible contingencies, and due to the need to counter opportunistic behaviour, leading contracting individuals to naturally correct for this through the socialization of risk.[56] As a consequence, long-term associations, or associations based on authority and long-term reciprocity, tend to form. The economy is full of such entities, including households and firms. The tendency towards the partial institutionalization of production is particularly notorious for welfare production, i.e. for life-cycle events that imply sudden dependence (age) long-term returns (skills) or that involve highly unpredictable and potentially disastrous risks (health, unemployment). Below we point to relevant problems of contingency contract markets in the areas of individual and aggregate welfare.

a. Individual welfare. It is fairly obvious that welfare delivery cannot proceed on the basis of presentialist contracts (pay over the counter) alone. It is precisely when the individual is weak (sick, unemployed, old, unskilled) that she is least likely to meet the cost of her welfare needs. Welfare insurance arose as a response to this high risk dilemma. The point of welfare insurance from the individual's point of view is that the ongoing cost is *independent* of life-cycle events. What happens then if marketization is encouraged into welfare insurance provision? Suppose the individual takes out a welfare contract only once, and chooses between rates in a competitive market. In that case, the individual's life risks would be evaluated only once, and the cost of insurance set accordingly. After that point the individual would not face the high risk dilemma.

Now suppose that the individual is able to change insurer at any time in a competitive welfare insurance market (as was the case for health and pensions in Chile, Chapter 7). As noted, the Friedmanite school sees this as preferable on the grounds of choice (equated with freedom) and price competition (this argument tends to get primacy). But we can immediately see that this logic pertains only when the insured is at a low risk juncture (in the case of health, young, male – not liable to pregnancy, and in a good occupational stream). Given that the features that constitute low risk junctures are unlikely to improve after a certain point (even the person described does not get younger or more male with time), it is unclear whether costs of changing insurance frequently outweigh the costs. The information required for optimal exchanges by both insurer (on individual's risks) and insured (on the services offered) are considerable. The sales, advertising and administration costs of shifts would be likely to put up equilibrium level prices. Hence even quite competitive social insurance markets require limitations on the briefness of insurance contracts. Chile's increase in the limit of shifts in pensions insurance (from *de facto* once a quarter to once a year) was a practical demonstration of this. Even supposing there are no transaction costs in shifts, it is questionable how safe and desirable is cut-throat competition in life-cycle goods.[57] Hence, both on the counts of price, quality for price, and general quality, the case for market process even within the narrow terms of neo-liberal theory (optimizing choice for the ideal *individual* consumer) is not strongly convincing.

(ii) Aggregate welfare and systemic efficiency

But what about the likelihood of performance at the aggregate level, to which neo-liberal theory also (if more implicitly) makes a claim? We are back to the question of how far optimization of market process in welfare would be likely to generate mainstreams in welfare. Even Pinochet's radical insurance reform was justified on such grounds. In this case, it is fairly clear that risk heterogeneity leads to the *de facto* exclusion from insurance markets of large groups of individuals, whose cost of insurance due to the relationship between their risk and income become insurmountable (Chapter 7).[58] In theory, even where entry inequalities are minimized (say, where incomes are roughly equal), 'natural' differences will produce highly unequal welfare outcomes in purely competitive social provision and insurance markets: in education the brightest will still be selected by specific schools, and in health the weak will still pay insurmountable insurance costs. But the salience of the efficiency claims for aggregate welfare are more tenuous still when set in the wider context of welfare production. As noted, the claim to markets as inherently cost effective excluded the creation of mainstreams as forming a goal for welfare policy. Specific (targeted) programmes might attempt to make up for entry inequalities, but could only perform this function at the margins, because the mainstay of society was to be governed by markets. This vision is inconsistent.

First, on a conceptual level, it is not compatible with the expectation that optimal (welfare) outcomes inhere in markets that marginal sectors should exist at all, and certainly not that markets produce them. Hence, the notion of cost effectiveness as inherent in markets cannot be maintained, (a) because markets are shown in this case not to be self-sustaining (in welfare), and (b) there is an in-built cost in taking care of excluded sectors (by states) on which the market design depends. Moreover, targeting represents a dead-weight cost in so far as no sustainable mainstreams exist, which the marginalized individual can be brought 'within'. We may compare this with a rights-based model, where targeting in principle is more cost efficient in terms of long-term outcome efficiency (the existence of mainstreams to bring the excluded within), but also less needed and hence less of an immediate cost (because exclusion does not systematically grow).[59] As we saw for Friedman on education, neo-liberal theory is not able to make this comparison. In reality the neo-classical model does not have a monopoly on concern even for immediate cost effectiveness. Pagano (following Hayek) has convincingly shown that all models of economic governance operate with principles of cost efficiency, and that the informational and transaction costs of either planning or pure markets tend to lead to intermediary management forms.[60] In a rights-based model, decisions also have to be made for instance about what citizens' package of learning materials best delivers a desired standard in relation to available monies. A reasoned analysis of the welfare and freedom states valued by the principal contenders to the welfare debate would also show that their implication in social terms justifies at least a minimal consensus on means.

IV.3 Market reformers' implicit recognition of the value of equity in welfare opens a possible passage for dialogue between proponents of neo-liberal versus holistic welfare models, based on the efficiency implications of more or less *a priori* welfare enhancing governance structures

As we have argued, the neo-classical welfare model formally denies, but implicitly accepts welfare mainstreams as a distinct outcome goal. As a consequence it does not have a mechanism for distinguishing between process and outcome (Figures 0.2 and 0.3), and hence it leaves the connection that it ultimately must make to outcome unexplored.[61] This can only be considered a fundamental methodological flaw. The key question is whether in fact efficiency in social policy is not equally judged, by market reformers and their critics, as optimal welfare outcomes for the population as a whole. There are differences, of course, in terms of exact distributional choices, yet to pose the above debate in terms of one between equity and inequity is methodologically misleading. Over-emphasis on such differences produces only circular reasoning: if goals (in this case about social development) are ultimately incomparable, there is no debate to be had about institutions and policy at all. Two libertarian claims (separate from the cost utilitarian arguments perused) are central to the natural superiority that the market neutral perspective asserts. First, markets are fairer because they are neutral and free from interference. Second, welfare outcomes are just that follow from just procedure; or rather, it is the only justice possible.[62] But this means that the neo-liberal (policy) position rests on the veracity of two positions: first, that market procedure is in fact neutral and hence more consistent (fair) than other forms of economic organization (including modified market procedure); and second, that the neo-liberal school makes no claim or prior commitment to any equity outcomes or ideals. As we have already argued, neither of these positions can be maintained, but they also conflict.[63] The two assumptions put the neo-liberal school in an untenable position, because it cannot claim at one and the same time that the trickle-down effect is justified as a measure due to (i) expected equity outcomes which would imply a justification in relation to a notion of outcome fairness, and (ii) that it is just because of the superior justice of market procedure. The important procedural question is: if markets in welfare do in fact systematically undermine mainstreams, is this compatible with neo-liberal theory? As noted, both classical liberalism and the cost accountancy strand of neo-liberal economic theory make implicit claims to outcome fairness in terms of economic utility or welfare. On the other hand, libertarians like Nozick defend market process (defined as *ad hoc* transactions) not just on the grounds that it will protect those of property, but on the grounds of the primacy of the liberty to act *of all*. In other words, libertarians would argue that absence of violations like tax and forced redistribution ultimately protect the (primary) antecedent rights of all, including the poor. Hence if markets *consistently* undermine welfare in either form (utility or freedom), both the utility and the freedom-enhancing strands of neo-liberal theory would need revision. In this case, to what method and sense of outcome equality could theorists in the neo-liberal tradition agree? We can focus on libertarians because they make the strongest claim to antecedent rights. Here arguments to establish and justify the finance and sense of outcome equality would have to be related to (i) justifications for tax; (ii) the necessity of specifying outcome goals to establish the effectiveness of antecedent rights; and (iii) the likelihood that such specifications do not in other fundamental ways violate rights to freedoms that libertarians value.

(i) Taxation and social cooperation

The basic problem is that libertarians like Nozick see all forms of running socialization of resources (except for security) as property theft. Nozick allows that individuals may voluntarily transfer resources, but no one can be obliged. On the other hand, Nozick does appear to accept implicitly that the state may intervene, even heavily, to correct past economic and social injustices – that is, to start individuals again on a more equal footing.[64] What Nozick seems to object to is regular taxation – because it is taking forcefully from an individual who has not wilfully or directly contributed to economic 'sin'. But, if it is accepted that modern market economies (which Nozick advocates) generate significant social inequalities, then the only feasible solution to the problems of entry inequalities is some regular remedy like the fiscal redistribution of means. Nozick's position ultimately falls foul of the fact that not all consequences of individual actions can be isolated (in fact, the larger part cannot) in modern complex economies, and hence more abstract measures of just distribution can be justified.[65] Hence, we can suppose that Nozick's third critique of Rawls (with which he defends his opposition to the financing of distributive justice) can be qualified. This is the idea that production does not entail cooperation.[66]

(ii) Outcome goals and antecedent rights

The justification of distributive taxes, however, ultimately is related to the fact that the distribution of means is necessary to the kind of freedom libertarians seek to protect. We may start by supposing that an intermediary form of outcome equality could be accepted even by libertarians, through the distribution of the given tax, if account is made of Nozick's two other critiques of Rawls.[67] That is, distribution of means may be acceptable when it aims to enhance the freedom of individuals (and not groups). And, this distribution is not directed at final end-states, but at some intermediary level of acceptable means designed to optimize the ability to freely choose. The question as to what is entailed in acting freely and freely choosing is complex. However, if in the interest of finding the basis of agreement between welfarist and libertarian positions we limit ourselves to minimal means in the sphere of work and exchange, we can argue that given the insecurity and complexity entailed for individuals (of no fault of their own) in modern market economies, a minimum redistribution should aim to generate effective occupational chances. On the one hand, this could be justified on the grounds of the simple economic outcome associated with the neo-liberal policy school (continuous access to income); and would include at the very least continuity in access to basic resources (health, pensions, basic education); and adequate transition resources (reasonable means of relocation: education, information, minimum transitional income). The libertarian justification on the other hand, would be made in relation to a notion of developmental freedom. The libertarian claim to the freedom to act is also often justified in relation to the ultimate value of individual human personality, the idea that each life is an end in itself,[68] and hence has strong affinities with notions of developmental freedom as the freedom to act, choose, and to choose freely and according to our nature.[69] This sense of freedom would not be possible within the economic domain without access to the personal growth arising from a freely chosen occupational trajectory, and in a modern economy this at a minimum entails a range of complex informational and educational connections in the economic realm and organisation of relocation resources (see note 49). Libertarians also make more complex claims, for instance, to the value of autonomously 'giving',[70] presumably as an aspect of personal freedom, which appear to have some affinity with freedom-oriented welfarist valuations of individual autonomy and truly independent initiative that libertarians criticize final end theories as lacking,[71] and which would entail a much more demanding conception of just distribution to provide a realistic basis for the development of the independent capacity to 'give', through command over personal and physical property. As regards a minimum income, libertarians should logically prefer an unconditional version, to minimize state interference and administrative costs. In summary, the libertarian conception of freedom thus conceived demands *at the very least* the measures entailed in the utilitarian valuation of mainstream welfare, and even have an unexpected affinity with more demanding interpretations of what is justly required in terms of the distribution of means to enhance personal freedoms.

(iii) Other freedoms libertarians value

But does this undermine other core antecedent rights stipulated as important by libertarians (beyond the issue of taxation discussed)? As already noted, freedom justifications of the distribution of means do involve access to property, to some level of effort-related gain, and some level of divergence in final means, and do not in principle conflict with freedoms to trade or contract. In this context, differences of opinion could be confined to issues like the level of taxation desirable, level of income inequality acceptable, mutual obligations under specific forms of contract, and such like. The point is that the just distribution of means and the rights to certain personal freedoms are important values in themselves, and it seems not practically feasible, and also undesirable, to evict one in favour of the other by logical extension of mono-variable and ahistorical theories of justice.

The problem of Nozickian libertarian theory is not its evaluation of freedoms, but that it sets out to defend an absolutist position, and one which it is not feasible to sustain in the context of modern economies. This is both a logical point and a pragmatic one. As we saw, Nozick's position is that the overall 'co-operation' (production's systemic nature) is not chosen by the individuals engaged in it (individuals only choose specific transactions). But this position can be questioned from a systems perspective since individuals engaged in exchange always make choices within systemic constraints. Therefore, in order to live out Nozick's ideal of purely voluntary exchange, individuals or other relevant units (like families) would have to live autarkicly, or in a manner of speaking the life of 'the little house on the prairie'.[72] The point of course is Nozick's justified worry as someone who values a variety of personal freedoms about conceding to systemic justifications for redistribution, because logically that might erode all rights to individual property (considering that most production is clearly systemic), which he sees as a fundamental violation of personal freedom. The case for pure planning based on the ultimately systemic nature of all production equally represents a logical extreme that is not only impossible but the desirability of which is also open to question.[73]

It follows that because both redistribution and personal freedoms (such as are highlighted) are values with independent worth – i.e. valued independently of economic systems – they need to be justified also relatively independently of economic systems; in other words, by reason and political choice, even if their modified realization (modified since their absolute realization is, as argued, untenable) depends on knowledge of and judgements about the workings of economic systems. If such evaluations are thus necessarily historically sensitive, specific valued freedoms cannot be given a universal *a priori* exact weight relative to other freedoms, but must be valued both concomitantly and relative to each other in specific contexts. Sen is closer to such an approach (the 'comparative importance' of rights) than Rawls, though Sen observes that political freedom may have a special procedural significance, given its social importance (though one individual may not value political liberty highly, others may).[74] This however may also be said of economic *vis-à-vis* political freedoms. Another way to make the point is that there is something special about political liberty because it is what allows individuals to voice their freedom (including their economic freedom) preferences. All else being equal this must be true. However, it must also be true that stark social deprivation prevents individuals from exercising this voice. If freedoms tied to economic and social well-being and political freedoms thus are interdependent, any action in one domain without some tangible regard for the other, would not ultimately be meaningful in a development perspective that values personal freedoms.[75]

The quality of this kind of debate depends on an understanding of the specific ways that freedoms relate and possibly conflict. This is particularly true for the welfare debate, which is characterized by the neo-liberal counter-position of individual (economic) liberty and state intervention. The neo-liberal position seems to imply that the maximization of all kinds of freedoms makes overall freedom more absolute. This is clearly misleading. Tax is a form of economic unfreedom, but the increase in welfare equality that taxes facilitate may co-relate positively with economic freedoms that libertarians value, like labour market flexibility, as in the Danish case where high welfare benefit access underpin a high degree of labour mobility.[76] Even in this case welfare benefit access varies with income.[77] These specific legal aspects of economic freedom in the Scandinavian welfare state undermine Friedman's critique that the notion of fairness of 'socialists' (in which he refers to countries like Sweden and pre-Thatcher postwar Britain) is 'vague',[78] and very likely resulting in political and economic repression.[79] But the neo-liberal argument against state-provided welfare in emergent economies is particularly surprising not only because entry inequalities to markets are greater here, which seems to make the classical liberal arguments in favour of (at least) public and standardized schooling on *efficiency* grounds especially compelling;[80] but also because there are strong arguments to suggest that such services are more efficiently delivered (as process) – especially in emergent economies – if they are delivered by right.[81] Our empirical concern in this volume, however, is the welfare effects that arise from atomized systems, specifically the possibility that presentialist contract markets in welfare are undermining of mainstreams. If such systemic effects are known, or *foreseeable*, then even Hayek would wish to accept some level of intervention to correct them, since he allows that the term injustice (which implies action to correct it) has meaning '... in so far as we [can] hold someone responsible for... *allowing it to come about.*'[82]

Many of the apparent greater differences between the libertarian and welfarist positions arise in fact from expected end-states rather than actual policy differences. A good part of Hayek, Nozick and Friedman's arguments against state intervention emanate from what *would* happen if giving in to policy measures that socialist proponents of them regard as merely instrumental to broader end states.[83] In short, if libertarians and welfarists argue long enough they will find that the welfare debate is about the exact nature of trade-offs like those discussed, and not about absolutes. Specifically, we have argued that neo-liberal theorists (and even libertarians) would have to accept the incongruence entailed in adhering to the good of welfare mainstreams and supposing these can be achieved through the maximization of market neutrality. They entail a rejection therefore of the radical extent to which market process was introduced in Latin America. This is significant.

V. Themes in Latin American welfare reform

A series of general concepts has been associated in the policy literature with the success of the welfare reforms and therefore require specific mention.

(i) Targeting

It is often suggested that the success of market reforms in welfare has been illustrated by the achievements of targeting (section IV.2). Indeed, there are undoubted results from policies that target vulnerable groups like expectant mothers and infants. On the other hand, such successes say little about targeting in a more general context or about the magic of individual incentives and market reforms. One might be justified in thinking that achieving some specific and visible results is merely what one would expect from a programme encouraging vaccinations and distributing milk to poor schools (Chapter 5).[84] The point is that targeting on its own can say little about the success of market reforms according to our terms of reference, since, as we saw, it usually aims only at those 'outside' the mainstream. Targeting is not a unique, or even a characteristic feature of market reforms. In most cases it involves a highly centralized policy, as Angell finds (Chapter 5). Targeting is compatible with a range of universal policies, and would not have seemed out of place in either developmental or welfare states.

In short, it is difficult to disagree with policies that seek to bring excluded sectors within the mainstream. It is the way in which, or extent to which, targeting is expected to complement – or even replace – other policies that differences of opinion arise. Targeting, as we argued, takes on a rather different dimension if the overall welfare (and economic) model consistently produces exclusion. The targeting of youth in training programmes in Chile suffered from both of these problems. The labour market itself found reception difficult because it lacked adequate standards (Chapters 1 and 4). This recalls the question raised above of whether market selection in welfare, the *ad hoc* cost accountancy model, is supportive of mainstreams. In the case of education, Chapter 4 herein shows that market selection, the 'choice model', produced polarization and the so-called 'waste-basket' schools. Targeting of poor schools at the primary level has been highly successful in Chile, as Chapter 5 depicts. However, Angell also finds that financial decentralization as the mode for the mainstream was a politically untouchable subject.

The debate has been narrowly posed because it has tended to present targeting and the mainstream as mutually exclusive ideas. Policy-makers, it is argued, face an essential choice between two poor constituencies. Policies are 'pro-poor' which help the poorest and evade middle sectors and mainstream provision. This is another example of the application of the 'inevitable choice' convention. This convention worked at a political level, but has become steadily less relevant as the differences between the two groups have grown decreasingly marked. As social policy has been withdrawn as a vehicle for the mainstream (the postwar cycle), the mainstream itself has dropped, making it more difficult for the excluded to 'enter' as competition at the lower end of the 'mainstream' labour market has grown. In the labour market this implies the bringing in of precariousness, of informality, to the formal sector (Chapters 1, 3 and 9). In education, as Helgø shows (Chapter 4), it entails the systematic creation of 'waste-basket' schools in every borough as well as weakly performing schools in poorer boroughs. At some point the mainstream ceases to be, and the standard to bring excluded sectors above disappears. As targeting becomes the mainstream policy, and the population of potential recipients grows, targeting cannot remain a precise and fair tool, but becomes a large-holed net or an arbitrary stab into poverty. In the case of Chile's youth training scheme the target population was so large that the beneficiaries were essentially selected at random (Chapter 1).

The chapters by Latapí and Badia pick up on other apparent inconsistencies in targeting policy. In the case of Mexico's PROGRESA, Latapí notes how poor individuals who qualify according to income for public aid were excluded from the programme if living in richer communities. In the case of policies for female heads-of-household in Chile, Badia found problems in policies actually reaching the women in need. The point to highlight here is that these features go against the two alleged merits of targeting, relative to mainstream (old-style) demand-based provision. First, that due to its narrow focus and precision, one may be sure that those who qualify (for targeted aid) are reached. And second, that targeted policies could not be exploited broadly, and would locate the poorest among the poor, who would not be sufficiently vocal to seek support in a demand-based scheme. On a more positive note, Mexico's PROGRESA at the very least set up a permanent register and improved state infrastructure. In that respect it provided a proficient base whereby poverty aid might change into a form of mainstream provision. But this was possible only in light of the programme's centralized features. This brings us to the core issue of consumer choice and decentralization.

(ii) Consumer choice and financial decentralization

Reference to consumer choice and individual freedom has been at the core of the platform for market reforms in the libertarian strand of the literature (section IV). Unfortunately, most analyses of the market reforms fail to pick up on the narrow understanding of freedom of choice that is presupposed here. The negative presentialist notion of freedom that is implied defends the simple right to contract. As a reformist goal this was suited to an age where the principal struggle of working people was to gain the right to a free contract of labour, to be geographically and socially mobile, and to be accepted as worthy on the basis of merit rather than status.[85] These, though, were all basic positive freedoms accepted in Latin American countries, certainly Chile, by the mid-1970s.

Returning to our efficiency standard, the core question concerns the effectiveness of negative freedom (as presentialist contracts) in welfare markets in providing access to welfare for all and in reproducing a mainstream. In each of the relevant areas of welfare covered in this book, slightly different problems of adverse selection apply. In the case of pension and health insurance, companies will de-select certain risk groups, or certain risk groups will end up paying unacceptable premiums, as argued above. The choice of how much you introduce distribution effects *ex ante*, for example, the difference highlighted by Barrientos and Lloyd-Sherlock between Colombia's and Chile's reforms may mark the difference between a system where, as unemployed, you lose your access to a pension or, as a certain age and risk group, your access to health, and a system in which you do not. Such technical details are significant in the context of individuals' lives. In education in Chile, we already noted how competitive selection had an inbuilt tendency towards polarization, in the production of 'waste-basket' schools (Angell and Helgø). It is difficult to find fault *prima facie* with the claim to freedom of choice for parents (in education) or firms (for training), which proponents of market reforms cite in defence of decentralized management. Most would agree that a reasonable freedom of choice is a good. The problem at hand is that the menu of choice does not form part of a mainstream. In education, for instance, freedom of choice is only real if schools do not de-select. In Chile the freedom of choice exercised by users of (those selected by) the better-performing schools was parasitic on the state schools' willingness to act as last resort and accept those unable to enter the better schools.[86]

This centrifugal system was deliberately promoted by market reformers, and reflects the simple choice to withdraw the state from reproducing the mainstream. The lack of mainstream standards in schools compounded problems of social integration through the labour market and training. Several of the chapters demonstrate the centrifugal tendency created as a result of atomization and competitive selection in welfare markets. 'Cream-skimming' (the selection by service providers of the better able, less sick, individuals) usually associated with insurance markets (Chapter 7) occurs in education as well. Private schools perform better because they are able to attract better students, not because they themselves produce a more optimal service. In a direct comparison of secondary privately- and state-run schools (Chapter 4), the latter were found more effective. In the case of training, simple territorial distribution (tax rebates) meant that existing power relations in firms exercised strong effects on the selection of the beneficiaries of public finance for training. In short, these cases are a practical representation of the (negative) welfare cycles depicted in section IV. They show how financial decentralization undermines the equity, which the setting of fixed per-unit subsidies and of minimum national standards is supposed to achieve. Financial decentralization allows vicious and virtuous circles, in schools or in firms, to become entrenched, and hence allows the segmentation in welfare outcomes to widen.

In summary, the contemporary pursuit of presentialist contracts has tended to go against the expansion of freedoms. As argued in section IV, improving the freedom properties of labour markets for individuals would demand, at the very least, the unconditional provision of basic services and of minimum incomes. In the sphere of work this occurs because of the lack of individual control over movement. In welfare markets presentialist contracts undermine freedom because of the ineffectiveness of choice for all bar the lowest risk groups. Presentialist contracts might have been expanded to some degree in one sphere, say in work, had welfare access been more secure. But a maximization of both was unfeasible.

It could be argued in the favour of the market reforms that the polarization produced by the choice model is a necessary trade-off to ensure diversity, local autonomy of schools and parental freedom of choice. In light of the experience of some centralized systems, this juxtaposition however, is false. Local state schools in the *Folkeskole* (state school system) in Scandinavia, to take one example, have considerable autonomy within a flexible but strongly supervised public curriculum.[87] Private schools exist, but form part of the mainstream, and charges are at a generally affordable level. What makes this kind of local autonomy compatible with national equity is the element of centralized finance. In this case parents have the assurance that should they choose a school of a particular kind (say, that concentrates more on language instruction, a school that places emphasis on play (like the Steiner) or one that values Catholic teaching), their children will (at least) form part of a mainstream. Problems of equity always remain: but parental choice is not restricted in this case in the same structural way, for example, by residence in a municipality with materially inadequate schools, due to resident poverty. An interesting point of comparison arises with Chile, in that in this case it was precisely through the 'marginal' programmes, discussed by Angell, which were financed in a centralized way, that local schools were given real space for developing difference. The idea, then, that full financial decentralization is necessary to expand individual choice is disputable. It is also questionable on efficiency grounds. In Chile and Mexico, targeting worked not because it expressed a 'minimal state' (i.e. because targeting focused on marginal sectors), but because in its style of delivery it imitated state-guided mainstream (centrally financed) provision. According to Angell, the programmes he assessed worked because they were at one and the same time a model of bureaucratic efficiency and designed to develop community input. Ironically, this is in many ways what state-guided, broad-based social development programmes in countries with strong social development records (Cuba, Japan, Korea, Kerala in India) have traditionally sought to achieve.[88] Therefore, both the example of Mexico's PROGRESA and Chile's MECE 900 suggest that Latin American states may do better to focus on reforming their states and turning targeting methods into mainstream provision than leasing the responsibility for mainstream welfare to markets.

(iii) Administrative efficiency, decentralization and fairness

The achievement of administrative (cost) efficiency is the central efficiency claim made by market reformers in favour of decentralization. The rationale is that low-level decisions produce better value for money. The case studies in this book attack this notion at different levels. For the case of the labour market, Haagh (Chapter 1) shows that sector-level agreements and the longer-term influence of unions can have important efficiency implications for training. But the argument has been particularly about the effects of decentralized systems in the public and mixed (public and private) sectors of education and health. Barrientos and Lloyd-Sherlock (Chapter 7) point to the high administration costs of Chile's atomized system, and its low quality-for-money for certain risk groups compared with the *ex ante* distributional aspects of Colombia's scheme. Gideon (Chapter 8) points to deficiencies in the public side of the system.

In the case of education, market reformers made the assumption that schools within the public sector would not have incentives to perform, and therefore private administration – given the same resources – would produce better results. But in Chile, in seeming contravention of Friedman's calculus, the state-owned municipal schools performed better than the privately–run, state-subsidized schools (in secondary education, Chapter 4). The explanation Helgø offers is that state schools were able to compete on a par with private schools at this level (less demand on the state schools to act as a last resort for bad students). On the other hand, availability of basic infrastructure resources and teaching materials did seem to matter to school performance. Similar findings come out of Parandekar's contribution on El Salvador (Chapter 6). These chapters therefore provide a practical insight into the working of negative or positive cycles (section IV) in respectively market-based and public sphere-centred welfare production.

A further rationale in favour of financial and administrative decentralization arises from the negative assumption of possible misuse of funds and, ultimately, corruption in bureaucracies that are far removed from the usury and the local community (the decentred consensus, section III). The question here is, why should one assume that decentralization, or greater local autonomy, gets rid of corruption? Chile's bureaucracy is well known as one of, if not the, cleanest public administration in Latin America, and at the same time it is one of the most centralized systems.[89] Angell's account indicates how a centralized targeting policy can be efficiently run. On the other hand, Gray-Molina's discussion of the participation programme in Bolivia provides a sobering insight into the possible inefficiency and political usage of public resources at community level. These two cases suggest that it is the political institutions, or institutional traditions, that matter to corruption and inefficiency, and not the level of the centralization of finance. In the case of Bolivia, the speed of the decentralization, it seems, was also a factor. It proves again that simple financial decentralization, unaccompanied by a process of institutional building and political learning, can be a dangerous and polarizing experience. On the other hand, Latapí's chapter for Mexico's PROGRESA suggests how the switch to a poverty programme based on neutral and centrally set (albeit locally managed) criteria improved the honesty of Mexico's notoriously bad record in the political management of development aid.

Fairness is the *sine qua non* of services like health. But fairness can also be narrowly conceived in ways that go against the concept of the mainstream itself. The notion of administrative efficiency used in the attempt at financial decentralization of large-scale services like health has introduced a new individualistic concept of fairness. The new concept is based on a strict territorial, as opposed to universal, distribution of public resources. An example is the introduction of the *Fichas CAS* discussed by Gideon (Chapter 8). In this case units of health services are divided equally by person over defined periods of time (per year), regardless in principle of whether the person is at that time in need of more or less than the stated amount. It is doubtful whether this health voucher concept would pass other tests of fairness that have become acceptable today. Taken to its logical conclusion, most people would not accept that a person with a terrible illness should be left to flounder because of his/her misfortune (having used up her credits).

An alternative way of keeping public resources at bay would be to establish access according to need, but adjusting entitlements to particular services according to reasoned priorities. As we have already observed (section IV), relative cost efficiency between such (purchased versus provided) systems cannot be given *a priori* according to neutral criteria. Efficiency in both cases depends on a range of administrative (including computational) tools. But it seems fairly clear that individualistic fairness systematically wastes resources in refusing even to make the attempt to match spending according to differential need; for instance, in the case of health (the *Fichas CAS*), to not consider that a large number of people receiving the 'stated amount' in fact are not ill or in need of preventive attention. This argument is very similar to the case for training subsidies that are sensitive to firm size (Chapter 1), as opposed to universal rates (another instance of individualistic fairness), that end up supporting only large firms (that train anyway), and hence waste public resources. In summary, the examples of health, education and training indicate that retaining a mainstream, and therefore efficiency, does require redistribution, and also that redistribution on demand (see note 81) may be less costly to administer than individualistic fairness.

(iv) Participation

We have already suggested how experiences of participation (loosely defined) have come to be seen as part and parcel of welfare policy. Methods of participation came to form a part of market reforms in the 1980s, partly as a savings device, partly as an aspect of multilateral aid and loan conditionality; in both cases, as a way of streamlining what was seen as ineffective bureaucracy. Idealistic aspirations, in the form of personal and community empowerment, territorial autonomy and self-help, fitted in conveniently (section III). An important question to raise is how important experiences of participation are for good quality services. Is it right or even possible to make (genuine) participation compulsory, an in-built part of the service? Is the fact that we value participation as a community or individual experience an argument for introducing participation as a welfare policy tool? This is where the confusion lies. An argument could be made that the aim of social services is to provide the basic means to enable people to choose freely how they want to participate and engage in productive activities. Its purpose is to provide access to freedoms, not to define how such freedoms are used. That kind of activity *should*, appropriately speaking, be separate from the state. Seen in this way, making an ill-defined participatory role a condition for obtaining social rights is patronizing as well as misplaced. Without pretending to resolve the 'participation debate', we wish to suggest that the participation term, though freely used, is not well defined, is romantically loaded, and more often than not does not fulfil the expectations it raises. What participation actually means, and how important it is, will vary depending on policy area and individual countries. The notion has been used in many different guises, from participation as 'stake-holding' in a more economic sense (owning a share, contributing to an insurance plan), to municipal and/or local school/health centre autonomy, to participation as the use of 'groups' (local communities, firms) as consumers in welfare markets, and to the involvement of (local) voluntary labour in policy implementation. In each case, the answer to the questions of how real participation is, how significant to qualitative welfare goals, to freedom, and to cost-accountancy, differs.

a. Participation as consumer choice/stakeholding

The idea of participation as consumer choice is most closely associated with the assumptions of a market rational model, which we discussed in section IV.

This is the 'economic' concept of participation. But we have already seen, looking at the Scandinavian case, that there is no necessary opposition between centralized redistributive systems and local autonomy. In Scandinavian settings (centrally financed), systems of income support can in practice give regions considerable autonomy in promoting particular lines of employment and training for unemployed people (in consultation with community actors, business and individual recipients).[90] We saw how the concept of participation associated with consumer choice and personal stakeholding is based on a negative (presentialist) notion of freedom, that is, a simple equation between freedom and choice. This kind of participation may provide good services (freedoms) to individuals in certain groups (of good income, low risk), but it does not necessarily provide a continuous service (and freedom), or one that is well connected with other welfare domains. In most welfare or social development markets consumer choice is in reality highly selective, as we saw for training (large employers vis-à-vis small ones and workers), education (parents living in richer communities) and health (certain risk groups). For other groups choice does not readily translate into freedoms. It is difficult to see in these cases where the alleged opposition between efficiency and equity (both as freedom and utility) lies. In each case the selectiveness of markets was negative.

b. *Participation as autonomy of service providers*
The idealistic idea of participation (making autonomous decisions about local development issues) has also been linked to the notion of administrative efficiency, when finance is decentralized to local municipalities or regional governments acting in education and health. In this case we have already discussed the problems that financial and administrative decentralization might occasion in the development of the mainstream. The area in which the term participation in welfare markets has been most in vogue is where local communities (groups) demand, and are in some way involved with, development programmes.

c. *Participation as groups in welfare markets*
The idea of participation of groups in welfare markets appears to unite the case for financial decentralization with idealistic notions about community spirit and growth. The assumption is that community infrastructure together with development of a 'say' (away from gloomy bureaucracies) coincide with fiscal savings as the most needy (communities) are given preference. Just as in the area of targeting, endeavours to bring deprived communities up to a certain standard appear worthwhile both on cost-effectiveness and fairness grounds. However, problems arise, as with targeting, when this community bias becomes or replaces general provision. The notion that higher participation and service quality is tied to autonomy from central management is not always borne out, as the chapter by Parandekar shows. As in the case of

corruption, problems of undemocratic leadership and imposition are as likely, or more so perhaps, to arise in a local community context, as at higher levels, creating the new problem that nebulously defined groups' rights override individual ones. Territorial versus universal redistribution also potentially scatters the infrastructure of welfare delivery, when 'community' wishes are not easily locked into a national network (Chapter 10). The chapter by Latapí shows an interesting aspect of discrimination against individual rights in a community-oriented programme (PROGRESA). In this case, although individuals were targeted on the basis of universal criteria, certain individuals duly eligible did not in practice qualify, because the programme was implemented only in *communities* defined as poor.

d. Involvement of voluntary labour

A romantic notion of participation has also been invoked in association with various forms of financial decentralization that involves the work of voluntary NGOs, without such NGOs gaining the influence to which they aspired. The chapter by Gideon discusses the experience of voluntary health groups within the decentralized health care system in Chile. This example shows how the process of participation can take on a duplicitous character, as the volunteers who clamour to participate to ensure an extended service for particular groups, end up merely supporting centralized cost-savings schemes. The case of the '*monitores*' in education (local school volunteers), discussed by Angell, provides perhaps a more positive case. But then again, their role was clearly defined from the outset within a nation-wide programme. Effectively they were acting as employees, not as a quasi-interest group seeking to influence policy, which is later co-opted.

Conclusion

We have argued that the debate about policy reforms today is not about substantive goals as much as it is about methods. Oye's 'great trade-off between efficiency and equity' therefore is particularly misplaced for the area of welfare.[91] Whilst it is generally accepted that trade-offs can exist between equity (as income inequality), on the one hand, and efficiency and valued freedoms, on the other, particularly in the medium term, it is more difficult to accept this as an obvious truth for welfare. To pose cost efficiency as an end in itself in the case of welfare is clearly absurd. Some consideration of acceptable welfare outcomes must logically enter a discussion of any policy with the explicit design to improve on welfare, whether as an end state or as a means. We have argued that a (historically sensitive) lowest common denominator between libertarian and welfarist positions might point to the right of access, irrespective of income, to a decent pension and health care, to a place in mainstream education, and the possibility of rejoining the mainstream, through training, unemployment benefit and/or access to targeted programmes designed to bring marginalized individuals 'in'.[92] Corresponding with a developmental conception of freedom (Haagh, 2002,a,d; Chapter 1) these would ideally emphasize choice over compulsion. Certain standards would also have to be set and followed in the occupational realm in order for work experiences to hold a reasonable level of currency, though these could in principle allow for the maximum possible flexibility at enterprise level that is compatible with an acceptable mainstream.

In the welfare debate, then, efficiency must be understood as the ability of given institutional designs to achieve such welfare goals as are compatible with our notion of acceptable mainstream levels of welfare. But a key methodological difference remains: whereas market reformers and critics both see the mainstream as a normative guide, the latter more explicitly see the mainstream as an *efficiency* guide. At the crux of the matter is the question of how far the social mainstream has to be defined and locked into institutional designs *ex ante*, where it can be predicted or shown that extreme financial decentralization is counter-productive. How this debate is resolved depends in part on what are considered legitimate levels and forms of governance, and particularly on the form and legitimacy of the state.

This points to another difference: whereas market reformers see the loss of the mainstream (for a period, until the market 'works') as a price that has to be and is worth paying for economic reform, critics of recent reforms believe this is a dangerous path to take for several reasons. Freedom-oriented welfarist positions would see it as dangerous because it implies the acceptance in principle of the complete submersion of the means necessary to certain (economic) freedoms that even libertarians must value. Objections can also be made on efficiency grounds. One such objection would point to the historical institutional and statistical evidence to suggest that recognizable standards of human development are a necessary incentive to broad-based productive economic investments.[93] We have pointed in more general terms to the need to recognize the wider systemic properties of welfare production, and their temporal character. The divisive impact of market process within and the general trend towards the atomization of welfare, through localized governance and markets, which this book seeks to depict, also points to the difficulty of re-introducing mainstream standards once such standards are lost. In other words, to postpone the mainstream is not only to postpone broad-based development, but also to erect actual *barriers* to it. Such barriers range from vested interests in the private sector, to political, financial and administrative pressures, and through to the way the challenge grows as social disparities make the introduction of mainstream standards an ever more distant goal. Financial decentralization separates the governance of welfare domains at all levels, including the local level. Whether through labour relations in firms (Chapter 1) or through local communities (Chapter 10), the case studies in this book provide evidence of the way financial decentralization embeds social service markets in relations of power. Chile again provides a good illustration of the difficulty of policy reversal (Chapters 2, 4, 5, 7 and 8). Though this country has retained an efficient and uncorrupt state apparatus it has not proved possible to return to a mainstream model of welfare, following the radical introduction of market reforms. The policymakers seeking to soften the original market model in Chile after 1990 refrained, on the whole, from touching the general choice-competition model in education and health. Re-reforming the structure of atomized welfare markets is an arduous and, above all, a political challenge.

Notes

1. Marglin and Schor (1990). On Latin America, see Thorp and Whitehead (1986).
2. Despite notable differences (section IV below) neo-classical economic thought (Friedman (1962,1980), Krueger (1983)) and libertarian thought (Nozick (1974), Hayek (1960,1973,1976)), share a market neutral perspective, based on (i) the primacy accorded to the individual freedom to contract (specifically its methodological detachment from social and individual consequences that may be valued); (ii) the belief in the superior (self-sustaining or neutral) function of market mechanisms in producing growth, and economic and social and well-being.
3. There is no authoritative definition of the governance term. We broadly adopt the Laskian (1936) tradition that sees markets as politically structured. Hence, market governance (markets as an 'economic governance structure') as defined by Bowles and Gintis (1996, p. 309) is a form of political governance: 'the rules of ownership, forms of competition, norms and conventions that regulate the incentives and constraints faced by economic actors, and hence that determine the nature of coordination failures and their solutions.' See further Pagano (1985), Solow (1990), Arestis et al. 1997, Marglin and Schor (1990), Putterman (1986, 1990).
4. Marshall (1949, p. 58) considered the dominance of the 'provided' minimum (unrelated to income except through taxation) relative to the 'purchased service' the hallmark of the development of more socially inclusive societies, that is, as a means of deepening social citizenship.
5. Social contract refers to the relationship between state and society in welfare production, both in the institutional sense and in the generation of welfare norms. Normally the content or depth of social contract would specify (tacitly or legally) the number and depth of standard welfare goods that the state guarantees, though these may in practice be delivered, partly financed and/or depend on non-state social arrangements.
6. That such effects exist is implied in Marshall's depiction as noted, and also in Esping-Andersen's (1990) work on the stratification effects of welfare states.
7. Titmuss (1958, 1974) and Esping-Andersen (1990) similarly defined differences in welfare systems to lie in the degree to which social rights replaced market provision (hence Titmus's 'residual' welfare state of minimums for the weakest versus the institutionalized welfare state, based on the tax-rights financial nexus, and Esping-Andersen's degrees of de-commodification (market dependence)).
8. The 'corporatist' social insurance-based model and the 'social democratic' universal model of welfare depicted by Esping-Andersen (1990) both aim explicitly to structure welfare outcomes according to specific egalitarian criteria (universally or within occupational groups) – and as such both are essentially rights-based, in contrast with the liberal model which separates process (market) from outcome.

9. A presentialist contract (Williamson, 1985, p. 69) is a form of contract that limits economic commitments as far as possible to the present, so in a business relationship, short-term pay-back or delivery, or in labour contracts, the day labourer contract (in the extreme form). Because of the immediacy and minimal 'human' or relational (temporal) commitment of the transaction, these represent the contractual form that most resembles the pure markets thought optimal by neo-liberal theorists.
10. For example, Mill ([1859] (1982), Applications, p. 176) despite his opposition to state intervention, was an early advocate of universal and compulsory schooling, as was Malthus (as explained in Donzelot (1997, pp. 73–4)).
11. See particularly Graham (1998, pp. vii, 1–3). Typically 'market reforms' are referred to in general, such as that arguments about the detrimental effects of the extent of the introduction of market principles in welfare, would be construed as a general attack on markets.
12. Graham (1998), p. 39.
13. Comment by Nancy Birdsall, Executive Vice President of the Inter-American Development Bank, back cover of Graham (1998). See also World Bank (1997), pp. 4–5, 26, 56 for a salutary evaluation.
14. See Huber (1996) for discussion of these two cases. Brazil's trajectory towards a rights-based regime is looking increasingly insecure following the conservative turn of economic policy since the mid-1990s.
15. Examples include Sen's focus on 'a life of meaningful options' (1992), and the centrality of freedoms attained through capabilities and functions (1999), and conceptions about the broad institutional framework for social integration, as conceived through different welfare regimes (Esping-Andersen *op. cit.*) or through different forms of occupational citizenship (Haagh, 2002). We refer to these as freedom-oriented welfarist perspectives.
16. Sen (1999), p. 74.
17. Sen (1999), p. 75.
18. Chile remains one of the most unequal countries in the world as defined by the distribution of income. Chile's gini co-efficient was 56.5 in 1994, surpassed (outside sub-Saharan Africa) only by Brazil, at 60 in 1993, and Paraguay, at 59.1 in 1995. (All mid-1990s figures.) World Bank (2000/2001), p. 282.
19. Pension coverage declined from close to 80 per cent in 1970 to less than 51 per cent of the labour force by 1998. Chilean courts were in 2001 (La Tercera April, 2001) stranded with over 150 000 claims for lost pensions contributions, a small portion of the 1.4 million pensions schemes (over 20 per cent of the economically active population) deemed to be in arrears or abandoned. Of the claims in court the majority take several years to reach a hearing, and a still significant number fall foul of a rule which allows debts to be cancelled after five years.
20. Hirst and Rhodes (2000) identify several uses of the term, of which the majority refer to what we could call business-functional uses (the new public management, corporate governance, and the minimal state).
21. Leftwich (2000, pp. 65–8) gives a summary of the post-modernist critique of development as a planned or even national process, and the associated valuation of localized governance.
22. For instance Sen (1999, pp. 153–4) sees political participation as constructive in generating substantive debate about development ends.
23. A clear expression of this tendency in the World Bank is the increasing use of participation conditionality in the use of social funds, for instance, conditioning

help for local school development on the participation of mothers (in Pakistan); or, in Chile, experiments with pro-poor policies through FOSIS (ILO 1998) that make communities bid for development funds. See also Chapter 5 in this volume.
24. On the style of flexibility in Denmark compared see Haagh (2001), ILO (1998).
25. As Esping-Andersen (1990, pp. 53, 67–9) depicts, Scandinavian societies resolved this tension in the postwar period by making public provision 'middle class' – good enough to deter middle earners away from the social contract.
26. And hence these differ from standard workfare campaigns, whose main focus is to compel individuals to work, without new projects, or with only weak projects, to organise the regeneration of occupational mainstreams and choice of work. The weight of the expansion of *opportunities* can be seen in the high level of voluntary mobility and voluntary take-up rates of new kinds of part-time, leave and job rotation schemes (Haagh, 2001). Hence, while certainly deplorable on freedom grounds, work conditionality may also be quite unnecessary (and a cost constraint) on efficiency grounds. Haagh (2001). Maurice *et al.* (1986).
27. 'Sensibly' because of the resistance in this paradigm (see below) to separate cost concerns from market process.
28. World Bank (1992), p. 3.
29. The Bank is not synonymous with the neo-liberal movement. It represents several sources of influence. Its adoption of policies consistent with neo-classical discourse is, however, a good indicator of the degree of influence on development policy generally of the neo-classical paradigm, and of the neo-liberal movement.
30. On how the state in East Asia went beyond 'market enhancement' and 'market friendly interventions' to organizing the market to suit developmental ends in general see Chang (2002) and in labour markets Chang and You (1993), Haagh (forthcoming b).
31. For a positive evaluation of the World Bank's (self-titled) 'comprehensive development framework', see Sen (1999) pp. 126–7.
32. As I explain elsewhere (2002 b,c, Chapter 1) this framework entailed a curious exchange of roles between business and state, whereby the latter came to finance (through tax breaks and leases), and the former to organize, welfare; in sharp contrast, for instance, with East Asia or Scandinavia, where business contributes to, and the state organizes, welfare.
33. In certain cases of authoritarian rule pro-democracy actors may be left significant space to engage with welfare issues, in so far as these are in principle recognized as political, as for instance in developmental states that have made fairly strong *ex ante*, political welfare commitments (to education, basic health) (Goodman *et al.* (1999), Park (1994), Haagh (2001)).
34. Sen (1999, pp. 66–7) discusses informational bases of social theories.
35. For early insurance systems, see Mesa-Lago (1978, 1989).
36. For general reviews on the politics, see Pollack (1998), and the economy Bosworth *et al.* (1994), Scott (1995).
37. Tamburi (1985), p. 60.
38. On the use of conventions in neo-liberal discourse in general, see Hirschman (1993).
39. With the exception of Brazil and Costa Rica, but with the caveats noted (note 14).
40. A good recent overview and summary of the literature is Tendler (1997). On political aspects, see Angell and Graham (1995).
41. For a discussion of different claims to decentralization in the debate, political, economic and social (referring to ideals of participation), see Haagh (2000).

42. For a good discussion of utility-based welfarist evaluation, see Sen (1991), pp. 2–3.
43. As arising from local (mainly larger) industrialists' ability to prevent the entry of cheaper goods from abroad, against the interests of the common man (lower prices and hence greater consumption). Smith (1998 [1776], pp. 315–16).
44. Apart from defence and justice, the state's duties included, according to Smith (1998 [1776], pp. 393–414) 'erecting... those publick institutions and those publick works, which, though... advantageous to a great society, are... such... [that the] profit[s] could never repay the expense to any individual... to erect and maintain.'
45. Even sympathetic readers of the liberal tradition in economics note that Friedman's aversion to state intervention was weakly supported by facts (Green (1987, pp. 73, 80), and more generally inspired in a normative aversion to the state.
46. Friedman suggests that the political determination of economic rules is necessarily, or inherently, more corrupting than the neutrality of market rules (1980, p. 292).
47. Friedman (1980), pp. 154–5.
48. 'Equality of outcome is in clear conflict with liberty'. Friedman (1980: p. 128, pp. 128–49).
49. On occupational streams, see Maurice et al. (1986). The notion of an occupational stream allows us to perceive how one stage in productive life can be institutionally connected to another, and how meaningful connections allow for self-sufficiency and sustainability in productive life.
50. Nozick (1974), but also Rand (1961) and Hayek (1973, 1976) strongly contributed to this revival of the idea of inalienable rights, which only a political order limited to free exchange between persons would protect. On this see also Green (1987), Sen (1991), pp. 12–14.
51. Hence the Thatcherite analogy with the household purse.
52. Nozick (1974), pp. 160–70, Rand (1964). And see note 14.
53. Hence Nozick's (1974, pp. 155–60) critique of 'patterned theories'.
54. Friedman's (1980, pp. 13–14) discussion of the role of voluntary exchange in the formation of prices also carries the tone of this advocacy.
55. This seems to entail an implicit assumption that private education both (a) enhances choice and (b) is more cost effective, and even that these are related. However, whether these never conflict is not clear.
56. Williamson (1985), pp. 62–72.
57. In the case of health, how does the non-health-expert consumer evaluate whether the cheapest possible service actually delivers services of reasonable *quality* and safety? The more dispersed the competition and services, the more difficult (costly) it would be for any public regulator to ensure good information and check the quality of services provided.
58. See also Haagh (2002b) on unemployment insurance.
59. For instance, because initial state schooling in principle aims at softening entry inequalities, and providing sustainable occupational channels for the more as well as the less academically gifted. On Germany, see Maurice et al. (1986).
60. Pagano (1985), pp. 139–62.
61. As in the case of the unspecified mechanism and time delay involved in the 'trickle-down effect'.
62. As we have already seen, this is Nozick's (1974) and Hayek's (1976) position.
63. Miller (1990, pp. 100–23) has convincingly argued that economic liberalism taken generally accepts notions of social responsibility, and an underlying morality of human equality, in the act of charity.

64. He premises his theory of the minimal (redistributive) state thus, 'If the set of holdings is properly generated...' (1974, pp. 230–1, 152–3), and his 'principle of rectification' entails the seemingly radical proposition to 'maximize the position of whatever group ends up least well-off in the society'.
65. Nozick justifies absolute individual rights to 'unheld' things individuals can claim (justice in acquisition, p. 152), but we can note that these are few in modern economies. Hence, if we are to follow Nozick strictly, most property does arise from economic 'sin' (p. 231). Tax, our just social contribution prior to indulging in free acquisition (consumption, property), therefore becomes possibly the only means in complex economies to free us from sin (and hence the relevance of taxation to protect the (just) right to own property, which Nozick values).
66. Nozick (1974, pp. 183–97).
67. Nozick (1974), p. 190 (and pp. 164–6, 190–6) on individual rights; and on end-state principles in general, pp. 153–5; and Rawls, pp. 198–204.
68. That libertarians potentially see this kind of freedom as fundamental is evident in Rand's (1964, p. 23) belief that 'thinking and productive work' are 'the two essentials of the method of survival proper to a rational being'. Cited in Green (1987, p. 52).
69. On developmental freedom as applied to economic democracy, see Archer (1995), and to occupational life, Haagh (2002a).
70. Nozick emphasizes the 'right to give' (1974, p. 168) that arises from legitimately owning individual property.
71. Sen (1992, p. 57) refers to agency achievement as 'the general usually social' goals (other than immediate social well-being) which the person has reason to value and 'the occurrence of such things [that one values, as] brought about by one's own efforts'. See note 15. The freedom-oriented welfare perspective entails an acceptance of the relevance of markets and market incentives to welfare; that is, to move and produce (labour), choose (consumption, activities), and to plan living (making savings, developing personal property and 'life styles'). Sen (1999, pp. 6–8, 75) and (1992, p. 14). On the freedom to contribute, see Haagh (2002a).
72. It is questionable whether this is possible (turning back the tide of systemic production), but it would also by extension limit freedoms libertarians possibly value to enjoy the full range of products and services entailed in modern economies.
73. It is impossible, as we have seen, due to the unfeasibility of computing all relevant economic variables and factors entailed in finding economically optimal solutions (Pagano, 1985, pp. 139–42, citing Hayek (1935)). Moreover, it may be undesirable in the context of the kind of human autonomy that derives from a certain level of economic (outcome) indeterminancy.
74. For this point and Sen's difference with respect to Rawls (1971), see Sen (1999), pp. 64–5. See also Sen (1991), on equity 'in the distribution of freedoms'.
75. This being said, the sense of a trade-off is clearly more prominent in countries of late development, and hence the tolerance say of economically ineffective democracies lower.
76. Denmark in 1998 spent 5.63 per cent of GDP on labour market programmes, the highest in a recent OECD comparison of selected countries (Haagh 2001, pp. 344 and 357). On the other hand, the degree of firing freedom in Denmark was only overtaken by the USA in a sample of 16 member countries assembled by the OECD (Smith 1998 p. 109) Close to 40 per cent of all existing jobs are opened each year. ILO (1999), p. 17. See further Haagh (2001) on labour market freedoms.
77. Income dependent variation in goods like unemployment and pension insurance co-exists with socialization of mainstream provision (basic income support).

78. Friedman (1980), pp. 95–6, 100–1, 140–5.
79. Friedman (1980), pp. 134–5. This critique builds on Hayek's discussion of the danger of 'made' orders (1973, pp. 35–54).
80. To take this somewhat elitist example from Alfred Marshall, 'the economic value of one great industrial genius is sufficient to cover the expenses of the education of a whole town...All that is spent during many years in opening the means of higher education to the masses would be well paid for if it called out one more Newton or Darwin, Shakespeare or Beethoven', Book Four, Chapter 6, Prgh 7.
81. Basic welfare services are (i) by nature standardized, (ii) cheap to deliver in human resources terms (wages in the social service sector are relatively low), (iii) not in need of means-testing (hence can simply apply to all); and can for all these reasons be delivered most expediently by the state. See also Sen (1999, p. 144).
82. Hayek (1976), p. 31.
83. In other words, if both libertarians and socialists ceased to imagine socialism as a necessary end outcome of social policy, libertarians could see some specified level of just distribution of means as the (just) bases for free experiments in utopias (Nozick 1974, pp. 330–4), and for 'achievements...greater than any single mind can foresee' (Hayek, 1960, p. 31) through the 'competitive efforts of many to induce the emergence of what we shall want when we see it (*ibid.*, p. 29)'; and democratic socialists might pursue their particular utopia in societies of individuals with a more enriched conception of solidarity, through the morality of a just distribution of means.
84. Cardoso (1994) and Raczynski (1991) have also questioned whether the positive indicators formed part of a general trend.
85. The classical sources are Polanyi (1944) and Marshall (1949).
86. See further Helgø (1999), Chapters 1 and 2.
87. A good source in English is Struve (1981).
88. Contrary to the tradition of public spending on urban luxury welfare in Latin America (Lloyd-Sherlock, 1998), such programmes entailed entitlement-based basic services, relying on the conditions mentioned in note 80. See also Tendler (1999) on similar programmes in Brazil.
89. See Angell (1988), (1995).
90. See Torfing (1999), and *Information* 19 July, 30 August 1998; *Socialforskningsinstitutet* (1998), No. 2.
91. Comment by Kenneth A. Oye, Director, MIT Center for International Studies, back-cover of Graham (1998).
92. Haagh (2002a).
93. On the theory of asset specificity and longer-term contracts, see Williamson (1985). The core statistical evidence remains centred on the Asian experience, as in Romer (1986), Lucas (1988), and Barro (1991).

Bibliography

Angell, A. and Graham, C., 'Can Social Sector Reform make Adjustment Sustainable and Equitable? Lessons from Chile and Venezuela', in *Journal of Latin American Studies*, Vol. 27, Part 1, February 1995.

Angell, A., 'Some Problems in the Interpretation of Recent Chilean History', *Bulletin of Latin American Research*, Vol. 7, No. 1, pp. 91–108, 1988.

Archer, R., *Economic Democracy – The Politics of Feasible Socialism*, Clarendon Press, Oxford, 1995.
Arestis, Philip, Palma, J. Gabriel., Sawyer, Malcolm C., Harcourt, Geoffrey Colin (eds), *Capital Controversy, Post-Keynesian Economics and the History of Economic Thought*, London: Routledge, 1997.
Barrientos, A., 'Has Latin America a Liberal Welfare Regime?', unpublished manuscript, 2002.
Bosworth, B.P. and Marfan, M., 'Saving, Investment and Economic growth', in *The Chilean Economy – Policy Lessons and Challenges*, Bosworth, B.P., Dornbusch, R., and Laban, R. (eds), The Brookings Institution, Washington, D.C., 1994.
Bowles, S. and Gintis, H., 'Efficient Redistribution: New Rules for Markets, States and Communities', in *Politics and Society*, Vol. 24, No. 4, December 1996, pp. 307–42.
Cardoso, E., Comment in '*The Chilean Economy – Policy Lessons and Challenges*, Barry P. Bosworth, Dornbusch, R., and Laban R. (eds), The Brookings Institution, Washington D.C., 1994.
Chang, H.-J., *Kicking Away the Ladder – Development Strategy in Historical Perspective*, Anthem Press, 2002.
Chang and You, J.-I., 'The Myth of Free Labour Market in Korea', *Contributions to Political Economy* 12, 1993.
Donzelot, J. *The Policing of Families – Welfare versus the State*, London, Hutchinson, 1977.
Esping-Andersen, G., *The Three Worlds of Welfare Capitalism*, Polity Press, Cambridge, 1990.
Friedman, M., *Capitalism and Freedom*, University of Chicago Press, Chicago and London, 1962.
Friedman, M., *Free to Choose*, Secker and Warburg, London, 1980.
Goodman, R., White, G., and Kwon, H.-J. (eds), *The East-Asian Welfare Model – Welfare Orientalism and the State*, Routledge, London and New York, 1998.
Graham, C., *Private Markets in Public Goods – Raising the Stakes in Market Reforms*, Brookings Institution Press, Washington D.C., 1998.
Green, David, G., *The New Right – The Counterrevolution in Political, Economic, and Social Thought*, Wheatsheaf Books, 1987.
Haagh, L., 'Chilean Social Reform', in *Learning from Reform Models*, Weyland, K. (ed.), Woodrow Wilson Center, Washington D.C., forthcoming a.
Haagh, L., 'The "Free" Labour Market and Korea's 1997 Financial Crisis', in collection based on the *Brazil–Korea Conference*, Institute of Latin American Studies, University of London, 9–11 December 2000, Amann, E. and Chang H.-J. (eds), Institute of Latin American Studies, forthcoming b.
Haagh, L., *Citizenship, Labour Markets and Democratization – Chile and the Modern Sequence*, Palgrave Macmillan, Basingstoke and New York, 2002a.
Haagh, L., 'The Emperor's New Clothes – Labour Reform and Social Democratisation in Chile', for *Studies in International Comparative Development*, University of Berkeley, 38:1, May 2002b.
Haagh, L., 'The Challenge of Labour Reform, in Korea: A Review of Contrasting Approaches to Market Enhancement', in *Labor Market Reforms in Korea: Policy Options for the Future*, World Bank, March 2001.
Haagh, L., 'Social Policy and Decentralizations: The Liberal Model in Chile Compared', Latin American Centre – University of Oxford, LAC-02-2000.
Haagh, L., 'Training Policy and the Property Rights of Labour in Chile: Social Citizenship in the Atomised Market Regime', in *Journal of Latin American Studies*, Vol. 31, Part II, May, pp. 429–72, 1999.

Haagh, L., D.Phil Dissertation, University of Oxford, 1997.
Hayek, F.A., *The Constitution of Liberty*, Routledge and Kegan Paul, London, 1960.
Hayek, F.A., *Law, Legislation and Liberty*, Vol. 1. Rules and Order. 1973.
Hayek, F.A., *Law, Legislation and Liberty*, Vol. 2. The Mirage of Social Justice, 1976.
Helgø, C.T., D.Phil Dissertation, Cambridge University, 1999.
Hirschman, A.O., 'The Rhetoric of Reaction – Two Years Later', in *Government and Opposition* 28:3, pp. 292–314, 1993.
Hirst, P. and Rhodes, R., in Pierre, J. (ed.), *Debating Governance*. Open University Press, London, 2000.
Huber, E., 'Options for Social Policy in Latin America: Neo-Liberal versus Social Democratic Models', in *Welfare States in Transition – National Adaptations in Global Economies*, Esping-Andersen, G. (ed.), UNRISD (United Nations Research Institute for Social Development) and Sage Publications, London, 1996.
International Labour Organization, 'Denmark: Flexibility, Security and Labour Market Success', Per Kongshøj-Madsen, ILO Employment and Training Papers, No. 53, Switzerland: Geneva, 1999.
International Labour Organization, *Chile – Crecimiento, empleo, y el desafío de la justicia social*, Geneva: 1998.
Krueger, A.O., *Trade and Employment in Developing Countries, Vol. 3., Synthesis and Conclusions*, Chicago University Press, 1983.
Laski, H., *The Rise of European Liberalism: An Essay in Interpretation*, London: George Allen and Unwin, 1936.
Leftwich, A., *States of Development*, Polity Press, 2000.
Lucas, R.E., 'On the mechanics of Economic Development', *Journal of Monetary Economics*, 22, pp. 3–42, 1988.
Marglin, S.A. and Schor, J.B. (eds), *The Golden Age of Capitalism*, Oxford: Clarendon Press, (1990).
Marshall, A., *Principles of Economics – An Introductory Volume*, Eighth Edition, Macmillan London, Melbourne, Toronto, 1966. [First edition 1890].
Marshall, T.H. *Citizenship and Social Class*, Cambridge University Press, 1949.
Maurice, M., Sellier, F. and Silvestre J.-J., *The Social Foundations of Industrial Power – A Comparison of France and Germany*, Cambridge, Mass. and London: MIT Press, 1986.
Mesa-Lago, C., *Ascent to Bankruptcy: Financing Social Security in Latin America*. Pittsburgh, Pittsburgh University Press, 1989.
Mesa-Lago, C. *Social Security in Latin America: Pressure Groups, Stratification and Inequality*, Pittsburgh, University of Pittsburgh Press, 1978.
Mill, J.S., *On Liberty*, The Penguin English Library, Richard Clay (The Chaucer Press), Bungay, Suffolk, 1982 [1859].
Miller, D., *Market, State and Community: Theoretical Foundations of Market Socialism*, Clarendon Press, Oxford, 1990.
Mills, C.W., *The Marxists*, Penguin Books, Middlesex, England; Victoria, Australia, 1962.
Nozick, R., *Anarchy, State and Utopia*, London, Blackwell, 1974.
Pagano, U., *Work and Welfare in Economic Theory*, Oxford, Basil Blackwell, 1985.
Park, Y.-B., 'State Regulation, the Labour Market and Economic Development: The Republic of Korea', in Rodgers, G. (ed.), *Workers' Institutions and Economic Growth in Asia*, Switzerland: Geneva, 1994.
Polanyi, K., *The Great Transformation*, Beacon Press, Boston, 1957 [1944].
Pollack, M. *'The New Right in Chile, 1973–97*, Palgrave Macmillan, 1999.
Putterman, L. *Division of Labor and Welfare – An Introduction to Economic Systems*, Oxford University Press, 1990.

Putterman, L., *The Economic Nature of the Firm – A Reader*, Cambridge: Cambridge University Press, 1986.
Raczynski, D., 'Decentralización y Políticas Sociales: Lecciones de la Experiencia Chilena y Tareas Pendientes', in *Colección Estudios Cieplan*, Número Especial, No. 31, pp. 141–52, Marzo 1991.
Rand, A., *The Virtue of Selfishness*, Signet, New York, 1964.
Rand, A., *For the New Intellectual*, Signet, New York, 1961.
Rawls, J., *A Theory of Justice*, Oxford University Press, 1971.
Romer, P.M. 'Increasing Returns and Long-Run Growth', *Journal of Political Economy*, 94(5), pp. 1002–37, 1986.
Scott, C.D., 'The Distributive Impact of the New Economic Model in Chile', revised version of paper presented to the Conference on 'The New Economic Model in Latin America and its Impact on Income Distribution and poverty', London, 11–12 May, 1995.
Sen, A. *Development as Freedom*, Oxford University Press, 1999.
Sen, A. (1992), *Inequality Re-examined*, Oxford, Clarendon Press, 1992.
Sen, A., 'Markets and Freedoms', Development Economic Research Programme, Suntory–Toyota International Centre for Economics and Related Disciplines, London School of Economics, DERP, No. 3, April, 1991.
Smith, A., *The Wealth of Nations*, Oxford/New York, Oxford University Press, 1998 [1776].
Smith, N. 'Det effective, rummelige og trykke danske arbejdsmarked?', in *Arbejdsmarkedspolitisk Årbog*, Denmark, Copenhagen, 1997.
Solow, R. *The Labour Market as a Social Institution*, Cambridge, Mass./Oxford: Basil Blackwell, 1990.
Struve, K., *Schools and Education in Denmark*, Det Danske Selskab, Copenhagen, 1981.
Tamburi, G., 'Social Security in Latin America: trends and outlook', in Mesa-Lago, C. (ed.), *The Crisis of Social Security and Health Care: Latin American Experiences and Lessons*, University of Pittsburgh, Centre of Latin American Studies, 1985.
Tendler, J., *Good Government in the Tropics*, Johns Hopkins University Press, 1977.
Thorp, R. and Whitehead, L., *Latin America – Debt and the Adjustment Crisis*, Basingstoke: Macmillan (now Palgrave Macmillan), St. Antony's, 1987.
Titmuss, R., *Social Policy*, Allen and Unwin, London, 1974.
Titmuss, R. *Essays on the Welfare State*, Allen and Unwin, London, 1958.
Torfing, J. 'Workfare, Danish-style?', *Centre for the Study of Democracy Bulletin*, 6(2), pp. 11–13, 1999.
Williamson, O.E., *The Economic Institutions of Capitalism*, New York, The Free Press, 1985.
Williamson, O.E., Wachter, M. and Harris, J. 'Understanding the Employment Relation: The Analysis of Idiosyncratic Exchange' in Putterman, L. (ed.), *The Economic Nature of the Firm*, Cambridge University Press, 1986.
World Bank (2000/2001) World Development Report, Oxford University Press, 2000/2001.
World Bank (1997) World Development Report, Oxford University Press, 1997.
World Bank (1993) World Development Report, Oxford University Press, 1993.
World Bank (1992) World Development Report, Oxford University Press, 1992.

Part 1
Labour Market and Social Policies

1
Human Resources and Decentralization in Chile

Louise Haagh

Three trends shaped social policy in Latin America from the 1970s to the millennium. The state withdrew from the provision of welfare, employers' flexibility over labour use was increased, and social policy tools were refined in an effort to make state activity complement rather than shape the role of markets in the production of welfare. The retraction of the state from the provision of welfare meant that social well-being became more sharply defined by individual performance in the employment sphere. Sustaining such performance on the other hand became a more difficult task as labour insecurities rose. In theory this situation should increase the importance of policy instruments that allow individuals to sustain their labour market connection. A key issue in the welfare debate in consequence is how far continuous (as opposed to fixed) employment is enhanced by new policy tools.[1] This must be the minimum performance criteria of a welfare model that sees social development as arising spontaneously from the working of markets.

In this chapter we will look at a policy area in which the direct prospects for building employability are especially good, namely workers' training post-schooling. Education for work and tradable training standards are the key to effective mobility, and therefore, as far as a market model that places a prize on individual mobility works, we should be able to deduce its effectiveness here. Moreover, the post-schooling stage in the development of human resources has the potential to involve firms directly, and hence the existence of an efficient link between social and labour policy is not only of particular importance in this field, but should also be more easy to build.

What policy instruments have been devised for the field of training reform, and what is peculiar about the Chilean case? Considering policy instruments decentralization represents beyond doubt the most popular trend (Introduction). Since the social policy reforms of the 1970s onwards, decentralization has represented one of the most persistent areas of policy and institutional change. Decentralization takes different forms, but the introduction of what we would call economic decentralization, the decentralization of the power to demand to smaller economic units, has featured prominently in the design of recent policy changes. Chile is usually considered not only as one of the earliest, but also the most successful proponent of such reforms. The country introduced a demand-based model early on, and the area of training was one of the first to undergo change. Chile therefore represents an optimal case for evaluating the success of decentralization; whereas training, as mentioned, must be considered the most plausible policy tool to aid the kind of de-regulated labour market that neo-liberal reforms set out to produce. Chile, moreover, is the only country in Latin America that has completed the liberal economic reforms that are pursued throughout the continent, as well as the country with the best macro-economic performance. This provides us with a good period of hindsight and fertile ground for evaluating the impact of economic decentralization, and the factors that have influenced this policy model's achievements.

The Chilean experience has been rich and varied. In some ways the success of macro-economic performance provides us with a best possible setting to evaluate welfare market reforms. For more than a decade following the recovery that began in the mid-1980s, real wages improved, unemployment steadily fell, and growth averaged 7 per cent. This success notwithstanding, structural weaknesses in the economy revealed the challenges to social policy that persisted. For instance, high unemployment (peaking at 13.8 per cent in Santiago for the month of March 2001, following over three years of two-digit figures) and the end of the period of easy re-integration of labour, cast doubt on the actual flexibility of the labour market, particularly in response to crisis. This means that the liberal thesis is no more so evident, even for Chile, that as long as maximized markets are allowed to get on with it, what is required in terms of human development and social integration will follow in time.[2] The emphasis on recycling human resources effectively within the neo-liberal paradigm only serves to underline the centrality of training policy within this equation.

The decentralizing reforms in Chile have some advantages, and the reasons for the model's overall weakness are complex. Nevertheless, we will stress here the excessively narrow focus on the economic component in decentralizing reforms. This has included an over-application of market principles that do not apply well to human (as opposed to physical) resources, and an under-application of political factors in decentralizing reforms (Introduction, section IV). An appropriate demarcation of property rights is important within any market in order to facilitate fluid transactions to occur. However, in the case of human resources, the definition of property rights is an especially delicate matter considering the particular requirements of reproduction that is tied to this asset, and hence the special need for longer-term contracts.[3] Greater involvement of political actors and aspects of planning are, therefore, particularly important to the success of policies that emphasize the mobility of human resources. The special conditions attached to the human commodity mean that it is not optimal on either freedom or efficiency grounds to centre economic flexibility narrowly in the freedom of firms, when this freedom can be exercised to the detriment of the long-term flexibility of the carriers of human resources, that is, individual workers. The political factors we will emphasize have to do with securing long-term flexibility in the development of human resources. These are: (i) the lack (or under-application) of mechanisms of institutional coordination (network efficiency) at the national level with other areas of social policy, and (ii) the lack of integration of labour institutions with social policy. The first may be explained by a strict adherence to a doctrine of non-intervention among the agents of labour policy, considering that Chile had a reasonable level of institutional capital in the area of training provision. Meanwhile, the second aspect can be explained by the weakness of social institutions (like unions) during the first decade-and-a-half of the new training regime. Together, these shortcomings suggest why there were not the necessary institutions and political will to develop a more efficient (in effect, a more democratic) structure of property rights in relation to human resources in Chile.

Below we first outline briefly the training regime developed since the 1970s. We then look at trends in the labour market and at general problems of property rights in relation to human resources that would indicate the possible problems in a demand-based model in Chile. Lastly, we look at the two sources of political failure mentioned above. In order to discuss the weak integration between labour and social policy reforms, we assess the evidence from a 1992 survey of union presidents.[4]

The 1970s training reforms

Efforts towards ensuring that workers have good access to training would seem on the surface to be compatible with a policy to make labour markets more flexible: adequate skills make workers better able to move in labour markets, thus reducing the costs both of quits and dismissals. However, the strict neoclassical vision of labour markets pursued in Chile since the 1970s precluded a more engaging role for the state. Training policy came early on to be perceived quite mechanically as an extension of labour management of individual firms, following the neoclassical theorem that all economic decisions are best made at this level.[5] Moreover, ministers of the first democratic government that followed authoritarian rule, in 1990, adopted broadly the liberal reforms and neoclassical thinking of the preceding regime. They emphasized the principle that social policy should be centred on poverty relief and the control of inflation. It could not be a 'welfare' or a 'labour market' policy.[6] Hence a neoclassical position has been consistently followed by policy-makers in Chile for the last three decades.

Radical deregulation of labour institutions was initiated upon Pinochet coming to power in a 1973 coup. INACAP, the government-controlled training corporation, was privatized and around 70 public training corporations (henceforth TCs) were passed over to private administration by entrepreneurial groups through renewable leases held by the state. The Pinochet government sought to create a competitive market in training provision and, by the mid-1980s, close to 800 establishments offering training had come into existence. A public body under the Labour Ministry, SENCE, was set up in 1976 to regulate the activities of the private TCs. The system of public finance devised for the emergent market in training shows that the new regime represented a particular (not a neutral) market design. It was decided, for instance, that the bulk of public resources should be channelled through a tax rebate scheme (Table 1.1). This represented an explicit choice about who should be consumers in training markets, by centring the power to demand directly and exclusively in the managers of individual firms. Hence, although the intended beneficiaries were individual workers, authority to demand resided in firms. This structure had two biases, the first between individual firms, which because of their differing size and market position would respond very differently as consumers, and the second between the government of firms (management) and individual workers. We could call these the between-firm and the labour relations biases. We could also identify a third bias, namely, the separate introduction of the training reforms from other reforms that are important to the development of human resources, including reforms to social security, to forms of unemployment protection and to programmes that target marginal sectors. Together, the between-firm bias and this broader coordination failure constitute the first kind of political weakness in decentralization highlighted earlier. Meanwhile the labour relations bias represents the second kind of political weakness in decentralization.

Table 1.1 Percentage distribution of participants and spending on different SENCE Programmes (selected years)

Years	Tax deduction Programme (%)		Apprentice Scheme (%)		Grant Programme (%)		Youth Training Scheme (%)		Total (%)
	1	2	1	2	1	2	1	2	
1977	41	40	–	–	59	60	–	–	100
1980	65	65	–	–	35	35	–	–	100
1985	86	91	–	–	14	9	–	–	100
1990	97	98	0.2	0.0	2.4	0	–	–	100
1991	91	74	0.3	0.3	2.2	3.6	6.5	22.3	100
1996	**94**	77	**0.1**	0.3	1.4	2.3	**3.8**	18.8	100

Notes: 1 Participants, 2 Spending.
Source: The Labour Ministry Chile.

The origin of these biases is ideological, reflecting a particular vision of markets and of the role of states, held by economic policy-makers at the time. It held that since state intervention was a form of unjust interference (Introduction section IV), such interference (including assistance) should be equal regardless of need. In this vision fairness is understood in the limited sense of equal benefits (to the target group, not to all), leaving at all times the structure of economic opportunities constant.[7] This approach was not deliberately selective, but the outcome, in terms of who would effectively have power to demand training resources, was. The concentration of power to demand in employers moreover was intensified by policy-makers over time. In 1977 at least 60 per cent of public funding for workers' training was channelled through a grant scheme targeting workers directly at the municipal level. By 1985 this was down to 35 per cent; by 1990 it had fallen to 3 per cent, and between 1996 and 2002 (at the time of writing) remained at this level (2 per cent (Table 1.1)). There were potential benefits in the new training reform, particularly in creating a more diversified set of training providers. The problems resided in the absence of guidelines to these, and in the nature of the demand structure created. These meant that training policy over time did not fit well with the direction that labour market flexibility actually took in Chile.

Precariousness as a social policy challenge

The form of labour market flexibility pursued in Chile increased corporations' immediate freedom in the use of labour. Corporations' freedom in labour use was seen as fixed. On the other hand, workers' access to welfare and related means to help increase their freedom to move and choose was considered a derivative unworthy of explicit policy consideration except in specific cases.[8] As a consequence, precariousness in working conditions within the Chilean labour market was allowed to increase markedly from the mid-1970s onwards. The distinction between formal and informal work became less relevant as a way of defining social exclusion, as informal conditions became general to working life. On the one hand, in the 1980s and up to the mid-1990s, Chile had one of the highest rates of re-formalization of labour markets, as contractual employment nearly doubled during the 1980s, following a deep economic down turn in 1982–83, to return to historical levels of just over 60 per cent by the end of the decade. On the other hand, precariousness, defined as the displacement of risks onto individual workers, became a permanent feature of formal (waged) work, as the burden of social security and risk-taking steadily shifted from employers, down from 40 to 3 per cent of their non-wage costs, from the mid-1960s to the mid-1990s.[9]

Precariousness intensifies the problems individuals face in retaining their links with labour markets, and increases the need for social interventions, including interventions to increase the tradable value of skills. Labour

Ministry data for Chile suggests that only 24 per cent of new contracts signed in 1998 were indefinite contracts, with 32 per cent being fixed-term contracts, and 50.1 per cent of work terminations caused by the expiry of fixed-term contracts. Of the total of the work-force that had indefinite work contracts, 81.6 per cent, half had been employed for less than five years. This fact conceals a high level of vulnerability in terms of social insurance and prospectively unemployment insurance as well.[10]

At the same time, the official data suffers from two kinds of drawbacks. Employers would be unlikely to reveal the true numbers of workers on precarious contracts, whereas workers might well feel compelled not to reveal conflictive information in an interview process openly involving employers. In this context, the author's 1992 non-official survey of union presidents proved a useful source on the organization of work because of the status of union presidents as full-time workers and their day-to-day involvement in the resolution of work disputes. Since conditions of work are generally found to be better in unionized firms, and since the survey was carried out some years before the official ENCLA survey (which represents a trend of intensified precariousness), labour relations and the organization of work in the local union survey could be said to represent a 'best possible' setting. The union survey indicated that in 41 per cent of the establishments investigated at least 20 per cent of the waged work-force had no employment contracts. Only 38 per cent of those interviewed cited a yearly wage variability of less than 25 per cent (in their own wage). Another 37 per cent experienced not only more than 25 per cent variability, but also reported a level of turnover within their establishment over the past two years that exceeded 30 per cent, and at least once the employer had fired workers in order that they may rehire them on different terms.[11] In all, it was only in 37 per cent of the companies studied that a formal wage structure could be identified. Moreover, in 34 per cent of firms (these were all manufacturing firms), union presidents could confirm that less than 1 per cent of workers had received training in the previous 24 months. This incidentally accords rather well with ENCLA figures, which suggest that 38 per cent of the firms had carried out some form of workers' training in the previous 12 months, although the survey also demonstrated that six out of every ten employers that had characterized the firm as well endowed with management training (55.2 per cent), had not carried out any training for workers.[12] The union survey further showed that greater precariousness tended to decrease the likelihood of investments in training. This kind of data has both freedom and efficiency implications that bear on our central debate (Introduction). It points to the low level of security and personal control, and therefore the low level of freedom, associated with working life, and suggests at the same time that this state constituted a barrier to the development of human resources, stating the case therefore for better specified interventions on both freedom and efficiency grounds.

This brings us back to the subject of the peculiar conditions attached to investments in human resources, and the questions this raises about the distribution of freedoms and responsibilities in the sphere of work. The distribution of freedoms and responsibilities in turn are hard to separate from economic considerations concerning investments in skills. Let us look at the question of individual freedom first. Human resources are inalienable from their owners. Scholars from the classical liberal school to the Marxist have recognized the problems of individual freedom that this condition entails. As Marx observed in an imaginary dialogue with an employer:

> The use of my daily labour power therefore belongs to you. But by means of the price you pay for it every day, I must be able to reproduce it every day, thus allowing myself to sell it again … Very well, like a sensible thrifty owner of property, I will husband my sole wealth, my labour power … Every day, I will spend, set in motion, transfer into labour only as much of it as is compatible with its normal duration and healthy development.[13]

The problem of continued existence that Marx raised is more complex today, concerning such issues as what happens with the health and pension insurance of the worker continuously on flexible contracts, or to women with long periods out of work.[14] Moreover, it is not a problem confined to developed societies. The problem of secure flexibility was certainly felt by local leaders in Chile:

> For me [modernization] ought to mean raising our standards. In the sense of taking advantage of the new technology that arrives, and making provision for workers' training, so that we will have skills (*conocimientos*) which will enable us to make out in any other place as well which is taking advantage of the new technologies.

On the other hand, the problem of continued existence of the worker (her developmental freedom) must also be seen as a broader economic problem, as we suggested. An economic problem arises, for example, when investments in skills cannot effectively be recycled in labour markets. The condition of asset specificity suggests that unless employers can safely expect to keep their workers on a long-term basis, or can easily acquire comparable aptitudes, they have no immediate incentive to invest in their skills.[15] In this sense, precariousness in the formal labour market can be regarded as a dynamic factor of inefficiency in the development of human resources.[16] In this instance, problems involved in securing individual freedom have a significant coincidence with economic problems associated with the investment in human resources.

Let us then look at the Chilean case. At a simple level, the problem of Chilean labour institutions can be expressed in terms of institutional coordination: both workers and employers, in surveys, have expressed a high level of demand for training. In the case of employers, a SERCOTEC survey of 1991 found that 43 per cent of employers of small-and-medium-sized manufacturing firms required access to better-skilled workers. Yet, as we saw, the avenues for attaining such access were not well established. Workers did not have the means to demand publicly funded courses for training, and the kinds of blanket demand-based incentives that existed for employers failed to take account of the special situation of small- and medium-sized firms. For small- and medium-sized firms the 1 per cent of wages which they could claim back from taxes for workers' training tended to be insufficient to realize skill investments, hence the between-firm bias in a training system that relies solely on individual initiative in the investment in skills. Moreover, employers feared losing the investment if workers should quit. Indeed, another important aspect of the between-firm bias was the lack of mechanisms in Chile to ensure that broadly recognized skills standards existed, which would facilitate the match between individual workers and firms. The point to note, however, is that demand for skills did exist in Chile. In other words, actual (low) investment levels could not be taken to indicate that Chile was at a stage of economic development where better skills were not in demand. The fact that there was a demand for skills from firms defies the natural sequence explanation for why firms invested little in workers' skills in Chile, that is, that at that stage of economic development skills were not really required. One of the weaknesses in the neoclassical tradition in economics is the inability to explain the social and political dimension in technological innovation. In this line of analysis, technological changes 'appear', which then change social and economic practices (for instance, towards more relational forms – Schultz, 1993, p. 244). Efficient contracts (like the relational or long-term form) are 'selected' (Williamson, 1985, pp. 211–15) if proven efficient. In these cases, therefore, new technology or efficient contracts appear always to be arrived at in socially and politically neutral ways, i.e. through some kind of spurious or natural sequence. Hence, despite the important acknowledgement in these analyses (see Introduction, section IV) that long-term contracts can be more efficient, no admission is made to the effect that social and political arrangements may also condition the rise of technology and contractual forms. The possibility is excluded that certain social arrangements make investments in skills more likely, or in the Chilean case, that the absence of associational practices made them unlikely.

The evidence from Chile suggests that the problem of low investment was indeed institutional in nature, and consisted, at least in part, in the failure to specify a more optimal distribution of freedoms and responsibilities in labour markets or, in other words, in the failure to establish a more sophisticated system to identify the property rights of labour. Such a system would have placed greater emphasis on the ability of workers and small- and medium-sized firms, respectively to exercise greater command over mobility and training resources.

Defining the property rights over human resources and implications for policy

The market reforms introduced in Chile since the 1970s can be seen as an attempt to reproduce the classical liberal system of property rights – what Miller has referred to as the liberal or 'proprietary' notion of property relying on 'unrestricted control', 'where a person is seen as a self-determining agent controlling his material environment and recognizing no obligations to others around him'.[17] Essentially, this is the notion whereby property rights over resources become concentrated to a maximum degree, through legal and other means, in the owners of physical capital. A relevant contrast can be made with other national systems of governance where this legal 'personification' of the firm, as Chomsky has called it[18] has been countervailed by the development of other forms of property right, chiefly of the agents of human capital, namely labour, for example in certain Scandinavian or East Asian societies, in the main by making individuals the key agents who demand from integrated systems, of one form or another, of social welfare.[19] In these cases, a higher degree of network efficiency (Introduction) is – inadvertently or directly – attached to the securing of individual (and not corporate) freedom.

The neglect of the development of the markets and the property rights of labour in Chile had a passive form (as in the structuring of public finance for training), and an active form, in terms of maximizing limited and unsophisticated forms of contract in the labour market – what Williamson has referred to as the presentialist or classical form which 'favours escape clauses, limited commitments and short-term relationships', 'to cause to be perceived or realised *at present*' (emphasis added).[20] Examples of the latter in Chile included: (i) the development of *ad hoc* forms of bargaining entities in Chilean firms;[21] (ii) the promotion of precarious contracting; and (iii) the prohibition of regulation of the working day and/or night as well as workload.[22] Other important aspects included (iv) the expansion of individual account social insurance without links to other forms of state-guaranteed welfare provision; and (v) the leasing out of training supply on short-term contracts to a multitude of private providers (one of the longest state-provided contracts to private institutes, through the Youth Training Scheme of the 1990s, being six months). A key element, finally, was (vi) the promotion of short-term contracting in the training market, by centring the power to demand in individual employers, in a context where the state or industry played no role in the setting of standards. Together these elements of institutional segmentation in Chile represent the over-application of market principles – what we have referred to as the dominance of the economic logic in decentralization. Below we assess the possible implications for the development of human resources of this dominance, by considering the two broad areas where political factors in decentralizing reforms were under-applied.

The first, lack of institutional coordination, that is, the weakness of social contract and of integration between welfare domains, had consequences at the *aggregate* level of policy. The weakness of employer and welfare institutions entailed ineffective responses to unemployment and weak incentives to training investments. The second area, lack of integration with institutions of labour, had consequences at the *local* level, in this case for the ability to establish long-term relationships at the level of firms. We look at these two levels in turn.

Political failures in decentralization I: weakness of institutional coordination

Given the problem of asset specificity, investment coordination above the firm is vital to the development of human resources in the case where labour markets are fluid (labour mobility high). Without investment coordination (henceforth IC) skills cannot be traded, and without the prospect of a trade (for firms, finding comparable skills, and, for workers, being able to move) investments in skills will not be made. Primary education is the most centralized, in a sense the ultimate example of IC, but IC also occurs when the state establishes a levy on firms to help finance re-training schemes, or where a collectivity of firms, such as in an industry, undertakes a similar action. Other examples include systems of apprenticeship, in which case the network of contracts that develop the property rights of labour tends to be cast even deeper and wider.[23] Such links help strengthen the control that individuals have over the use of their human resources, but also help other entities in the market to develop a share in them, by establishing a band of universally recognizable (and therefore *tradable*) standards.

Investment coordination in skills may take a variety of forms in different national contexts: (i) bureaucratic identification of skill requirements and their co-financing among firms (as in Germany); (ii) a combination of state-initiated relocation of labour with decentralized administration of training programmes (as in Denmark); or (iii) the top-down orchestration of developmental guidelines (as in Korea).[24] The more decentralized decisions are (as in Denmark), the more sophisticated institutional links are required to be between different providers (training centres, municipal offices), and relevant users (employers and workers). This is necessary in order to make the demands of local autonomy and the maintenance of standards compatible. Ensuring the continuance of an equilibrium between these two potentially contradictory trends is not simple. It requires mechanisms of continuous mutual adjustment between the evolving realities and needs of localities (firms and regions), and efforts to maintain a network of recognizable standards that enable workers to trade the skills developed in one particular area more widely. In Denmark the regional labour market council, comprising representatives of the public administration, and employers and union organizations has played such a role. This institutional centre has helped set up apprenticeship schemes in the regions' firms (employers' initiative) which have a broader occupational content (union initiative).[25] However, in contrast with both Germany, Korea or Denmark, investment coordination in Chile was weak. In this case the tension between standards and local autonomy was posed in the terms of a stark opposition. Hence, only one of the two extremes, namely local autonomy (defined in this case as the decentralization of decisions to firms), was attempted. At the same time countervailing measures were not developed to ensure that firm decisions would be compatible with the development of an effective market in skills. In other words, the greater power of decision of firms was not matched with a political component that would provide firms and workers with training options that had a secure and tradable value through time. Socio-economic councils functioned in some regional governments in Chile, but employers vested no power in them, and local bureaucracies have consistently been unable to gather information about firm needs, as employer organizations did not support information sharing.[26] The problem of investment coordination in a country like Chile, then, was not the strength of private training corporations *per se* (investment coordination requires that supplier organizations be strong). Rather, it was the fact that links between them and other groups in the training market were weak. This meant that decisions made were rarely debated or accountable and hence tended not to be long-term in nature. Below we attempt to illustrate various aspects of the weakness of investment coordination in Chile.

(i) Lack of tradable standards

As we have argued, lack of tradable standards is both a key cause and a consequence of weak IC. The establishment in Chile of an atomized training system as described above, in which employers demand training in isolation, helped to fuel the reluctance in the private sector to finance workers' training, and specifically to participate in institutions to coordinate economic activities to that effect. They were unlikely to perform this function because they were themselves isolated in the training market.

In fact, it is doubtful how far it would be correct to say that a market for skills existed in the Chile of the 1990s, in the sense of a market truly governed by supply and demand. Surveys of small- and medium-sized firms have found high levels of dissatisfaction with course supply. One study of the early 1990s, for instance, revealed that more than 90 per cent of firms rejected the management courses on offer on the Chilean market as incompatible with the situation of their sector or business.[27] The construction of an intermediary between providers (OTEs – *Organismos Técnicos de Ejecución*) and firms did exist in Chile, the so-called OTIRs (*Organismos Técnicos de Intermediación Reconocidos*). In theory, these should aid in the aggregation of preferences and bridge market failures like information scarcity. However, the key OTIRs in Chile did virtually no investigative market research in terms of identifying demand. Nor could they play the role of *incentivizing* demand, by producing the kind of long-term time-horizons that make investments by firms in particular skills worthwhile. Since channels of information were weakly developed between these and the training institutes, the latter ended up effectively structuring supply.

The consumers involved in the Chilean case, moreover, were in the main larger firms and employers. This helps to explain how roughly 65 per cent of the courses offered by registered training corporations have tended to go to the training of management rather than workers (Table 1.2). The reason for this focus on management training is not an underlying economic need for management skills, but rather the existence of adverse incentives to invest in workers in a labour market composed of short-term and exclusive contracts. The exclusivity of the initial investment and the disproportionate concentration of consumption (demand) in the Chilean case in the employers/owners of larger firms, led to a concentration of the ownership over human resources in firms. At the same time, this sense of ownership was only a benefit to firms in the immediate term. Over time, ownership would be rendered diffused and uncertain, as the individual separates from the firm. In summary, low trust in labour relations, the likelihood of losing the investment in workers through quits, combined with the absence of a market in comparable skills (lack, therefore, of a future replacement of equal value) have combined to deter the investment in workers in Chile.

(ii) Weakness of employer association

There are important political factors behind the weak institutional coordination one finds in the training market in Chile. The OTIRs with the most dense institutional capacity (links to firms, and so on) are associated with

Table 1.2 Percentage distribution of participation of occupational categories through the tax break scheme (selected years)

Year	Management			Sub-Total	Work-force			Sub-Total	Total
	1	2	3		4	5	6		
1977	14	18	20	52	27	16	5	48	100
1985	21	25	17	63	28	6	3	37	100
1990	21	26	14	61	30	7	2	39	100
1996	18	34	12	64	29	5	2	36	100

Notes: 1 Executives/professionals, 2 Administrators, 3 Supervisors, 4 Skilled workers, 5 Semi-skilled workers, 6 Unskilled workers.

Source: Up to 1992, handwritten sheets from SENCE archives, and since *Boletí Estadístico 1994–1996*.

entrepreneurial groups, and have been encouraged by these to retain a market-neutral role. [Note: on market neutrality see Introduction.] The Head of Studies of the SOFOFA (the *Sociedad de Fomento Fabril*, the Industrialists' Association in Chile) confirmed in the early 1990s that activities that implied coordination of economic activities between firms (particularly training) had 'always been viewed as something remote'.[28] The view expressed by him and other influential employers' leaders interviewed in 1992 was that training had to be guided by activities and demands generated inside individual firms.[29] This view has also dominated efforts at the national level to deepen training policy, as successive attempts to establish clearer standards and involve the labour sector in training policy, first through the yearly social accords between 1990 and 1994, and later through other fora (like the *Foro del Desarrollo Productivo* and, in 2000, the *Consejo de Diálogo Social*), have failed.

(iii) Failure of simple tax rebate schemes to provide sufficient incentives

The design of the tax rebate scheme in Chile in the 1970s, by market reformers, was an attempt to make public policy 'follow the market'. Later democratic governments were unable to reverse this trend, which was even somewhat intensified after 1990, when left-centre governments vowed to upgrade skill development as a public priority. Course supply (Table 1.2) has continued to mirror almost exactly the occupational distribution (between workers and management) found among the total of private TCs in the private market. (This also showed a distribution of 65 per cent of courses for managers against 35 per cent for workers, Haagh 1999.) The importance of labour relations was acknowledged in a 1997 reform of SENCE, which established higher public deductions in firms for workers' training on the tax rebate scheme, and which also required consultation with unions.[30] In practice, however, the reforms were weak because the locus of decision-making remained centred in individual firms. The new committees were advisory only. Even a legally required body, such as the health and safety committee (*comité paritario*) was found, in our union survey, not to function in 67 per cent of firms. These changes to the tax rebate scheme failed to make up for the tendency for training to be located mainly in larger firms, and in courses to do essentially with administration rather than production or the innovation of production technique.

(iv) Unemployment insurance and the link to training

While institutional innovation has taken place in labour policy in recent years, as with the introduction of compulsory unemployment insurance (finally legislated in April 2001), the link between this and training policy remains theoretical. In one way the proposed insurance does promote flexibility for workers by allowing, for the first time, for the deduction of contributions for workers voluntarily leaving employment.[31] Still, the prospects for linking the scheme to training and job relocation efforts depend on the development of institutional links between service providers. Employers insisted from the first on a 'market neutral' administration of the scheme, by either the banks or the private pension providers (AFP), and in this way curtailed the future prospects for developing integrated and redistributive systems of social and employment insurance. Unlike a similar new insurance scheme in Korea (introduced in 1995), the unemployment benefit was not administratively tied to efforts in relocation and training. As we noted, unwillingness on the part of employers to pass on the information necessary had upset previous attempts to create so-called *bolsas de trabajo* and to make the local employment relocation offices (*oficinas de colocación*), on the one hand, and training policy, on the other, more effectively linked. Moreover, the resources of the unemployment insurance finally put through parliament were far more limited than envisaged even after several modifications at employers' insistence had been made since a scheme was first proposed in 1993.[32]

(v) **Absence of strategic initiative by the state in its largest new programme – the Youth Training Scheme (YTS)**

Arguably the area of social policy where policy-makers have gone furthest in Chile since 1990 in trying to link the fight against poverty (pro-poor policy) with the labour market and training is in the Youth Training Scheme. Throughout the 1990s, this scheme commanded roughly a quarter of SENCE's resources (Table 1.1). The scheme was focused on young people with special difficulty in emerging from poverty. It even appeared to have an apprenticeship element, as the youth selected would spend half their course (a total of five months) practising in an actual firm. Because of these ostensibly superior features, it is important to note how an over-application of market principles (presentialist contracts – see Introduction) negatively affected the design and impact of even this ostensibly superior scheme.

The public auctioning of resources on the YTS leased out decision-making on training policy to individual suppliers and this economic decentralization was not matched with a political element. SENCE's director confirmed that the only criteria for distribution that the state entertained was an effort to ensure financial equi-parity between Chile's twelve regions.[33] There was essentially no involvement at the local or regional level of representative institutions that might be able to begin building an infrastructure capable of policing tradable skills. The Labour Ministry did not actively link the information from other ministerial surveys (such as from the Economy Ministry) of demand for skills in the regions, but relied on the training institutes themselves and their existing capacity, as the core mechanism for the selection of training. Because the latter tended to be offered only short-term contracts (at most, six months), individual centres had more incentive to keep information secret from one other than to cooperate in identifying demand.

When comparing figures it was found that less than 7 per cent of the courses offered in most regions fell in areas of skill development in which the Economy Ministry's surveys had found that local firms had expressed an interest. 41 per cent of curricular items on one of the auctions implied activities with little future prospect of providing a tradable work experience, such as vigilance and office helper (the two largest categories in this group).[34]

There was from the outset little chance that the YTS would operate in practice as an apprenticeship scheme. The programme placed no obligations on firms to provide personnel trained to carry out apprenticeship-teaching duties, and there was virtually no precedent to draw on in the private sector itself (outside selected sectors, like metal). The 1998 ENCLA survey revealed that of all labour contracts a mere 0.1 per cent were apprenticeship contracts.[35] In earlier surveys some 13 per cent of employers actively complained that they lacked the technical expertise to carry out apprenticeship duties. On the YTS itself, the quality of courses was extremely varied and weakly monitored.[36] Skill certificates were dubious in value at best, since there was no attempt made to establish a band of recognizable standards. Moreover, the target group of youth was explicitly 'marginal youth with social–psychological problems', thus stigmatizing this group from the outset, through a parallel training structure deemed of low value relative to mainstream employability norms. This, together with the low re-employment rate on the YTS, and the remaining high youth unemployment in Chile, suggests that the lack of links to a mainstream on the YTS conceivably entailed a diffusion, if not a loss, of a good deal of the investments in human resources that this scheme entailed.

(vi) The exception to the rule – political learning in the metallurgical sector

As in other areas of policy it is the exception that confirms the rule. Not surprisingly, it is in sectors with a political history of development policy and union–employer accords, in short where the political element in decentralizing reforms is more strongly felt, where we find an explicit attempt to develop the property rights of labour. In the case of metal, a sectoral accord of 1992, initiated by the entrepreneurial group, ASIMET, was furnished with plans to discuss union participation in the design and implementation of training schemes. The accord asked all ASIMET members to give more information to unions for collective bargaining, and the parties agreed to study an unemployment insurance scheme and an information bank on employment. They also proposed that joint national institutions be established to share in training policy and deal with the problems that high turnover entails.[37] Political pragmatism among entrepreneurial leaders allowed steps of this kind to be taken. In turn, this political pragmatism had developed through the experience over several decades of engaging directly with labour issues by entrepreneurial leaders.[38] This experience allowed entrepreneurs to see beyond political affiliations and to focus on practical matters. For instance, ASIMET leaders were able to recognize the pragmatism in labour leaders, even when these were linked to the Communist Party. According to the president of ASIMET, the inclusion of the main, Communist Party-led, union federation, CONSTRAMET, was the key to the success of the pact-making process. Theirs was the most powerful federation and the Communists could be trusted.[39]

The effect of political decentralization in the training market is exemplified in this sector by the programme initiated by ASIMET (top-down) to develop an actual qualification of 'foreman' (*maestro calificado*) to undertake the special responsibility to carry out training activities in firms. This initiative showed that effective local development that is also successfully linked to the wider economy does depend on a strong centre. This is true in more ways than one. First, and as a general rule, it is only by establishing a uniform qualification as apprenticeship teacher that it is possible to ensure that general standards of apprenticeship, and therefore tradable skills, are developed within any sector of economic activity. But, more than that, the experience of sectoral accords in Chile appeared to have increased the chances of workers having a say in the training that occurs inside the firm. In the union survey quoted before, it was found that workers in the metal sector generally were more likely to have a voice in the kind of training demanded at the level of firms compared with other sectors without any accords or dialogue at the sectoral level, although in the latter the same amount of training was reportedly carried out.[40] Therefore, it can be said that the metal sector accords and the development of skill markets in this sector represented a case of leadership and organizational innovation rather than of self-selection of efficient contracts by firms. At the same time, the metallurgical sector remains a counter-factual case within the landscape of labour relations in Chile. The extension of similar accords has been strongly and consistently opposed by the Industrialist Association (SOFOFA).[41]

Political failures in decentralization II: weaknesses in the representation of labour

(i) The problem of long-term contracts in firms

The third domain of contracting over human resources we highlighted was the establishment of long-term relationships at the level of firms. Such relationships are crucial in order to make investments in training appear worthwhile to employers. In addition, they are important as a source of support of the national training system. Consider, for example, the case where workers in a firm have gained some participation in decisions on workers' training, and have therefore been able to divert the tax incentives administered by SENCE towards the training of workers (as in the case of metal). Secondly, relationships at the level of firms are important because they represent an important avenue through which agreements between firms, on training and other matters, are reached.

At a simple level, we might say that the kinds of relationships that are likely to promote the development of human resources are long-term relationships, because of the specific investment conditions pertaining to human resources, and because they generate a sense of commitment that fosters agreements. An obvious indicator, then, apart from actual numbers of workers trained, would be the level of turnover of workers as well as the usage, or not, of short-term presentialist contracts. Although medium levels of turnover may be compatible with a certain level of investments in skills (say of particular groups of workers) we can suppose that very high levels, say over 20 or 25 per cent per year, begin to have a significant effect on training investments, and in general on the company culture that breeds a sense of commitment. Accordingly, in this section we use relatively lower levels of training and higher levels of turnover as indicators of a short-term time-horizon of management.

These factors are not always of equal importance, however, nor are they in themselves sufficient to describe a relationship (between employer and workers). First, short-term contracts in different settings are not equally pernicious to investments in training. Or, to put it differently, the implication of a long-term relationship at the level of the firm for the development of human resources also depends on institutions at the national level. When there is investment coordination between firms (in apprenticeship, for example, as in the German or Dutch cases, as noted) short-term contracts in individual firms do not necessarily hinder investment.[42] In the case of Chile, however, short-term contracting at firm level generated disincentives to invest in training. Presentialist forms of contracting produce instability not simply because contracts are short term, but because the individual contract is isolated, not part of a network. Since the level of the effective unemployment benefit (or its equivalent) depends on the length of employment, the short-termism of contracts was, moreover, a direct source of instability, and therefore precariousness, for the individual worker.

On the other hand, specifying the length of a contract alone does not amount to explaining the relationship that gave rise to the contract. Or, to put it in a different way, as we saw for Germany and Denmark, many kinds of relationships are compatible with long-term or short-term time-horizons of management. However, because short-term relationships impose great instability on workers in Chile, they are likely in this case to be accompanied by higher levels of friction. In this case, the labour relationship within the individual firm, its social capital, matters; or at least it matters relatively more than in other cases. Below we will discuss what evidence there is to support this assertion. The question that interests us is simply how far labour relations influence the time-horizon of labour management. In order to assess this question we explore first how far labour relations in general matter, and then (in section (ii)) we isolate the influence of representation. There are various examples to illustrate the existence of short-term or presentialist contracting forms at the level of firms, starting with indicators of precariousness such as those we mentioned in section I, as well as the evidence of high turnover rates. Turnover is a problem, as indicated, if it occurs in a context of non-comparable standards of skill development and work between firms, because gained skill and experience is systematically lost in the economic system. The question then is, how far did labour institutions serve to sustain this problem in Chile? Data from the survey of local unions mentioned earlier indicated that high precariousness (understood as instability in working conditions) was closely linked to low formalization. The lowest level of formalization identified in Table 1.3 is where more than 20 per cent of workers do not have formal contracts, where a formal wage system does not exist and where no management can be identified as separate from the owner. In all, 30 per cent of firms surveyed fell within that group. On the other hand, the highest level of precariousness was identified as obtaining in firms in which the respondent had not only experienced more than 5 per cent fluctuation in earnings last year, but, moreover, where dismissals in the firm had increased and/or the respondent had experienced at least once that workers in the firm had had their contracts terminated in order to be hired on different terms. In all, 39 per cent of firms fell into that

Table 1.3 Union survey: formalization correlated with precarious flexibility

Chi Sq. ##		Formalization# – from high to low, 1–3*		
		1. 23% 55 cases	2. 47% 113 cases	3. 30% 70 cases
−2306**	1. None of the below.	53%	38%	27%
Precariousness	2. Respondent had more than 5% fluctuation in earnings last year.	31%	23%	19%
	3. (2) and dismissals have increased and/or at least one experience of re-hiring with new contract.	16%	39%	54%
		= 100%	= 100%	= 100%

Notes: # 1. Firms which have none of the characteristics below. 2. Firms in which more than 80% of workers have formal contracts and (possibly) only *one of* the two characteristics cited under 3. 3. More than 80% of workers have formal contracts, a formal wage system exists and management is identified as separate from owner or shared between owner and professionals ## (* indicates significant (below 0.05), ** indicates highly significant (below 0.01).

Source: Survey of Union Presidents, Haagh (1997).

group. Only 16 per cent of the firms with high levels of formalization also had a high level of precariousness. In summary, the data indicates that instability (precariousness) in Chile hinged to a significant degree on *arbitrariness in work rules*. This association is what we would expect because of the tensions associated with short-term contracts for workers in Chile.

Moreover, there was a strong direct association between the arbitrariness of work and the time-horizon of labour management. High levels of turnover as defined above were associated with various indicators of low formalization of work rules, for example, the existence or not of a formal wage system. In the group where the size of the work-force had varied by more than 30 per cent, only 18 per cent of firms had both a formal management and a formal wage system (Table 1.4). This compared with 50 per cent and 62 per cent in the two lower groups of turnover. The relationships varied little with size of firm, sector differences or the ratio of workers to machine.[43]

Finally, as we noted earlier, strong associations were found to point to the existence of a relationship between the number of workers that had received training in the previous two years and indicators of representation (Table 1.5). For instance, in the group where a large proportion of the work-force had received training, that is, more than 10 per cent, only 17 per cent did not have

Table 1.4 Union survey: labour turnover (#) correlated with level of formalization

Chi Sq. ###		Turnover – from high to low, 1–3. (#) Selected cells from cross-tabulations		
		1.** 46% (107 cases)	2. 31% (72 cases)	3. 23% (53 cases)
−2529**	1. (2) and formal wages (a) & contracts (b).	18%	50%	62%
Formalization ##	2. Owner is not or only partially involved in management and (a) or (b).	52%	27%	21%
		30%	23%	17%
	3. None of the above.	= 100%	= 100%	= 100%

Notes: # refers to turnover levels above 30%, ## to turnover levels between 15 and 29.99%, and ### to turnover levels under 14.99%. These figures were derived from the union survey carried out by the author, using a proxy for labour turnover calculated as the difference between the maximum level the work-force had reached in the previous two years and the minimum level during the same time. The advantage of this method compared with official statistics (which in any case cannot be obtained at firm level) is that workers without contract would also be considered, and rather than recording the number of workers on a particular day in the year (as the National Statistics Institute does) the actual (though approximate) maximum and minimum levels would be recorded. ** indicates highly significant (below 0.01).

Source: Survey of Union Presidents, Haagh (1997).

Table 1.5 Work-force training correlated with indicators of workers' representation

Chi Sq. ###			Level of workers' training from low to high, 1–3##		
			1 (%)	2 (%)	3 (%)
−2549**	Formalization#	1. (2) and formal wages (a) & contracts (b).	14	24	31
		2. Owner is not or only partially involved in management and (a) or (b).	40	50	51
		3. None of the above.	46	26	18
−3488**	Workers' Health and Safety Committee (WHSC) (*comité paritario*)	1. Functions	20	26	53
		2. Exists only in name	29	53	30
		3. Does not exist	51	21	17

Notes: # As defined in Table 1.3, ## Workers trained in the last two years (i) non – 0.00%; (ii) 1–9.99%; 10% < ### *Significant below 0.05, **Significance below 0.01.
Source: Survey of Union Presidents, Haagh (1997).

a *comité paritario*, compared with 51 per cent in firms with low levels of training. The *comité paritario*, or the Workers' Health and Safety Committee (Table 1.5), was legislated in the 1980s as a mandatory bi-partite forum of consultation at firm level on health and safety matters. It constituted a weak form of representation usually at the employers' discretion (in practice, only one-third of these committees met). The committees nevertheless are a useful indicator of the quality of labour relations precisely because they are not enforced. In summary, the existence of short-term contracts and short-term relationships in Chile appeared to deter the investment in workers.

(ii) **The social factors behind long-term contracts in the Chilean case**

In what way do labour institutions enter the picture? It is highly plausible that the relationship between labour management and labour relations is a cyclical one. Indeed, it seems a reasonable assumption that labour relations are formed over time and hence that they have important self-sustaining elements. On the other hand, the fact that a relationship is self-sustaining says little about causality, about time order.[44] Union age works as an instrumental variable here, in the sense that we cannot directly associate union insertion with training or turnover some 20 years later. The strong statistical relationship which was found between the two (Table 1.6) would have to be explained instead through the influence that union age over time had on the level of precariousness and hence the time-horison of labour management. Union age is clearly a prior condition, and the strong relationship with low precariousness had been established over time.[45]

Table 1.6 Age of union crossed with labour turnover and training #

Chi Sq. ##			Date of union establishment			
			>1969 (%) (48 cases)	>1973 (%) (75 cases)	>1988 (%) (51 cases)	>1992 (%) (47 cases)
−2033*	Percentage of ordinary workers who experienced training in previous two years	− none or >0.99%	27	26	36	50
		−1–9.99%	35	30	39	17
		−10% and >	38	44	25	33
			= 100	= 100	= 100	= 100
−1801*	Level of labour turnover	− more than 30%	48	36	50	67
		− between 15 and 30%	28	34	38	22
		− between 0 and 10%	24	30	12	11
			= 100	= 100	= 100	= 100

Notes: # Turnover as defined under Table 1.4 and training as defined in Table 1.5, ## * significance level below 0.01.
Source: Survey of Union Presidents, Haagh (1997).

The importance of this variable (union age) cannot be understood without some reference to Chilean labour history. Essentially, unions inserted before 1973, and which had survived right through the dictatorship years (the survey in question was conducted in 1992) would generally have developed a much stronger influence on labour management in the firm, compared with unions that had been formed in the 1980s and which had arisen at a time when union growth was subject to presentialist forms of contract. Moreover, with the exception of seven cases (less than 3 per cent of the sample), the firms in which unions were interviewed in the fall of 1992 had all been established before the Pinochet reforms. This means that we have a long period over which to assess the differences between firms that had had a union established sometime after a new labour code came into effect in 1980. We should point out here that there were only four unions in our sample established between 1973 and 1980 (when most union activities were banned). Hence, the difference both in context and time between the two epochs of union insertion is clearly marked.

This also eliminates the most plausible alternative explanation for the difference between firms with old and new unions, namely that the nature of labour management in firms with older unions was more likely to be, for example, long-term, *because* the firms themselves were older and had therefore been able to develop over a much longer period of time, or that conceivably they were strong organizations because they had managed to survive through the crisis years of the 1970s. The possibility that their tolerating unions prior to dictatorship could have been because they were already more successful economically also cannot be discounted. However, it is unlikely that such differences of over two decades prior to the interview would still be the explaining cause of the differences in labour management in the early 1990s. Following the economic success explanation as a cause for accepting unions, we would have to assume that it applies even more after dictatorship when, again, employers had much greater manoeuvre to avoid unions if they did not want them in their firm. If this economic argument were correct, then the firms with new unions should be relatively more likely to be governed by long-term relationships and negotiation; but we saw that the obverse was the case, at least in the economic sphere (turnover and training).

Finally we have run a regression to illustrate the significance of union age. The significance of union age alone (not considering, for example, contracts) was most clearly evident in the case of training, and not as clear in the case of turnover (Table 1.6). Table 1.7 shows that its removal from the regression seeking to explain the levels of training in the firm would imply

Table 1.7(a) Logistic regression to explain high levels of work-force training

Variable to be explained (dependent): Training of more than 5% of work-force in the last two years.

Explanatory factors	B	S.E.	Wald	Sig.
(i) Basic factors:				
*Sectors with a higher level of technology [dumhil1]	− 0.6093	0.4240	2.0649	0.1507
*Sectors with a lower level of technology [dumhil3]	− 0.6314	0.4389	2.0694	0.1503
*Big firms (rt. medium or small) [big1]	− 0.8118	0.4030	4.0568	0.0440
*Small firms (rt. medium or big) [small1]	0.8779	0.4276	4.2144	0.0401
(ii) Union presence:				
* Union established after 1979 (rt. before 1973) [duman3]	0.9895	0.4399	5.0590	0.0245
(iii) Labour management:				
* Existence of WHSC [whsc]	− 1.6551	0.3642	20.6560	0.0000
* Low levels of turnover [r]	− 0.2580	0.1127	5.2412	0.0221
* Not measurement of individual piece-rate output [meas]	1.1948	0.3939	9.2002	0.0024
Constant	0.4077	0.4543	0.8054	0.3695

Classification table = explained 62.73% for value 0 of training and 82.6% for value 1 of training.
= overall 74.39%

Note: See Haagh (1997) (Appendix B) for regression model and definition of all variables.

a: A single dummy was used here for simplicity, distinguishing between two levels of training, low and high. Standing also uses variables with just two values in his analysis of training in Malaysia, but distinguishes between presence or absence of training activities. Standing (1992), p. 342.

Louise Haagh 69

Table 1.7(b) Parsimonious model
Variable to be explained (dependent): Training of more than 5% of work-force in the last two years.

Explanatory factors:	B	S.E.	Wald	Sig.
(i) Basic factors:				
* Big firms (rt. medium or small) [big1]	−1.2238	0.3441	12.6506	0.0004
(ii) Union presence:				
* Union established after 1979 (rt. before 1973) [duman3]	0.8983	0.4283	4.3999	0.0359
(iii) Labour management:				
* Existence of WHSC [whsc]	−1.6688	0.3457	23.2987	0.0000
* Low levels of turnover [r]	−0.2717	0.1054	6.6463	0.0099
* Not measurement of individual piece-rate output [meas]	1.2710	0.3862	10.8332	0.0010
Constant	0.3597	0.3360	1.1465	0.2843

Classification = explained 61.39% for value 0 of training and 81.47% for value 1 of training. = overall 73.17%.

Note: See Haagh (1997) (Appendix E) for regression model and definition of all variables.

Table 1.7(c) Significance of the reductions of the original model when progressively controlling for the least significant factors*

Original and reduced models		Size and significance of reduction			
Model	Variables remaining	Sum of squares (explained)	Degrees of freedom	Reduction	Sig.
1 Original	Meas, whsc, r, dumhill, dumhil3, small1, big1, Duman3.	76.376	8	–	–
2 minus: dumhill		74.291	7	2.085	0.96
3 minus: dumhil3		74.265	7	2.111	0.96
4 minus: dumhil1 and dumhil3		73.640	6	2.736	0.83
5 minus: dumhil1 dumhil3, small1***		69.722	5	6.654	0.25
6 minus: dumhil1, dumhil3, small1, duman3.		65.041	4	11.335	0.03

Note: * See text under (a)(b)(i). In the present table, model 5 (***) is the parsimonious model.

a significant reduction in its overall significance (see Haagh (1997) for regression model and definition of all variables).

In summary, the evidence presented here indicates that local unions retained a quiet, but qualitatively significant, role throughout the dictatorship years. The lessons in economic history are also important. In this case, the persistence of social capital in some firms during periods of extreme liberalization of labour relations seems to indicate the impossibility of creating 'pure' market relationships. What liberalization appeared to create instead was very high levels of differentiation. In addition, there seems to be evidence of negative cycles (short-term time-horizon and low formalization) in the firms that did not have unions prior to liberalization. This apparent existence of self-reinforcing relationships in the firms (the negative cycles) is at odds with the explanations that many economists tend to give for the development of particular forms of contract, as noted. For example, Theodore Schultz assessed the importance of institutions to the development of human resources, and Oliver Williamson explained the importance of long-term contracts in the markets of idiosyncratic goods, but both have rejected explanations that posit long-run political obstacles to the development of efficient contracts (or institutions) in favour of explanations of self-selection.[46]

In contrast the evidence presented supports the thesis mentioned earlier, of dynamic inefficiencies in labour relations. This was the idea, adopted from Amsden's work, that institutional deficiencies in labour relations can become self-sustaining (in the case of Chile they were reinforced under rapid economic liberalization) and hence may deter the development of human resources.

Conclusion

The Chilean case highlights the importance of distinguishing between different components in decentralizing reforms. The problems we encountered in the demand-based provision of training had to do with the dominance of a classical market relative to a political logic. The fact that the original reforms were based in a narrowly conceived market logic, one which selected the managers of firms as the primary consumers and which exalted local-level decision-making to the detriment of intermediary forms, made demand-based provision dysfunctional in terms of the development of human resources. If it is accepted that the development of human resources hinges on the existence of a *network* of contracts, we can see how the expansion of presentialist forms can engender a negative pattern. The more diffused the contracting over human resources, the more difficult it is to recreate a common basis from which links between services can be drawn, establishing a classic Olsonian fix.[47]

The other political weakness in the reforms was the absence of a link with labour policy. The missing political component here was the lack of participation from unions. We found that only in firms where presentialist forms of contracting had been *counteracted* over a period of time (such as in firms with older unions) were positive cycles between labour relations and time-horizon in evidence. The example of the enterprise unions demonstrates the importance of local participation in market-enhancing welfare reforms. At the same time, it also shows where local participation does not suffice. The influence of local unions remained confined to the enterprise level. Essentially there were not enough influential local unions to spark off a shift in the relations *between* individual firms. This indicates the limitations that arise from understanding participation in narrow territorial terms. It was in the sector with sector-wide agreements (that is, metal) that local participation had the most consistent influence on training policy inside individual firms. In other words, it was only in the context of the building of universal standards that local participation could assert itself, and attain a wider mainstream generating effect.

This confirms again the relevance of institutional linkage, between one level of social policy and another, to the development of labour's property rights, and its importance both to efficiency – in this case the development of human resources – and to the expansion of individual freedoms. Skills and work experience which are not tradable are easily lost to society as well as to the individual firm. They also restrict the freedom of movement, and hence the developmental freedom of workers. The social reforms of the 1970s continue to exert influence today. By delegating decision-making power away from the public sphere a process had been set in motion that, if not impossible, will nevertheless be difficult to reverse.

Notes

1. Fixed employment refers to a single workplace, and continuous employment to the state of being employed.
2. Neoclassical statements can be found in Hayek (1980) and Krueger (1983). Lall (1995) has summarized the representation of this view within the development field under the heading of 'neoclassical development economics'.
3. For a discussion of asset specificity and investments in human resources, see Pagano (1991).
4. This survey was carried out by the author.
5. A discussion of different notions of labour market flexibility is beyond our purpose here (see Haagh (2001) and forthcoming a, b) for such a discussion. Suffice to note that flexibility in the neoclassical vision is confined to the immediate freedom of employers to choose in the management of labour. This, then becomes the hallmark of efficiency. The neoclassical view does not include a consideration of flexibility as the greater freedom for workers to choose and move in labour markets, and is therefore blind to how this may affect the notion and measurement of efficiency.
6. Interview with Minister of Government under the Aylwin Government, Enrique Correa, 1992.
7. And, as we noted, in this case the final beneficiary group, individual workers, was not directly targeted but reached through employers.

72 Social Policy Reform and Market Governance in Latin America

8. As discussed in the Introduction, problems in the association of individuals with labour markets were only acknowledged *ex post*, in the case of policy programmes that targeted extreme marginality from labour markets, for instance, which sought to integrate marginal youth or female heads of households, as discussed in this chapter and in Chapter 2.
9. Díaz (1997, pp. 171–2) accordingly defines formal work as waged work covered by a work contract and granting access to social security. This definition, though, excludes workers in waged employment working without contracts (as the legislation permits for a short period) or on short-term contracts, which may or may not provide access to social security coverage paid for by workers.
10. Encuesta Laboral, Informe de resultados (ENCLA), Dirección del Trabajo, Santiago, Chile, 1998, pp. 13, 21–3. This survey covered 1241 firms.
11. According to firm-level data obtained from the National Statistics Institute (henceforth INE) of a sample of 300 manufacturing firms (based on the sample of the union survey), the average variation in the total size of the formally employed work-force between 1988 and 1989 was 19.4 per cent. The INE data is unlikely, however, to reflect actual minimum and maximum levels (being based on the figure of one day in the year). The survey of union presidents came up with an average variation (this time between 1990 and 1992) of 31 per cent. See further Haagh (1997), pp. 204, 238.
12. ENCLA 1998, pp. 63, 71.
13. Marx ([1859] 1976), Chapter 10, 'The Working Day', p. 343. T.H. Marshall's concern with providing 'second chances' (1950) and Macpherson's interest in developmental freedom (1973) express essentially the same kind of reflection.
14. As women have entered the labour force in increasing numbers, with a participation rate of 34.5 per cent in 1996, up from 29.3 per cent in 1986 (compared with a participation rate of 54.5 per cent for both sexes in 1996). ILO (1998), p. 78.
15. Williamson (1985), pp. 52–5.
16. Dynamic inefficiency was a terminology employed by Amsden (1989, chapter 10) in her characterization of negative cycles in investment and management patterns in the Korean cotton, spinning and weaving industries. We employ the idea of embedded disincentives to investment within the specific area of investment in the development of human resources of workers in Chile.
17. Miller (1990), chapter 1.
18. On the personification of the firm, see Eggertson (1990), p. 7, and Chomsky in Burchill (1998), p. 19.
19. For example, in Scandinavia, unemployment insurance is directly tied to other social assistance and training at national level, whereas in East Asia, national training systems and 'copying' have tended to set an occupational welfare standard between firms. On the theory of property rights of labour in different national systems, see Pagano (1991).
20. Macneil (1978, p. 863, n. 25, 890), cited in Williamson (1985), p. 69. Please note our earlier discussion of presentialist contracts (Introduction).
21. In the 1990s, the percentage of workers involved in collective bargaining through 'bargaining groups' (set up with the 1979 labour code) rather than unions has fluctuated between 20 and 25 per cent (up from 10 per cent in 1987). Dirección del Trabajo, Santiago, Chile. Bargaining groups are *ad hoc* formations which by law must dissolve following the signing of a convention (a legally weak bargaining instrument compared with collective contracts, for example excluding the right to strike).

22. For example, decree law 942 (article 3) of May 1975 made any agreement on the limitation of daily work illegal, and Article 345 prohibiting night work, was repealed.
23. On apprenticeship see Maurice *et al.* (1986).
24. On these countries, see further Haagh (2000, 2001).
25. For this particular result, see Haagh (2001).
26. On the difficulties of gathering information and carrying out planning, see CINTERFOR (1990), V. 29–54.
27. SERCOTEC (1991), op. cit., p. 18.
28. Interview with Jaime Alé, Santiago 8 April and 14 September 1992.
29. Interviews with Manuel Feliú, Pedro Lizana, José Antonio Guzman and Eugenio Heiremans, all present or past leaders of the SOFOFA or the national employers' federation, the CPC (*Confederación de la Producción y el Comercio*).
30. Ley Num. 19.518, Fija Nuevo Estatuto de Capacitación y Empleo, *Diario Oficial*, 14 de octubre 1997.
31. The scheme also allowed for the spread over time of employers' costs, by setting up compulsory individual accounts with workers' and employers' contributions, respectively, of 0.6 and 1.6 per cent.
32. The 1997 government proposal had envisaged contributions of 0.8 and 3.6 per cent, respectively, by employees and employers. Proyecto de Ley Sobre Sistema de Protección al Trabajador Cesante (PROTRAC), 7 July 1997. For a full discussion of the unemployment insurance, see Haagh (forthcoming a).
33. Interview with Mario Cerda, Director of SENCE, Santiago, 24 August 1992.
34. See Haagh (1997), pp. 199–201 for further detail.
35. ENCLA 1998, p. 21.
36. For a detailed report, see ILO (1998), pp. 333–6.
37. Acuerdo Marco entre ASIMET, Consfetema – Fentema y Constramet. May 1992, pp. 3–7. For further detail, see Haagh (1997), pp. 136–40.
38. Even in the context of dictatorship when entrepreneurs in general held back from the development of associational practices, following the market conventions pursued by the Pinochet regime, ASIMET had created three new corporations, a corporation for sport and culture, *Corporación Deportiva y Cultural de ASIMET* (CORDEMET), one for education, *Corporación Educacional de ASIMET* (COREDUCMET), and one for workers' training, the *Corporación de Capacitación Ocupacional y Desarrollo Laboral de la Industria Metalúrgica* (CORCAPLAM), of 1979. CORCAPLAM trained over 5000 workers in 1991, and had 283 member firms. ASIMET (1991) p. 47. The example of one firm, the *Indústria Procesadora de Asero, S.A.* (IPAC) is typical. The firm joined CORCAPLAM in 1988, and since then it had not only begun to use the yearly tax rebate available to firms for workers' training, but had also invested an additional 32 per cent of its own profits. With a stock of 145 workers in 1992, it had offered training for 302 individulas since 1988, with an average of 24 courses a year purchased through CORCAPLAM. ASIMET (1992), pp. 8–9.
39. Interview with Jaime Paredes, President of ASIMET, Santiago, 28 July 1992.
40. The odds were 6 to 1 that unions in the metallurgical sector (57 in all) with a strong relationship with the union federation would have a say on training in the firm, compared with the unions surveyed (60 in all) in the group of new export industries (wood, fish, fruit and vegetable products). See further Haagh (1997), pp. 291, 337.
41. See Haagh (1997), chapter 2.

42. For Germany, see Maurice *et al.* (1986), and for Denmark, Haagh (2001).
43. For example, the association within the sectors of higher technology (paper products, metal chemicals, textiles, furniture and confectionery) had a Chi Square of 0.00746 compared with 0.00023 (both being highly significant) in sectors of lower technology (fruit, forestry, wood and fishing industries, copper and bread production). See Haagh (1997), Appendix B, p. 357.
44. On causality, see Agresti and Finlay (1997), p. 357.
45. The use of an 'instrumental variable' has been applied recently in the economics of crime and education. For example, Levitt (1996) uses the electoral cycle (which has a direct influence on numbers of police officers) to demonstrate the link between the level of policing and crime rates.
46. Williamson (1985); Schultz (1993).
47. Olson (1965).

Bibliography

Agresti, Alan and Finlay, Barbara, *Statistical Methods for the Social Sciences*, Third Edition, Prentice Hall, New Jersey, 1997.
Amsden, A., *Asia's Next Giant: South Korea and Late Industrialization*, New York, Oxford University Press, 1989.
Angell, A., *Politics and the Labour Movement in Chile*, Oxford University Press, 1972.
ASIMET, Memoria, ASIMET, Santiago, 1991.
ASIMET, *Guía de la industria metalúrgica-metalmécanica*, ASIMET, *Publicaciones Lo Castillo*, Santiago, Chile 1992a.
Barrera, M., *El Sindicato Industrial: Anhelos, Metodos de Lucha, Relaciones con la Empresa, Universidad de Chile, Edicion Publicaciones INSORA*, No. 48, Santiago, Chile, 1969.
Burchill, S., 'Human Nature, Freedom and Political Community: An Interview with Noam Chomsky' in *Citizenship Studies*, Vol. 2, No. 1, pp. 5–22, February 1998.
CINTERFOR, (ILO), *La formación profesional en el umbral de los 90*, Vol. I., Montevideo, ILO, 1990.
Cortázar, R. *Política Laboral en el Chile Democrático – Avances y Desafíos en los Noventa*, Ediciones Dolmen, Santa Magdalena 187, Santiago, 1993.
Díaz, A., 'Chile: Neoliberal Policy, Socioeconomic Reorganization, and Urban Labor Market', in *Global Restructuring, Employment, and Social Inequality in Urban Latin America*, Tardanico, R. and Larín R.M. North-South Center Press, 1997.
Eggertson, T., *Economic Behavior and Institutions*, Cambridge University Press, 1990.
Haagh, L., 'Market Neutrality and Social Policy – Unemployment Insurance and Resistance to Comprehensive Learning in Chile', in *Learning from Reform Models*, Weyland, K. (ed.), Woodrow Wilson Center, Washington D.C., forthcoming a.
Haagh, L., 'The "Free" Labour Market and Korea's 1997 Financial Crisis', in collection based on the *Brazil–Korea Conference*, Institute of Latin American studies, University of London, 9–11 December 2000, Amann, E. and Chang, H.-J. (eds), forthcoming b.
Haagh, L., *Citizenship, Labour Markets and Democratization – Chile and the Modern Sequence*, Palgrave Macmillan, Basingstoke and New York, 2002a.
Haagh, L., 'The Emperor's New Clothes – Labour Reform and Social Democratisation in Chile', for *Studies in International Comparative Development*, University of Berkeley, 38:1, May, 2002b.

Haagh, L. 'The Challenge of Labour Reform in Korea: A review of contrasting approaches to market enhancement', in *Labour Market Reforms in Korea: Policy Options for the Future*, World Bank, 2001.

Haagh, L. 'Social Policy and De-Centralisations – The Liberal Model in Chile Compared', Working Paper LAC-02-2000, The Latin American Centre, University of Oxford, 2000.

Haagh, L., 'Training Policy and the Property Rights of Labour in Chile (1990–1997): Social Citizenship in the Atomised Market Regime', *Journal of Latin American Studies*, Vol. 31, pp. 429–72, 1999.

Haagh, L. D.Phil Dissertation, University of Oxford, 1997.

Hayek, F.A., *1980s Unemployment and the Unions – The Distortion of Relative Prices by Monopoly in the Labour Market*, Hobart Papers, No. 87, Institute of Economic Affairs, London, 1980.

ILO, *Chile – Crecimineto, empleo y el desafío de la justicia social*, Geneva 1998.

Inter-American Development Bank Report, *Modernizar con Todos: Hacia la Integración de lo Social con lo Económico en Chile*, Washington, January 1994.

Krueger, A.O. *Trade And Employment in Developing Countries, Vol. 3: Synthesis and Conclusions*, Chicago University Press, Chicago, 1983.

Labour Ministry of Chile, SENCE, *Boletín Estadistico*, 1994–96.

Labour Ministry of Chile, Encuesta Laboral, Dirección del Trabajo, 1998.

Lall, S., 'Paradigms of Development: the East Asian Debate', Plenary Paper to Queen Elizabeth's 40th Anniversray Conference: The Third World after the Cold War, Queen Elizabeth House, Oxford University, July 1995.

Levitt, S.D., 'The Effect of Prison Population Size on Crime Rates: Evidence from Prison Overcrowding Litigation', *Quarterly Journal of Economics*, pp. 319–51, May 1996.

Macneil, I.R., 'Contracts: Adjustments of Long-Term Economic Relations under Classical, Neo-Classical and Relational Contract Law', in *Northwestern University Law Review*, No. 72, pp. 854–906, 1978.

Macpherson, C.B., *Democratic Theory*, Clarendon Press, Oxford, 1973.

Marshall, T.H., *Citizenship and Social Class*, Cambridge University Press, 1950.

Marx, K., *Capital*, Vol. I., Penguin books, 1976 [1859].

Maurice, M., Sellier, F., and Silvestre, J.-J., *The Social Foundations of Industrial Power – A Comparison of France and Germany*, MIT Press, Cambridge, Mass.; London, England, 1986.

Miller, D., *Market, State and Community: Theoretical Foundations of Market Socialism*, Clarendon Press, Oxford, 1990.

Olson, M., *Logic of Collective Action*, 1965.

Pagano, U., 'Property Rights, Asset Specificity, and the Division of Labour under Alternative Capitalist Relations', *Cambridge Journal of Economics*, No. 15, pp. 315–42, 1991.

Park, Y.-B., 'State Regulation, The Labour Market and Economic Development: the Republic of Korea', in Rodgers, G. (ed.), *Workers' Institutions and Economic Growth in Asia*, Geneva, 1994.

Schultz, T.W., *The Economics of Being Poor*, Basil Blackwell, Oxford, England and Cambridge, Mass., 1993.

SERCOTEC (Servicio de Cooperatión Técnica – Economy Ministry – Chile), Antecedentes sobre la capacitación empresarial y laboral en la pequeña y mediana indústria y artesenado. Document no. 9, Santiago, March, 1990.

Standing, G., 'Labour Flexibility and Insecurity: Towards an Alternative Strategy', in *Labour Relations and Economic Performance*, Brunetta, R. and Dell 'Aringa, C. (eds), Macmillan (now Palgrave Macmillan), 1990.

Valenzuela, J.S., 'Labour Movements in Transitions to Democracy: A Framework for Analysis', Kellogg Institute for International Studies, Working Paper #104, June 1988.

Williamson, O., *The Economic Institutions of Capitalism*, Free Press, New York, 1985.

2
Gender and Development Policy in Chile: the Aid Programme to Female Heads of Households

Mònica Badia Ibáñez

The Chilean neo-liberal approach to welfare has received much attention due to its emphasis on poverty reduction and on income generation through increasing access to the labour market. This chapter focuses on the Aid Programme to Female Heads of Households (*Programa Mujeres Jefas de Hogar de Escasos Recursos* or PMJH), in order to examine the potential of this strategy to alleviate poverty. The core elements of the programme constitute what are considered at present to be the main aspects of an innovative social policy – an integrated approach, targeting, decentralization, and participation. The analysis of the PMJH as a case study is appealing because it reflects the particular policy and strategy that the Chilean government has adopted as the means to achieve gender equity and poverty alleviation. It is also interesting to examine the extent to which the PMJH has achieved its stated goals of interlinking policies of equality of opportunities with those of poverty alleviation and of decentralization. This analysis of the PMJH raises five main issues that are pertinent to wider debates about poverty reduction policy. First, the PMJH illustrates the tensions that exist between innovative programmes and the institutional framework in which social policy operates. Secondly, it draws attention to the way in which gender issues in development appear to have collapsed into a poverty trap. Thirdly, it addresses the controversial question of targeting female heads of households for anti-poverty interventions. Fourthly, it contributes to the debate about the role of broad-based social welfare provision *versus* targeted relief and assistance. Finally, the Programme provides a new model of social intervention for comparative purposes.

I. The 1990s: the institutional strategy for poverty alleviation

Chile's first two democratic governments of *Concertación*[1] in the 1990s faced constraints in their efforts to introduce measures favouring the poor.

These constraints stem from the legacy of a free-market system and the attempt by the present government to avoid a total rupture with the preceding conservative dictatorship in making the transition to democracy (Weyland, 1997).[2] Previously, the neo-liberal attempts to dismantle the Chilean welfare system[3] and to 'modernize the state' during the military regime of Pinochet (1974–89) were characterized by several features, including the subordination of social policy goals to the requirements of economic policy; the interplay of market forces in the allocation of public resources; a shift from universal social programmes to targeting state resources at those designated by the state as being 'in need' (selectivism); and decentralization of state functions from a single centre to smaller units, together with the transfer of social welfare to local governments and private agents, including NGOs and local community associations.

Although there is an underlying continuity in the economic and social policy model in the post-Pinochet era (Vergara, 1993; Oxhorn, 1994), there has been a new strategy to promote fairness, encapsulated by two slogans: 'a Process of Integration to Development' (Aylwin government, 1990–94) and 'a Policy of Opportunities and Quality of Life' (Frei Ruiz-Tagle government, 1994–2000). The present social strategy is based on the idea that economic growth alone is not enough to guarantee an equal distribution of its benefits (Pizarro et al., 1995; Lloyd-Sherlock, 2000). Therefore, two main elements of social policy design seek to establish a complementary relationship with economic policies. First, policies aim to reinforce sectorial programmes such as education, health, housing, social security and legal assistance (Irarrázabal, 1995). Secondly, policies are geared towards the implementation of specific initiatives to break the structural limitations that prevent the integration of vulnerable groups into development (Figueiredo and Shaiheed, 1993). The current administration has emphasized an array of 'social investment' programmes to provide the poor with the means to attain an income. These programmes do not take the form of subsidies, but instead adopt a 'help for self-help' approach at the heart of the anti-poverty strategy.

During the 1990s in Chile, there was an increase in social spending through increased taxation and institutional reforms (Hardy, 1997).[4] The reforms included the creation of the Planning and Development Ministry (MIDEPLAN) and of new instruments of social action under its authority, such as the Social Investment Fund (FOSIS), the National Women's Bureau (SERNAM), the National Institute of Youth (INJ), the National Commission for the Indigenous Population (CONADI), and the National Fund for the Disabled (FONADIS). Each of these institutions design and coordinate social programmes directed at their respective targeted group. There are two principal criteria for targeting: territorial (poor municipalities or areas) and specific vulnerability. Rather than implementing their own programmes, these new institutions invite competitive tenders from NGOs, municipalities and profit-making organizations. In this way they can transfer the responsibility of programme implementation and of stimulating collaboration between public and private sectors and NGOs (Bebbington and Lehmann, 1998). The underlying idea is that the central government designs the goals and priorities of the programme which are then implemented by decentralized governmental entities, municipalities and by the private sector.

In 1994, the National Plan for Alleviating Poverty (PNSP) was established to bring about increased coordination of public aid in the poorest municipalities, in order to increase the quality of life of the low-income strata. The PNSP hoped to achieve its objectives by prioritizing social investment through policies that promoted equality of opportunity, rather than compensatory social programmes (Sheahan, 1998). It also provided an innovative social model of administration based on an integrated approach in order to promote decentralization and social participation (Castañeda, 1992; CEPAL, 1992a). Decentralization was justified on the grounds that it enhances democratic accountability, policy innovation and administrative efficiency (Whitehead, 1993; Larrañaga, 1995; Jordana et al., 1998). Similarly, social participation was viewed as a means of addressing poverty and social exclusion through strengthening community participation and planning at the regional and local levels (Graham 1996, Gaventa 1998).

II. The feminization of poverty

The feminization of poverty is usually taken to mean that the poorest are mainly women, rather than to signal how the experience and implications of poverty are different for men and women. This section provides insights into the severity of poverty among women and the greater difficulties that women face in comparison with men in lifting themselves and their children out of situations of extreme poverty.

Poverty affects proportionally more women than men, owing to the inequitable integration of women into the labour market and the failure of public policies to recognize the economic contributions women make through non-wage-earning productive activities, particularly the unremunerated work of food production, child-rearing and housekeeping (Elson, 1991; Benería and Feldman, 1992; Araiz et al., 1998). The assumption of household responsibilities and the incompatible schedules of child care establishments and schools mean that women are greatly overloaded with work. This double work-burden makes the integration of women into the formal labour market difficult, rendering them economically dependent. Women are often employed in jobs requiring low qualifications and offering low remuneration. These factors, coupled with the perception that women are not viable candidates for access to credit, and the low estimation of women's work in maintaining and caring for the family, result in high female unemployment. It also leads to women's absence from the labour market's most dynamic sectors and to their lack of support in entrepreneurial ventures (Vogel, 1995;

Clert, 1996). Educational programmes further contribute to this situation by failing to consider changes in gender roles during recent decades and therefore do not equip women for the demands of the labour market. Additionally, there are low numbers of professional women because of restricted access to higher education (Bustillo, 1993).

Women's poverty is also reflected in their relationship with their environment. The surge of expanding urban centres has resulted in serious problems of overcrowding, pollution and the decay of infrastructure and public services. In cities, women face new dimensions of poverty owing to the gender-based division of work. For example, the collection of refuse falls primarily to women and such tasks expose them directly to environmental pollution. Since women bear the brunt of the problems of family survival and health care, they feel more acutely the impact of the deterioration in drainage systems, air pollution and the existence of rubbish dumps. In having to deal with these growing problems, they also face an increase in their work-load (Moser, 1996).

In rural areas, several factors encourage women's poverty. These include non-ownership of land; lack of education and a high rate of illiteracy; geographic isolation; minimal public services; and the direct impact of the environmental degradation of the production base. For indigenous women, rural poverty reinforces the effects of ethnic discrimination. These women are often the worst off in terms of their access to production resources such as land, water, capital, technical assistance and training in order to fulfil their basic needs (Matear, 1997). Furthermore, women in rural areas are particularly badly affected by the extensive use of chemical pesticides, which frequently cause poisoning and are particularly harmful for pregnant women. Of particular note are the unstable working conditions of the *temporeros* (seasonal workers). The problems facing this group have been compounded by the fact that the fruit sector has made excessive use of pesticides and fertilizers that affect workers' health. Since most of these workers are women, this has a severe impact not only on their personal health, but also potentially on the well-being of future generations (Barrientos *et al.*, 1999).

The feminization of poverty is further exacerbated by the increase in the number of households headed by women. In Chile there are 1 269 868 female-headed households (FHHs). That is, 28.3 per cent of households are headed by women (CASEN, 1998). The economic crisis of the 1980s in Latin America and the Caribbean proved to be a catalyst for the emergence of FHHs as a visible social phenomenon. Recent processes of globalization have aggravated the long-standing problem of the migration of men in search of employment, leaving many families headed by women (Afshar and Barrientos, 1999). Furthermore, the consequences of the displacement of family members include rural stagnation, family dislocation and homelessness among children, leading to the inter-generational reproduction of poverty (Buvinic *et al.*, 1992).

The crisis of the 1980s led to the adoption of family strategies for dealing with poverty in a process that came to be known as the 'invisible adjustment'. The practice of expanding household size to include relatives as well as non-relatives (known as *via allegamiento*) was clearly a survival strategy. Many of the psychological problems of the urban poor are related to the lack of privacy and safety in overcrowded households. Poverty is greater when there are more dependants, and the likelihood of falling into poverty is greater in households where the mother is less well educated (UNICEF, 1990; CEPAL, 1992b).

A household is defined as a person or group of persons who inhabit the same home and have a common nutritional budget. A household can have one or more family units (principal and secondary). A female head of the principal family unit is the woman who is in charge of a household's maintenance and who is primarily responsible for its economic upkeep. Sometimes there is more than one family unit within a single household, as a result of such diverse situations as extended families or unmarried mothers. A female head of a secondary family unit is understood to be a woman who has dependants and who shares, along with them, a household with other individuals (either relatives or non-relatives), one of whom is the head of the household. According to CASEN 1996, households or family units in urban zones are considered to be below the poverty line when their *per capita* monthly income is equal to or below two basic family shopping baskets (36 964 Chilean pesos). When this *per capita* monthly income is equal to or below one basic family shopping basket (18 482 Chilean pesos), the household or family unit is in absolute poverty.

Female headship is a common feature of poor households. This situation can arise for a number of reasons. In most cases, female household headship is determined by the absence of a partner, since FHHs are mostly mothers who are single, separated or widowed, which obliges women to assume the role of provider that is traditionally assigned to men, in addition to domestic and child-rearing tasks. The woman may have no partner or, if she has one, he may have a lower income or no income because of unemployment problems, alcoholism, drug addiction and/or physical disability. Female headed households are some of the most vulnerable to poverty; 20.2 per cent of FHHs (256 591) are below the poverty line (CASEN, 1998). The percentage of destitute households is slightly higher when led by women (5.1 per cent compared with 4.5 per cent of those led by men), while the percentage of destitute family units led by women (6 per cent) is nearly double those led by men (3.2 per cent) (CASEN, 1998).

The role women play as providers and their need to access income sources accounts for the fact that their rate of participation in the labour market (48 per cent) exceeds that of women in general (35.5 per cent). Yet, in spite of these higher percentages, FHHs' numerous difficulties of integration into the labour market partly determine their socio-economic situation. Poor or deprived FHHs' rate of participation in the labour market is only 20.1 per cent, less than half that of men in the same socio-economic situation (44.2 per cent) and less than a third of that of FHHs with higher income (63.9 per cent). This indicates that the barriers encountered in accessing the labour market are greater among poorer women. In the same way, their unemployment rate (31.5 per cent among the destitute and 13.5 per cent among the non-destitute poor) is significantly higher than that of male headed households (MHHs) (23.3 per cent among the destitute and 4.7 per cent among the non-destitute poor) and of FHHs with higher income (CASEN, 1996). Unemployment particularly affects FHHs in the age range 15–44 (see Table 2.1).

The link between poverty and FHHs is reinforced by the way that women's reproductive roles (care-giver, home-maker) and productive roles (income earner) clash with one another. Female headed households generally have fewer working members, a greater number of dependants, a limited resource base and more responsibilities and burdens concentrated on the head of the household. Social deprivation, such as the lack of educational opportunities, housing, reliable health care and direct discrimination, worsen the predicament (Chant, 1997; Geldstein, 1997; Vecchio, 1998). In addition, it is more difficult for FHHs to escape poverty because these women tend to be less well educated and therefore have major disadvantages in terms of access to the labour market. According to CASEN 1998, FHHs of poorer households have lower levels of education than MHHs (5.6 years on average). FHHs, like all women, have differentiated access to employment, since the labour market is segregated according to gender. Their integration into the labour market takes place mainly in the informal economy and in domestic services (around 60 per cent of them are concentrated in these forms of employment), which translates into high poverty levels (Bravo and Todaro, 1995; Espinoza *et al.*, 1996). There is a significant income differential according to gender (when comparing MHHs and FHHs) and to status (when comparing FHHs of different socio-economic strata) (see Table 2.2). According to data from CASEN 1998, the average income of households headed by women is

Table 2.1 Distribution of female headed households by activity and range of ages (in %, 1998)

Range of ages	Employed	Unemployed	Inactive	Total
15 to 29	65.6	5.4	29.0	100.0
30 to 44	73.9	6.8	19.3	100.0
45 to 59	57.7	4.3	38.0	100.0
60 and over	14.0	0.7	85.3	100.0
Total	44.2	3.5	52.3	100.0

Source: MIDEPLAN in CASEN 1998.

Table 2.2 Average work income by gender of the head of household (in Chilean pesos, November 1998)

Income quintile	Male	Female
I	89 751	74 179
II	192 442	165 926
III	290 767	218 501
IV	471 563	367 125
V	1 465 371	888 257

Source: MIDEPLAN in CASEN 1998.

equivalent to 66.4 per cent of the income earned by households headed by men, and the income of FHHs in the first quintile is 22.1 per cent of FHHs in the fifth quintile. Likewise, the percentage of employed MHHs amounts to 81.3 per cent while that of FHHs is only 69.2 per cent; this percentage decreases even more in the lower income strata.

Contributing factors to the link between poverty and female headship include increasing female migration from rural to urban areas, increasing numbers of single mothers and incidence of teenage pregnancy, and high female life expectancy. Given this situation, policies oriented towards decreasing the barriers to poor FHHs' stable work is essential in facilitating their exit from the vicious circle of poverty and discrimination in which they live. Income generation, access to quality social services and to adequate living conditions are indispensable for their social and economic participation. Although the diversity of household types in Chile comes across in censuses and surveys, social policy has been designed on the basis of a nuclear family (Valenzuela *et al.*, 1994). As a corrective, measures are necessary that consider FHHs' specific difficulties and potentials for integration into the labour market under suitable conditions. This cannot be achieved solely with greater economic growth and a lower rate of unemployment, since this group does not reap the fruits of greater growth, as it is outside the economy's more formal and dynamic occupational activity (Inhen, 1998). To meet this challenge, since 1992 SERNAM has developed the Aid Programme to Female Heads of Households (*Programa de Apoyo a Mujeres Jefas de Hogar de Escasos Recursos* or PMJH). After a pilot phase in five districts and validation of its proposals, the PMJH began its phase of national implementation. It is now operating in 94 districts of Chile's 13 regions.

III. The Aid Programme to Female Heads of Households (PMJH)

The PMJH is part of the strategy adapted by the Chilean government in its efforts to achieve its stated goal of interlinking policies of equality of opportunities with those of poverty alleviation and decentralization. The PMJH is based on the assumption that FHHs' vulnerability is associated with their precarious position in the labour market. In this sense, the PMJH coordinates policies from different ministries designed to implement labour training for women with initiatives to satisfy women's demands for other services (housing, health, legal aid and child care). The core elements of the PMJH constitute what are currently considered to be the main aspects of an innovative social policy – an integrated approach, targeting, decentralization, and participation. An *integrated approach* implies that social programmes should consider several, mutually complementary initiatives, in order to achieve an effective improvement of the quality of life of the population involved. Inter-sectoriality constitutes an operational strategy derived from the integrated criterion, to foster a significant degree of inter-institutional coordination which is indispensable given the State's compartmentalized structure. In turn, this requires a basic synchronization of objectives, initiatives and operational patterns with the sectors involved. *Targeting* describes the identification of population and territorial sub-sectors which, being in particularly vulnerable situations, deserve to be considered as priority groups for direct social investment, and requiring specific interventions to respond to their particular characteristics. *Decentralization* relates to the increasing involvement and autonomy of the local and regional levels in the design, administration and evaluation of social policies and programmes. In this sense, the municipality is considered as a key actor, as it is most directly linked to the population and is most likely to perceive its real needs. Finally, *participation* refers to the active involvement of potential participants in the design, implementation and evaluation of policies and programmes. This is thought to be the most appropriate way of ensuring that participants' real needs are met, of making use of their knowledge and experience, and of encouraging them to cooperate. Although these characteristics have currently achieved governmental consensus as essential to social policy formulation, the PMJH was the first programme in Chile to apply them in practice.

The PMJH was first initiated as a pilot project lasting two years (1992–93) targeted at those women from low-income strata who are responsible for supporting their household and family economically. The aim was to develop and experiment with a model of intervention that tackled poverty and discrimination against FHHs. This model then formed the basis for the elaboration of a nation-wide programme. SERNAM implemented a pilot plan in five districts for a period of two years,[5] with the aim of testing a model of local intervention. This pilot plan, which benefited from funds that SERNAM transferred to the municipalities, comprised five initiatives. The central initiative was labour training, oriented towards improving the quality of women's employment and, especially, their income levels. The other four PMJH initiatives – child care, health, housing and legal aid – were initially conceptualized as supports to women's incorporation into the labour market, and also as ways to improve their own standard of living, and that of their families.

By the end of 1997 the PMJH had been started in 80 districts of the country's 13 regions, and reached a coverage of 20 000 women. In 1998, the PMJH become institutionalized as a government programme; that is, as an interministerial programme not 'a SERNAM programme'. It was coordinated by SERNAM but implemented in districts by the municipality. The PMJH from 1998 – the year phase II began – is called 'Programme for Labour Training for Women from Low-Income Strata, especially Heads of Household'. In the four-year coverage (1998–2001) it is hoped that the coverage will increase to 41 000 new participant women. The average number of children under 15 in households headed by women on low income is 2.08, so that it is estimated that the second phase will have 85 000 children as indirect beneficiaries. The PMJH is targeted to women with children in their care who are economically active and with expressed disposition to work (they work, are between jobs or are looking for work for the first time). 75 per cent of participants must be FHHs; women who are not household heads will thus be able to participate, if they are economically active. Participants need to live in the districts where the PMJH is implemented. The PMJH will be preferentially implemented in urban districts, and prioritized for those with more than 30 000 inhabitants with a concentration of FHHs. Territorial reach will be extended to rural and semi-rural districts if they meet the requirements.

IV. Assessment of the PMJH

An integrated approach

The heterogeneity of poverty means that policies have to be sensitive to the particular characteristics of the target groups. In the case of women in the PMJH, poverty is the result not only of their socio-economic situation, but also of their family situation and gender. The PMJH proposes to intervene with respect to the cluster of factors that enhance FHHs' vulnerability. Operationally, this translates into five initiatives: labour training, child care, housing, health and legal attention. This integrated approach aims to support and facilitate the fulfilment of the central objective: improving FHH's standard of living and achieving FHHs' labour (re-)integration. However, at the central level, there are institutional obstacles and resistance to the setting up of a coordination network with the sectors responsible for the five initiatives. A lack of coordination tends to inhibit local creativity.

Inter-sectorial coordination has proved to be an innovative and unusual way to conduct public policies. Coordination occurs institutionally – various sectors focusing on the same target group, and coordinating with the municipality – and in terms of policy content and target population. Traditionally, the sectors dealt with their target groups' needs fragmentarily, without considering the different interrelated aspects – labour, health, education, and housing – affecting each targeted group. This perspective rendered problematic the design of policies to deal with the structural problems underlying their poverty situation. As a consequence of this, there was a lack of formal and stable means of coordination among the different sectors during the PMJH's implementation. Given the lack of institutional mechanisms, the PMJH established coordination through informal mechanisms related to the decision-making power of coordinators, and to their influence in decision-making circles.

The PMJH has a clearly defined target population, and a cluster of activities and initiatives related to the population's characteristics and needs. However, the analysis performed makes it clear that the PMJH has another target population, which in its formulation has remained more or less implicit. These are the institutions with which SERNAM cooperates in order to develop the PMJH. For legal reasons SERNAM acts to coordinate policies and programmes, and only exceptionally does it execute them. The execution of these policies must necessarily be entrusted to third parties, but there is no formal mandate to regulate this. Deficiencies of coordination have been observed, both between sectors in the national, regional, provincial and local spheres as well as inter-sectorially, between national, regional and provincial levels of the same sector. In addition, there are difficulties within the same ministry among the different services, and therefore coordination is also required at the sub-sectorial level (Holz, 1999).

The central challenge is to achieve a pace of development that harmonizes the five initiatives in three senses: coherence of content, focus and styles of implementation. This is not an easy task, given that execution can and should involve more than one institution, that all the initiatives are updated concerning each other's progress, and that activities corresponding to each initiative do not hinder each other, but rather articulate with each other and work together. This requires not only that institutions be strong and well organized, with secure financial and human resources, but also that they have the capacity to achieve cooperation with the rest of the public administration. Furthermore, they should have expedited information channels and decentralized structures to permit the influence of the PMJH in the various bodies implementing policy. SERNAM's inter-sectorial coordination has experienced difficulties deriving from multiple factors, such as the compartmentalized and non-integrated work styles that characterize state action; insufficient recognition and visibility of FHHs as subjects; lack of effective coordination mechanisms between the various sectors; and lack of coordination between the national, regional and local levels. These difficulties constitute important obstacles for any programme proposed in a strategy of inter-sectorial action.

If coordination in the public sector is difficult, coordination of gender policies is even more so. The promotion of equal opportunities is still insufficiently integrated with sectorial priorities. Experience has shown that in order to achieve positive results, SERNAM–PMJH had to try to integrate itself continuously into the priorities and interests of the coordinating institutions, rather than the reverse. In other words, it has not been enough to present initiatives pertinent to the PMJH's objectives, but the proposals must, above all, be relevant and transparent to the third parties with whom coordination is sought. Therefore, there is the additional difficulty of building acceptance of the gender perspective as a useful orientation to the design and execution of social policies Guzmán and Salazar, 1992). The PMJH's professional team thus needs to have a very precise knowledge of the activities of each institution with which it seeks coordination, including the relevant technical knowledge and awareness of inter- and intra-institutional rivalries. Accumulating all of this information makes great demands on the limited number and relatively low profile of the PMJH's personnel. Such demands are not easy to meet for any public institution, and definitely not for SERNAM, which suffers significant restrictions in this area (Waylen, 1996). Meeting the goals of intersectorial coordination has depended greatly on the effort and commitment of the municipal employees in charge of and/or linked to the implementation of the PMJH. Although these personal efforts should not be underestimated, it is no less true that the PMJH's future success necessitates that they be provided with more solid institutional support.

Decentralization

From the perspective of decentralization, the people responsible for PMJH administration at the different levels function quite autonomously in planning and programming. However, attempts to decentralize at the municipal level have been hindered by a lack of training, combined with endemic patterns of political manipulation and clientelism (Márquez and Rosenfeld, 1996). In addition, channelling resources to the municipalities and delegating tasks of coordination of human and financial resources at the local level has clashed with the established structures of municipal work. Evidence suggests that it is still necessary to pursue the decentralization of public management in order to give scope for planning at the local level and to improve the coordination between institutions. As one coordinator describes the situation:

> The most difficult aspect of the PMJH has been its implementation at the local level. The municipal authorities still regard it as a programme of SERNAM, and additionally it reaches only part of the municipality, not all of it. Thus, it is usually run by the local women's bureau, with the little power that women have in the planning of the district. Furthermore, the administration of State funds remains a very difficult issue. For instance, the authorities cannot understand the relevance of a course on personal development for women, so the funding from SERNAM is used

to finance other projects. This means than you might plan something and at the last minute the money has gone to another project. (Coordinator A)

The innovative and integrated design is not congruent with the traditional forms of social policies; the proposal to focus on FHHs means making visible a subject group previously invisible to the municipality; and the PMJH's modalities of coordination are often opposed to the predominant compartmentalized practices. Decentralization, in its most political sense, must first ensure that the PMJH is fully integrated into the municipal structure. The PMJH is effectively integrated when the sectorial structure of municipal work is broken and the PMJH's interdisciplinary and inter-departmental focus is imposed. To implement the PMJH communally, it is necessary to define explicit strategies for the executive institutions. These strategies should take into account the institutions' characteristics as well as actual conditions. The executing municipalities represent an important segment of the PMJH's 'institutional target population'. In particular, this is because the PMJH proposes to the municipality a cluster of requirements that mostly cannot be fulfilled spontaneously, both due to their content and their methodology. The PMJH certainly cannot integrate communal diversity into its implementation design. But the inherent diversity of already incorporated municipalities, according to the significant differences in the districts' development level, must be considered in defining and programming activities. Two main differences emerge between the municipalities that implement the PMJH: the availability of financial resources to contribute to the PMJH's development and the ability to administrate an innovative social programme in terms of content and work methodologies.

Territorial targeting

Targeting is understood as the relationship between the programme strategies and objectives, and the territories (geographical spaces) and people (FHHs) in vulnerable situations. With respect to territory, the targeting criterion cannot be applied uniformly in all districts. In small districts, identifying FHHs in one sector alone makes no sense, because potential participants are dispersed all over the geographic area. In large districts, by contrast, it is possible to identify priority geographical sectors with many FHHs. Although the PMJH has also considered communal poverty among the criteria of territorial targeting, it has confronted the contradiction that in the poorest territories it cannot be implemented, as the minimum social infrastructure necessary to develop the different initiatives (i.e., kindergartens, schools, outpatient departments) does not exist. As a result, the criterion of communal poverty has had to be applied in a pragmatic and flexible way. Criteria of territorial targeting, therefore, need to be defined with reference to the existence of minimal conditions, which would lead to the exclusion of certain kinds of districts.

At the local level, the potential of the municipalities to contribute to social development is undermined by a shortage of both human and monetary resources, and of working instruments (Serrano, 1995). Some local women's bureaux (*Oficinas Municipales de la Mujer* or OMM) were established without telephones, office furniture or enough money to cover the staff salaries. These difficulties have been discussed by a coordinator of the PMJH:

> Success in the implementation of the PMJH greatly depends on the commitment and ability of the persons in charge of the PMJH to negotiate with the municipal authorities. The stability of the team is a very important factor to achieve better organization over the years. When there is a high level of turnover, you lose information and records about the participants of the PMJH. There is a huge staff turnover with average employment periods of less than a year. (Coordinator B)

The PMJH needs to be legitimized at the local level and be capable of accessing external resources in order to ensure its perpetuation, even beyond the funding period guaranteed by SERNAM. Only with this legitimization and increased access to resources will the coordinators believe that the continuity of the PMJH is secured, and so be willing to make long-term plans.

Social targeting

There have been problems related to the fact that some poor women hide their real status in order to access the services and resources offered by the programme. In particular, the incorporation of health and child care services in the PMJH has attracted women who are not FHHs. For example, day care centres built in their neighbourhoods enable them to work as *temporeras* in nearby fields without worrying about their children. Additionally, for the first time in their lives they may have access to dental and other health services offered to them in connection with the new employment programmes. This confirms the relevance of an integrated approach based on offering multiple services such as housing, legal support, access to employment and earnings, and provision for child care, which are vital in strengthening the position of women from lower socio-economic strata. In addition, some women's precarious situations lead some teams to soften the selection criteria, and the needs and demands of some non-FHHs correspond to the services offered by the PMJH.

This aspect of the PMJH raises the issue that targeting of social programmes is not a comprehensive solution since a concentration of resources on the needy is not always achieved. It also raises the possibility that targeting FHHs may be suboptimal or may even be counter-productive, because of a failure to take into account other women who are also in need. Furthermore, targeting has a problematic effect because, in order to gain access to the programme, women are required to meet a series of conditions and to have a level of information that is unlikely to be possessed by the most marginal people. This also leads to the importance of taking actions to eradicate female illiteracy since the poorest women, who are often illiterate, are deterred by the stigma attached to means-testing procedures. In this regard, it is important to reduce women's drop-out rates and to encourage women, especially rural and indigenous women and teenage mothers, to remain in the educational system. Neither are universal and targeted policies exclusive opposites and, in fact, it might well be better to assist the poor by a tandem strategy using both approaches.

In the near future the government will measure the results in quantitative terms, for example, by assessing the programme in terms of labour market insertion. This strategy will force the coordinators of the PMJH to identify those women with better potential to enter the labour market, resulting in changes in what is required of participants.

> To rethink the goals of the PMJH implies restructuring the profile of the participants. During the first stage of implementation of the PMJH, the main aim was to establish the programme as part of a social strategy to alleviate poverty. However, in the second stage of the PMJH, you need to show immediate results: that these women are inserted into the labour market and are increasing their income level. Therefore, we will feel forced to choose those women with better chances to be integrated into the labour market; for example, a woman who has two children instead of six, with a higher level of schooling and enterprising capacity, rather than a woman excluded from all the social systems...We have been working over the years with the poorest women. How do you say to them that now the programme is restructured? (Co-ordinator C)

Therefore, the poorest are likely to be excluded again as a result of such targeting.

Participation and empowerment

With respect to women's participation, the PMJH has promoted a new type of relation with the municipalities, through dialogue concerning the PMJH's contents and means of implementation. Empowerment calls for approaches that seek to build an increased sense of self-confidence and self-esteem among women (Molyneux, 1998). However, the present approach to social programmes places emphasis on 'outcomes' rather than on a dynamic 'process' of change, and problems arise from the resulting short-termism and the need to achieve rapid results. These target-driven strategies focused on performance indicators has resulted in a dilution of participatory and empowerment objectives. Furthermore, those in charge of the OMMs are predominantly female social workers who often have extensive experience in women's organizations or grass-roots groups. Social workers are perceived by women from poorer sectors as professionals from whom to ask for assistance and services. The management of the PMJH at the local level remains *'asistencialismo'* (paternalistic or assistance-based). Thus, women have been perceived as objects of social policies rather than subjects, as the means to provide services and to reach the rest of the family. Most of the measures to alleviate female poverty have been through state subsidies, assuring subsistence but not social mobility. The traditional understanding of the role of the woman as wife and mother underpin local policies (Weinstein, 1996). This attitude stems from historical conceptions of the poor based on ideological and cultural models reinforced under the dictatorship, rather than from the professional bias of the social workers themselves. It is interesting to note that in some cases women themselves desert the programme when they realize that they are required to play an active role and to be trained for work to receive further services. This shows that the participants themselves are expecting a paternalistic and palliative approach rather than 'a hand up, not a hand out' approach. In sum, the modification of this assistance-based model, not just at the municipal level, but in all public and private institutions closely linked with the poor, represents one of the main challenges to the development of a 'participatory relationship' of women's decision-making processes at the local level.

> Women in the PMJH build their identities as heads of households along with their self-esteem rather than as 'victims' – a view which stereotypes them as women who have been abandoned and have no options. In some municipalities, the PMJH plays an empowerment role for these women as social agents in the local context. However, in other districts this is not an issue for the municipality. There is a lack of skills and attitudes among municipal staff about how to work in a participatory way in communities. Then the municipality works like a service provider, but without long-term expectations of positioning these women as social agents in the communal space and as an interlocutor to the authorities. There is resistance from traditional power-holders to turn over the control of the programme to the participants. Accountability and representation of these women remain key problems. (Coordinator D)

However, to develop participation effectively, it is not enough that the women meet, talk, criticize and propose; all this must have concrete results, otherwise such participatory experiences come to an end. In fact, regional and communal reports recurrently demand operationalization: what is participation, exactly? What are the specific mechanisms through which it can be sustained over time? This requires SERNAM to clarify which women can participate in the PMJH, as well as what the goals of participation are. On these grounds, public assistance needs to be subordinated to the requirements of the participants, and to be accountable to them in order to encourage genuine social participation. In this respect, the decentralization of social programmes at the level of regional departments and municipalities should allow the delivery of the correct combination of services according to local characteristics and demands by encouraging the involvement of participants at the planning stage.

Labour training

There are no studies to measure the achievements of the PMJH concerning the quality and type of insertion into the labour market of the participants. The evaluation of social programmes in Chile is a task that is just being initiated. However, current results based on evidence from research interviews are not encouraging when considering the emphasis of the PMJH on paid and stable occupations in the formal labour market in poor areas where there are not many firms at the local level. In general, the programme is unlikely to make a strong impact. There is a lack of knowledge about the range of training courses offered and a lack of flexibility in adapting the courses to the particularities of the labour market at the regional and local levels. In general, women are taught those skills that require less financial outlay owing to limited resources, and these skills may not challenge gender stereotypes of women's work. As a result, the training courses undertaken reinforce women's occupational segregation and do not improve their socio-economic condition, leaving women to prefer social benefits to this new type of social intervention. There is a gap between the emphasis of the programme in the sphere of labour training and the major significance for the participants of other spheres of intervention, particularly health care. This makes them positively value the access to health and other services to meet their most urgent needs rather than the training courses.

The PMJH's services are provided as a function of improving their own labour performance. However, this focus cannot be applied homogeneously to each and every communal reality. Different demands emerge that question the labour initiative as the PMJH's axis. The group discussions reveal that not all women understand or feel that labour training is what they must focus their efforts on. One finds instead a multiplicity of perceived needs, and therefore, a great diversity of demands made on the PMJH. For many participants the most relevant and desired support was in the area of health services. Participants valued preferential attention in the outpatient departments. By contrast, they did not always see labour training as relevant and central to the PMJH. One often found that training was a good opportunity for acquiring new skills that had nothing to do with labour integration, but rather with the execution of domestic chores. In this sense, training loses its sense as training for remunerated work. The social characteristic of districts also influenced how women prioritized the PMJH's initiatives. Child care, for instance, was not a perceived need in the rural districts, where there is still a family tradition of support in child care.

These considerations of the labour training component reflect back upon the suitability of the integrated approach discussed earlier. On the whole, the integrated approach is fundamental to appropriate social policy intervention in the problem of FHHs' vulnerability. Although labour integration should continue to be the PMJH's axis, this does not necessarily presuppose labour training as a principal support channel. To insist principally on labour training implies a lack of awareness of the diversity of demands made by and needs felt on the part of FHHs.

For this reason, rather than make integration into a rigid concept, it should be understood and applied according to specific *relevance*. The requirement of integration should remain, but the relevance and priority given to elements of each initiative should depend on the participants' profile and on the local context. Diagnosing local conditions and refining the profiles (demands) of participants to accommodate families of diverging structure and composition – who are traversing different stages of the family life cycle – is necessary to make integration an effective and adequate principle.

V. Conclusion

This analysis has sought to identify the successes and obstacles that represent some of the limits and potentials of what are currently called 'innovative' social programmes. Although some of the PMJH's components and orientations are derived from the specific requirements of the target population, the lessons learned from the PMJH can be used to facilitate the administration of other municipal programmes. It clearly demonstrates the advantages and difficulties that may confront similar programmes that have been implemented subsequently, unless the modalities of public administration and of relations between the state and private sector change. This analysis of the PMJH raises five main issues that are pertinent to wider debates about poverty reduction policies.

First, the PMJH illustrates the tensions that exist between innovative programmes and the institutional framework in which social policy operates. This is the result of the nature of a public apparatus that is marked by a culture of corporatism and with a lack of experience in the implementation of horizontal relations between the different sectors. There is a considerable amount of resistance on the part of policy experts to consider the gender dimension of key policy areas like health, education, and particularly labour. Gender-blind administrative arrangements and bureaucratic practice often become a key factor in limiting SERNAM's range of actions. This shows a lack of information and familiarity with the concept of gender-aware planning among civil servants, and inadequate human and financial resources allocated to the PMJH. The PMJH has been criticized by opponents for destroying the family and SERNAM has had to couch its language of support for the programme in terms of the better results for social policies which can be obtained by increasing the income-generating capacity of the needy. It is important to understand the wider political context and the wider cultural framework to comprehend the outcomes. The formulation and implementation of the PMJH has been framed with reference to the difficulties facing FHHs in overcoming poverty, rather than with the aim of creating gender equity. This has resulted in policies targeting women, which in reality belong to areas of poverty alleviation and social welfare.

Secondly, this analysis draws attention to the way in which gender issues in development appear to have collapsed into a poverty trap (Jackson 1998). Because regional planners do not consider the gender dimension, they visualize the problem as a subjective one, which is difficult to address in terms of planning or social policy. Their opinions differ as to the existence of discrimination against women. Ignorance also results in the delegation of women's issues exclusively to women and institutionally to SERNAM, although gender issues need to be integrated as part of sectorial agendas and require coordination between the different public services. SERNAM's exclusive responsibility is linked to its legal status as the government institution responsible for women, but is not compatible with its technical and economic capacities. Therefore, technical insufficiencies and the devaluation of gender issues contribute to a lack of recognition of the differential impact of social policies on women and men.

Many of the operational problems and obstacles have their origin and solution in the policies and procedures elaborated at the regional and national levels, in the institutions that integrate or collaborate with the PMJH's work. It is far from clear that, at the municipal level, there is a willingness to integrate the gender perspective into their policies and an interest in developing the PMJH. The fact that the gender contents incorporated into the PMJH's design are reflected in its implementation is taken more as an achievement than as a starting point. Experience has shown that it is not enough that the PMJH (and perhaps other programmes) has been designed with the unequal structural conditions of poor woman in mind for its execution to reflect its orientation.

Thirdly, the PMJH addresses the controversial question of targeting FHHs for anti-poverty intervention. Local diversity – its cultural, social and economic specificities – seems relevant in two spheres. First, the subject of FHHs' visibility and valuation is closely linked to the district's socioeconomic characteristics. In rural districts, recognition of female household headship generates more resistance and suspicion than in urban districts, especially more modern ones. Visibility of the target group is closely associated with the PMJH's credibility inside the municipality and thus with its capacity to generate resources from the community to ensure its sustainability. The strategies of developing a social identity of female household headship cannot be assumed to have had a uniform impact in all districts.

Thus, aiming to change gender conceptions profoundly affects each person and her or his cultural surroundings.

A second sphere where the communal context is important concerns the training initiative's success. The difficulty is that this initiative does not consider the district's socio-economic context or the participants' interests. The difference between the available resource (training courses) and the women's and district's demands and needs is considerable. It is difficult to integrate women into the labour market if the training they receive is not adjusted to their needs and expectations or to the demands of the labour market. Interviews stated that programmes that favour labour market integration should aim to improve low-income women's standard of living by promoting employment and vocational initiatives that support women's cooperatives, associations of female producers, self-managed enterprises and other forms of productive organization. Participants were aware of the need to establish credit systems for small businesses run by women, and to eliminate obstacles to women's access to all productive resources, particularly training, technical assistance and basic social services.

Fourthly, the PMJH contributes to the debate about the role of broadbased social welfare provision *versus* targeted relief and assistance. Overall, there is a need to institutionalize a gender-planning approach in government policy by shifting away from one that targets welfare at vulnerable groups, and towards one that mainstreams a gender perspective across all sectors. In effect, this means operationalizing higher levels of gender awareness in the government's decentralization process and developing bases in government and civil society to promote gender equity. Once again, gender awareness requires work at the level of cultural attitudes as well as policy areas. In this regard, progress has to be made in conducting broad-based campaigns on the gender perspective and making use of the local and international media and public education programmes, in order to make society sensitive to the need for more balanced, egalitarian participation by women and men in development planning and in social and economic policies. An integrated approach based on multi-impact inter-sectorial policies, which address the task of alleviating poverty and include the dimension of gender equity, is therefore necessary. Moreover, it is important to take advantage of the state reform processes, particularly decentralization, that can help advance the cause of equal opportunities for men and women. In this regard, municipal governments have a decisive role to play in bringing the gender perspective into the mainstream in order to reach a more local level.

Fifthly, the PMJH provides a new model of social intervention for comparison. Institutionalization means strengthening the different administrative levels of the PMJH. The PMJH proposes a non-bureaucratic administrative model with a high degree of autonomy, which permits adaptation to municipal characteristics and to the regional public sector, as well as to the particular conditions of FHHs in each locality. For an important part of the PMJH's administration, the communal directors act in a decentralized and autonomous way. However, in order that this autonomy does not become isolation, the PMJH needs to be effectively integrated into the municipality. In practice, the PMJH has to overcome the many bureaucratic obstacles in each municipality, but has little and sometimes no coherent means of attaining institutionalization. In particular, this translates into a social programme that tends to function autonomously and alone inside the municipality. In this sense, the PMJH, more than an independent programme, is an 'island' inside the municipality. This isolation also results in difficulties in adapting this new type of social programme (integrated, inter-departmental, inter-disciplinary, supra-institutional and participatory) to municipal realities.

It is paradoxical that the state's investment strategy, which bestows a central role to 'innovative' programmes (since they are supposedly more advanced than traditional welfare subsidies provided by the municipalities), does not provide as stable financing channels for innovative programmes as it does for welfare subsidies. This has considerable relevance for the future projection of the PMJH, for two reasons. First, the financial support SERNAM currently provides for the municipalities implementing the PMJH cannot last indefinitely. Secondly, although the PMJH's institutional development strategy is based largely on the relocation of resources, it does not eliminate the need to incorporate fresh resources. On the one hand, it is necessary to finance and coordinate these institutions. On the other hand, if one wishes to achieve real progress in the design of specific policies, it is also necessary to develop new programmatic initiatives in the different sectors. One last general conclusion of the analysis is the necessity of reinforcing, within the poverty alleviation strategy, the complementing of universal and targeted policies. This raises challenges that go beyond the PMJH, in which the regional governments – that are also a part of the PMJH's 'institutional target population' – are called on to fulfil a far more active role.

The PMJH confronts a disjunction between the maintenance of traditional patterns of social administration at the different state levels, and the search for new ways to counter poverty and social inequality. In general terms, the new social strategy has tended to become watered down during the execution process. There are two problematic aspects in the implementation of these types of innovative programmes. First, the lack of coordination between sectors causes delays, mixed signals and conflicting procedures that would be avoided by an integrated approach. Secondly, there is concern about the suitability of this type of programme to the specific socio-cultural and economic environment in which it is implemented and expected to improve the quality of life. These aspects point to the need to ensure flexibility in the programmes, to strengthen the role of municipalities in the tasks of local development, and to incorporate poor sectors in the prioritization of local needs.

Notes

This paper forms part of a PhD thesis submitted to the University of Cambridge in January 2001. I wish to acknowledge the financial support of the Centre of Latin American Studies at Cambridge University for research carried out in Chile on which this paper is based. I am grateful to the Latin American Faculty of Social Sciences (FLACSO, Chile) which offered a stimulating setting in which to base my work. In addition, I wish to thank Glen Rangwala, Bryan Turner and David Lehmann for their comments.

1. The parties forming the *Concertación de Partidos por la Democracia* – a party pact between the centre and left forces – were led by the *Partido Demócrata Cristiano* (PDC) in the centre, the *Partido por la Democracia* (PPD) on the centre-left, and the *Partido Socialista* (PS) on the post-Marxist left.
2. Under the military regime of Pinochet (1973–90), Chile was the first country in Latin America to embrace economic neo-liberalism. The crisis of the political economy model of import substitution industrialization (ISI) and the economic crisis afflicting the economy in the mid-1970s and the early 1980s, led to a combination of austerity measures and liberalization policies within a framework of severe structural reforms. Restructuring during the 1980s increased economic growth, but at the cost of an increasing disparity in the distribution of income, rising poverty, and declining public and social spending (Bulmer-Thomas 1996, World Bank 1997, Schkolnik and Teitelboim 1998).
3. The neo-liberal philosophy behind the restructuring was a marked departure from the traditional Chilean belief that the state should play a progressive role in income distribution and welfare. A comprehensive description of the pre-Pinochet social welfare system can be found in Arellano (1985). For an extensive analysis of Chile's adjustment and social policies during the 1980s and 1990s, see Raczynski and Romaguera (1995) and Hiscock and Hojman (1997).
4. In this context, the taxation reform in 1990 provided an expansion of the resources directed to social ends. The first government of *Concertación* had a budget fixed by the military government that was 7 per cent lower than in the year 1989 (at the end of the dictatorship), when the social priorities were different (Raczynski 1998:214).
5. The five districts were: Arica (Region I); Conchalí and Santiago (Metropolitan Region); San Antonio (Region V) and Coronel (Region VIII).

Bibliography

Afshar, H. and Barrientos, S. (eds). 1999. *Women, Globalisation and Fragmentation in the Developing World*. Basingstoke: Palgrave Macmillan.

Araiz, S., Mercado, O. and Wayser, M. 1998. 'El Caso de Chile', in R. Lagos and C. Arriagada (eds) *Población, Pobreza y Mercado de Trabajo en América Latina*. Chile: OIT.

Arellano, J.P. 1995. 'Política Fiscal y Desarolle Social', in Pizarro, Raczynski and Vial (eds) *Políticas Económicas y Sociales en el Chile Democrático*, CIEPLAN and UNICEF, Santiago.

Barrientos, S., Bee, A., Matear, A. and Vogel. I. 1999. *Women and Agribusiness. Working Miracles in the Chilean Fruit Export Sector*. Basingstoke: Palgrave Macmillan.

Bebbington, A. and Lehmann, D. 1998. 'NGOs and the Development Process: Dilemmas of Institutionalization', in M. Vellinga (ed.) *The Changing Role of the State in Latin America*. Boulder, Col.: Westview.
Benería, L. and Feldman, S. (eds). 1992. *Unequal Burden: Economic Crises, Persistent Poverty, and Women's Work*. Boulder, Col.: Westview.
Blumberg, R.L., Rakowski, C., Tinker, I. and Monteón, M. (eds). *Engendering Wealth and Well-Being: Empowerment for a Global Change*. Boulder, Col.: Westview.
Bravo, R. and Todaro, R. 1995. 'Las Familias en Chile: Una Perspectiva Económica de Género'. *Proposiciones* 26. Santiago de Chile: SUR.
Bulmer-Thomas, V. 1996. *The New Economic Model in Latin America and Its Impact on Income Distribution and Poverty*. London: Institute of Latin American Studies, University of London.
Bustillo, I. 1993. 'Latin American and the Caribbean', in E. King and A. Hill (eds) *Women's Education in Developing Countries: Barriers, Benefits and Policies*. Washington D.C.: Johns Hopkins University Press for the World Bank.
Buvinic M., Valenzuela J., Molina T. and Gonzalez E. 1992. 'The Fortunes of Adolescent Mothers and their Children: The Transmission of Poverty in Santiago, Chile', *Population and Development Review* 18(2): 269–97.
CASEN 1998. Encuesta de Caracterización Socio-Económica National (National Economic Survey).
CASEN 1996. Encuesta de Caracterización Socio-Economica National (National Economic Survey).
Castañeda, T. 1992. *Combating Poverty: Innovative Social Reforms in Chile during the 1980s*. San Francisco: ICS Press, International Centre for Economic Growth.
CEPAL 1992a. *Social Equity and Changing Production Patterns: An Integrated Approach*, Santiago.
CEPAL 1992b. *Major Changes and Crisis. The Impact on Women in Latin America and the Caribbean*, Santiago.
Chant, S. 1997. *Women-Headed Households. Diversity and Dynamics in the Developing World*. Basingstoke: Palgrave Macmillan.
Clert, C. 1996. 'Pobreza, Género y Exclusión Social en Chile', Supporting Document for a Report on 'Women's Poverty'. Santiago: Universidad de Chile.
Elson, D. 1991. 'Male Bias in Macroeconomics: The Case of Structural Adjustment', in Elson, D. (ed.) *Male Bias in the Development Process*, pp. 164–90. Manchester, UK: Manchester University Press.
Espinoza, V., Márquez, F. and Nuñez, L. (eds). 1996. 'Las Mujeres y el Empleo Informal: Profundización de Algunos Aspectos para el Diseño de Políticas Sociales'. Discussion Paper no. 51. Santiago: SERNAM.
Figueiredo, J.B. and Shaiheed, Z. 1993. 'Reducing Poverty through Labour Market Policies', paper presented at the symposium on 'Poverty: New Approahes to Analysis and Policy', Geneva.
Gaventa, J. 1998. 'Poverty, Participation and Social Exclusion in North and South'. *IDS Bulletin* 29(1): 50–7.
Graham, C. 1996. 'Gender Issues in Poverty Alleviation: Recent Experiences with Demand Based Programmes in Latin America, Africa and Eastern Europe'. *Issues in Development* No. 11. Geneva: OIT.
Geldstein, R.N. 1997. *Mujeres Jefas de Hogar: Familia, Pobreza y Género*. Argentina: UNICEF.
Guzmán, Virginia and Salazar, Rebeca. 1992. 'El Género en el Debate de las Políticas Públicas'. *Proposiciones* 21: 250–62.

Hardy, C. 1997. *La Reforma Social Pendiente*. Santiago: Las Ediciones de Chile 21.
Hiscock, J. and Hojman, D. 1997. 'Social Policy in a Fast-Growing Economy: The Case of Chile'. *Social Policy and Administration* 31(4): 354–70.
Holz, P. 1999. 'Evaluación y Seguimiento del Programa de Habilitación Laboral para Mujeres de Escasos Recursos Preferentemente Jefas de Hogar' Discussion Paper no. 65. Santiago de Chile: SERNAM.
Ihnen, P. 1998. 'Reflexiones sobre la Magnitud de la Pobreza en Chile', CEP Discussion Paper No. 100, Santiago: Centro de Estudios Públicos, Benson Collection.
ILPES. 1993. (Instituto Latinoamericano y del Caribe de Planificación Económica y Social) *Evolución de las Políticas Sociales en Chile, 1964–1980*.
Irarrázabal, I. 1995. 'Habilitación, Pobreza y Política Social'. *Estudios Públicos* 59: 99–165.
Jackson, C. 1998. 'Rescuing Gender from the Poverty Trap', in R. Pearson and C. Jackson, (eds) *Feminist Visions of Development. Gender Analysis and Policy*. London: Routledge.
Jordana, J., M. Lasagna, and M. Salvador. 1998. 'Descentralización del Estado en America Latina: Participación versus Políticas Públicas'. *Agenda. Revista de Gobierno y Políticas Públicas*, pp. 33–57, Bogotá.
Larrañaga, O. 1995. 'Descentralización y Equidad: el Caso de los Servicios Sociales en Chile'. *ILADES Research Document*. Georgetown University.
Lloyd-Sherlock, P. 2000. 'The Need for New Approaches to Welfare to Promote Development'. *Journal of International Development* 12(1).
Márquez, F. and Rosenfeld, A. 1996. 'Seguimiento Evaluativo de la Implementación Municipal del PMJH'. Discussion Paper no. 43. Santiago de Chile: SERNAM.
Matear, A. 1997. 'Gender and the State in Rural Chile'. *Bulletin of Latin American Research* 16(1): 97–106.
MIDEPLAN. 1999. *Resultados de la Encuesta de Caracterización Socioeconómica Nacional 1998*. Santiago.
MIDEPLAN. 1997. *Pobreza y Distribución del Ingreso en Chile, 1996: Resultados de la Encuesta de Caracterización Socioeconómica Nacional*. Santiago.
Molyneux, M. 1998. 'Analysing Women's Movements'. *Development and Change* 29(2): 219–45.
Moser, C. 1996. 'Pobreza Urbana, Políticas Sociales y Género en un Contexto de Crisis Económica', in M.E. Ducci, V. Fernández and M. Saborido (eds) *Asentamientos Humanos, Pobreza y Género*, pp. 32–45. Santiago: GTZ, MINVU, PGU.
Oxhorn, P. 1994. 'Understanding Political Change after Authoritarian Rule'. *Journal of Latin American Studies* 26(3): 737–59.
Pizarro, C., Raczynski, D. and Vial, J. 1995. *Políticas Económicas y Sociales en el Chile Democrático*. CIEPLAN/UNICEF.
Raczynski, D. and Romaguera, P. 1995. 'Chile, Poverty, Adjustment and Social Policies in the 80s', in N. Lusting (ed.) *Coping with Austerity. Poverty and Inequality in Latin America*. Washington, D.C.: The Brookings Institution.
Raczynski, D. 1998. 'Para Combatir la Pobreza en Chile', in R. Cortazar and J. Vial (eds) *Construyendo Opciones: Propuestas Económicas y Sociales para el Cambio de Siglo*, 191–231. Santiago: CIEPLAN/DOLMEN.
Schkolnik, M. and Teitelboim, B. 1998. *Pobreza y Desempleo en Poblaciones: La Otra Cara del Modelo Neoliberal*. Chile: Programa de Economía del Trabajo, Benson Collection.
Serrano, C. 1995. 'Municipio, Política Social y Pobreza', in C. Pizarro *et al.* (eds) *Políticas Económicas y Sociales en el Chile Democrático*. Santiago: CIEPLAN–UNICEF.

Sheahan, J. 1998. 'Changing Social Programmes and Economic Strategies: Implications for Poverty and Inequality'. *Latin American Research Review* 33(2): 185–97.

UNICEF. 1990. *Los Escenarios de Vida de los Niños y Mujeres de Chile*. Santiago de Chile: UNICEF.

Valenzuela, M.E, Venegas S. and Andrade, C. 1994. *De Mujer Sola a Jefa de Hogar: Género, Pobreza y Políticas Públicas*. Santiago: SERNAM.

Vecchio, N. 1998. *Poverty, Female Headed Households and Sustainable Economic Development*. Westport, Conn.: Greenwood Press.

Vergara, P. 1993. 'Ruptura y Continuidad en la Política Social del Gobierno Democrático'. Discussion Paper no. 44. Chile: FLACSO.

Vogel, I. 1995. 'Gender and the Labour Market: Women's Experiences of Labour Force Participation in Chile', in D. Hojman, (ed.) *Neoliberalism with a Human Face? The Politics and Economics of the Chilean Model*, pp. 82–92. Liverpool: Institute of American Studies.

Waylen, G. 1996. 'Democratization, Feminism and the State: The Establishment of SERNAM in Chile', in Rai, S. and Lievesley, G. (eds) *Women and the State: International Perspectives*. London: Taylor and Francis.

Weinstein, M. 1996. 'Estado, Mujeres de Sectores Populares y Ciudadanía'. Series *FLACSO-Duncplas*.

Weyland, K. 1997. '"Growth with equity" in Chile's new democracy'. *Latin America Research Review* 32(1): 37–67.

Whitehead, L. (ed.). 1993. 'Economic Liberalization and Democratization: Explorations of the Linkages', in *World Development* XXI(8) Special Issue.

World Bank. 1997. 'Poverty and Income Distribution in a High-Growth Economy: Chile 1987–1995'. Washington D.C.

3
New Labour Market Challenges to Social Policies in Mexico

Maria Cristina Bayon, Bryan Roberts and Georgina Rojas

Introduction

From the late 1980s, economic restructuring accompanying trade liberalization reshaped Mexican labour markets, eliminating jobs in many traditional manufacturing industries. The number of job creations in manufacturing declined. There was an overall reduction in wage jobs and an expansion of informal employment (Rendón and Salas, 1993). Job growth occurred in the services and in transnational manufacturing sectors, such as the automobile industry or the *maquiladora* (in-bond) sector (Tardanico, 1997; Oliveira and García, 1997).

Mexican labour and social policies were designed with the full-time male worker in mind. Current changes in labour markets thus make these policies increasingly obsolete. Nowhere is this clearer than in the case of female participation in the labour force, which has increased in Mexico as in other Latin American countries (Valdés *et al.*, 1995). Whereas female workers represented 19 per cent of the Mexican labour force in 1970, their numbers increased to 32.8 per cent by 1995 (INEGI, 1999a).

The characteristics of women's labour market participation also changed in this period. Women's incomes became an increasingly essential part of family income as both male real incomes and the contribution of children declined. The latter trend resulted from the combined effects of children staying on in education and of declining fertility leading to fewer children. The family status of employed women shifted from being predominantly that of dependent or independent single women to a higher participation of married women with children (Pedrero and Rendón, 1982; García and Oliveira, 1994a). However, female participation in the labour market remains concentrated in low-income occupations and Mexican labour markets show segregation by gender in terms of occupations and lower wages for women than for men (Pedrero *et al.*, 1997; García, 1999).

We will explore these changes in the labour market and the challenges they imply for social policy in Mexico. Although some changes apply equally to men, we focus on women to illustrate the shortcomings in current directions in labour and social security policy. We argue that the key role of working women in household income generation has not been acknowledged either by traditional social policies or by the new targeting policies adopted as part of economic adjustment policies. However, the changes in the nature and scope of women's labour market participation create an urgent need for policy to take account of their needs.

Social and labour policy in Mexico

In the Latin American context Mexico is at the medium level of social expenditure together with Colombia and Venezuela (ECLAC, 1999).[1] Differences in the extension of social security coverage among countries has been largely a result of their level of development and composition of their labour force: those with the largest urban, salaried, formal sectors have presented the widest coverage, while those with the biggest rural, non-salaried, informal sectors have had the smallest coverage (Mesa-Lago, 1997). Mexican social security coverage has been less extensive than that of the countries of the Southern Cone, which have the highest levels of social expenditure. During the period 1988–91, 54 per cent of Mexico's economically active population had pension, disability and health coverage compared with 86 per cent, 80 per cent, and 72 per cent of the Chilean, Uruguayan and Argentinian population respectively (Mesa-Lago, 1997: 504).

These differences are explained in part by Mexico's more recent and more compressed period of urbanization and industrialization compared to the Southern Cone countries. Rapid urban growth outpaced the provision of social services and infrastructure in Mexico. Moreover, despite Mexico's rapid industrialization, a substantial part (approximately a third) of urban employment in Mexico remained in self-employment and in micro-enterprises – the so-called informal sector – which remained outside social security provision and state regulation of the labour market. Mexico's mainly peasant rural population was, until recently, largely excluded from social security provision.

Mexican social welfare and labour policies provide universal protection for those in formal employment. This includes *aguinaldo* (extra month's salary paid at Christmas), housing (INFONAVIT), and social security (health insurance, pensions, and child care). There has been, however, little or no protection for non-standard employment statuses, such as part-time or intermittent work, which are particularly common among women. Mexican labour law guarantees permanent contracts, allowing temporary contracts only when the nature of the activity is not permanent. However, in practice, an employer can arbitrarily impose a temporary contract on a worker whose function is a necessary part of the firm's activities. The use of temporary contracts has increased since the 1980s. In the early 1990s, 12 per cent of manufacturing industry workers were employed temporarily. At the same time, the extension of subcontracting practices (such as cleaning, cafeteria, transportation, surveillance, and maintenance) has resulted in an increasing labour insecurity and a means of avoiding employers' legal obligations (Bensusan, 1999). The percentage of workers working more than 35 hours a week who received less than a minimum wage increased from 4.7 per cent to 8.2 per cent between 1992 and 1996, and more than 25 per cent of the economically active population (EAP) worked more than 48 hours a week during 1996 (OCDE, 1997: 98).

The changes experienced in the Mexican system of labour relations have been characterized as a process of transition from a system of *selective inclusion* – linked to the ISI model and the internal market – to a system of *generalized exclusion* in the context of the outward oriented model of development. The emergent system promotes competitive strategies based upon labour cost reduction, employment precariousness, and weakening of labour unions; in sum, external flexibility (Bensusan, 1999).

These market changes have had both direct and indirect effects on health and other welfare services. As described by Gómez-Dantés (1998) and in the official text, *Seguridad Social* (1998), the 1995 social security reform included administrative de-concentration, budgetary autonomy of health zones, a reduction in employer contributions, services subcontracting and the privatization of some. However, González Bock and Gutiérrez (1998: 7) show that the proportion of the GDP spent on health did not increase in the 1990s. Thus, health and other welfare services continued to suffer from deficiencies in infrastructure despite reforms and decentralization. This was the case in both the sector providing services for the uninsured population (approximately 50 per cent of the total population) and the 40 per cent of the population that is insured. These changes are described by González Block and his collaborators (1989), Cardozo Brum (1993), Leyva (1993), Albro, 1996, by Gómez-Dantés, 1998 and by Gershberg (1998). These deficiencies probably explain the finding of the 1994 Health National Survey that the private sector appears to provide services for many more than the 10 per cent of the Mexican population that is neither covered by the insured or uninsured plans. Thus, 23 per cent of the people enrolled in social security agencies reported a private provider as their usual source of primary care, as did 46 per cent of the people with no social security benefits.

Up to now health and social security reform in Mexico has focused on financial viability through the separation of financing and services. Gómez-Dantés (1998) argues that apart from the recent (1995) Family Health Insurance plan for uninsured workers, reform has given little attention to achieving more equity in coverage, to improving the quality of services or to expanding services for working women. The case of child care provision illustrates this failing.

Only a very small percentage of working women in Mexico are entitled to public child care services, which are limited to formal workers. This limitation forces working women to look for alternative strategies of child care, which tend to rely on other family members, friends or neighbours. They include accepting a part-time job or working in the informal sector where work schedules tend to be more flexible, and allow mothers to take their children to the work-place. As described by Tolbert et al. (1993) and Knaul and Parker (1996) private services are scarce and too expensive for most working women.

By the early 1970s all female government workers and all female workers who were enrolled in the social security programme had, in principle, a right to day care services provided by the state. The critical policy concept in public-sector day care in Mexico is the provision of services to *women who work* and their children. Day care is available to increase the productivity of women workers, not to enable women to take up training opportunities, seek jobs or attend to household responsibilities. It is thus the service and not the policy that is child centred. Tolbert et al. (1993: 359) argue that child care policies aimed at *workers* and not at *children* are likely to be incomplete in terms of equal opportunity and social justice.

Child care provision shows high levels of segmentation according to the category of workers protected. The main provider of child care for those women working in the formal private sector is the Mexican Institute of Social Security (*Instituto Mexicano del Seguro Social*, IMSS). Another public provider is the Institute of Social Security for State Workers (*Instituto de Seguridad y Servicios Sociales de los Trabajadores del Estado*, ISSSTE) which offers child care services for public employees. If we consider the total population under 6 years in 1997 (13 million) and the population of this age group receiving child care services, which was 96 020 children (67 315 covered by IMSS and 28 705 by ISSSTE) according to official figures, then less than 1 per cent of Mexican children have access to day care services provided to formal working women (CONAPO, 1997; Poder Ejecutivo Federal, 1997).

Child care services for working women who are not entitled to social security are provided by the agency for the Integral Development of the Family (DIF). It covers just a minimum proportion of the non-insured population, which is mainly a low-income population without the capacity to pay for child care services (Tolbert et al., 1993; Knaul and Parker, 1996).

An example of the low levels of child care coverage is the case of Mexico City where there are approximately 20 000 publicly financed places for all children under five, compared with the estimated 500 000 children from birth to three years of age in the metropolitan area whose mothers work. Tolbert et al. (1993: 359) claim that in the border region the waiting list for IMSS day care is so long that some facilities have ceased accepting names. In the private sector, unregulated child care results in large differences in facilities, quality and price structure. Informal family day care and kindergartens serve mostly the middle and upper classes, as their fees and hours make them inaccessible to low-income working mothers. Private day care fees range from 40 per cent to 200 per cent of the minimum wage. It is clear that private child care services are unobtainable for the working poor and is not a cost-effective alternative for government workers or private employees (Tolbert et al., 1993).

Mexican provision of child care services is very poor, not only in absolute terms but also in regional terms, at least when compared with countries such as Argentina and Brazil. In Brazil the potential clientele for day care programmes is estimated to be 13.2 million children (newborn to age three) and for pre-schools approximately 10.5 million children (age four to six). In terms of coverage, in the early 1980s less than 10 per cent of children less than seven years of age were attending day care centres or pre-schools. In metropolitan areas this number had increased to 23 per cent in 1985 (Rosemberg, 1993: 46). Thus, while Brazilian levels of coverage are still very low, they are high when comparing with Mexico. In Argentina, 35 per cent of children between three and four years of age attend day care centres and pre-schools; 58.3 per cent of these children are in the poorest 40 per cent of the population, and 40 per cent of them are covered by public food programmes (SIEMPRO, 1999: 43).

Economic restructuring and regional labour markets

In this section we consider recent trends in working conditions in Mexico and their differential impact on men and women. We look at these trends in terms of the various forms of non-standard employment (temporary contract, part-time work, informal employment, intermittent employment) that depart from the norm of the full-time worker on stable contract on which social and labour policy in Mexico was constructed. We introduce regional contrasts to emphasize the diversity of both men and women's employment situations and thus the need for a regionally sensitive labour and social policy.

The Mexican urban system has been historically characterized by the population and economic dominance of Mexico City and sharp regional inequalities (Garza, 1990 and 1991). With the growth of foreign direct investment, Mexico City has strengthened its role as the country's dominant city given its importance as a financial centre. This role may mean better labour market opportunities for women with high qualifications, but increasing income inequality in the city is likely to mean worsening conditions for most working women. We also look at labour market conditions in Guadalajara and Monterrey, the two main regional centres of Mexico, with long-standing manufacturing bases and important service and commercial functions. We expect labour market opportunities for women in these cities to be less polarized than in the case of Mexico City.

As a further point of contrast we consider four northern border cities (Matamoros, Nuevo Laredo, Ciudad Juarez and Tijuana). These cities are characterized by the predominance of the *maquila* industry and by their proximity to the United States. The rates of population growth in the border cities surpassed that of Mexico City during the 1970s and 1980s since the massive creation of jobs in the *maquiladora* plants attracted population from all around the country. The *maquiladora* plants are mainly concentrated in activities such as the electronic, garments and the automobile industries. These cities provide stable jobs in large manufacturing operations for young women entering the labour market. For this age group, labour market conditions for women in terms of social security provision and permanent work contracts are likely to be the most favourable of any of the cities. However, opportunities for older women are less favourable than for younger women.

Working conditions

On our first dimension of non-standard employment – informal employment – women and men show broadly similar trends with important regional variations. Overall, both men and women are more likely to be informally employed in 1999 than in 1987, thus increasing the proportion of the uninsured population. Informal employment defined as the self-employed and those employed in micro-enterprises, is historically a salient characteristic of the Mexican labour market (Roberts, 1991 and 1993b).[2] The economic restructuring and trade liberalization of the 1990s has not lessened the importance of informal activities, particularly in Mexico City. Between 1987 and 1999 male informality increased in Mexico City from 31 per cent to 42 per cent, whereas female informality increased from 28 per cent to 31 per cent, with the percentage of women employed in domestic service remaining constant between 11 and 12 per cent. In the border cities, informal work has remained constant among women at 22 per cent and declined among males from 43 per cent in 1987 to 35 per cent in 1999. In the regional centres, males were as likely to be informally employed in 1999 as in 1987 with approximately 36 per cent so employed in both years. Female informality, however, has declined from 35 per cent in 1987 to 30 per cent in 1999, with an additional 11 per cent of women employed as domestic servants in the former year and 9 per cent so employed in the latter year.

The National Survey on Urban Employment (ENEU) began to record the nature of the employment contract in 1994, recording whether the contract was a written contract for an indefinite period, a fixed-term contract or a verbal contact. Categorizing those on fixed-term contracts and verbal contracts as temporary workers, we find that overall women are no more likely than men are to be employed on temporary contracts (Table 3.1). As in the case of informal employment, the characteristics of the local labour market, not gender, appear to be the major determinant of temporary employment. The proportions of men and women with temporary jobs remain constant between 1994 and 1999 in Mexico City. According to Table 3.1, in the regional centres, there were more female temporary workers than male in all six years, but the proportions working temporarily declined for both males and females. In the border cities, women who are still the mainstay of *maquiladora* employment were less frequently hired on a temporary basis than were men throughout 1994–99. The border cities had both the lowest proportions of temporary employment among the three regions and the sharpest decline in temporary employment between 1994 and 1999 (Table 3.1).

On two other dimensions of non-standard employment – part-time work and intermittent employment – women clearly differ from men. A shorter schedule is one means by which women cope with their work inside and outside the household, particularly in the absence of adequate child care service. In Mexico as well as some other countries – Argentina (Marshall, 1992), Western Europe (Marshall, 1989), and the US (Tilly, 1996) – evidence shows the concentration of female workers in part-time activities (García, 1999). Table 3.2 shows that women are hired on a part-time schedule more frequently than are men in the three regions for 1987 as well as for 1999. As with temporary employment, the border cities show the lowest levels and largest declines over time in part-time work.

Moving in and out of the labour market or intermittent labour force participation is a common pattern of female participation in Mexico as well as in other Latin American countries (Cerrutti, 1997). We created two panels from ENEU, one beginning in 1987 and the other in 1996, containing observations of changes in the economic activity of the population over one year.

Table 3.3 shows that the large majority of males in all three regions are economically active throughout the year. In contrast, women show a high degree of intermittent participation. The lowest intermittent participation

Table 3.1 Temporary workers* by sex and region, 1994–99 (percentages)

Region	1994 M	1994 F	1995 M	1995 F	1996 M	1996 F	1997 M	1997 F	1998 M	1998 F	1999 M	1999 F
Mexico City	44.5	45.0	44.7	41.0	47.2	41.1	46.4	44.9	46.7	45.3	45.6	44.6
Regional centres	41.8	42.2	43.7	45.0	40.7	41.4	39.1	42.6	39.2	41.9	33.3	36.8
Border cities	30.7	22.4	27.5	20.1	25.9	21.6	24.6	18.7	22.6	15.5	22.0	15.8

Notes: * Temporary jobs are defined here as those under written contract for a fixed-term period or *obra*, and those under verbal contract. These figures correspond to any firm size. By each category, the rest of the workers (by sex and region) hold a permanent and written contract.

Source: Mexican National Survey on Urban Employment (ENEU), third quarter of each year.

Table 3.2 Part-time* workers by region and sex (percentages)

	1987		1999	
Region	M	F	M	F
Mexico City	13.6	28.1	12.0	27.2
Regional centres	14.3	30.9	11.4	29.5
Border cities	13.7	19.3	4.9	13.9

Note: * Part-timers are those who worked less than 35 hrs during the week of reference in the survey. Any firm size.

Source: Mexican National Survey on Urban Employment (ENEU), third quarter of 1987 and 1997.

Table 3.3 Intermittence* in the labour force (entries and exits) by sex and region during one year of observation (percentages)

	Mexico City		Regional centres		Border cities	
	M	F	M	F	M	F
1987–88						
Always in the labour force	72.0	40.7	72.4	36.6	70.9	39.4
Out–In	5.6	12.7	7.8	16.0	6.3	18.6
In–Out	7.0	12.1	5.9	13.3	7.6	16.7
Intermittent	15.4	34.5	13.9	34.1	15.2	25.3
Total	100	100	100	100	100	100
1996–97						
Always in the labour force	74.7	38.2	76.8	47.2	75.3	35.2
Out–In	4.7	13.7	5.8	13.8	4.6	17.5
In–Out	6.2	14.8	4.9	11.2	6.9	15.4
Intermittent	14.4	33.3	12.5	27.8	13.2	31.9
Total	100	100	100	100	100	100

Note: * Intermittence is defined as two or more movements in and out of the labour force during the year of observation.

Source: Mexican Urban Employment Survey. Panels constructed from the third quarter of the respective years throughout the third quarter of the following year.

during 1987–88 is in the border cities (15.2 per cent male and 25.3 per cent female workers). In the regional centres and in Mexico City, 34 per cent of women worked intermittently. In 1996–97, the proportions of male intermittent workers decreased in the three regions. For women the trend is less clear. Women from the regional centres became less intermittent, from 34 per cent in 1987–88 to 28 per cent in 1996–97. The proportion of intermittent participation among Mexico City women slightly decreased from 34 per cent to 33 per cent. However, women's intermittency on the border increased from 25.3 per cent in 1987–88 to 31.9 per cent in 1996–97.

In summary, there are contradictory trends in working conditions in terms of full-time employment and job security in the period 1987 to 1999. The striking contrasts are between the regions and between men and women's working conditions. Women are less likely to work informally, but more likely to be part-timers and to work intermittently. Mexico City shows the most unfavourable employment conditions for both men and women and the least improvement over time. Thus, Mexico City is the only region to experience an increase in informal employment by 1999. In the border cities, and to a somewhat lesser extent in the regional centres, working conditions improve by the end of the 1990s, with less temporary work, less part-time work and less informal employment.

A preliminary analysis of trends in the earned income of men and women in Mexico City between 1987 and 1999 provides additional insight into the impact of economic adjustment in this period.[3] We grouped workers into four major categories: (a) the non-professional self-employed and owners of small-scale enterprises, (b) workers in enterprises of less than six workers, (c) workers in enterprises of five or more workers and (d) owners of enterprises of more than four workers and self-employed professionals. The first two categories can be labelled informal sector workers and the third, formal sector workers. We also calculated the average earnings of each quintile of the income distribution within each group.

In the period 1987 to 1994, real incomes increased for all categories and for almost all quintiles. The major exception was the lowest quintile of formal sector workers whose real income declined in these years. The largest increases in income were in the top quintiles of the income distribution.

Two separable trends are evident. Income inequality increases between categories of workers and income inequality increases within categories. The income gap between formal sector workers and owners and the informal sector (the self-employed and micro-enterprise workers) increases in these years. Whereas, in 1987, the average earnings of the two top quintiles of the self-employed were higher than were those of the two top quintiles of formal sector workers, they had dropped behind by 1994. Also, there was an increase in income inequality among the self-employed, formal sector workers and owners, but not among the micro-enterprise workers. Thus between 1987 and 1994, the ratio of the average earnings of the top quintile to the average earnings of the bottom quintile increased from approximately four times to 10 times for formal male workers and from about three times to seven times for formal female workers.

After 1994, following devaluation and increased inflation, there are drops in the real incomes of all groups, and income inequality within groups diminishes slightly between 1994 and 1999. However, the earnings of all informal sector workers fall further behind those of formal sector workers by 1999.

Females have lower average incomes than males in all quintiles of income. In both the lowest and the highest quintiles of income distribution, our analyses show an increasing inequality of average income between men and women by 1999 in comparison with 1987. By 1999, female formal sector workers earn on average just under 30 per cent less in both the highest and the lowest quintiles than do male formal workers.

The labour market and income findings for 1987 to 1999 suggest that trade liberalization and economic adjustment have different consequences for informal and formal sectors of the work-force and for different regions of the country. Informal sector workers are earning relatively less in comparison with formal workers than they did at the end of the import-substitution period in the 1980s. Even though the informal sector increases its real income in the 'boom' years up to 1994, it is formal sector workers and owners who show the most rapid rise in incomes. After the economic decline accompanying the devaluation of the end of 1994, the incomes of all labour market sectors decline, but these declines are somewhat less severe among formal sector workers. Despite market liberalization, there is also no evidence, except in Mexico City, for a decline in the proportions of workers who enjoy full-time protected employment.

These positive trends for the formal sector need, however, to be qualified. There is some suggestion that within the formal sector, certain categories of workers have become more disadvantaged with time. Thus the lowest income quintile of formal sector workers, both male and female, show the sharpest drops in average income from 1987 to 1999, even when compared with the informal sector. We noted that incomes for women workers in the formal sector have declined in comparison with male incomes. Economic liberalization has thus not expanded formal sector employment sufficiently to offset the depressant effects of an increasing competition for even low-end jobs.

These findings can be interpreted in terms of the changing economic structure and economic geography of Mexico in this period. The expansion of export manufacturing occurs mainly in the north of the country, but is also present in the regional centres. Mexico City grows economically as a centre of trade, finance and services, but loses manufacturing jobs. Cheap imports and the increase in large retailing chains undermine the economic basis of craft production, small-scale commerce and services. In Mexico City this leads to a greater polarization of the labour market as relatively high wages in the formal service and commercial sectors contrast with the low wages in the informal sectors. This contrast is less accentuated in the regional centres and in the border cities because of the offsetting employment growth in the new types of manufacturing.

Female work and household responsibilities

With the increasing entrance of women into the labour market there have been demographic changes in the composition of the 'supply side' between

1987 and 1999. Cerrutti (1997) shows that in comparison with Argentinian women, Mexican women have had relatively low labour force participation and are more likely to withdraw from the labour force once they start having children (Cerrutti, 1997).

Figures 3.1 and 3.2 show the age specific female participation rates between 1987 and 1999 for the three regions. In 1987, the participation rates in the 12–19 and 20–24 year age groups are similar in the three cities. In the older age groups, Mexico City shows the highest participation rates. By 1999, the regional centres had the highest participation rates for the two younger age groups. However, the most striking shift is towards higher participation rates among older women in all three regions, suggesting that women are staying longer in the labour force.

This increase in volume of women in the labour force as well as the duration of their participation implies a series of further changes. One of these is that the historic predominance of childless single women in the female labour force in Mexico (INEGI, 1999b), is giving way to that of married women with children. Table 3.4 shows that the proportion of the female labour force who were married women with children grew in Mexico City between 1987 and 1999 from 34.4 per cent to 37.4 per cent. The increases were sharper in both the regional centres and in the border cities where married women with children increased from 31.6 per cent in 1987 to 37.0 per cent in 1999 and from 29.5 per cent to 38.9 per cent, respectively. By 1999, women with children, whether married, single, or separated/divorced, form

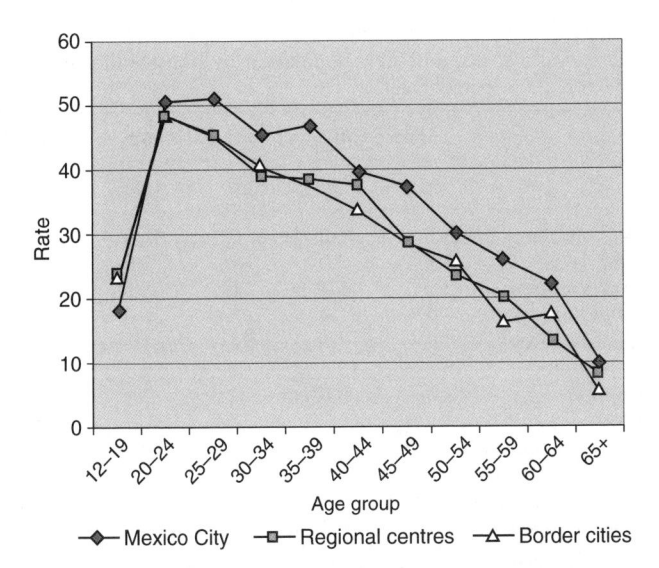

Figure 3.1 Age-specific rates of female participation in the labour force by region, 1987

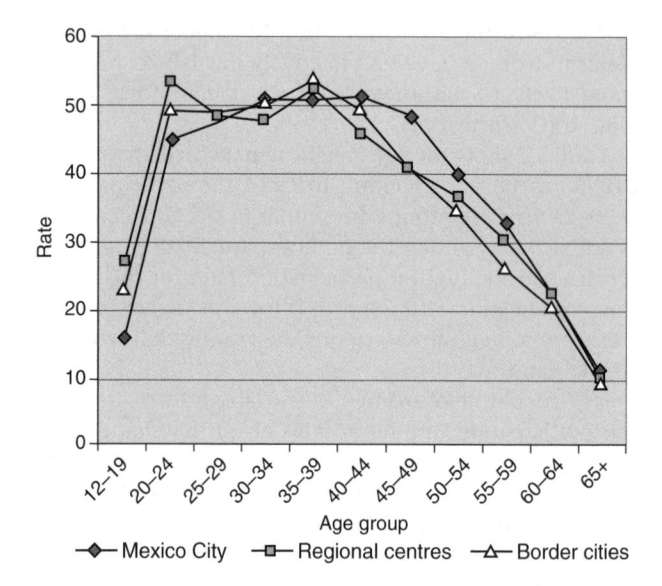

112 *Social Policy Reform and Market Governance in Latin America*

Figure 3.2 Age-specific rates of female participation in the labour force by region, 1999

Source: Mexican National Survey on Urban Employment (ENEU), third quarter of 1987 and 1999.

Table 3.4 Economically active female population by household status and region, Mexico, 1987 and 1999 (percentages)

Household status	Mexico City 1987	Mexico City 1999	Regional centres 1987	Regional centres 1999	Border cities 1987	Border cities 1999
Single w/out children	43.2	36.2	52.3	42.8	48.6	33.5
Single w/children	1.7	3.0	1.6	1.9	3.1	2.7
Married w/out children	3.7	5.4	4.0	4.6	5.0	5.7
Married w/children	34.4	37.4	31.6	37.0	29.5	38.9
Ex-marr w/out children*	1.4	1.6	0.8	1.3	1.8	2.1
Ex-marr w/children*	13.1	13.6	7.5	10.3	9.2	13.0
Other non-single members**	2.5	3.0	2.2	2.1	2.8	4.1
Total	100	100	100	100	100	100.0
n	2 104 802	2 574 859	601 637	994 480	209 971	428 297

Note: * Ex-married women: those divorced, separated or widowed.
** Other non-single women: those non-direct relatives or friends who live in the household.

Source: Mexican National Survey on Urban Employment (ENEU), third quarter of 1987 and 1997.

the majority of the female labour force. In Mexico City they accounted for 54 per cent of the female labour force. Women with children were 49.2 per cent of the female labour force in the regional centres in 1999. In the border cities, where hiring policies supposedly discriminate against women with children, women with children were 54.6 per cent of the female labour force in 1999 as compared to 41.8 per cent in 1987.

Single (never married) women with children, although a small percentage of the female labour force, have particular needs in the labour market, mainly in terms of child care provision. Since this category of mothers is very unlikely to receive child support from the father or relatives, women who are single parents have very high rates of labour market participation. In Mexico City in 1987, 70 per cent of never-married mothers participated in the labour force and, by the end of the 1990s, that proportion had increased to 77 per cent. On the border, the labour force participation of never-married mothers grew from 61 per cent in 1987 to 64 per cent in 1999. There was also an increase in the participation of never-married mothers from 70 per cent to 75 per cent in the regional centres between 1987 and 1999.

A slightly less vulnerable category is once-married women (separated, divorced or widowed) with children. These are more likely to receive aid from relatives and to live with them. In Mexico City, 44 per cent of such women were economically active in 1987 and 47 per cent in 1999. In the regional centres, 34 per cent of once-married women with children were employed in 1987 and 45 per cent in 1999. In the border cities 31 per cent of once-married women with children were part of the labour force in 1987 and 48 per cent in 1999.

There is, then, a consistent trend over the three regions for an increased labour force participation of women with children, whether or not there is a spouse present. The border cities provide the highest degree of social security protection for employed women, as might be expected given the predominantly formal nature of women's employment there. Between 1987 and 1999 there are slight declines in the proportions of single mothers, married women with children and once-married women with children who are not covered by the social security system on the border from 39 per cent to 38 per cent, from 32 per cent to 31 per cent and from 45 per cent to 41 per cent respectively. In Mexico City, lack of social security coverage increased for both currently married with children and once-married with children from 43 per cent to 52 per cent and 52 per cent to 57 per cent respectively. However, lack of coverage diminished from 1987 to 1999 for single mothers from 47 per cent to 44 per cent. In the regional centres also, lack of coverage decreases for single mothers from 51 per cent to 41 per cent in this period. The proportions of those currently married with children without coverage increases from 48 per cent to 51 per cent between 1987 and 1999, while the lack of coverage among the once-married remains the same at 53 per cent. As in other indicators of employment conditions, Mexico City shows the least favourable trends for women.

Gender and local labour markets: two dimensions of inequality

The findings on the trends in women's labour force participation show a change in the demographic profile of female workers. There are proportionately more older women working and there are more married women with children. In general terms, women are clearly more educated than in the past and stay in the labour force despite their household responsibilities. Female participation in the labour market has also implied a double burden in order to fulfil domestic and extra-domestic tasks. But it is also shaped by regional inequalities in the structure of work opportunities.

The heterogeneous industrialization in Mexico that concentrated more favourable job opportunities in big cities – such as Mexico City, Guadalajara and Monterrey, and the border cities – is being reconfigured by Mexico's integration into the global economy. NAFTA has accentuated internal inequity between those areas that are structurally integrated to the North American market and those that are marginal (Alba, 1999). Given the importance of the *maquiladora* in the border cities' productive structure, this region still represents the best opportunity for low-income women to get a stable and protected job in manufacturing industry. Mexico City has the most diversified structure in terms of services, commerce and manufacturing, but it also has an increasing gap between the opportunities for the better qualified and the less qualified workers. The regional centres – Guadalajara and Monterrey – are not as diversified, but they are increasingly attracting in-bond industries and are becoming important sub-centres for services and commerce in Mexico. As expected, the most disadvantageous labour opportunities are found in Mexico City given the polarization of the economic structure there.

Up to the beginning of the 1980s, basically the period of the Import Substitution Industrialization model (the period from approximately the 1940s to the 1980s when Latin American countries promoted industrialization, particularly in basic goods production, though limited imports by tariff protection), public policies talked about the need to reduce the socio-economic gap between regions in Mexico. In practice, only some isolated actions, that is, the foundation of industrial districts as 'development poles', were undertaken but were not effective enough to reduce inequality significantly (Garza, 1992). In the current economic restructuring in Mexico, there are no public policies that seek to reduce social and economic inequality among regions. The new, more targeted policies may have a regional impact but such regional effects are not planned (Alba, 1999). Internal inequality in Mexico is likely to deepen.

New directions in state policy in Mexico: limitations and challenges

Although a commitment to the realization of a comprehensive welfare state has not been entirely abandoned in Mexico, the boundaries of state action have been redrawn. Two closely interrelated trends can be observed. One is a contraction of real welfare expenditure as a consequence of austerity programmes, and the emphasis on self-help and delegation of responsibilities.[4] The other trend is primarily ideological: a move from the concept of universal welfare to the prioritizing of managerial efficiency within a framework of delegation and privatization, and the dogma of minimalist social action (Abel and Lewis, 1993).

Social policies that have been applied during the 1990s in Mexico as elsewhere in Latin America correspond to the World Bank's political recommendations, which include inflation control, economic growth, and the construction of social safety nets. Three main definitions summarize how the new social policies visualize social problems. First, they are identified almost exclusively with extreme poverty. Secondly, macro-economic policies must not be used to achieve social and redistributive goals. Finally, poverty reduction is a by-product of economic growth and social policy has to be focused only on the poorest of the poor (Lo Vuolo, 1997).

At the same time, the new approach emphasizes the role of family, community and the voluntary sector (NGOs), in the design and implementation of decentralized social programmes. The aim is to reduce costs and to seek the cooperation and participation of local communities. Targeting is based on the hypothesis that focused social policies are more efficient in alleviating poverty than are universal ones. Franco (1996: 18), for instance, claims that 'universally-oriented policies have a high cost and low impact'.

Although the Mexican state reduced its direct economic involvement in the market in the 1980s and 1990s through privatization and market de-regulation, it has been much slower to relinquish direct control of social welfare provision. The continuity of an authoritarian state-based welfare system in Mexico is a point of contrast with Chile where the experience of dictatorship provided some impetus under democracy to experiment with decentralization and with involving non-governmental organizations and community groups in policy formulation and implementation. In Mexico, decentralization and targeting policies have been heavily dependent on the central state and on direct links between local communities and central government agencies. There is little use for non-government organizations to implement policies.

The programme that best illustrates the new kind of social policies in the Mexican context is the National Solidarity Program (*Programa Nacional de Solidaridad*, PRONASOL), implemented during the Salinas de Gortari administration (1988–94). The PRONASOL emerged in a context of increasing poverty and inequality that accompanied the application of economic adjustment policies from the early 1980s.[5] The target of the programme was the population in extreme poverty, that is, non-waged earners with the lowest income levels, and its actions were restricted to the micro-level of economic activity. It had a territorial base, concentrating its actions basically in the poorest states and on the rural population. The programme represented

45 per cent of social investment and 18 per cent of the total investment of the federal administration (De Gortari and Ziccardi, 1996; Gordon, 1996; Garza, 1999). The resources committed to the programme were considerable, indicating one of the advantages of Mexico's centralized decision-making over public policy. There is, however, one key absence in the National Solidarity Programme: working women, and especially those with children, are not included in the 'target population' of the programme.

The projects for labour legislation reform from the governing as well as the opposition parties are focused mainly on two aspects: the introduction of labour flexibility and the democratization of labour relations.[6] However, in none of these projects are there special provisions for specific categories of workers that are an increasingly normal part of the labour market – such as part-time workers, a category in which women concentrate. While equal opportunity is included in the Mexican Labour Law (*Ley Federal del Trabajo*), there are no enforcement mechanisms to promote it. The implementation of mechanisms to ensure equal opportunity, the provision of social protection for part-time workers, as well as cumulative rights to social security for intermittent workers represent important issues to be included in a new labour policy agenda, which is able to meet the challenges of the new labour market realities.

There are projects to complement government provided day care facilities by child care services provided by non-profit organizations. However, while the efforts are noteworthy, and often innovative, they are isolated and local, serving small communities and groups. Registration with the Ministry of Education of child care centres in the private profit and non-profit sectors is not mandatory. No organizations exist to coordinate policy-making, public relations or fund raising. Nor are there mechanisms for sharing lessons learned in community involvement, training programmes, financing strategies, child development, or pedagogical techniques. As Tolbert *et al.* (1993) argue, financing remains the primary obstacle to successful non-profit child care efforts for low-income families. One of the main policy implications suggested by the previous overview of child care provision in Mexico is the need for a coordinated effort among the public, social, and private sectors involving government and non-governmental agencies with expertise in the area.

The new directions of social policy in Mexico promise greater flexibility, more individual choice and greater community participation. Yet, in labour reforms or in community development, they have to date relatively little to offer women in the labour market who are working under the conditions described in the previous sections: women with children, many of whom work intermittently, informally and part-time. Community development programmes need to focus on the needs of working mothers and labour and social security policies need to provide protection for non-standard employment situations. Indeed the focus on community caring is likely to entail greater burdens for women, who are the primary care-givers both for the elderly and for the young. It is unlikely that social problems can be solved in the private sphere because the market does not tend to produce collective goods and, as Garcia Delgado (1994) argues, because working with social networks constructed exclusively from civil society makes it difficult to go beyond short-term or local problems. At the same time, informal sources, such as family, community and the voluntary sector, have a limited capacity to provide social welfare. The role of social policy cannot be limited to residual functions and oriented exclusively to the final phase of poverty ignoring its causes.

Notes

1. Countries with high and medium-high levels assign between 17.5 per cent and 19.5 per cent of their GDP to social expenditures; those with a medium level between 7.9 per cent and 8.5 per cent; and countries with the lowest levels of social expenditure between 5.3 per cent and 7.7 per cent (ECLAC, 1999: 97).
2. We use as a definition of informality non-professional workers in firms with less than five employees, owners of firms of five or fewer employees, the self-employed and family workers.
3. This analysis is not complete with respect to the regional centres and border cities. We used the Consumer Price Index to standardize the incomes reported in the National Urban Employment Survey (ENEU). Our calculations are based on the Third Quarter Surveys for 1987, 1994, 1997 and 1999.
4. Between 1980 and 1993 there was a decrease of 24.3 per cent in public expenditures although, according to official data, spheres such as education, health and urban services were targeted and received most public investment during 1990–93 (INEGI, 1999b).
5. Between 1982 and 1988 the minimum wage dropped 53.3 per cent in real terms and contractual wages decreased by 38.2 per cent during the same period. From 1988 to 1994 contractual wages dropped 10 per cent in real terms and the Gini Index increased from 0.49 in 1989 to 0.51 in 1994 (Cortes, 1997).
6. There are the three different projects for labour legislation reform, one coming from employer organizations, and the other two from the opposition parties (PAN and PRD). These projects vary according to the degree of labour flexibility, the kind of relationship among the state, labour unions, workers, and employers, and the system of labour justice they seek to promote (Bensusan, 1999). The employers' project is the one that promotes the lowest levels of protection in respect to labour stability and general labour conditions, proposes a more individualized and depoliticized relationship among firms, labour unions and the state, and has an authoritarian approach to conflict regulation. The projects coming from the opposition parties advocate the dismantling of corporatist relations between the state and labour unions as well as the establishment of more autonomous and democratic organizations, differing basically in the degree of discretion that they give employers.

Bibliography

Abel, C. and Lewis, C. 1993. 'Introduction', in C. Abel and C. Lewis (eds) *Welfare, Poverty and Development in Latin America*. Basingstoke: Palgrave Macmillan.

Alarcón, Diana and Terry McKinley, 1998. 'Mercados de trabajo y desigualdad del ingreso en México. Dos décadas de restructuración económica', *Papeles de Población*, Año, 4(18): 49–79

Alba, Fracisco 1999. 'La cuestión regional y la integración internacional de México: una introducción', *Estudios Sociológicos*, 17(51): 611–31.

Albro, K. 1996. 'Reform of the Mexican Health System: Decentralization of Public Health Services in the 1990s', Master Thesis, University of Texas at Austin.

Bayon, M.C., Roberts, B., and Saravi, G. 1998. 'Ciudadania Social y Sector Informal en America Latina', in *Perfiles Latinoamericanos*, No. 13, December 1998, pp. 73–111.

Bensusan, G. 1999. *El modelo de regulacion laboral mexicano*. Mexico City: Plaza y Valdes, Fundacion Friedrich Ebert.

Bensusan, G., Von Bulow, M., and Garcia, C. 1996. *Relaciones laborales en las pequenas y medianas empresas en Mexico*. Mexico City: Fundacion Friedrich Ebert, Juan Pablos Editor.

Caire, Guy, 1989. 'Atypical wage employment in France', in Gerry Rodgers and Janine Rodgers (eds), *Precarious Jobs in Labour Market Regulation: The Growth of Atypical Employment in Western Europe*, International Institute of Labour Studies, Free University of Brussels, pp. 75–108

Cardozo Brum, M. 1993. *Análisis de la Política Descentralizadora en el Sector Salud*, Buenos Aires: Asociación de Administradores Gubernamentales.

Cerrutti, Marcela Sandra 1997. 'Coping with Opposing Pressures: A Comparative Analysis of Women's Intermittent Participation in the Labour Force in Buenos Aires and Mexico City', PhD Dissertation, University of Texas at Austin.

Consejo Nacional de Población y Vivienda (CONAPO), 1997. *La situación demográfica de México 1997*. Mexico: CONAPO.

Cortes, Fernando, 1998. 'Politica economica y desigualdad. Distribucion del ingreso segun su origen', *Demos*. Carta demografica sobre Mexico, pp. 26–8.

ECLAC. 1999. *Social Panorama of Latin America 1998*. Santiago de Chile: United Nations.

Franco, R. 1996. 'Social policy paradigms in Latin America', *CEPAL Review* # 58, April 1996, pp. 9–23.

García, Brígida, 2000. 'Economic Restructuring, Women's Work and Autonomy in Mexico', in Harriet Presser and Gita Sen (eds), *Women's Empowerment and Demographic Processes: Moving Beyond Cairo*, Oxford: Clarendon Press, pp. 261–86.

García, Brígida and Orlandina de Oliveira, 1994a. 'La medición de la población económicamente activa en México al inicio de los años noventa', *Estudios Demográficos y Urbanos*, 9(3): 579–608.

García, Brígida and Orlandina de Oliveira, 1994b. *Trabajo femenino y vida familiar en México*, Mexico: El Colegio de México.

Garcia Delgado, D. 1994. *Estado & Sociedad. La nueva relacion a partir del cambio estructural*. Buenos Aires: FLACSO, Tesis Grupo Editorial Norma.

Garza, Gustavo, 1990. 'El carácter metropolitano de la urbanización en México, 1900–1988', *Estudios Demográficos y Urbanos*, 5 (1): 37–59.

Garza, Gustavo, 1991. 'Dinámica industrial de la Ciudad de México, 1940–1980', *Estudios Demográficos y Urbanos*, 6(1): 209–14.

Garza, Gustavo, 1992. *Desconcentración, tecnología y localización industrial en México. Los parques y ciudades industriales, 1953–1988*, México: El Colegio de México.

Garza, Gustavo 1999. 'Globalización económica, concentración metropolitana y políticas urbanas en México', *Estudios Demograficos y Urbanos*, 14(2): 269–312.

Gershberg, A. 1998. *Decentralization and Recentralization: Lessons from the Social Sectors in Mexico and Nicaragua*, Final Report, Inter-American Development Bank.

Gómez-Dantés, O. 1998. 'Health Policy for the Poor in Mexico', paper presented at the International Conference 'Health and Social Exclusion in Latin America', London School of Hygiene and Tropical Medicine and Instiute of Latin American Studies, London, April 1998.
González Block, M. and Gutiérrez, E. 1998. 'State government and federal health expenditures for the uninsured in Mexico. Their contribution to equity and efficiency', *FUNSALUD*, México D.F.
González Block, M. *et al.*, 1989. 'Health services decentralization in Mexico: formulation, implementation and results of policy', in *Health Policy and Planning* 4(4): 301–15.
Gordon, S. 1996. 'Entre la eficacia y la legitimidad: el PRONASOL como politica social', in *Las Políticas Sociales de México en los Años Noventa*. Mexico: PyV Editores, Instituto Mora, UNAM, FLACSO.
Gortari, H. de and Ziccardi, A. 1996. 'Instituciones y clieutelos de la politica social: un esbozo historico, 1867–1994' in *Las Politicas Sociales de Mexico en los Años Noventa*, Mexico: Plaza y Valdes-Instituto Mora – UNAM–FLACSO.
INEGI, 1999a, *Estadísticas Históricas de México*, Tomo I, México: INEGI.
INEGI, 1999b, *Perfil estadístico de la población mexicana: Una aproximacióna a las inequidades socioeconómicas, regionales y de género*, México: INEGI.
Knaul, F. and Parker, S. 1996. 'Cuidado infantil y empleo femenino en Mexico: evidencia descriptiva y consideraciones sobre las politicas', in *Estudios Demograficos y Urbanos*, Vol. 11(3), 577–608.
Leyva, R. 1993. *La descentralización municipal de los servicios de salud en México*, Guadalajara, México: Editorial Universidad de Guadalajara.
Lo Vuolo, R. 1997. 'El Enfoque del Banco Mundial en el Sector de la Seguridad Social', in C. Filgueira, C. Midaglia and J. Petersen-Thumser (comp.) *Desafíos de la Seguridad Social*, Montevideo: DSE, CIESU, Trilce, pp. 115–41.
Marshall, Adriana, 1989. 'The Sequel of Unemployment: the Changing Role of Parttime and Temporary Work in Western Europe', in Gerry Rodgers and Janine Rodgers (eds), *Precarious Jobs in Labour Market Regulation: The Growth of Atypical Employment in Western Europe*, International Institute of Labour Studies, Free University of Brussels, pp. 17–48.
Marshall, Adriana, 1992. *Circumventing Labour Protection: Non-standard Employment in Argentina and Peru*, International Institute for Labour Studies, Geneva, pp. 1–13.
Martínez, G., González, E., and Parker, S. 1996. 'The New Mexican Social Security Law', paper presented for the seminar 'Social Security Reform in Mexico', sponsored by the Brookings Institution and Inter-American Dialogue, June 10, 1996.
Mesa-Lago, C. 1997. 'Social Welfare Reform in the Context of Economic-Political Liberalization: Latin American Cases', in *World Development*, 25(4): 497–517.
Nueva Ley del Seguro Social, 1995. México D.F.: Diario Oficial de la Federación, December 21, 1995.
OCDE, 1997. *Estudios Economicos de la OCDE*, Mexico City: OCDE.
Oliveira, Orlandina de and Brígida García, 1997. 'Socioeconomic Transformation and Labour Markets in Mexico' in R. Tardanico and R. Mejívar Larín (eds), *Global Restructuring, Employment, and Social Inequality in Urban Latin America*, Miami: North-South Center Press.
Palacios L. Juan José, 1990. 'Maquiladoras, reorganización productiva y desarrollo regional: el caso de Guadalajara', in B. González-Aréchiga and J.C. Ramírez (eds), *Subcontratación y Empresas Transnacionales. Apertura y Restructuración en la Maquiladora*, Mexico: El Colegio de la Frontera Norte-Fundación Friedrich Ebert.
Pedrero, Mercedes and Teresa Rendón, 1982. 'El trabajo de la mujer en México en los setentas' in Secretaría de Programación y Presupuesto (SPP), *Estudios sobre la Mujer*

1. *El empleo y la mujer. Bases teóricas, metodológicas y evidencia empírica*, Mexico: SPP, pp. 437–56.
Pedrero, Mercedes, Teresa Rendón and Antonieta Barrón, 1997, *Segregación ocupacional por género en México*, Mexico: CRIM-UNAM.
Poder Ejecutivo Federal. 1995. *Programa de Reforma del Sector Salud 1995–2000*. Mexico D.F.: Poder Ejecutivo Federal.
Poder Ejecutivo Federal. 1997. *Tercer Informe de Gobierno*. Mexico D.F.: Poder Ejecutivo Federal.
Rendón, Teresa and Carlos Salas, 1992. 'El mercado de trabajo no agrícolaen México. Tendencias y cambios recientes', in *Ajuste estructural, mercados labourales y TLC*, Mexico: El Colegio de México-Fundación Friedrich Ebert-El Colegio de la Frontera Norte: 13–31.
Rendón, Teresa and Carlos Salas, 1993. 'El empleo en México en los ochenta: tendencias y cambios', *Comercio Exterior*, 43(8): 717–30.
Roberts, Bryan 1991. 'The Changing Nature of Informal Employment: The Case of Mexico' in Guy Standing and Victor Tokman (eds), *Towards Social Adjustment*, Geneva: ILO, pp. 115–40.
Roberts, Bryan 1993a. 'Enterprise and Labour Markets: The Border and the Metropolitan Areas', *Frontera Norte*, 5(9): 33–65.
Roberts, Bryan 1993b. 'The Dynamics of Informal Employment in Mexico', in *Work without Protections: Case Studies of the Informal Sector in Developing Countries*, Washington: US Department of Labor, pp. 101–25.
Rosemberg, F. 1993. 'Day Care Policies and Programs in Brazil', in M. Cochran (ed.), *International Handbook of Child Care Policies and Programs*, Westport: Greenwood Press, pp. 33–56.
Sassen, Saskia, 1994. *Cities in a World Economy*, California: Pine Forge Press.
Seguridad Social, 1998. Organo de Difusión del Sindicato Nacional de Trabajadores del Seguro Social. Epoca XV, Volume 1, Mexico D.F., April.
Sistema de Informacion, Monitoreo y Evaluacion de Programas Sociales (SIEMPRO), 1999. *Encuesta de Desarrollo Social* (version 06/16/99), Presidencia de la Nacion, Secretaria de Desarrollo Social: Buenos Aires, Argentina.
Soria, V. 1988. 'La crisis de la proteccion social en México. Un análisis de largo plazo con énfasis en el período 1971–85', in E. Gutierrez Garza (coord.) *Testimonios de la Crisis. La Crisis del Estado de Bienestar*. Mexico: Siglo XXI.
Tardanico, R. 1997. 'From Crisis to Restructuring: Latin American Transformations and Urban Employment in World Perspective' in R. Tardanico and R. Mejívar Larín (eds), *Global Restructuring, Employment, and Social Inequality in Urban Latin America*, Miami: North–South Center Press.
Tilly, Chris, 1996. *Half a Job. Bad and Good Part-Time Jobs in a Changing Labour Market*, Temple University Press.
Tolbert, K. *et al.*, 1993. 'Day Care Policies and Programs in Mexico', in M. Cochran (ed.), *International Handbook of Child Care Policies and Programs*, Westport: Greenwood Press, pp. 353–76.
Valdes, T. *et al.*, 1995. *Mujeres Latinoamericanas en cifras; tomo comparativo*. Santiago de Chile: Ministerio de Asuntos Sociales/FLACSO.

Part 2
Education and Decentralization Policies

4
Market-Oriented Education Reforms and Social Inequalities among the Young Population in Chile

Camilla T. Helgø

The aim of this chapter is to determine some of the sources of inequalities within the Chilean secondary education sector following the introduction of market-oriented educational reforms at the beginning of the 1980s. Chile as a case study is appealing because of its many innovative policies and the country's reputation as a successful example of social and economic transformation, not least in the field of education, within the international donor community. An analysis of the functioning of the Chilean secondary education system is also highly relevant given the relationship between education and social and economic status and considering the country's continuing struggle with conspicuous income inequalities.

In line with the economic adjustments of the time, Chile introduced privatization, a voucher scheme and decentralization into the education system. Chile was one of the first countries to introduce such reform on a national scale. While much effort has been devoted to analysing the effects of the policies on the Chilean primary education sector, until now research has largely ignored the impact on the secondary education system. The primary education studies available have focused primarily on the impact of privatization on variations in academic standards and have, on the whole, been positive about the market transformations which have occurred.[1] The current study goes beyond the areas of focus of the primary school studies, as it examines not only the impact of privatization on academic standards in secondary school but also the effect of other aspects of the education models, such as decentralization and 'choice'. In addition, this investigation is not only concerned with academic standards as is the case with the primary school studies, but also post-school status variables such as total years of education, hourly salary and occupation, all of which are pertinent to the ongoing inequality debate.

This study investigates sources of educational inequalities at two different levels. The quantitative part of the study analyses how the type of school, within the pluralistic Chilean secondary education system, influences test scores, level of education, hourly salary and occupation of students. The empirical analysis underpinning this research is a survey of 300 former secondary school students, between 20 and 28 years of age in 20 municipalities in Santiago. The statistical research explores two sets of questions: the relative advantages or disadvantages associated with attending municipal, semi-private (private-subsidized) and private fee-paying schools and the variations in attainment of students whose schools were located in municipalities of different economic status. The two issues are particularly relevant given the relationship between education and earning. Previous studies of primary schools have argued that private-subsidized education is superior to that offered in municipal schools; but the question has yet to be addressed in relation to the secondary education sector. Finally, almost two decades after the financial decentralization reform, the link between school location and attainments remains unexplored.

The second part of this empirical investigation is based on detailed interviews in 12 secondary schools in six municipalities in Santiago. The analysis of the in-depth interviews sheds light on how factors such as selection methods, student profiles, family characteristics, teaching staff and school resources interact and influence academic outcomes in academic secondary schools in Santiago. The overall objective of this part of the analysis is to determine why educational institutions with relatively similar characteristics in terms of secondary school stream (academic/vocational), geographical location and financial resources still differ with regard to academic results.

Together the quantitative and qualitative analyses explore the significance of structural educational factors as well as more complex, individual, school-based variations in the production and reproduction of social and economic inequalities among the young population in Chile.

Institutional changes within the secondary education system

From the beginning of the 1980s, the state altered its education strategy from authoritarian control to policies guided by neo-liberal principles in which the role of the state was reduced. On a general level, the basic principles of the 1980 social policy reforms were: decentralization of the management of social programmes from central to local governments (municipalities); encouragement of private-sector participation in the provision of social services; a change in emphasis from broad coverage to programmes targeted on vulnerable groups;[2] and, in some cases, changes in social services from direct provision to subsidy on demand by users.[3] In addition to the education system, important institutional reforms were initiated in the areas of social security, housing and the health care system.

At the beginning of the 1980s the military government reviewed its highly centralized education system and instituted decentralization and privatization reforms. The reforms consisted of transferring control of schools from the central government to the municipalities, and encouraging private individuals and non-governmental organizations (NGOs) to set up tuition-free schools. The design of the education policy emphasized the incentives provided by the 'invisible hand' of the market.[4] Below we will outline how these changes, possibly the most profound transformation ever experienced in Chilean public education, were conceived, designed and implemented.

The Chilean educational reform was introduced to increase the quality and level of efficiency within the educational system. The main pillars of the privatization reform were the expansion of the private-subsidized school system[5] and the introduction of a *voucher* or a per-student subsidy scheme. After the reform, parents and students had the choice between (i) a municipal school (decentralized state school), (ii) a free, private, state-subsidized school, or (iii) a generally superior-performing 'private fee-paying' school. The basic idea of the voucher scheme was that a state-funded voucher would follow the student wherever he or she decided to study (in the case of both the municipal and private-subsidized schools). It was hoped that by giving schools financial incentives to improve their performance records, the quality of the state-funded education in the country would improve. For the schools, a higher academic rating would mean more students, and increasing the number of students would, in turn, lead to greater financial gains.

During the educational decentralization process, all aspects of public schools, including infrastructure, equipment and personnel, were transferred to municipalities, private organizations or corporations.[6] The decentralization policy came in response to the highly centralized welfare system. The underlying rationale of the general decentralization policy was that by transferring financial resources and responsibilities to smaller geo-political units, the system would respond more efficiently to client demand, and enable people to request better services.[7] Similarly, the justification for the educational decentralization process was to improve participation (an interesting policy inconsistency seeing that the military government had already broken with the historical trend of raising the levels of teacher, parent and students participation), administrative efficiency and academic quality of the educational institutions.[8]

From the beginning of the 1980s the autonomy and, at least in theory, the financial power of the municipalities increased. However, in practice, the financial means to cover municipal schools' deficits, contribute to the supply of education materials and ensure school building maintenance were often lacking. The revenues of the municipalities were derived partly from local taxes, and partly from government funding and the Common Municipal Fund (FCM). The FCM is a redistribution scheme which was introduced to reduce differences in the financial capacities of the municipalities.

Larrañaga maintains, however, that even after the establishment of the FCM, the financial advantage of the richest 10 per cent of municipalities is still significant.[9] In fact, according to his figures, the educational contribution of the 10 per cent richest municipalities is as much as three to four times higher, on average, than that of the remaining 90 per cent.[10] As a consequence, in the upper-income municipalities, the municipal education transfer represents just under 40 per cent of the central contributions, whereas in the remaining municipalities the transfer represents on average around 10 per cent of the state education subsidy. Other authors, such as Rounds Parry (1996), Winkler and Rounds Parry (1993) and Hojman (1993) have also pointed out that, despite the operation of the FCM, poorer municipalities contribute fewer financial resources to their local schools compared with the higher-income municipalities.

The administrative roles of municipal and private-subsidized schools were extended after 1980. With the decentralization reform, most of the decisions regarding the operation of schools were passed to local government and the private-subsidized schools. Municipal governments and private school owners were granted complete autonomy in deciding issues such as which teachers to hire, salary levels, class sizes (up to a maximum of 45) as well as what repairs and general expenditures to make.[11] Even so, the central government continued to be in charge of setting national minimum standards in the case of the primary schools and general standards for secondary schools, and also to distribute a per-student contribution to all municipal and private-subsidized schools.

Structural inequalities in the Chilean secondary education system

Aims of the study

The main aim of the first part of this empirical research is to investigate how structural aspects of the secondary education system in Santiago influence the social and economic status of individuals after finishing secondary school. The two main areas of research are:

(i) *The three-tiered education system*. How do standardized test results, *Prueba de Aptitud Académica* (PAA), years of education and hourly salary vary among the secondary municipal, private-subsidized and private fee-paying graduates?

(ii) *Decentralization*. Do students at schools located in higher-income municipalities have greater prospects of achieving higher test scores, a higher level of education and higher salaries?

In the regression analysis, variables linked to family background and school resources (in the case of the three-tiered education system) were controlled for.

In this way I sought to determine to what extent the inequality patterns that arise may be attributed to external background factors, as opposed to the type of school attended by the former secondary student. The sample consisted of 300 former academic and vocational secondary school students between 20 and 28 years of age. All of the individuals had studied at a secondary school in one of 20 pre-selected municipalities in Greater Santiago. The 20 chosen municipalities were those that first embarked on educational decentralization. Fortunately, the distribution of the municipalities in question resembled that of the municipalities in Greater Santiago as a whole, with only a slight bias in favour of the highest- and lowest-income municipalities. The respondents were either working or unemployed. The interviews were conducted in December 1997 and January 1998.

Results of the statistical analysis

The econometric model

Fifteen former secondary students were interviewed in each of the 20 municipalities. In each municipality, three pre-selected areas were visited, and in each catchment area five individuals were interviewed. The issue of response rate is not relevant here because the interviewers went from door to door within the pre-determined area until the requirement of five responses had been fulfilled. The method of choosing equal numbers of respondents in each of the municipalities may be criticized on the grounds of unequal selection probability, as the wealthier municipalities generally have a smaller number of inhabitants. Nevertheless, it was believed that the variation in the young population would be greater in the higher-income municipalities than in the lower ones and thus that this over-representation would be justified (Fowler, 1993). Later, however, the respondents were weighted on the basis of a cross-tabulation of home municipality (high, middle, low income) and type of school (municipal, private-subsidized and private fee-paying) to eliminate the bias.[12]

The generalized economic model is provided in the Appendix. Whereas multiple regression analysis is used to test for statistical relationships for the first three dependent variables (academic test results, years of education, average net hourly salary), in the case of occupation, logit analysis is employed to test the likelihood of achieving non-manual occupations. The likelihood is calculated from logistic regression analysis, with the coefficients converted by taking their exponential values so they express more comprehensible likelihoods. As the exponential values are used, a coefficient higher than one implies that the explanatory variable has a positive impact on the dependent variable; a coefficient with a value lower than one signals that the explanatory variable has a negative effect.

Owing to space constraints, only the findings with the greatest implications for education policy are presented here.[13]

Privatization

Table 4.1 shows that, in the 20 municipalities included in this study, the benefits of attending a private fee-paying school (the last of the three dummy variables in the 'type of schools' category) as opposed to a municipal school (the base category) are significant and substantial. More surprisingly, the results reveal that, on average, the former private-subsidized students score slightly lower on the PAA test (around 20 points lower out of a maximum of 800) and earn somewhat less per hour (151 pesos or 20 pence) than do the former municipal school students. 151 pesos represent a 13 per cent variation on the average wage in the sample (1 150 pesos) and suggests that the former municipal school students do have a significant earning advantage compared to the private-subsidized school students. Moreover, the private-subsidized students are only 0.72 times as likely (or 0.28 times less likely) to have a non-manual as opposed to a manual occupation. Thus, the prospects of obtaining non-manual employment were better for the municipal school students. Only in the case of total years of education is the difference between the municipal and the private-subsidized school students insignificant.

When including further socio-economic variables as well as school resource factors in the regression analysis, the basic pattern noted above stays the same. However, the value of the private fee-paying dummy variable decreases (Table 4.2). Hence, part of the explanation for the higher PAA results, more years of education, higher salaries and a greater likelihood of obtaining a non-manual job, lies with the family background of the fee-paying students as well as the more abundant resources they enjoyed at school.

These results conflict with the conclusions of other studies on the issues of the relationship between SIMCE (National Measurement System for the Quality of Education) result and type of primary education institutions.[14] These studies agree that when socio-economic factors are excluded, primary private-subsidized students perform slightly better than the municipal ones.

Table 4.1 Impact of type of secondary school on generalized inequalities

	PAA results[a]	Years of education[b]	Hourly salary	Manual/non-manual occupation[c]
Private-subsidized school	−19.99*	−0.056	−150.79*	0.72*
Private fee-paying school	70.17*	1.80*	990.06*	2.02*
R-squared	0.12	0.11	0.16	66.02%

Notes: * = significant at 1% level, ** = significant at 5% level, *** = significant at 10% level.
[a] PAA results refer to post-secondary school standardized test results (similar to the Scholastic Aptitude Test (SAT) in the United States). Only the mathematics scores have been considered here.
[b] Education refers to years of education, excluding years repeated.
[c] We are testing for the likelihood of obtaining a non-manual occupation. This series is based on logistic regression analysis. The coefficients have been converted by taking their exponential values (see text for explanation).

Table 4.2 Impact of type of secondary school on generalized inequalities – controlling for socio-economic background and school resources

Variable	PAA results	Years of education	Hourly salary	Manual/non-manual occupation[e]
Type of school:				
Private subsidized	−7.59***	−0.02	−81.94*	0.77*
Private fee-paying	40.17*	0.49*	445.79*	1.30*
Years of education				
Mother's	1.80**	0.04*	3.60	0.91*
Father's	4.44*	0.10*	43.38*	1.03*
Occupation				
Father's[a]	29.87*	1.06*	318.09*	2.68*
Family resources				
Room per person	14.53*	0.70*	250.74*	5.56*
No. of cars	16.86*	0.49*	312.42*	0.88***
No. of televisions	−11.98*	−0.19*	−103.06*	1.23*
School resources				
Textbook[b]	14.94*	0.09*	154.63*	0.90*
Library[c]	25.05*	0.47*	98.09*	1.18*
Class size	0.37**	0.02*	−2.77	1.07*
Gender[d]	44.69*	−0.09***	280.67*	0.40*
R^2 adjusted	0.39	0.42	0.37	78.17%

Notes: * = significant at 1% level, ** = significant at 5% level, *** = significant at 10% level.
[a] Father's occupation is a dummy variable that takes the value of 1 where father had a non-manual job when the respondents attended the first year of secondary school, and 0 otherwise (i.e. father had a manual job).
[b] Textbooks: measures the impact of the number of mathematics textbooks used in the first year of secondary school.
[c] In the case of the logistical regression analysis (when occupation is the dependent variable), library takes the form of a categorical variable.
[d] Gender is a dummy variable that takes the value of 1 if the respondent was male and 0 otherwise (female).
[e] We are testing for the likelihood of obtaining a non-manual occupation. This series is based on logistic regression analysis. The coefficients have been converted by taking their exponential values (see page 127 for explanation).

There are several plausible reasons for the contrasting results. An obvious but crucial point to bear in mind is that, whereas the 'other' studies have examined the situation in the primary education sector, the present research is based solely on secondary education institutions. In other words, the sample is different. Primary schools must incorporate all students because of the law of obligatory primary education. Also, at the primary level, private-subsidized schools tend to be more selective than municipal schools.[15] Consequently, primary municipal school students are left with the majority of the disadvantaged students.[16] At the secondary school level, however, most of the least able students have left the education system. This means that municipal and private-subsidized schools operate under more similar conditions. It is interesting to note that when this is the case municipal school students generally perform better then their private-subsidized school peers. This would suggest that municipal schools are, in fact, more effective: the problem is simply that, at the primary level, this category of schools is hampered with a greater proportion of the disadvantaged students.

Another issue which could explain the above finding of the municipal students out-performing their private-subsidized counterparts is that the municipal schools in the capital are in a unique position because of the often very good reputation they have acquired over the years. Thus, contrary to arguments relating to the primary sector,[17] it might be that parents prefer one of the traditional and well-established municipal establishments to the recently introduced, and therefore less experienced, private-subsidized schools. If this were the case, we could be dealing with a pre-selection bias, in terms of the academic abilities of students, in favour of the municipal schools.

Moreover, the fact that our sample is restricted to schools in Santiago, whereas other studies have covered the whole of the country, may also explain some of the conflicting conclusions. That is, if the better-performing municipal secondary schools are restricted to the Santiago area, and if we were to increase the sample to cover the whole of the Chilean population, the advantage of the secondary municipal students would be significantly reduced. In support of this argument, it is mainly the municipal schools that operate in the more rural, isolated and disadvantaged areas. This pattern lowers the average national performance record of the municipal schools.[18]

Finally, the result could be deemed invalid by variations in the level of education in the sample. For instance, if a higher percentage of the private-subsidized students (compared to the municipal school students) attended higher education institutions after finishing secondary school, their test results, years of education, hourly salary and occupation would be negatively biased as a larger proportion of the 'better performing' students would be excluded from the sample for not having finished their education.[19] For a thorough response to this see Helgø, 1999, chapter 4. Here, I will note only that it appears that the percentage of students who go on to study in a tertiary education institution is higher in the case of the former municipal school students, thus ruling out this point as potentially invalidating the results of this analysis.

Decentralization

To test for the effect of decentralization we restricted the sample to include only former municipal secondary school students, as these are the students who would have been most directly affected by the decentralization policy. Table 4.3 shows the effects on the dependent variables (mathematics PAA

Table 4.3 The decentralization effect on municipal schools

	PAA results	Years of education	Hourly salary
School municipality			
High income	72*	2.01*	853*
Middle-high	6	1.18*	142
Middle income	22	0.89*	226*
Middle-low	72*	0	202*
Years of education			
Mother	−11*	0.07*	−3
Father	−1	0.02	21**
Occupation			
Father's[a]	110.3*	0.45*	163*
Family resources			
Rooms per person	33*	0.69*	251*
Car	39*	0.24*	36
Television	−15*	−0.04	−95*
Gender[b]	64*	0.58*	379*
R^2 adjusted	0.68	0.53	0.58

Notes: * = significant at 1% level, ** = significant at 5% level, *** = significant at 10% level.
[a] Father's occupation is a dummy variable that takes the value of 1 where father had a non-manual job when the respondents attended the first year of secondary school, and 0 otherwise (i.e. father had a manual job).
[b] Gender is a dummy variable that takes the value of 1 if the respondent was male and 0 otherwise (female).

test results, years of education, hourly salary and occupation) of studying in a low-, middle-low-, middle-, middle-high- and high-income municipality. Dummy variables – where the low-income municipality is the base category – have been used to test for the impact of the income level of the municipality in which the student's school was located. Socio-economic background variables (mother's and father's education, father's occupation, room per person in the family home, number of cars, televisions in the family home and gender) have been controlled for to attempt to single out the net effect of studying in a municipality of a certain economic level. Table 4.3 shows that the students who studied in the very highest income municipalities achieved significantly higher PAA test results, more years of education and higher salaries than those who studied in lower-income municipalities. The impact of the income level of the school municipality is much less pronounced for the other municipality categories. It is interesting to note that the pattern is also maintained after controlling for socio-economic background. That is, the benefit of studying in the very highest-income municipalities in Santiago is significant even when considering family background factors. This finding agrees well with Larrañaga's (1995) argument, discussed above, that the financial bonus of the richest 10 per cent of the municipalities is highly significant even after redistributing municipal funds through the FCM. In contrast, the funds of the remaining 90 per cent of the municipalities, he argues, are relatively equal. Thus it appears that possessing greater amounts of financial capital, useful for supplementing education material provided by the state and the upkeep of the physical school environment, does have an impact on the three outcome variables. A quite possibly superior quality teaching force in the more prosperous municipalities may also contribute to the above finding. That is, the higher-income municipalities may, as a result of both the payment of extra financial bonuses, supply of additional training courses[20] and the superior social standing of their schools, attract higher-quality and better-motivated teachers.

Qualitative research

In the last section I analysed and determined the extent to which numerically or categorically quantifiable school and background variables influence present social and economic status. The purpose of this part of the analysis is to acquire a better understanding of how variables such as selection method, student profile and school resources interact and influence academic outcomes in secondary academic schools in Santiago. In particular, the aim is to explore why educational institutions with relatively similar characteristics in terms of secondary school stream (academic/vocational), geographical location and financial resources still differ with regard to academic results. Only an abstract of the analysis will be presented here. The full discussion can be found in Helgø, 1999.

The sample consisted of 12 academic secondary schools: 10 private-subsidized and two municipal schools; that is, two, either private-subsidized or municipal secondary schools, in each of six municipalities of varying socio-economic status (ranked according to the National Institute for Statistics (INE), 1995). The municipalities were chosen from among the 20 municipalities included in the quantitative study. In designing the sample, the aim was to include municipalities of differing income status. In each of the six municipalities selected, the private-subsidized/municipal schools with the lowest and the highest mathematics and Spanish scores were selected. The academic ranking was made on the basis of SIMCE second-year, secondary school results. The schools, and their academic ranking, are listed in Table 4.4.

Selection practices

According to the Ministry of Education's regulations, municipal and private-subsidized schools are expected to accept all students who apply. Furthermore, schools are prohibited from using entrance exams or other means of selecting students. However, the regulation is not strictly enforced. The use of selection enables some schools to attract more high-performing students, maintain full enrolment and, therefore, maximize income (as the schools are being paid a sum per student). Schools who seek to produce better test results, improve their reputation and increase the number of students will have a better chance of succeeding if they ensure that their co-producers (the students) are of the highest possible calibre. In this section we analyse the functioning and effects of selection practices. Finally, we discuss the concept of the 'waste-basket school'; the lowest quality, most stigmatized schools in the municipalities. We will argue that these schools are the result of the present 'free choice' education system. Ironically, they also ensure the continued existence of the system by taking on 'left-over' students who would otherwise have nowhere to go.

In most of the 12 schools included in the sample, some form of selection was practised. However, the majority of the low-achieving schools in the sample faced a situation where they were forced to accept all students who applied as a result of lack of demand. However, even these schools often exercised some form of selection so as to be perceived as an attractive school in demand. Still, in the 12 schools included in the sample, selection procedures were more common, and stricter in terms of academic requirements, in the higher-performing schools than in the lower ones. This finding is in line with the logic of the per-student subsidy. The intention of the subsidy is to encourage improvements in the quality of the schools, as higher academic quality would attract more students and parents, and increased numbers of students would lead to financial gains by the school. By rejecting students with lesser abilities, the high-achieving schools secure their academic standing, attract more students and consequently gain financially. Many of the low-achieving schools, on the other hand, find themselves with such a poor reputation that the selection process they still claim to employ has become something of an absurdity given their obvious inability to select students. Similar to the labour training case presented by Haagh earlier in this volume (Chapter 1), the example of the school voucher system shows how allowing the market to manage social policies may produce unexpected outcomes. In this case it is because, unlike other commercial products, the consumers (the students) will have a direct impact on the quality of the output (test results and reputation), and thus the school will be encouraged to reject students of lesser ability.

In each of the municipalities it appears that a 'waste-basket' school is being created. Over the course of time at least one school in the municipality seems to fall into the vicious cycle of low academic quality, falling demand, inability to select and reject students, poor motivation of students, increasing financial pressure, low academic morale and deteriorating quality. From a pragmatic standpoint, the 'waste-basket' school, or the school that reluctantly takes on students none of the other schools are ready to accept, is perhaps the most pivotal component in the functioning of the system. Without them the high-achieving school could not exist, and thus, one of the motives behind the pursuit of *la libertad de la enseñanza* (freedom of education),[21] would vanish.

Wexford College in Providencia (the highest-income municipality in Santiago, according to INE, 1995) is an example of how a pattern such as that encountered by the 'waste-basket' schools may arise. During my conversation with Irene Morén, a Spanish teacher at Wexford, she stated that had she been in charge she 'would have been stricter with the selection' (*'Yo haría una selección más estricta'*). The question is simply whether she would have been able to, and the answer, according to the following testimony, is probably not.

> We are quite different (...) we receive children who have practically been thrown out of other schools, they are children with problems such as separated parents, from higher classes who are now unable to pay for a private fee-paying schools.[22] Irene Morén, Spanish teacher, Wexford College.

Another example of a typical 'waste-basket' school is Avenida Principal, in the middle-low income municipality of Conchalí. The headmaster at the school, Carlos Gonzáles, explained that, in practice, the school does not have a selection process: 'the students enrol without taking any kind of entrance exam, 90 per cent of the students who enrol are repeaters'(*'el alumno ingresa sin tener ningún tipo de examen previo, el 90% de los alumnos que ingresan son alumnos repitentes'*). Over a period of time the school has gained a reputation as a typical 'waste-basket' school. The headmaster commented on the situation:

> Of course it is a difficult situation, we do it because of a necessity more than anything, so that the college can exist. If we don't absorb them, the other colleges won't either.[23]

In other words, the school accepts these less able students simply because it must do so if the school is to survive. As discussed above, the financial structure of the Chilean voucher system is such that schools receive contributions depending on the number of students in the school. Hence, because of lack of demand the headmasters, particularly in the 'waste-basket' schools, are forced to take on all students who apply. The 'waste-basket' school in Peñalolén, Colegio York, is in a similar situation:

> They pay on the basis of student attendance, so, it is important for the proprietor to have a quantity of students...it is not possible to carry out a selection process.[24]

Headmaster Carlos González also stressed that the reason for taking on the repeated students is that if the school failed to do so, the youngsters in the area would have nowhere else to go. This sobering statement clearly supports the hypothesis of the 'waste-basket' school.

Had it not been for schools such as Avenida Principal, Colegio York, Wexford or any other of the many 'waste-basket' schools in the country, the education system would have been subjected to a greater pressure to create more schools. Alternatively, selection would be prohibited, and the outcast students would have begun to mix with students in the high-achieving schools.

The peer group effect

I argued above that, as a result of the schools' use of selection methods, academically disadvantaged students are prevented from having equal access to schools of higher academic quality. Virtually all of the recent Chilean education research supports the argument that selection practices have the effect of segregating students according to academic ability.[25] What this study shows is that the formation of high- and low-performing schools, with student bodies of matching capabilities, occurs in every municipality. Low-quality schools are not exclusively situated in low-income areas and *vice versa*. In both the affluent municipality of Providencia and the much poorer municipality of Peñalolén, the least motivated and able students are channelled into the stigmatized 'waste-basket' school either in their own, or another, municipality.

This is quite a disheartening tendency considering that research indicates that segregation of students by ability has additional detrimental effects on the education of the poorer students.[26] That is, the peer group effect may further exacerbate the academic variations between the low- and the high-performing schools. The suggested link between selection process, student composition and SIMCE results accords with studies carried out in Britain. In research conducted on secondary education in London, Rutter *et al.* (1979) and Rutter (1983) found a significant relationship between the balance of the intake, student behaviour and examination results. Similarly, studies of streaming[27] have concluded that the method propagates initial academic variations among students.[28] This system of segregation of students into study groups, or academic bands, it is suggested, has particularly detrimental effects on the least able students.

The resource base of the schools

There is a vast body of literature on the subject of education financing. In this section, rather than discussing the financial management of schools, I will investigate variations in physical and financial resources in the two different categories of schools (high- and low-achieving).

All of the municipal and the private-subsidized schools receive a fixed per-student attendance-based state subsidy.[29] In addition, all private-subsidized and municipal secondary schools have the opportunity to charge a fee of up to US$88 (£52.70)[30] a month (Ministry of Education)[31] or 2.5 times the subsidy per student.[32] However, if a school decided to demand contributions, their state subsidy would decrease on a sliding scale depending on the amount the school wished to charge.[33] All 12 schools in the sample, except one, operate a so-called Shared Finance (*Financiamiento Compartido*) System.[34] In Carmela Carvajal, the only school without monthly fees, parents still paid $42 000 (£93.33) a year to the Parents' Association. Contributions to the Parents' Association were also required in six other schools in the sample.[35]

Below, I explore whether the lower-achieving schools are forced to charge lower fees as a result of lack of demand. I will argue that the level of fees is divided more clearly along the lines of the income level of the municipalities than the academic status of the schools. However, another issue to consider is the number of students per class. Because of the generally smaller class sizes in the 'waste-basket' schools, compared with the higher-performing schools in the more prosperous areas, these schools are likely to lose out financially, compared with their higher-performing counterparts.

Table 4.4 shows the income level of the municipality, the school's academic ranking and, finally, monthly Shared Finance and Parents' Association payments (for parents who did not have special exemption from fees), for the twelve schools included in the sample.[36]

Table 4.4 Academic ranking and monthly fees

Name	Category[a]	Results[b]	Rating	Payment[c]
Carmela Carvajal	High income	77.07	1	5.60
Wexford College	High income	32.83	12	50.67
Presidente Errázuriz	High income	68.85	3	25.33[d]
Rafael Sotomayor	High income	47.48	7	16.00
La Salle	Middle-high	70.19	2	29.33
Mauricio Rugendas	Middle-high	36.93	9	28.00
Leonardo Murialdo	Middle-low	67.65	4	13.07
Alejandro Flores	Middle-low	37.60	8	3.33
Cristóbal Colón	Middle-low	56.87	6	24.00
Avenida Principal	Middle-low	35.86	10	3.33
Colegio Jorge Prieto L.	Low income	57.48	5	4.67
Colegio York	Low income	33.83	11	6.80

Notes
[a] The income status of the school municipalities are based on INE's personal income ranking data.
[b] Mathematics and Spanish SIMCE, second-year, secondary school results (1993), added and divided by two. *Source*: Ministry of Education, Chile.
[c] Monthly, Shared Finance and Parents' Association contributions in pounds. Exchange rate: 750 pesos to the pound.
[d] At Presidente Errázuriz parents paid contributions on a sliding scale depending on their income level. As we did not have information about parents' average contributions, the mid-point on the payment scale (8000 to 30 000) was used in the table.

Interestingly, there does not appear to be a significant relationship between SIMCE results and monthly charges. Although in a number of cases one has to pay more to attend a higher-achieving school (La Salle and Presidente Errázuriz in the high-income municipality of Las Condes), several schools contrast with this trend. The most obvious exception is Wexford College, the school with the lowest academic rating in the high-income municipality of Providencia, whose fees far exceed the contributions demanded by any other college. Also in contrast to the proposed trend, the low-performing Mauricio Rugendas in the middle-high income municipality of La Florida charges relatively high fees. Still, in comparison with the higher-achieving schools in the richer municipalities, these financially 'more advantaged' 'waste-basket' schools still suffer as a result of the lower number of students in each class.

In terms of monthly charges, it appears that one must distinguish between the 'waste-basket' schools in the higher- and lower-income municipalities. The 'waste-basket' schools in the more prosperous municipalities charge relatively high fees, perhaps to make up for low student numbers. The 'waste-basket' schools in the lower-income municipalities, on the other hand, are not in a position to compensate for lack of funds through co-financing, and therefore their fees are much lower.

In line with this trend, we find a positive (albeit weak) correlation between the income levels of the municipalities and monthly payments. Of the six schools in the upper payment region (between £16 and £51), all except one (Carmela Carvajal),[37] are situated in middle-high or high-income municipalities. The government would surely be content to find such a result seeing that one of the purposes of the Shared Finance Scheme is that one would move closer to the ideal of making parents pay according to financial ability.[38]

Moreover, five of the schools, four of them high-achieving, received extra resources from other sources. First, the high and middle-high income municipalities (Providencia and Las Condes) in which the two municipal schools in our sample, Carmela Carvajal and Rafael Sotomayor were located, paid for teacher-training courses and other 'necessities'. Furthermore, three of the high-achieving schools received either extra financial assistance from their religious congregations (Presidente Errázuriz and Leonardo Murialdo) or from the state-run Montegrade Project (Cristóbal Colón) for dynamic schools who make the effort to apply for resources.[39] While the exact amount of extra resources, which these mostly high-achieving schools (with the exception of Rafael Sotomayor) received, is unknown, it is plausible that the additional assistance may have contributed to the academic quality differences between the high- and the low-achieving schools in our sample.

Further interesting variations in the high- and the low-achieving schools are found in the areas of textbook use, and the number and quality of the laboratories and libraries in the schools. Again, for a full discussion of these issues see Helgø, 1999. Here, it will simply be noted that the in-depth schools interviews showed that the students in the high-achieving schools were equipped with a greater number of textbooks than their counterparts in the low-achieving schools. The interviews also demonstrated that the teachers and headmasters in the superior-performing schools were more concerned with the benefits of using such books. In contrast, some of the teachers in the lower-performing schools found the use of textbooks to be inappropriate given the chaotic atmosphere in their classrooms.

In sum, the most revealing finding in the qualitative analysis is that 'waste-basket' schools develop in every municipality as a result of school selection and the parental choice policy. Students and parents are encouraged to select the school of their choice, and the schools are, in practice, able to decide which students they wish to accept into their academic community. However, because of their lack of desired credentials – in this case, academic ability – some students are unable to exercise their choice freely. Also, the 'waste-basket' schools, because of their negative reputation, are unable to select students. The most unfortunate consequences of the formation of these low-quality schools are the exacerbation of the peer group effect, the intensification of the teachers' negative perception of their students and the more difficult financial situation facing these schools as a result of the lower levels of demand (Figure 4.1).

The situation of the 'waste-basket' schools in the higher-income areas differs somewhat from the model in Figure 4.1. Parents' greater financial capacity allow the schools to charge substantially higher Shared Finance and Centre for Parent fees to make up for the lower state subsidy per class. Even so, in comparison with the higher-achieving schools in the richer municipalities,

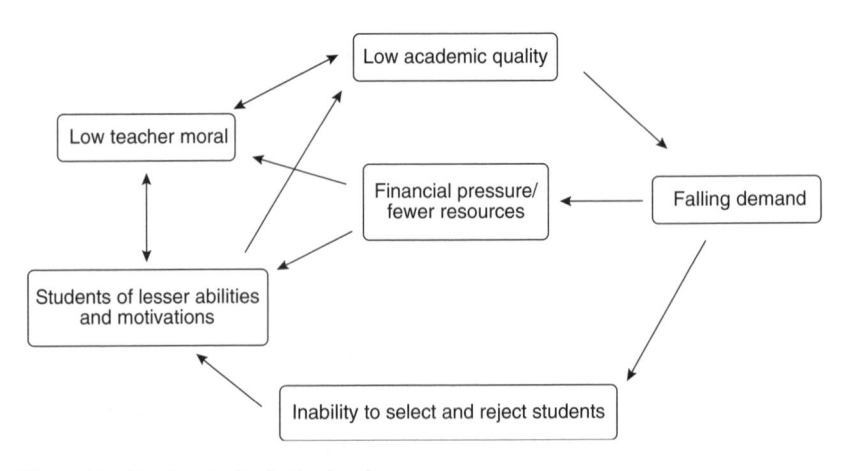

Figure 4.1 The 'waste-basket' school

the financially 'more advantaged' 'waste-basket' schools still suffer as a result of the lower number of students in each class.

Having identified the problematic aspects of the Chilean secondary education model, one might wonder what would constitute a superior education model in terms of equality of opportunities. The most common alternative to a 'choice model' such as that pursued in Chile, is one in which the students and their families are assigned to a school depending on the catchment area in which they live. Although conceivably successful in Scandinavian countries where economic inequalities are relatively low, several authors disagree that such a policy constitutes a superior alternative in terms of educational opportunities.[40] This is because, they argue, in most countries families are segregated residentially according to level of income. Thus, if poorer families want to choose a better public school in a middle-class municipality, they would need to purchase a house in that area. However, this would typically be difficult because of the prohibitive house prices in these municipalities.

An alternative voucher model, in which negative effects are reduced, would be one in which schools are forced to accept all students who apply and in which a lottery mechanism would be in place where applications exceed available places. In addition, instead of distributing a uniform subsidy per student, schools that cater for a higher number of disadvantaged pupils would receive compensation (Krashinsky, 1986). While the issue of compensation may be complicated to administer, this model may still represent the best conceivable option considering the complex demands for choice, efficiency and equality of opportunity of education.

Another question that springs to mind is to what extent students who attended a 'waste-basket' school would suffer in terms of future possibilities. This issue is discussed further in Helgø, 1999. Here, I will briefly mention that a high percentage of wealthier low-achievement secondary students tend to continue their education at a private university because of the excess supply at many of these institutions. As a result of the high number of private groups and individuals having responded to the invitation by the Pinochet government to set up private higher-education institutions after 1980, a situation has developed in which many private universities, much like the 'waste-basket' schools, are forced to accept virtually all applicants. Owing to these circumstances, the 'waste-basket' students with the means and the motivation to avoid social degradation do have the opportunity of continuing their education at the tertiary level.

Conclusion

The different research questions pursued throughout this analysis can perhaps be summarized as: what are the sources of inequalities within the Chilean secondary education system? The question has been answered on the basis of an empirical analysis of young secondary education graduates currently enrolled in the labour force as well as of the situation in academic secondary schools in Santiago today. While the first, quantitative study investigates the relationship between type of school and present education, economic and occupational status, the qualitative investigation examines the factors that determine outcomes in schools of differing academic status.

While the sample of the qualitative study is too small to shed light on the issue of privatization, the statistical analysis clearly demonstrates that the pattern of the secondary schools in Santiago differs from that of the primary education sector. Among the students who had attended academic and vocational secondary schools in the capital, the municipal school graduates actually performed better than the former private-subsidized school students in terms of academic results, years of education, hourly salary and occupational status. When their parents'/families' education and economic status are controlled for, the trend persists.

This last finding in fact agrees with Rounds Parry's (1994) and Carnoy and McEwan's (1997) primary school research. In her study, Rounds Parry concluded that private schools have superior achievement records only when they enrol students from higher socio-economic backgrounds. She also found that public municipal schools out-perform private-subsidized schools when both enrol disadvantaged children. Similarly, Carnoy and McEwan argue that Chile is in a unique position compared with other countries in that their private-subsidized schools do not have an achievement advantage for students of similar levels of abilities.

In the qualitative analysis it was suggested that, as a consequence of having provided students and schools with the opportunity to choose their 'counterparts', a system of 'waste-basket' schools has developed in each municipality. The main feature of these schools are students who, because of the system of selection and their poor performance record, have no choice but to attend the least popular school in the area. The development of 'waste-basket' schools has a number of negative implications ranging from increased peer group effect, exacerbation of teachers' negative perceptions of, and attitudes towards, their students and even financial disadvantages. In the high-income, poorly achieving schools, the financial disadvantages are caused by their smaller class sizes, whereas for the 'waste-basket' schools in the lower-income municipalities, the greater financial difficulties stem partly from the lower fees these schools are able to charge.

Financial inequalities in municipal schools are not only related to the factors outlined above, but are also a consequence of the decentralization policy. The decentralization policy has implications for the level of resources held by the individual municipality and, consequently, by the municipal schools. In the quantitative analysis it was also shown that, in line with Larrañaga's (1995) argument, students whose schools are situated in the very highest income municipalities perform better in terms of all three outcome variables: standardized test (PAA) results, years of education and hourly salary. Even when socio-economic background factors are controlled for, this finding remains constant. That is to say, municipal school students do not perform better simply because of their family background, as proclaimed by so many sociologists and education specialists;[41] the results indicate that the financial capacity of the municipal schools also has a powerful independent effect on the outcome variables.

With regard to the level of school resources, several interesting trends emerge. Both textbooks and libraries were of the expected positive sign in the quantitative analysis. Having more of such resources is positively associated with all four outcome variables. The in-depth schools interviews not only showed that the students in the high-achieving schools were equipped with a greater number of textbooks than their counterparts in the low-achieving schools but also that the attitudes towards such teaching aids vary between the higher- and the lower-performing schools.

Several policy lessons regarding inequalities of educational opportunities may be drawn from this study. Both West (1996) and Friedman (1955) suggest that the voucher system represents a superior alternative to a system in which families are assigned to schools depending on the catchment areas they live in because the poor then have a chance to choose whatever school they prefer in whichever area they want. However, as argued in this analysis, there are several complications attached to this proposition. Had there been no preferences and hierarchical formations, then of course freedom of choice would have constituted the ideal situation. However, as choices themselves influence the reputation, demand for and ultimately the quality of the institutions, voucher systems create new sets of hierarchies no longer confined to geo-economic areas, but instead embedded in each municipality. Thus, a traditional voucher system will never eradicate educational inequalities, but will rather render the structure of inequalities more complex, as educational hierarchies become as much a feature of inter- as intra-municipality variations. In this situation, the schools themselves come to symbolize the excluding factor, as lower-ability students are denied the educational opportunities available to their brighter counterparts.

In terms of other policy lessons, the most obvious would be that governments should be particularly cautious in implementing financial decentralization schemes. It is apparent from this analysis that such schemes have a harmful impact on the distribution of resources to schools in municipalities of lower-income status. Administrative decentralization, on the other hand, is far less problematic from an equity point of view and may improve management efficiency and sense of 'ownership' of the schools.

Finally, the introduction of semi-private (privately-administered, state-funded) schools may produce additional educational inequalities if either the state or private-subsidized system achieves a superior performance record because of factors such as experience, public preferences and legal framework.

In this analysis it was found that the municipal schools perform better than private-subsidized secondary schools do as a result, particularly, of experience and public preferences. However, in the Chilean primary education sector, the situation is reversed owing to a combination of preferences and legal framework.[42] Even so, it is important to remember that the most significant source of inequalities continues to be the operation of the private fee-paying schools. By contrast, the quality differences between the municipal and private-subsidized schools are very small indeed.

Appendix

The generalized econometric model.
Note that in Tables 4.1 and 4.3 only some of the variables listed here have been included in the analysis.

$$Y_{ni} = \beta_0 + \beta_{n1}D_{1i} + \beta_{n2}D_{2i} + \beta_{n3}D_{3i} + \beta_{n4}D_{4i} + \beta_{n5}D_{5i} + \beta_{n6}D_{6i} + \beta_{n7}D_{7i} + \beta_{n8}X_{1i} + \beta_{n9}D_{8i} + \beta_{n10}D_{9i} + \beta_{n11}D_{10i} + \beta_{n12}D_{11i} + \beta_{n13}X_{2i} + \beta_{n14}D_{12i} + u_{ni}$$

where:
- Y_n = Standardized test results (Prueba de Aptitud Académica, PAA), years of education, average hourly salary (net), and occupation (non-manual or manual)
- $n = 4$. That is, the equation will be used to measure four different types of dependent variables (listed above)
- i = The individual case
- D_1 = Type of secondary school (1 = private-subsidized school, 0 = all other schools)
- D_2 = Type of secondary school (1 = private fee-paying school, 0 = all other schools)
- D_3 = Secondary school stream (1 = academic, 0 = vocational secondary school)
- D_4 = School municipality (1 = middle/low income municipality, 0 = all other municipalities)
- D_5 = School municipality (1 = middle-income municipality, 0 = all other municipalities)
- D_6 = School municipality (1 = middle/high income municipality, 0 = all other municipalities)
- D_7 = School municipality (1 = high-income municipality, 0 = all other municipalities)
- X_1 = Socio-economic background – (i) mother's years of education (ii) father's years of education (iii) father's occupation (iv) number of rooms in the house per person (v) car (vi) television[43]
- D_8 = Home municipality (1 = middle/low income municipality, 0 = all other municipalities)
- D_9 = Home municipality (1 = middle-income municipality, 0 = all other municipalities)
- D_{10} = Home municipality (1 = middle/high income municipality, 0 = all other municipalities)
- D_{11} = Home municipality (1 = high-income municipality, 0 = all other municipalities)
- X_2 = School factors – (i) classes per week (ii) class size (iii) textbooks (math.) (iii) libraries
- D_{12} = Gender (1 = male, 0 = female)

Notes

1. Rodrígues, 1988; Aedo and Larrañaga, 1994a; Rounds Parry, 1996, 1997; Mizala and Romaguera, 1998.
2. In the case of the education system, such programmes were only introduced after the return to democracy. The first set of education programmes that targeted a specific group was the *Programa de las 900 escuelas* (The programme of the 900 schools), P900, which was launched to raise levels of standards in the schools with the lowest academic results (Angell, Chapter 5, this volume, de Kadt (1993), Carnoy and McEwan (1997), Rounds Parry (1997), Cox and González (1998)).
3. Marcel and Solimano (1994: 226).
4. Egaña and Magendzo (1983).
5. However, private-subsidized schools were not a new phenomenon. Subsidies to private schools were introduced in the primary and secondary education systems as early as the 1950s (Helgø, 1999: chapter 1). However, by increasing the value of the subsidy and by giving schools greater flexibility in administrative matters, the reform of the 1980s was more effective in encouraging private groups and individuals to establish schools (Espinola (1992), Helgø (1999: chapter 2)).
6. Espinola (1992: 38).
7. Goddard (1996).
8. Egaña and Magendzo (1983).
9. Still, it should be pointed out that the FCM represents the only attempt to distribute municipal funds in Latin America.
10. Larrañaga (1995: 358).
11. Rounds Parry (1997: 217).
12. The information which formed the basis of the weights was extracted from the 1987 CASEN survey. The 1987 survey was used as it represents the mid-point between 1983 and 1991, that is, the mid-point in the range of years the respondents attended first year of secondary school. All the questions in the survey relate to the situation of the former students in the first year of secondary school.
13. For a detailed discussion of the findings see Helgø, 1999.
14. Rodríguez (1988), Aedo and Larrañaga (1994a,b), Ministry of Education (1995), Mizala and Romaguera (1998), Rounds Parry (1994, 1997).
15. Rounds Parry (1994, 1996, 1997), Angell (2001).
16. Mizala and Romaguera (1998), Carnoy and McEwan (1997).
17. Arancibia (1994), Centro de Estudios Públicos (CEP) (1997).
18. Arzola et al. (1993: 6–12), Carnoy and McEwan (1997), Rounds Parry (1996), Angell (2001). This point is particularly relevant in the case of the primary school sector, given that municipal primary schools are even more widespread in the most remote areas than secondary schools.
19. Recall that only individuals who had finished their education and were currently employed or unemployed, were included in the survey.
20. Interview with headmistress Inés Huerta, at Carmela Carvajal, in the high-income municipality of Providencia (March, 1998). For a more thorough treatment of the two last points see chapter 6 in Helgø, 1999.
21. For a discussion of this point, see chapters 1 and 2 in Helgø, 1999.
22. '*Nosotros somos bien particulares (…) resulta que nosotros recibimos niños que son prácticamente expulsados de otros colegios, son niños que tienen problemas como separación de papás, de clases altas que ahora no han podido cancelar en los colegios particulares pagados.*'

144 Social Policy Reform and Market Governance in Latin America

23. 'Por supuesto que es una situación difícil, lo hacemos por una necesidad más que nada, para que el colegio exista. Si no los absorbemos nosotros, no los absorben los otros colegios.'
24. 'Le pagan por asistencia de alumnos, entonces para la sostenedora es importante tener una cantidad de alumnos ... no es posible hacer un proceso de selección.'
25. Carnoy and McEwan (1997), Mizala and Romaguera (1998), Rounds Parry (1996, 1997).
26. Coleman et al. (1966), Henderson et al. (1978), Summers and Wolfe (1977), Winkler (1975), Murnane (1986).
27. The practice entails dividing students into groups according to their academic abilities. The argument in favour of streaming is that each student will be in an appropriate and benefiting environment and will be challenged according to his or her individual academic capabilities.
28. Hargreaves (1967), Wright (1985).
29. In 1995, the subsidy was US$27.70 (£16.58) per student, per month, in the academic secondary schools and US$35.20 (£21.08) in the vocational schools (Peirano, 1998: 5). The distribution of the monthly subsidy contribution is based on the average number of students who attended school in the previous three months.
30. Exchange rate: 1.67 US dollar to the pound sterling (January, 1998).
31. Quoted in Peirano, 1998: 5.
32. Rounds Parry (1997).
33. For details see Quiroz and Chumacero, 1997. If a school decides to charge fees, the subsidy per student decreases as follows (in £):

Monthly payment	% reduction
0–6.58	0
6.58–13.18	10
13.18–26.35	20
26.35–52.7	35

Note: US$ – £ exchange rate: 1.67.

Source: Ministry of Education; in Peirano, 1998.

34. Peirano (1998), González (1998).
35. The contribution varied from $1000 (£1.33) a year at Colegio York, to $90 000 (£120) at Mauricio Rugendas and $80 000 (£106.67) at Cristóbal Colón. Examples of the utilization of Parents' Association funds are: subsidies towards books and other facilities (bus fares, sanitary towels etc.) for students of lesser financial means, school events (e.g. annual celebrations) and infrastructure maintenance.
36. The yearly Parents' Association contribution was divided by 10 to be comparable to other monthly contributions which were paid 10 times a year before being included in the table.
37. The low monthly tuition payment in Carmela Carvajal is likely to be due to its meritocratic ideology, thus portraying itself as welcoming to brighter girls from lower-income families. However, as discussed in more detail in chapter 6 of Helgø, 1999, it is interesting to note that despite the relatively low monthly contributions that the school receives from the students' parents, Carmela Carvajal was far from poor. The school was among the three most well-equipped (regarding textbooks, laboratories and libraries) in the sample (together with Presidente Errázuriz and La Salle).
38. González (1998), Helgø (1999, see chapter 2).

39. See chapter 2 in Helgø (1999).
40. Friedman (1955), West (1996).
41. Coleman *et al.* (1966), Wells (1987), Bernstein (1971).
42. Carnoy and McEwan, 1997.
43. The variables listed under X_1 and X_2 are included as individual factors in the regression analysis.

Bibliography

Aedo, C. and Larrañaga, O. 'The Chilean Experience', *Social Service Delivery Systems: An Agenda for Reform* (eds) C. Aedo and O. Larrañaga, Washington D.C., IDB, Ilades and Center for Research in Applied Economics, 1994a.
Aedo, C. and Larrañaga, O. *Educación Privada vs. Publica en Chile: calidad y sesgo de selección*, Ilades/Georgetown University, Santiago, Chile, 1994b.
Angell, A. 'Bringing the State Back in: Education Reform in Chile – *The Programa 900 Escuelas and the MECE-Basica*, St Antony's College, University of Oxford, 1997.
Angell, A. 'Education and Decentralisation', *Decentralizing Development: The Political Economy of Institutional Change in Chile and Colombia* (eds) A. Angell, P. Lowden and R. Thorp, Oxford University Press, Oxford, 2001.
Arancibia, V. 'La Educación en Chile: Percepciones de la Opinión Pública y de Expertos', *Estudios Públicos* 54, CEP, Santiago, 1994.
Arzola, S. *et al.* Proyecto MECE IV.2 *Destino Educativo Laboral de los Egresados de Enseñanza Media*, MECE/Ministry of Education, Santiago, 1993.
Bernstein, B. *Class Codes and Control*, Vol. 1, Routledge and Kegal Paul, London, 1971.
Carnoy, M. and McEwan, P. *Is Private Education more Effective and Cost-Effective than Public: The Case of Chile*, Standford University, 1997.
Centro de Estudios Públicos (CEP) 'Educación en Chile: ¿Que Piensan los Padres?' Estudio Nacional de Opinión Pública No. 5, November–December, 1996. Documento de Trabajo No. 268, 1997.
Coleman, J. *et al. Equality of Educational Opportunity*, US Department of Health, Education and Welfare, US Office of Education, Washington D.C., 1966.
Cox, C. and Gozález, P. 'Educación: De programas de Mejoramiento a Reforma' *Construyendo Opciones; Propuestas Económicas y Sociales para el Cambio de Siglo* (eds) R. Cortázar and J. Vial, CIEPLAN/DOLMEN, Santiago, 1998.
de Kadt, E. *Poverty – Focused Policies: The Experience of Chile*. Institute of Development Studies, Sussex, 1993.
Egaña, L. and Magendzo, A. *El Marco Teoretico-Político del Proceso de Decentralización Educativa (1973–1983)*, PIIE, Santiago, 1983.
Espinola, V. *Decentralization of the Education System and the Introduction of Market Rules in the Regulation of Schooling: The Case of Chile*, CIDE, Chile, 1992.
Fowler, F. *Survey Research Methods* Vol. 1, Newsbury Park, London, Sage, 1993.
Friedman, M. 'The Role of Government in Education', *Economics and the Public Interest*, (ed.) R. Solow, Rutgers University Press, New Brunswick, 1955.
Goddard, J. 'Between technocracy and democracy; decentralization and the challenge of urban governance in Santiago, Chile', PhD thesis, University of Cambridge, 1996.
González, P. *Finaciamiento de la Educación en Chile*, Ministerio de Educación, mimeo, 1998.
Hargreaves, D. *Social Relations in a Secondary School*, International Library of Sociology and Social Reconstruction, Routledge and Kegan Paul, London, 1967.
Helgø, C.T. 'Sources of Inequalities with the Chilean Secondary Education System', unpublished PhD thesis, University of Cambridge, 1999.

Henderson, V., Mieszkowski, P. and Suavageau, Y. 'Peer Group Effect and Educational Production Function', *Journal of Public Economics*, 10, 97–106, 1978.
Hojman, D. *Chile: The Political Economy of Development and Democracy in the 1990s*, Basingstoke, Macmillan (now Palgrave Macmillan), 1993.
Instituto Nacional de Estadístas (National Institute for Statistics) (INE), Santiago, Chile, 1995.
Krashinsky, M. 'Why Educational Vouchers May Be Bad Economics', *Teachers' College Record*, 88(2) 139–51, 1986.
Larrañaga, O. 'Decentralización y Equidad: El Caso de los Servicios Sociales en Chile', *Documento de Investigación*, ILADES, Georgetown University, 1–84, 1995.
Marcel, M. and Salimano, A. 'The Distribution of Income and Economic Adjustment', *The Chilean Economy; Policy Lessons and Challenges* (eds) B.P. Bosworth, R. Dornbusch and R. Labán, Brookings Institution, Washington D.C., 1994.
Ministry of Education, *La Reforma Educative en Marcha*, Santiago, Chile, 1995.
Mizala, A. and Romaguera, P. 'Desempeño escolar y elección de colegios: La Experiencia Chileana', *Documento de Trabajo*; Serie Economía, Centro de Economía Aplicada. Departamento de Ingeniería Industrial. Universidad de Chile, No. 36, 1998.
Murnane, R. 'Comparison of Private and Public Schools: The Critical Role of Regulations', *Private Education: Studies in Choice and Public Policy* (ed.) D. Levy, Oxford University Press, New York and Oxford, 1986.
Peirano, Claudia. 'Esquema de Licitación para la Admnistración de Colegios Municipal Subvencionados', Master thesis, Ilades, Georgetown, 1998.
Quiroz, J. and Chumacero, R. 'El Costo de la Educación Particular Subvencionada en Chile', *Documento de Trabajo*, Centro de Estudios Públicos, 1997.
Rodriguez, J. 'School Achievement and Decentralization Policy; the Chilean Case', *Revista de Análisis Económico*, 3(1), 75–88, 1988.
Rounds Parry, T. 'The Impact of Decentralization and Competition on the Quality of Education: An Assessment of Education Reforms in Chile', PhD thesis, University of Georgia, Athens, 1994.
Rounds Parry, T. 'Will Pursuit of Higher Quality Sacrifice Equal Opportunity in Education? An Analysis of the Education Voucher System in Santiago', *Social Science Quarterly*, 74(4), 821–41, 1996.
Rounds Parry, T. 'Achieving Balance in Decentralization: A Case Study of Education Decentralization in Chile', *World Development*, 25(2), 211–55, 1997.
Summers, A. and Wolfe, B. 'Do Schools Make a Difference?', *American Economic Review*, 67, 639–52, 1977.
Wells, G. *The Meaning Makers: Children Learning Language and Using Language to Learn*, Ontario Institute for Studies in Education, Hodder and Stoughton, London, 1987.
West, E. 'Education Voucher in Practice and Principle: A World Survey', *World Bank. Human Capital Development Working Papers*, HCDWP 64, 1996.
Rutter, M. 'School Effect on Pupil Progress: Research Findings and Policy Implications', *Child Development*, 54, 1–29.
Rutter, M., Maughan, B., Mortimore, P. and Ouston, J. *Fifteen Thousand Hours: Secondary Schools and their Effects on Children*, Open Books, London, 1979.
Winkler, D. 'Educational Attainment and School Peer Composition', *Journal of Human Resources*, 10, 189–204, 1975.
Winkler, D. and Rounds Parry, T. 'Municipal and Private Sector Response to Decentralization and School Choice', International Symposium on the Economics of Education, Manchester, England, 18–21 May, 1993.
Wright, C. 'Who Succeeds at School – And Who Decides?', *Multicultural Teaching*, 4(1), 17–22, 1985.

5
The Politics of Education Reform in Chile: The *Programa 900 Escuelas* and the MECE-*Básica*

Alan Angell

Education is central to the reform agenda of governments throughout Latin America. Investment in education is seen as crucial for long-term economic growth and overcoming sharp income inequalities. Yet rhetorical commitment has been greater than achievement. Reforming education is difficult. Well-organized teachers' unions oppose reforms that weaken their power. The supposed agents of reform, the Ministries of Education (MINEDUC), are frequently corrupt, inefficient and more concerned with bureaucratic self-preservation than with implementing reform. It is also extremely costly – after pensions the single largest item in the government budget is normally education.

Chile has been a pioneer of innovative social policies, including education, but too often this is seen as an achievement of the authoritarian government of General Pinochet (1973–90). This chapter examines, by contrast, the education policies of the democratic governments of President Aylwin (1990–94) and of President Frei (1994–2000), and argues that the reforms initiated in 1990 have succeeded in improving the quality and equity of education in Chile, and by doing so have contributed to strengthening democracy.

It is true that key elements of the Pinochet reforms such as decentralization of primary and secondary education to the municipalities, and involvement of the private sector remain in place. Yet there have been innovations. Two interrelated reforms in education differ from those of Pinochet both in their objectives – those of improving the quality and equity of education – and in their method of implementation. They are, firstly, a targeted programme to provide special assistance to primary schools in poor areas – the *Programa de Mejoramiento de la Calidad de las Escuelas Básicas de Sectores Pobres* (P900): and, secondly, a comprehensive programme to improve the overall quality and equity of primary education – the *Programa de Mejoramiento de la Calidad y Equidad de la Educacion Básica* (MECE-*Básica*).[1]

These two programmes are bold initiatives, yet they far from exhaust the range of policies to improve quality and equity. Education in Chile, for all the increased expenditure since 1990, remains under-financed. Equity-enhancing measures require even greater attention to the needs of poor regions and poor families, and much more emphasis on pre-school education. Teachers would no doubt respond positively to a massive increase in salaries. No government, however, least of all a transitional government facing a hostile majority in congress, is in a position to take all these measures simultaneously. Hence the focus of this chapter is to evaluate what the government did rather than what it might have done. Resources did increase, teaching materials were both more abundant and more imaginative, the teaching curriculum was improved, teachers were better trained and motivated, and poorer schools received preferential treatment. But other aspects of the reform were less well implemented – municipalities remained reluctant to assume their responsibilities in education, school autonomy remained limited and restricted, and parental and communal participation fell short of expectations. Educational policy since 1990 has been a combination of innovation and timidity, of imagination and of reluctance to change old habits. Yet the new policies did change Chilean education substantially for the better – and that can be said of few governments in Latin America.

This chapter will not discuss the reforms of the Pinochet government as Camilla T. Helgø discusses them in the previous chapter in this volume. Whatever the fiscal and administrative merits of the Pinochet government reforms, they were not accompanied by any real improvement in the quality of education.

Education reform under democracy

The major challenge facing primary education in Chile is no longer coverage but quality and equity. Primary education is almost universal for the 2 million children between the ages of six and 13, divided into eight grades. The incoming democratic government faced widespread concern about out-of-date curricula, old-fashioned and mechanical methods of teaching, and under-motivated teachers. The nationally applied tests for measuring educational attainment showed low levels of attainment.[2] These tests (known by their Spanish acronym SIMCE – *Sistema de Medición de la Calidad de la Educación*) applied to students of the 4th and 8th grades of primary education in 1991, showed averages of 60.1 per cent for mathematics, and 61.2 per cent for Spanish in the 4th grade; and for the 8th grade the respective averages were 51.6 per cent and 55.1 per cent. The level should have been in the order of 80 per cent (the private fee-paying schools reached 70 per cent). In rural schools the level is only about a third of what it should be.[3] There is also a problem of repetition of grades and of desertion.

The problem of improving quality overall is made more complicated by the sharp inequalities that exist in Chilean society and in the provision of education. National averages disguise sharp variations between town and country, and between different regions. There are mechanisms of redistribution between municipalities, but they are inadequate to deal with the growing inequality. Hence the incoming democratic governments faced not only the challenge of improving the quality of education overall, but also of redressing the inequality in access to education between different areas and social classes.

Whatever their intentions, there were severe restraints facing the incoming government in its efforts to improve education. The initial need for overall macro-economic stability was so pressing – both for political as well as economic reasons – that it was clear that there the increase in resources would be modest. Another problem was that municipalities had received little training to help them assume their responsibilities in education and many resented the lack of appropriate additional financial resources. Civil servants in the ministry, both at central and provincial level followed routines more concerned with making sure that the rules were applied than with support for new initiatives.

No reform can work without the cooperation of teachers. Teachers in Chile were poorly paid, suffered low morale, and years of authoritarianism had stifled any spirit of innovation. Many had been arbitrarily dismissed. They wanted to return to centralized bargaining and a wage increase. They obtained partial satisfaction with the *Estatuto Docente* (ED) in 1991 that established a national minimum salary and additional payments for seniority, professional qualifications and working in difficult areas. If this measure did reduce teacher discontent and protest, there was a cost in terms of pushing ahead with the reforms. The most controversial item of the ED was the creation of stability of employment (*inamovilidad del trabajo*) which prevented flexible use of personnel in the schools.[4] Moreover it was an expensive concession – the cost of the ED between 1991 and 1995 was US$300 million – which is more than the two reform policies discussed here.[5] The ED did little to solve the real problem of the poor quality rather than the quantity of teachers. Even with the salary increases of the ED, they are still low and it has been hard to attract the better graduates into teaching. What the ED did do, however, was to gain some breathing space for the government from pressure from the union of teachers (*Colegio de Profesores*) in order to be able to implement the P900 and the MECE-*Básica*.

Yet if there were obstacles in the way of reform, there were also factors that worked in favour, not least the political climate of the return to democracy. The new government enjoyed an initial powerful legitimacy. What better way than to begin, immediately, with programmes to improve the schooling of the poorest sector of society, and, not long after, with programmes to improve the general quality of education by methods that stressed discussion and participation rather than centralized imposition? The new policies dovetailed neatly with the spirit of the times.

Moreover, if the increase in educational expenditures was inadequate to deal with the accumulated problems, there was nevertheless an increase. Taking 1982 as the base year, the expenditure of the MINEDUC has risen in real terms from a low of 73 in 1990 to 160 in 1997. The value of the education voucher (*subvención*) has risen from a low of 77 in 1990 to 149 in 1997. Investment in infrastructure has increased four-fold between 1990 and 1996. Teachers' salaries have increased by 80 per cent in real terms between 1990 and 1996.[6] Yet, in terms of public expenditure overall, education accounted for 13.7 per cent of the total in 1987 and 15.3 per cent in 1996. Moreover, as a percentage of GDP, it rose only from 2.5 per cent in 1990 to 3.1 per cent in 1996. In other words, educational expenditure has grown apace with overall economic growth. Such fiscal prudence was perhaps inevitable when the major challenge facing the government was that of maintaining macroeconomic stability. The governments sought to attract private funding to education through tax incentives for business (which has had only marginal success) and systems of voluntary parental contributions to schools (which have had more success and produced an estimated US$170 million in the three-year period 1994–96). The Frei government, coming to power in 1994, made a commitment to increase spending on education (public and private) to about 7 per cent of GDP over an eight-year period. The government also enacted a fundamental, and expensive, change in the structure of education in Chile with an increase in the school day so that there is now to be a *jornada única* – a single school day rather than separate attendance either in the morning or afternoon, a process well advanced by 1999.[7]

However, it is misleading to equate quality of education with total expenditures (Venezuela is a cautionary example of gross misspending on education). Education reform is not necessarily very expensive, and the main thrust of the reform policies discussed here went far beyond a simple increase in resources. At the centre of the new policies was a redefined role for the state in education, and one very different from that envisioned by the government's critics on the Right. The state was given the role of planning the overall strategy of educational reform but in such a way as to encourage schools to take more initiatives themselves. The state also assumed the role of improving equity and that meant targeting resources to poor schools. These new policies were designed by *ad hoc* teams rather than by MINEDUC officials. After the reductions of the Pinochet years, the ministry was perceived as too weak, and with morale at too low a level, to plan such innovative programmes. It was the intention from the start, however, to begin a parallel process of modernization of the ministry, so that the reform policies could eventually be incorporated into the normal functioning of the ministry itself.[8]

If the proposed reforms were far-reaching in terms of curriculum innovation and new teaching methods, there were areas left untouched by the reforms. It was not envisioned that the schools should have any extra responsibility in managing its own finances, or in managing teacher supply – that remained the function of government, local and national. Such caution is understandable and perhaps even desirable in the early stages of a reform process. Too all-embracing a reform would run into opposition – from teachers, from the Right, from vested interests – capable of blocking the process. Proposals for increased participation of the community were rather vague and created the impression, confirmed by developments, that this was not central to the overall design of the reforms. They were more concerned with re-establishing the legitimacy of central state action than they were with radical decentralization of the educational process.

(i) The P900

The P900 programme that started in 1990, was aimed at improving the quality of schools in rural areas, and in areas of extreme urban poverty. Initially it targeted the 10 per cent of schools (900) that performed worst on the tests of educational achievement, but it was extended to cover a total of 1500 as some schools improved their overall performance sufficiently to leave the programme and other schools entered.

The objective was to improve the learning of children from grades 1 to 4 in reading, writing and mathematics, to improve the quality of teachers, and to increase the supply of educational materials and to improve school infrastructure. One welcome innovation was that of libraries of 40 books per classroom for first and second year pupils; and provision of tape recorders. This was completely new in Chilean education, and after some initial concern – were these books too good for the children? – was warmly welcomed.

It was considered vital to provide continuous training courses for teachers (*talleres de profesores*) to improve their ability to teach effectively taking into account the local cultural environment, relations between the school and the local community, and the need to stimulate the creativity and self-esteem of pupils. Another departure from traditional practice is the remedial classes (*talleres de aprendizaje*) for 3rd and 4th grade children with special needs. The classes are of 15/20 pupils led by young local volunteers (*monitores de la comunidad*). They function between July and December each year, twice a week, in three-hour sessions, held outside the normal school hours, using specially designed and attractive teaching materials. The *monitores* are chosen by the director of the school and the teachers, and trained by officials of the MINEDUC. By 1994 about 8000 *monitores* had been appointed nationally, receiving a small payment of US$50 per month.

By 1991 the P900 incorporated 1278 schools, 7267 teachers and 222491 pupils from the 1st to 4th grades, about 20 per cent of the total number of pupils at that level.[9] The administrative costs were low – about 4 per cent of the total cost of the programme. In the first four years, the annual average cost of the programme was US$4.8 million, of which $3.2 million came from abroad.[10]

The SIMCE tests show a marked educational improvement in the target schools and a narrowing of the difference between them and the rest of the schools. In tests administered to pupils in their fourth year of study in 1988, the poorest 900 schools reached grades of 43.15 per cent, while the national average (excluding fee-paying schools) was 54.70 per cent. By 1996 there was a marked overall improvement of both levels: the national average had risen to 67.93 per cent, but the P900 schools had significantly narrowed the gap with grades of 64.34 per cent.[11]

According to one evaluation,

> P900 was a model of how to do things. It was important in changing the expectations of the teachers and of the children. It helped to change the traditional methods of teaching by rote. It helped to break down the iron curtain between teachers and pupils, and school heads (*directores*) and teachers. The system was like a number of layers with very little contact between them. With P900 for the first time there was a real interaction between the layers.[12]

(ii) **The MECE programme**

The MECE programme is defined officially as 'the principal method of the government to improve the inputs, processes and results of the school system at the primary level, and to make the distribution of resources more equitable'.[13] The programme cost US$243 million between 1992 and 1998, of which the World Bank loaned US$170 million. Of the total sum 74 per cent was spent on primary education over six years; 16.3 per cent on pre-primary education over five years; and 10 per cent over five years to modernize the Ministry of Education and plan a similar programme for secondary education.

There are two basic objectives – to improve the physical conditions for teachers and pupils, and to improve the quality of education by encouraging initiatives taken at the local level.[14] These are to be achieved by the encouragement of participation; an improved role for the ministry combining regulatory functions and direct intervention; and the use of market mechanisms to promote coordination and innovation. Educational attainment evaluations should be widely available to parents so that they can question school performance and suggest improvement. The programmes apply equally to state-funded private schools as well as to municipal schools, except for the costs of infrastructure, which apply only to municipal schools. How far reality matched the promise will be discussed later but, at least on the most measurable aspects, the targets were met.[15] On those aspects less easy to measure, such as projects to transform the relations of the teachers with their local community, less progress has been reported.

The most innovative policy is called *Descentralización Pedagógica*, encouraging schools to design and implement their own programmes of educational improvement, known as *Proyectos de Mejoramiento Educativo* (PME). The PME are intended to change the highly centralized nature of the Chilean educational system to one in which schools and teachers enjoy some autonomy over curriculum and teaching methods. In the first round of 1992 there were 1200 schools presenting projects; and 440 were approved, between a minimum of US$2700 to US$8000 maximum (not including educational technology to the value of $1500).[16] A PME lasts for two to three years. In the period 1992–6 a total of 4178 projects had been approved, of which 591 were awarded to rural schools that cooperated in competing for them.[17] Over a million pupils were involved.

The benefits of participating in a PME are held to be, firstly, an increase in communication between teachers of different disciplines. Secondly, teachers acquire experience in diagnosing problems, designing and evaluating them. Thirdly, teachers adopt more imaginative teaching methods and take more initiatives. Fourthly, it has encouraged involvement of parents and of the community.[18] In the opinion of the National Coordinator of the MECE-*Básica*, the level of school participation in the PME has been 'spectacular'.[19]

Although the aims of the MECE programme are broader than those of the P900, the targeting policy of the P900 is sustained, notably through the MECE-*Rural* programme designed for rural schools of one to three teachers which fall outside the terms of reference of P900, as they do not cover the complete educational cycle. The aim is to create a curriculum and a teaching methodology relevant to the needs of these schools, supported by newly designed textbooks. There is also a special training programme for rural teachers aimed at combating the problems of isolation. By early 1996 the MECE-*Rural* was covering all the incomplete rural schools, and thereby reaching 25.4 per cent of the rural school population.

The MECE programme achieved its basic targets. There has been a massive increase in supply of textbooks: three for each pupil in grades 1–4; and four for each of the remaining grades. The total is more than 6 million texts annually – three times the level of the 1980s. There are small libraries of 35–60 books in each classroom of the first four grades. Teachers check on the state of health of their pupils, sending them to the local health clinic if necessary. By 1994 the level reached for attention to health problems of children was 91 per cent of the target, covering 100 per cent of children in the 1st to 3rd grades; in infrastructure the level reached was 71 per cent of the target (1178 schools repaired); for the provision of classroom libraries the target had been surpassed with a level of 109 per cent (33 606 classroom libraries, covering all classes in the 1st to 4th grades); there was complete coverage in the distribution of teaching material, covering all 1st to 4th grades, so that all children had adequate access to textbooks.[20]

It is too early to evaluate in any systematic way the long-term benefits of the MECE programme. Furthermore, the effect on factors such as school culture is far from easy to measure, not least because the policy was based upon persuasion. According to the Coordinator of the MECE-*Rural*,

> We are not imposing a dogma, there are no rules. We reorganized the grades, we had teachers work in smaller groups, and we had completely new teaching texts prepared by Chilean specialists. We tried to get teachers to use local experiences and cultures to link these to broader issues. On the whole teachers were enthusiastic.[21]

Explaining the success

The political mood in 1990 with the return to democracy was appropriate for reforms to improve the quality and equity of education. A democracy of pacts and of reconciliation would replace dictatorship. Education reform involving equity was an excellent way of embodying the political mood. The language used to launch the reforms was intentionally consensual and non-antagonistic. In the words of the Coordinator of the P900, 'we talked about improvement and equity, but not about reform. We did not want to revive fears that this was a new dogma being imposed from above, yet another ideological transformation'.[22] Yet it was also a way of linking the new democracy with the old – the state, once more, would assume its responsibility of providing adequate education.

The challenge was to put it into operation and quickly. The P900 could start immediately, and this was important in order to win support from teachers, school directors, supervisors, and the public. Above all, P900 brought immediate material benefit to poor schools in terms of improvement of buildings and of books and teaching aides.

One positive legacy of the previous government was the considerably improved statistical database of the ministry, making it possible to locate areas of greatest need and targeting resources. But the previous government had set the national budget for 1990 and there was no margin for expenditures on special programmes. Fortunately, there was immediate foreign funding available for the P900 to start, and this was a welcome vote of confidence from external donors both of the efficient design of the programmes, and of the political will to carry them out. The education reforms were also a beneficiary of the tax reform of the government in 1990, negotiated with the opposition parties in congress precisely to fund social programmes. That it was negotiated successfully meant that more resources were available for education, but it was also a further sign that there was national consensus on the need for such programmes.

Support from the World Bank, although obviously important in financial terms, also helped to legitimize the programme nationally and internationally.

The relationship with the World Bank is summarized by Cristián Cox, the National Coordinator of the MECE-*Básica*.

We had a level of expertise equal to that of the World Bank. We could talk with them on equal terms. However, the main negotiator, Juan Prawda, was a man of great international and governmental experience, and he was an enormous help and support to us. At first, the World Bank was rather worried about PME and the informatics projects – they thought that the people would run away with the money, that there would be widespread clientelism. But Chile is not like that, there are strict controls, and public officials are generally honest. Now the World Bank is recommending the PME to other countries.[23]

Executive support for such programmes is crucial and, in this respect, the Chilean experience was very positive. The Education Minister, Ricardo Lagos, who was both politically powerful and sensitive to the need for education innovation, backed the programmes. He remained in post for three years and was a strong defender of his ministry in the cabinet.

The reforms consciously sought to incorporate the strengths of the existing system and to take institutions and give them a new role. For example, the category of supervisor was created by the Pinochet government to work at the provincial level to oversee the schools in the area. The reforms changed what was largely a role of bureaucratic oversight to one of involvement in change and improvement. The supervisors had few difficulties in adapting to a role of greater professional interest, and one that they felt also gave them greater status.[24]

Arguably the most crucial factor in the success was the existence of a small group of educationalists of high professional ability, agreed both on what had to be done and on how to do it. During the dictatorship, several small research centres had conducted extensive research on Chilean education, and had experimented with ways of improving it. When the Aylwin government was elected, this group formed a closely-knit, united and dedicated team anxious to put into practice on a national scale what they had been doing on a small scale for years. There was, as many of them indicated, a real sense of *mística* (combination of commitment and belief). Moreover, the composition of the group remained stable.

Two major issues remained to be resolved – the relationship between the reform programme and the MINEDUC, and with the teachers. Creating *ad hoc* agencies to perform roles that ideally a ministry should be performing, invariably creates tension between the newcomers and the career functionaries of the ministry. The reforms of the 1980s did not help the ministry to assume a supervisory, regulatory role. It was limited to financial and administrative oversight with little attention to technical and educational responsibilities.

The design of the MECE attempted to minimize the tension with MINEDUC and included an element for the modernization of the ministry. The programmes sought to involve the agents of the ministry as closely as possible in the execution of the programmes. It was made clear that when the special funding was over the programmes would be incorporated into the normal operations of the ministry. The fact that the programmes were central to the education policy of the government, and that they were eventually to be incorporated into the ministry, helped to win over support from within the ministry, especially in the provinces. The P900 became part of the operating structure of the ministry after 1995 and, in a sense, the final success of the programmes would be the way in which, over the long term, they changed the procedures and culture of the ministry itself.

Teachers were another possible obstacle to the progress of the reforms. It is easy to understand the opposition of the teachers to the process of decentralization under Pinochet, given that it was implemented in an authoritarian way, and gave unelected municipal authorities the power to hire and fire teachers. Hence, for the success of the new programmes, it was important to win over the teachers, and this was achieved by the material results that the programmes brought, and by the access given to teachers for professional training. It is also likely that the effect of the *Estatuto Docente* was to make salary concerns less pressing, although there have been strikes by teachers over salaries notably in 1994 and 1996. This is certainly the opinion of the then Minister of Education, Ricardo Lagos, who argues that such action, paradoxical as it may seem, was necessary to save the process of decentralization. Faced with a powerful union of teachers who simply wanted to return to the old centralist model, the ministry had to assume national control of some activities, above all, those dealing with pay regulation. If there had not been some move towards levelling salaries there would have been a crisis and a return to the past model.[25] Although the *Colegio de Profesores* remains officially lukewarm about the reforms, there is widespread evidence that most teachers do view them positively.[26]

Criticisms of the programmes

The Right initially saw the policies as political reforms aimed at increasing the power of the government rather than as educational reforms. If they became the centre of political controversy, as had previous reforms, then the necessary confidence and trust for implementation would not have been created. This was a problem that seriously worried the then education minister, Lagos. Indeed, he was taken aback by the hostile response of the Right to the *monitores*, and had he realized beforehand the extent of opposition then he might have thought twice about going ahead with the scheme. Nevertheless, these criticisms lasted a relatively short period, and once the reforms were welcomed by the school community, and that there was no sinister political intent, then they became generally accepted.[27] The reformers did not respond directly to political attacks, and avoided polemics.

The policies have been criticized because they do not provide economic incentives for teachers. This may be one of the project's major drawbacks, given the current low status of teachers' salaries. Moreover, the project provides for only temporary, rather than incremental, or permanent assistance.[28]

These criticisms, however, miss the point. If the MECE programme had explicitly involved economic incentives for teachers, then it would have been lost in the controversial pay issue. And there were incentives – notably the PME, which was an incentive for the school as a whole, though more in terms of professional satisfaction than in terms of remuneration.[29] Although the form of the MECE is intended to be temporary, the content is not – it will gradually be incorporated into the MINEDUC's normal operations.

Indeed, if the programme were to have effects only during the period of special funding it would be a failure. According to Cristián Cox, the programmes have the broad-based political support necessary to ensure their continuation.

The MECE is the programme of the government in education – more, it is the programme of the *Concertación* in education. It would have taken place with or without the support of the World Bank. It was our programme.[30]

The Right has a series of criticisms of P900 and the MECE, arguing that they cost too much, are too centralized, and too directive. Although the idea behind the P900 is applauded, it is claimed that it has been implemented in too centralist a fashion. Another criticism is that the programmes have ignored the municipal governments, and this has eroded the principle of decentralization. Key to their thinking (and this point is shared more widely) is greater emphasis on autonomy for the school – not least for the school to have more resources of its own to manage. 'The school should be the protagonist, and not the state'.[31] The Right fears that unless there is a real change in school autonomy, the benefits of the programme will disappear when the special funding ends. The PME are seen as a real innovation, but too limited – there should be broader projects involving the school as a whole. Incorporating these programmes eventually back into the ministry is seen as a potential disaster – a return to old-fashioned centralization.

How fair are these criticisms? Central state action can be defended because, given the weakness of the municipalities and of the schools after years of authoritarianism, there was an initial need for central design and execution. There was also a need to act rapidly, and that too meant central initiatives. There have been moves towards school autonomy, though admittedly modest ones. Municipalities are taking a more positive attitude towards their responsibilities in education. Moreover, the assumption that decentralization is the crucial ingredient of education reform is by no means uncontested. As far as cost is involved, the MECE programme is not expensive – less than 5 per cent of the overall public education budget; or about half the increase in educational spending since 1992.[32] Hence the amount of the increase in the direct funding to schools if there were no MECE programme, would not be enough to make a real difference to the schools – and clearly there would have been no World Bank support simply for an increase in educational expenditure alone. The criticism of the Right also ignores the fact that one aim of the two programmes was to enable schools to make better use of the resources that they had. The issue of the integration of the programmes into the MINEDUC is clearly crucial, but clearly it can only be answered with the passing of time.[33]

Another criticism has been the relative failure to increase parent participation in schools. This is a difficult issue in Chile where a 17-year authoritarian regime had very negative effects on the level of participation, and where there is a general tendency to look to the state to solve problems. The schools visited in the course of this research, however, all indicated that there was, as a by-product of P900 and MECE, more parent involvement than before – generally adding that before there was practically none. One head teacher reported that the *Centro de Padres* raised money for a computer, paved the road in front of the school, and built a football pitch. However, this was only possible because the teaching staff made a great effort to involve the parents – and P900 was crucial in helping them to do that.[34] MECE-*Rural* is encouraging schools to develop projects in which the parents can participate making use of their local knowledge. However, it remains the case that these activities are by-products of other successful activities.

The P900 has also been criticized for concentrating on the first cycle of primary education, grades 1 to 4, and neglecting the second cycle, grades 5 to 8. Indeed, directors of schools have made this criticism as well, although the entire school benefits from the infrastructure improvements. However, targeted programmes always face this kind of criticism – could not the limits be more generous and include more groups? The P900 was seen as an emergency programme of recuperation for the most disadvantaged groups and there are good educational reasons for concentrating on the first cycle.

Educational reform and the municipalities

Relations between the reform programmes and the municipalities have not been easy. The role of the municipalities in education was to administer resources, and not to improve the quality.[35] The Pinochet government had appointed mayors, and it was not until 1992 that mayors would be directly elected. For many mayors educational responsibility was a nuisance rather than an opportunity – and not an area that allowed them to dispense much patronage. It is hardly surprising that the education policy-makers on the whole tried to bypass this structure, at least until mayors were democratically elected; but this tension reduced the possibility of integrating decentralization into the core of the reform process.

An integrated reform process should link municipal financing and educational financing; but in practice this does not happen – municipalities run up deficits and cover them by transfers from central government or by their own resources. Within the municipalities there is often administrative conflict between the Education Department, which in theory has oversight over education, and the Administration and Finance Department, which receives the money. It is hardly surprising in the words of one commentator that, 'The P900 had no interest in the municipalities'.[36] But if understandable given the political composition of the municipalities, there is no doubt that the conflict between municipalities and reformers was to the detriment of the smooth operation of education improvement.[37]

As the programmes became more established, and with a change to elected mayors in 1992, there has been a gradual shift of emphasis to cooperation and assistance. For example, in the MECE-*Rural* programme, there is a *convenio de coparticipación* (joint participation agreement) with the municipalities: it has no legal standing, but it is a moral commitment to cooperate. Within P900 there are efforts to develop local participation by bringing together mayors, teachers, supervisors and community groups in order to secure improvements in the schools.[38]

However, the most systematic attempt to involve the municipalities in education planning is the *Plan Anual de Desarrollo Educativo Municipal* (PADEM) – a local diagnosis of the educational needs of the municipality, and proposed solutions. Pilot projects had to be presented by September 1995, and full projects by 1996 – at least in theory, as it proved over-optimistic to assume that all municipalities would be able to present a viable document in the initial years. It is novel in that it attempts to involve the municipality in educational matters other than mere administration, and that it asks schools to make a diagnosis and recommendations to the municipality. Not least among problems that the PADEM are supposed to solve is that of efficient deployment of teachers in the municipalities, for there is a surplus of possibly as many as 8000 primary teachers.[39]

Yet the initial results were not promising. Municipalities tended to ask the officials of the MINEDUC how to complete their plans, or to seek help from outside consultants; once completed, the plan tends to be forgotten. The demand for an annual plan complicates the municipal budget, as the two periods do not coincide. None the less, in the larger municipalities, there is evidence that it is tending to shift municipalities away from purely administrative matters to those involving education quality and performance as well. This whole area, however, remains a challenge for the future.

Conclusions

Both the P900 and the MECE-*Básica* have attracted international attention and agencies as diverse as UNICEF and the World Bank have urged other countries to follow these examples.[40] Attention has focused on the lessons that can be drawn; but caution should be exercised in assessing their overall contribution to education improvement, and indeed the extent to which other countries could realistically copy these models.

The reforms in Chile represent a successful exercise in planning by the central state. In terms of achieving certain goals in social policy there is nothing wrong with that – although the prevailing concentration on the supposed virtues of decentralization and participation has tended to push the central state into the background. Few countries in Latin America, however, can emulate the Chilean state in terms of its relative efficiency, honesty and accountability. The Chilean reforms did not require a profound initial transformation of the state in the way that would be required – for very different reasons – in Peru or Venezuela. A sustained period of economic growth allowed the Chilean government to increase real expenditures on education without having to sacrifice expenditures in other areas – an unusual positive-sum game in Latin America. Moreover, the teachers' union in Chile was dominated by members of the governing parties, at least until the late 1990s, and inclined to support the government. Many countries cannot afford such substantial increases in teachers' pay and face fierce hostility from unions ideologically opposed to the government.

The Chilean experience does contain an important lesson: unless there is a reform of the central ministry, *ad hoc* programmes, however worthy they are in the short term, are unlikely to be sustainable in the long run. Admittedly, changing the Chilean Ministry of Education is a far less daunting task than those of most corresponding ministries in other countries, but it remains a necessary task. Even targeted programmes need, for their efficiency and sustainability, to be eventually incorporated in a central permanent government institution. It is too soon to say if the P900 and the MECE programmes (for the MECE-*Media* programme will be followed by one for higher education) have transformed the culture of the MINEDUC so that fundamental programmes of reform can easily be accommodated within the normal operations of the ministry, but it is important to recognize the need for such a transformation.

On many tests – the improvement in the SIMCE results, the improvement in infrastructure, the increase in textbooks, the attention given to teacher-training – there can be little doubt that the reform policies achieved their stated aims. On others, perhaps, the story is less convincing. Decentralized administration ran into the hostility or indifference of the municipalities, the suspicion of the central planners, and the strong desire of the Ministry of Finance to maintain strict control over all levels of fiscal expenditure. Participation by parents in the running of schools ran into the problems of a low level of social participation in a society still scarred by dictatorship, and to school authorities unaccustomed to, and not much in favour of, external influences in their area of activity. School autonomy was quite limited in theory – schools do not enjoy a separate legal status that would allow them to manage funds, for example – but even the limited amount on offer, over curriculum matters, was not taken up by school authorities used to dependence on the centre, and nervous about taking initiatives.

Were these reforms the optimal ones to obtain equity in access to education? The problem in answering such a question is that it depends on factors that have little to do with education – such as family income and employment, or the provision of adequate health care. Undoubtedly the P900 was a major advance in targeting resources to poor areas but other proposals would face political difficulties. Varying the voucher payments to favour poorer areas, for example, would have run into opposition from the richer, and much more politically powerful, municipalities. Social policy reform has to take into account the balance of political forces, and the government had a weak base given the way that the Constitution of 1980 over-represented the political Right. Measures such as the extension of the school day are more likely to be of benefit to poor families, as long as there is not an economic imperative for children to work part-time (as rural children do during the harvest). One area where there could have been more advance was in that of pre-school education. Such education in Chile only starts at four years of age, and the coverage has increased only from 20 per cent of the age group in 1990 to 29.8 per cent in 1996, although most of the increase has been concentrated in the poorest 20 per cent of society. Increasing the possibility for such children to attend nursery school in greater number and at an earlier age would make a positive contribution to equity.

Education reform cannot by itself produce an equitable society. It is one component of a series of interrelated measures involving health reform, labour market reform, and improvement in housing. The democratic governments in Chile have experienced great difficulty with health reform and, for political and economic reasons, have been reluctant to engage in much labour market reform. So, in a sense, what has happened in education has been in advance of reforms in other areas. Few, if any, social policy reforms achieve all their objectives, and sometimes there are unreasonable expectations of what they can achieve. Judged in this context the education reforms of the democratic governments in Chile are a major step towards improving the overall quality of education in Chile, and a significant, if partial, step towards securing greater equality of access to education.

Acknowledgements

The Social Agenda Policy Group of the Inter-American Development Bank commissioned this research. I am grateful to the members of the study group for their comments and especially Antonia Silva who coordinated the project. A preliminary version of this article appears in Antonia Silva (ed.), *Implementing Policy Innovations in Latin America* (IDB, Washington D.C., 1996). For their comments on this text I am grateful to Samuel Valenzuela, Gloria Pollack, Dagmar Raczynski, Carol Graham and Christopher Abel. Greatest thanks, however, must go to the members of the MECE team, above all, Cristián Cox and Marianela Cerri.

Notes

1. Within the MECE-*Básica* programme US$2.5 million was allocated to devise a programme for secondary education, which later was the subject of another reform programme and World Bank loan.
2. The SIMCE tests are criticized for not measuring the 'value added' by each school, and so may favour choice of those schools which train specifically for the tests rather than aim at an all round education.
3. Figures from Comité Técnico (1994: 24). The Chilean school year is relatively short – 800 hours annually, whereas most countries at the same level of development spend 10 per cent more time in school. Taiwanese children spend 1177 hours each year in school.
4. For an acute criticism of the *Estatuto Docente* see Larrañaga (1995: 263).
5. Cox (1994: 164).
6. Mena and Bellei (1998: 381–4).
7. This is a profound change and was strongly resisted by the teachers' union. It also involved for the first time state-funded private schools receiving financial support for infrastructure improvements. This change consumed a great deal of the time and energy of the education minister in charge, Sergio Molina. Interview, Sergio Molina, 11 December, 1996.
8. Interview with Pedro Serra, Coordinator, *Fortalecimiento Institutional*, MECE-*Básica*, 15 September, 1995. He adds that when some functions were devolved to the ministry, the results were poor – the officials were too cautious, too conscious of bureaucratic rules, though not particularly obstructive.
9. Figures and details from the Ministry of Education *Atención Preferencial* (nd 1993). In 1995 there were 988 schools in the P900 programme, with 288 271 pupils attending and 5135 teachers on training courses. For the views of the first National Coordinator of P900 see García-Huidobro (1994).
10. Gajardo (ed.) (1994: 81).
11. Mena and Bellei (1998: 366).
12. Interview with Johanna Filp, Researcher of the *Centro de Investigación y del Desarrollo de la Educación* (CIDE), and member of the P900 evaluation team, 1 September, 1995.
13. Cited in the Ministry of Education, *Orientaciones Básicas* (1994), which also gives full details on the programme.
14. Cox (1995).
15. Another programme increases the use of computers in schools, with a pilot project to create a *red escolar de communicaciones por computador* (school computer network system) intended to expand the horizons of the rural and isolated schools.

16. The 1281 projects operating in 1994 fell into six broad categories: communication (radio programmes, newspapers, audio visual aides); projects involving small gardens or raising of animals; artisanal workshops; small laboratories (computing, language, science); cultural activities: and experiments in improving expressive skills (literature, music, theatre). Cox (1995: 10).
17. Mena and Bellei (1998: 367). Over the six-year period it is estimated that 90 per cent of schools eligible for a PME will receive one. The element of competition is to be first in the queue, rather than to run a serious risk of failing to get a PME. There are 3443 rural schools with three or fewer teachers who have separate programmes.
18. Cox (1995: 11).
19. Interview, Cristián Cox, 21 August, 1995. The exception to this high level of participation has been at the level of the community where it has been more modest, partly because this element was marginal to the aims of the reforms.
20. Cox (1995: 8).
21. Interview with Javier Sanmiguel, Head of the MECE-*Rural* programme, 28 August, 1995. He added that getting teachers to change their teaching practices inevitably takes a long time but they had received positive feedback, which allowed them to improve their teaching materials.
22. Cecilia Jara, National Coordinator of the P900, interview, 22 August, 1995. There are clear echoes here of the damaging controversy over educational reform during the Allende period.
23. Interview Cox, 6 September, 1995.
24. Interview with Ignacio Jara, *Jefe de Programación del Programa Mece*, 21 August, 1995. 'P900 was seen by the local functionaries as, at last, the chance to do something positive. It was for the supervisors a chance to resume work as professional educationalists and move away from their role as controlling bureaucrats, and in the end they were more *profesores* than they were *Pinochetistas*.'
25. Interview, Ricardo Lagos, 24 August, 1995. Lagos argues that levelling salaries is a form of positive discrimination. He added that the battle to get the ED approved in Cabinet was a fierce one, and that he succeeded only with the support of the President. Subsequent amendments in Congress made the ED more rigid than he would have liked.
26. Interview, Javier Sanmiguel, 28 August, 1995. According to the head of MECE-*Rural*, the *Asociacion de Profesores Rurales* (affiliated to the *Colegio*) is so keen on the programme that it wants it to continue for ever.
27. Interview, Ricardo Lagos, 24 August, 1995. He added that congressmen, who initially complained that they had *monitores* in their constituency, soon began to complain that they did not have enough.
28. Aedo and Larrañaga (1994: 19).
29. In the end, of course, teachers' salaries have to be increased to ensure an adequate teaching supply. Both teachers and government agree on this, but disagreed about how much and how quickly – hence the strikes.
30. Interview, Cox, September, 1995.
31. Ema Budinich, economist at the research institute *Libertad y Desarrollo*, 'Our idea is that each school should make up its own budget and negotiate with the Educational Department of the municipality how much of the educational resources of the municipality it should have. The criteria would be those of efficiency and merit. That would give the mayors a more direct role in the educational administration of the municipality. School directors should have control over the appointment of teachers – at present they have none'. Interview, 15 September, 1995.

32. Valenzuela (1995).
33. Interview, Cox, 6 September, 1995. The vice-minister in 1995 declared that his special role will be that of modernization of the ministry. A commission has been set up to make recommendations about modernization – the first time since 1990 that internal ministerial reform has been firmly on the agenda.
34. Interview with the Head of the *Escuela Alejandro Graham Bell*, Pudahuel 26 August, 1996.
35. Cox (1994: 159). Also, interview with Juan Pablo Valenzuela, *Director de Estudios para Servicios Descentralizadas, SubDere, Ministerio del Interior*, 3 September, 1995.
36. Interview, Viola Espinola, researcher at CIDE, 6 September, 1995. She added that lines of authority are very blurred, and there is a great deal of confusion and conflict. 'We have reproduced centralization at the local level as far as the schools are concerned with the mayor having too much power.'
37. Interview, Juan Pablo Valenzuela, 3 September, 1995.
38. Interview, Cecilia Jara, 22 August, 1995.
39. However, according to former education minister, Sergio Molina, there is little evidence so far that municipalities are re-deploying teachers. Interview, 11 December, 1996.
40. Gajardo (ed.) (1994: 16), refers to UNESCO and UNICEF efforts to persuade other countries to adopt parts of the P900. Judith Tendler (1997) has argued that we know a lot more about bad government than about good, and that there has been too much emphasis on failure and insufficient attention paid to analysing success.

Bibliography

Aedo, Cristián and Larrañaga, Osvaldo (1994), *Social Service Delivery Systems*, Washington D.C.: Inter-American Development Bank.
Comité Técnico Asesor del Diálogo Nacional sobre la Modernización de la Educación Chilena (1994), *Los Desafios de la Educación Chilena frente al Siglo 21*. Santiago.
Cox, Cristián (1994), 'Las Políticas Educacionales del Gobierno de la Transición (Chile 1990–1994)', *Proposiciones*, 25.
Cox, Cristián (1995), *Programa de Mejoramiento de la Calidad y Equidad de La Educacion (MECE): Experiencia Exitosa en el Sector Educativo de Chile*. Santiago: Ministry of Education.
Gajardo, Marcela (ed.) (1994), *Cooperación Internacional y Desarrollo de la Educación en Chile*. Agencia de Cooperación Internacional de Chile: Santiago.
García-Huidobro, Juan Eduardo (1994), 'Positive Discrimination in Education: Its Justification and a Chilean Example', *International Review of Education*, 40.
Larrañaga, Osvaldo (1995), 'Descentralización de la Educación en Chile: Una Evaluación Económica', *Estudios Públicos*, 60.
Mena, Isidora and Bellei, Cristián (1998), 'El Desafio de la Calidad y la Equidad en Educacion', in C. Tolosa and E. Lahera (eds), *Chile en Los Noventa*. Santiago: Ediciones Dolmen.
Ministry of Education (nd 1993), *Atención Preferencial a las Escuelas Más Pobre de Chile*. Santiago.
Ministry of Education (1994), *Orientaciones Básicas, Objetivos y Componentes del Programa MECE*.
Tendler, Judith (1997), *Good Government in the Tropics*. Baltimore: Johns Hopkins University Press.
Valenzuela, Juan Pablo (1995), *Financiamiento de la Educación en Chile*. Santiago: mimeo.

6
Democratic Decentralization and People's Participation: an Examination of the EDUCO Programme in El Salvador

*Suhas D. Parandekar**

1. Introduction

Decentralization in social services is increasingly popular as a key element of a reform strategy to improve service delivery, and the education sector has been at the forefront of this strategy. The presence of a world-wide trend to give greater autonomy to schools in the interest of improving school performance is the focus of a growing literature.[1] One shortcoming of the literature is the paucity of empirical data to evaluate the impact of reforms based on decentralization and greater people's participation. Such an evaluation would provide insights into the context where decentralization reforms have made a difference. An empirical evaluation of a decentralized model of school management would also suggest avenues for improvement of school performance in decentralized settings. This chapter is based on a data set that has been compiled for a research project on the decentralization and privatization reforms in education, carried out in five countries under the supervision of the World Bank's Development Research Group. We present an investigation of the case of the Central American nation of El Salvador, which instituted the *Educación con Participación de la Comunidad* (EDUCO) programme in 1991. The EDUCO programme has received wide acclaim as a successful example of educational reform in a poor country with a history of deep inequality and resulting civil strife. It would be of great interest to uncover lessons derived from the EDUCO experience about the strengths and limitations of decentralization as a tool to improve school performance. The key hypothesis of this paper is that while a school-based management model with heavy parental involvement does have positive aspects, the impact of decentralization is heavily influenced by the context of available resources for the educational system as a whole.

The data set used here comprises an evaluation of a random survey sample of 311 primary schools.[2] The interesting aspect about the school decentralization programme in El Salvador is the continued co-existence of traditional schools run under the centralized institutional arrangement of the national Ministry of Education and community managed or EDUCO schools. The data set consists of information collected from school principals, teachers, students and parents from both EDUCO schools as well as the traditional Ministry of Education (MOE) administered schools. This chapter is based on a subset of the data comparing EDUCO and traditional schools in rural areas.

EDUCO and traditional rural schools are compared on the following lines of investigation. First, the two groups of schools are examined for differences in educational *inputs*. Data is compared in this section regarding the physical infrastructure of the schools and the human resources available for education. Secondly, the schools are compared in order to uncover differences in *outcomes*. In this case, an examination is made of basic efficiency measures such as repetition, in the inculcation of values which forms an important educational objective in El Salvador, and finally in the learning achievement test scores of students. The analysis is concluded with a comparison of differences in *technology* – by means of an educational production function linking measured educational inputs to the production of test scores.[3]

The rest of the chapter is organized as follows. Section 2 briefly presents background information about El Salvador and the EDUCO programme. Section 3 presents a comparison between EDUCO and traditional rural schools for educational inputs, and Section 4 does the same for educational outcomes. Section 4 also presents results from analysis of the production function for test scores. A summary of the main conclusions is presented in Section 5.

2. Community managed schools in El Salvador

The decentralized mechanism of service delivery discussed in this chapter did not originate in the boardrooms of the World Bank, nor in the offices of policy planners with the government of El Salvador, nor even in the halls of academia. This participatory model of provision of basic education literally was founded in the killing fields of the long civil war in El Salvador in the 1980s. In parts of the country gripped by war, the official machinery of the Ministry of Education had ceased to exist, and a number of communities of rural workers (*campesinos*) organized themselves for the schooling of their children. These voluntary associations of households were entrusted with the task of finding a place for the children to attend class, which could be an old school building, any other public place such as a church, and even spaces within private residences if a suitable benefactor was available. The community associations also had the responsibility of hiring and retaining a school teacher, as well as acquiring whatever basic educational inputs that the parents could afford. In the beginning of the 1990s, the civil war had ended but hundreds of thousands of school-aged children were out of school. While most communities had very few resources to provide for education in their makeshift schools in a sustained way, some had not even a hint of access to basic education.

The government of El Salvador was saddled with tremendous expectations for reforms in the provision of services at the end of the war. In 1991, the Ministry of Education set up a pilot programme which co-opted the concept of a community managed school. This pilot programme was progressively rolled out to other rural areas where it was determined that the lack of access to schools was the main cause behind the non-enrolment of children of school age. Whereas the major proportion of schools continued to be managed centrally, a mechanism was set up whereby resources could flow directly from the MOE to a bank account in the name of a community association or ACE (*Asociaciones Comunales para la Educación*) which was responsible for running the school. The World Bank provided help to the MOE in bringing the EDUCO model to scale, with resources for institutional strengthening, school construction, provision of textbooks and didactic materials and the training of teachers. Resources were also provided for the training of the Community Associations for varied activities from financial management to helping the teacher in classroom activities. In general, the magnitude of resources made available to EDUCO schools does not differ substantially from the resources provided to traditional schools.[4] Both EDUCO and traditional schools use the same curriculum and didactic materials, including textbooks. The only additional resource for EDUCO schools is a token amount of money to provide remuneration to parents for time spent in training for school management. The key difference between EDUCO schools and traditional schools is not the magnitude of available funds, but the degree of autonomy and flexibility afforded to the communities that run the schools. The organization of EDUCO schools has evolved over the years, but the basic elements include the following.[5]

ACEs enter into a one-year renewable agreement with MOE whereby they receive funds on a monthly basis to cover teacher salaries and operating costs, including school materials.[6] In this contract, ACEs agree to follow MOE guidelines for the distribution of funds to the schools, and its criteria for selecting teachers. In addition, MOE provides the schools with teaching/ learning materials, training materials for teachers and ACE committees, and supervision. The ACEs have autonomy to make decisions regarding: (i) hiring and firing of teachers, who in turn have annual renewable contracts; (ii) obtaining supplemental funds; and (iii) choose their own mix of school materials from within the MOE approved list. In addition to the formal responsibilities of the ACE, parents play an important role by supplementing the resources made available for the school by the MOE. Parents organize voluntary fund-raising efforts and make contributions in kind, but by far the most important contribution of parents comes through the voluntary contribution of manual labour. An important contribution of manual labour is in the form of parents helping to prepare and distribute school lunches. The ministry provides basic raw ingredients such as rice or corn flour, but parents provide supplements such as vegetables and fish. Parents also derive benefits from the training which helps them better organize and co-ordinate the voluntary contributions of time. Activities not directly related to the academic function of the school are an important way for parents to participate in the school. However, an analysis of the benefits of decentralized management needs to focus on the improved performance of the more traditional actors, such as the school director and the teachers.

3. Decentralized management and educational inputs

The first question investigated here is the extent to which the autonomy and flexibility of choice available to community associations has led to differences in the educational inputs chosen for EDUCO schools as compared with traditional MOE administered schools. The hypothesis that EDUCO schools would perform better because of greater autonomy is based upon the implicit assumption that ACEs which run the EDUCO schools would exercise the freedom of choice made available to them.

Do EDUCO schools in fact prefer certain characteristics among their directors and teachers, or is there no difference between the characteristics of educational inputs provided in EDUCO and traditional schools? If the inputs chosen by EDUCO schools are indeed different, it is of interest to examine the nature of the differences. If the inputs appear to be the same, some further interesting questions would be raised. It is possible that the autonomy available to EDUCO schools exists only in principle – if the supply of educational inputs to the EDUCO school is heavily constrained, autonomy and flexibility scarcely have any meaning. For instance, if there are only two or three teachers willing to work in a particular school in a remote mountainous location, and the school needs to employ three teachers, the ability to 'hire and fire' teachers would remain a theoretical ability. However, there is an important policy consideration which would follow if we find that ACEs end up with the same choices as traditional schools. It then becomes an imperative for the central ministry to actively seek ways to broaden the menu of options available to the community. Using the example regarding teachers, the ministry could consider schemes of compensatory 'hardship allowances' for teachers to work in remote areas, and could subsidize and coordinate local recruitment efforts.

Another explanation of similarity of inputs between EDUCO and traditional schools would be that even though EDUCO schools do choose a different mix of educational inputs, the differences are not observable to researchers using a quantitative survey instrument such as the one used here. If this explanation were true, we would expect to find differences when we compare EDUCO and traditional schools from other perspectives, especially when we examine final educational outcomes. In order to try to control as much as possible the factor of differing supply, given the fact that EDUCO schools exist only in rural areas, the comparison in this paper is restricted to traditional schools only in rural areas.

Four groups of educational inputs are discussed in this section: the school director, the school infrastructure and didactic materials; the teacher; and finally the home environment of the student. At this stage of the investigation, attention is restricted to a descriptive comparison of two groups – a sample of 54 EDUCO schools (with more detailed student level data from 182 students) and a sample of 127 traditional rural schools (323 students).

3.1 School directors

Table 6.1 presents a comparison of school directors from the two groups of schools. EDUCO directors are younger, less experienced, and more likely to be classroom teachers with an additional administrative duty as director. Such a difference would be expected given the recency of the programme, and the fact that EDUCO schools are smaller schools while traditional rural schools would be larger schools with multiple sections. On the other hand, it is plausible to assume that schools run by democratic community associations would prefer to hire someone from within the community. Such a local director or teacher would have closer knowledge of the problems and opportunities facing the community, and one can posit that such a director would have a greater stake in the success or failure of the school. Yet, one finds that there is practically no difference between the two groups of schools in the location of residence of the director. Again, given the strong and creditable emphasis that the Salvadorean authorities put on training, one would have expected to find that EDUCO directors would have sought and obtained more training, especially as they are younger and more inexperienced.

Table 6.1 Comparison of school directors

Variable	Type of school	
	EDUCO	Traditional rural
Age of director*	31.4 years	40 years
Experience of director*	3.3 years	8.2 years
Director also teaches class*	100%	71%
Director is female	48.2%	41.7%
Director lives in community	20.4%	16.5%
Training in previous year	2.9 modules	3.2 modules

Note: * Indicates statistically significant difference.

The comparison of observable characteristics of directors indicates that increased flexibility of the community in appointing directors has not automatically led to better directors being chosen, at least on key observable characteristics. School directors who live outside the community face long commuting times from their residence to the school, and their involvement with the community would be restricted to their official hours of duty. Training opportunities for directors from EDUCO schools need to be increased if directors are expected to be more effective, and incentives should be made available for directors to avail themselves of existing training opportunities. Community associations need greater assistance from the central ministry for providing relevant training to directors as well as the provision of incentives which encourage local residence.

3.2 School infrastructure

The cross-sectional view presented in Table 6.2 is a 'snapshot' of infrastructure in 1998, many years after the beginning of the EDUCO programme. Table 6.2 provides evidence of the fact that the EDUCO programme has been successful in targeting the poorest rural communities. The fact that fewer EDUCO schools had electricity and that none had a telephone are only two of the signals about the type of communities that have EDUCO schools. Although figures from earlier years are not presented here, there has been an increase in the number of EDUCO schools that now have school buildings of their own, which bodes well for the future of the programme. The last item on the table, 'School is clean', is based upon the observation of trained interviewers who visited the sampled schools to collect data. Even though the variable is a subjective measure of school cleanliness, the magnitude of personal bias is reduced by the fact that the same interviewers visited both EDUCO and traditional schools.

One of the criticisms of decentralization is the potential for it to exacerbate existing inequality. In the educational sector, it is commonly held that giving local communities complete freedom to invest their own resources in schooling leads to richer communities investing more and poorer communities

Table 6.2 Comparison of school infrastructure

Variable	Type of school	
	EDUCO (%)	Traditional rural (%)
School is electrified*	39	85
School has telephone*	None	8
School is in MOE building*	69	84
All students have desks	63	63
School is clean*	31	22

Note: * Indicates statistically significant difference.

investing less, thus undermining the key equalizing objective of free public education. While such a criticism is often valid, in the case of El Salvador, the data shows that the EDUCO programme is indeed targeted towards very poor rural communities. A more valid criticism of the EDUCO programme relates to the defence often put forward by proponents of the programme to justify poor school performance – the poverty of communities that have EDUCO schools. It is of interest to note that EDUCO schools have been able to overcome these disadvantages when it comes to the provision of basic infrastructural inputs. Even though the community associations that run the schools cannot make electricity available to their schools, the ACEs have been effective in improving conditions under their control, such as the availability of desks and school cleanliness, a finding that is reinforced in the following subsection.

3.3 Didactic materials

Table 6.3 indicates the absence of dramatic differences in the quantity of didactic materials available for the use of students from the two groups of schools. EDUCO communities are poor – as shown by the data on electrification, provision of drinking water and sewerage. In context of such poverty, the parity in the availability of didactic materials shows the clear advantage of parental management. It is interesting to note again the presence of qualitative differences in the provision of didactic materials. More EDUCO schools have libraries for third grade students, and the libraries are better stocked in terms of the variety of materials. Since very few households of EDUCO students would be wealthy enough to own extra reading material for children, it is also helpful to such students to be allowed to take books home,

Table 6.3 Comparison of didactic materials

Variable	Type of school	
	EDUCO (%)	Traditional rural (%)
Less than 1/2 students have language textbooks	33	38
Less than 1/2 students have mathematics textbooks	42	41
Maps in classroom	56	57
Charts in classroom	58	61
Globe in classroom	35	38
Library*	48[†]	35
Texts allowed to be taken home*	52	40

[†] EDUCO school libraries had a richer variety of books, with more magazines, reference books and encyclopaedias.
* Indicates statistically significant difference.

which is often a problem in centralized systems where teachers are held accountable for the upkeep of the stock of books in the school's possession.

3.4 Teacher empowerment and professional development

In a recent study of student achievement with a very high quality longitudinal data set with value added test scores, Eric Hanushek has written about the importance of teachers in driving gains in student achievement.[7] The literature borrows from evidence in the field of management and organizational design that shows that empowering front-line workers is a key to improved educational quality. Teacher empowerment was measured in this study through a set of two questions about a series of administrative and pedagogic decisions in which teachers may have a role to play. The first question asked teachers for their perception of the *locus of decision-making*. For each decision, such as the setting of school goals and determining student–teacher ratios, the sampled teachers were asked their opinion about the level at which the decision was made – the options being: (a) at the head office of the Ministry of Education; (b) the provincial directorate; or (c) at the school level. A follow up question asked teachers about the *influence that they could bring to bear on the decision*, regardless of the administrative level at which the decision was made – with choices ranging from 'Much influence' to 'No influence at all'.

This study found the peculiar result that the traditional school teachers were more likely to think that decisions were taken at the school level, whereas, by the very articles of association of the ACE, it would seem that EDUCO teachers would think this way. For instance, 74 per cent of EDUCO teachers thought that school goals were set at the school, compared with 87 per cent of traditional school teachers. Similarly, 56 per cent of EDUCO teachers had the opinion that student–teacher ratios were set at the school level, compared with 70 per cent for traditional school teachers. It is important to note that only 7 per cent of EDUCO teachers thought that teacher-training decisions are taken at the school level, similar to 6 per cent of traditional school teachers.

However, EDUCO teachers were more likely to think that they personally had much influence in decision-making. This finding was particularly acute in the case of deciding what mix of didactic materials to use (81 per cent of EDUCO teachers ascribed 'much influence' to themselves in this decision, compared with 55 per cent of traditional school teachers). Teachers from both groups of schools did not think that they were empowered in decisions about their own training (19 per cent for EDUCO and 12 per cent for traditional schools reported 'much influence' for this decision.)

Training of teachers is one crucially important educational input where localized school management has not had much impact on student scores. This finding is not merely an artifact of the particular way that the empowerment question was asked. Teachers were also asked to list the areas in which they had received professional training in the previous year, and the results shown in the Table 6.4 are illustrative of the generally low levels of training.

With clear deficiencies in the professional development programme, it is perhaps not surprising to observe that EDUCO teachers are not doing better when it comes to 'active' teaching practices, such as assigning project work for students and using group writing exercises, as shown in Table 6.5. Interestingly, EDUCO teachers seem to rely less on the outmoded teaching practice of students having to read aloud from their texts.

The findings regarding teacher professional development and teaching practices are central to a key hypothesis made in this chapter – decentralization and participation have important benefits in certain areas, but these tools do not have a major impact in other critical areas of service delivery. EDUCO school teachers, the front-line workers in this industry, have clear advantages in terms of higher levels of parental support and potentially have greater flexibility in arranging their work, but the data indicates that the teachers do not feel empowered to turn in the expected performance. In a finding that reflects their greater youth and inexperience, as well as their lack of job stability, compared with traditional school teachers, EDUCO teachers actually feel that they have less influence in deciding about school goals and the optimal number of students in their class. EDUCO teachers know for a fact that they are accountable to the local community for their performance in the job and, at the same time, they are saddled with the realization that the same community is powerless to provide access to the training that they need in order to provide a good performance.

There is an unambiguous policy implication of the findings regarding teachers and educational inputs more generally. If the decentralized model

Table 6.4 Comparison of teacher professional development

Variable	Type of school	
	EDUCO (%)	Traditional rural (%)
Formation of values	20	23
School–community relationships	6	14
School nutrition	33	35

Table 6.5 Comparison of teaching practices

Variable	Type of school	
	EDUCO (%)	Traditional rural (%)
Project work	13	15
Writing exercises	45	47
Reading aloud	51	63

of service delivery is to lead to improvement in the quality of education, a greater effort should be made to include the needs and aspirations of teachers in the delivery of the educational programme. Decisions about 'how much paper to buy *vs.* how much chalk' may well be important but, for school quality to improve, teachers need to be involved in more important decisions, such as the design of the curriculum and how many students can be taught effectively in a classroom. The evidence indicates that EDUCO teachers will not be able to provide a better education unless they get more and better training, especially training that provides them with the tools to handle specific contexts, such as teaching children from poorer communities.

4. Educational outcomes

We now turn to a discussion of educational outcomes. Three sets of outcomes are considered in this section of the chapter.

4.1 Efficiency related outcomes

Problems of internal efficiency plague educational systems in Latin America and other parts of the developing world. The roots of the problem of efficiency lie in high rates of student absenteeism and grade repetition. Consequently, over-age students clog up the flow of students through the grades. Higher repetition leads to higher drop-out rates and lead to excessive duration in school to get to school completion.

Community associations such as the ACEs in El Salvador are uniquely placed to help resolve the problem of inefficiency: owing to their proximity to the school, it is easier for ACE members to monitor the intensity of teacher effort. If ACEs have good working relationships with teachers, as is found in most cases, EDUCO teachers can expect greater cooperation from parents in sending their children to school. Some efficiency indicators available from the comparison of EDUCO and traditional rural schools are shown in Table 6.6. The table presents a somewhat counter-intuitive finding regarding measures of efficiency. Rather than performing better compared with traditional schools, EDUCO schools appear to be doing worse. Students from EDUCO schools repeat grades at a rate twice as high as traditional rural

Table 6.6 Comparison of absenteeism and repetition

Variable	Type of school	
	EDUCO	Traditional rural
Rate of repetition	10.91%	4.91%
Student absenteeism	18.8%	22.9%
Teacher absenteeism	5.3 days/year	3.2 days/year

schools. Similar findings can be seen regarding absenteeism, although the magnitude of the difference is smaller. A probable explanation can be the existence of confounding factors other than type of school management. Even though we have reduced the existence of these confounding factors by focusing the comparison of EDUCO schools with only *rural* traditional schools, we have not been able to control for other measures of the socioeconomic background of students. Higher repetition could be due to relatively more children from poor families in EDUCO schools. Low nutrition and low readiness for learning associated with poverty would lead to poor children having problems at school which are unrelated to the type of school management. Table 6.6 does not present counter-factual evidence of what absenteeism would have been in EDUCO schools under traditional management. Such evidence would require an experiment with a control and test group. While it is not feasible to implement an experimental design, some patters can be recovered from simple econometric tools, such as multivariate regression analysis. Further research, including an accounting for confounding factors that lead to inefficiency, would shed more light on the subject.

4.2 Formation of values

The formation of values is seen as an important goal of public education in El Salvador, and the government has tried a number of innovations to encourage children to learn individual, civic and social values in school. In the current study, teachers were asked a question about the values they thought were of primary importance for teachers to inculcate. It is interesting to note the presence of some difference between the two groups of schools in this regard: EDUCO teachers were more likely to stress the value of friendship (*amistad*), whereas traditional teachers were more likely to stress the value of respect (*respeto*). 15 per cent of EDUCO teachers cited *amistad* as the primary value, compared with 6 per cent for traditional school teachers. Likewise, 18 per cent of EDUCO teachers mentioned *respeto*, compared with 38 per cent for traditional school teachers.

There is some evidence to suggest that EDUCO teachers were more concerned than traditional school teachers with the inculcation of values. 16 per cent of EDUCO teachers reported organizing school campaigns to promote values, and 18 per cent of EDUCO teachers said that they organized festivals around the theme of values. (The corresponding percentages for traditional school teachers were 12 per cent and 5 per cent.) However, both types of teachers, in roughly equal proportion, complained about the lack of both time and training in the task of imparting values. The 'true spirit of community' that is found in EDUCO schools makes for a fertile breeding ground for the formation of values, especially civic values regarding an individual's responsibility to the community. Training for teachers about how to integrate values into the curriculum, and follow up evaluations of the effect on children's attitudes and practices, would be very useful to capitalize on existing advantages in EDUCO schools. The formation of values is another area where policy intervention from the central level would be required to realize the benefits of decentralization.

4.3 Learning achievement scores

As part of the evaluation of the EDUCO programme, an achievement test was administered in 1998 to third grade students from both traditional schools as well as EDUCO schools. Learning achievement was measured according to the number of curricular content goals achieved by the student out of a possible maximum of 10, for each of the two subject areas of Language and Mathematics. Figures 6.1 and 6.2 indicate the average learning achievement scores of students. The figures show that EDUCO schools had slightly inferior results compared with traditional rural schools, but the differences are statistically insignificant. Proponents of the EDUCO programme hold that the absence of superior academic achievement of EDUCO schools should not be construed as a criticism of the EDUCO model because of the disadvantaged backgrounds of EDUCO students. One method to test this hypothesis is to run a regression model of test scores on a set of school and family background variables. This 'production function' model is a popular econometric tool used to uncover the possible impact of educational inputs used in the 'production' of test scores.[8]

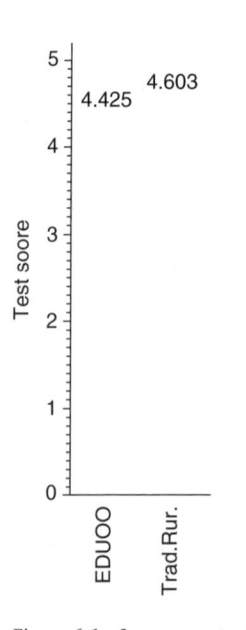

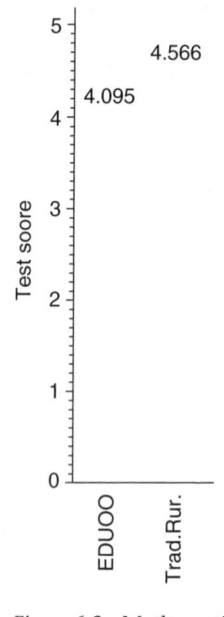

Figure 6.1 Language test score

Figure 6.2 Mathematics test score

Table 6.7 reports the results of the regression of test scores for 643 students from both EDUCO and traditional schools. Among the variables used to explain test scores, the regression specification uses a 'dummy' variable for EDUCO. The EDUCO dummy variable takes on a value of 1 if the student is attending an EDUCO school and 0 if the student is attending a traditional school. A positive coefficient on the EDUCO dummy would indicate that if the student attends an EDUCO school, he or she would get a positive benefit in terms of academic achievement. Conversely, a negative coefficient would indicate that being in an EDUCO school has a harmful effect on test scores. Since the multivariate regression includes other school and family background variables, the coefficient on the EDUCO dummy is an 'independent' EDUCO effect, controlling for the other explanatory variables.

After controlling for a set of school and family background variables, the EDUCO dummy has a positive coefficient. The regression results can be interpreted as a comparison of a pair of hypothetical EDUCO and traditional school students with identical family backgrounds (or characteristics such as father's schooling and durables owned) and identical school inputs (such as the available infrastructure and teaching materials). Such a comparison yields the finding that on average the student attending an EDUCO school would show better academic achievement. The explanatory power of the regression is low, which reflects the large variance in explanatory variables associated with the same level of academic achievement. Two statistically significant school infrastructure variables are the presence of electricity and sanitation facilities. While not directly related to the pedagogical process, the two variables proxy for the relative wealth of the school and the community in which the school is located. The negative coefficient on the presence of a

Table 6.7 Educational production function (OLS) (dependent variable: language score)

Variable	Coefficient	Std error	p for H_0 of 0
Constant	4.7459	0.4460	0.0001
Experience of director	0.0085	0.0157	0.5860
Director also teaches	−0.8663	0.2551	0.0007
Training of director	−0.0294	0.0380	0.4401
School is electrified	0.4936	0.2386	0.0389
School lacks sanitation	−0.5001	0.2211	0.0239
All students have desks	−0.1834	0.1947	0.3466
Classroom has maps	0.2813	0.1975	0.1548
No. of books in library	0.0000	0.0015	0.9642
Training of teacher	0.0291	0.0438	0.5066
Father's schooling	0.0336	0.0302	0.2663
Number of durables owned	0.0405	0.0424	0.3396
Family education expenses	0.0000	0.0001	0.5296
Dummy for EDUCO	0.4555	0.2398	0.0579

$N = 643 \quad R^2 = 0.0655$

director who also works as a classroom teacher is also a more general reflection of the fact that such a school would be smaller and located in a more remote and relatively less thickly populated area. The absence of statistical significance of variables, which would seem *a priori* to be important, can be explained by the fact that all rural schools in El Salvador, whether traditional or EDUCO schools, suffer similar conditions of poverty, low education of parents and low quality of critical educational inputs, such as teacher training. The results show that the EDUCO model does have some positive impact on children's learning, but that the favourable influence is constrained by the more general weakness of poor quality of educational inputs.

5. Conclusions

This chapter set out to answer the question of whether a decentralized mode of service delivery in an educational system, as represented by the EDUCO model in El Salvador, led to measurable differences in the quality of the schooling experience. The balance of the evidence suggests that the EDUCO model has been successful in certain aspects. Looking first at educational inputs, we found that even though the quantitative provision of basic inputs is much the same under the EDUCO model, there are *qualitative* effects, such as in EDUCO schools being neater, EDUCO libraries having better variety of books, and children being allowed to take books to their home. On the side of outcomes, we found the presence of subtle differences in the weight attached by community managed schools on the *formation of values*. The production function analysis of test scores supports the hypothesis that any positive impact of the decentralized mode of service delivery is swamped by a more general problem of the poor quality of educational inputs. In particular, the analysis of teacher empowerment and training indicates that key *deficiencies in the educational programme* have not been resolved with decentralization. Greater authority of the community in running schools has had a positive impact but, for this authority to be truly effective, more attention needs to be paid to upgrading the quality of educational inputs available to the community.

Notes

* The views expressed in his chapter are the author's personal views, and not to be attributed to the World Bank.
1. Fiske (1996); Burki *et al.* (1999); CEPAL (1999).
2. Detailed background information about the data set can be obtained from the World Bank, February, 1999.
3. The word 'technology' is used here in the economic sense, meaning the arrangement of a given set of educational inputs put together to produce an educational outcome, here taken to mean the production of the academic achievement of students.

4. The cost per student for traditional schools in about $75 per year and, for EDUCO schools, about $81 per year. The difference in costs of $6 per year is the additional cost for training of parents (which does not include the opportunity costs of parents' time, estimated annually to be a further $4 per student). Of about 1.2 million students in the basic education system, approximately 540 000 were enrolled in rural schools in 1998. The enrolment in EDUCO schools contributes nearly 200 000 to the total rural enrolment.
5. World Bank (1994).
6. The ACE is the key administrative unit that runs an EDUCO school. An ACE has five members: president, vice-president, secretary, treasurer and spokesperson. Members are elected for two-year terms by the community, either through a show of hands at a general assembly meeting, or through secret balloting. The process of selection appears to be genuinely democratic – there has not been any evidence of the elections being manipulated. Genuine participation is engendered because ACE members bear a twin burden of substantial responsibilities and commitment of time, which potentially outweighs any narrow political benefits of ACE membership. Further, the larger parent community continues to bring influence on the ACE members through monthly general assembly meetings of parents.
7. Hanushek et al. (1998). The authors find that teacher quality is the key factor explaining differences in the academic achievement of students. A number of other authors have highlighted the importance of teacher empowerment, teacher professional development, and incentive mechanisms linked to classroom practices. For instance, see Murnane and Levy (1996).
8. See Hanushek (1995: 227–46) for an overview of the literature of education production functions for developing countries.

Bibliography

Burki, S.J., Perry, G. and Dillinger, W., *Beyond the Center: Decentralizing the State*, Latin American and Caribbean Studies, World Bank, Washington, D.C., 1999.

Comisión Ecónomica para Americá Latina y el Caribe (CEPAL), *Descentralización de la Educación en America Latina: Un Análisis Comparativo*, Santiago, Chile, 1999.

Fiske, E.B., *Decentralization of Education: Politics and Consensus*, Directions in Development Series, World Bank, Washington, D.C., 1996.

Hanushek, E.A., 'Interpreting Recent Research on Schooling in Developing Countries', *World Bank Research Observer*, 10: 227–46, August 1995.

Hanushek, E.A., Kain, J.F. and Rivkin, S., *Teachers, Schools, and Academic Achievement*, NBER Working Paper No. 6691, National Bureau of Economic Research, Cambridge, USA, 1998.

Murane, R. and Levy, F., *Teaching the New Basic Skills*, Free Press, New York, 1996.

World Bank, *El Salvador Community Education Strategy: Decentralized School Management*, Report No. 13502-ES, World Bank, 1994.

World Bank, *Impact Evaluation of Education Reforms: El Salvador Case Basic Information*, Development Research Group, World Bank, 1999.

Part 3
Health Sector Reforms

7
Health Insurance Reforms in Latin America: Cream Skimming, Equity and Cost-Containment

Armando Barrientos and Peter Lloyd-Sherlock

Recent social insurance reforms in Latin America aimed at enlarging the scope for private sector involvement have produced structural changes in the provision and financing of health care. Private provision of health care is already long established in the region for middle to high income groups. The changes in health care financing go further, and represent a radical departure from traditional social insurance models of protection towards establishing health insurance markets. The aim of this chapter is to consider the implications of these changes in health care financing for health care access, demand and costs.

The health care reforms encourage the expansion of for-profits health insurance providers, which collect payroll contributions (both compulsory and voluntary), and insure individuals against specified health risks. Individuals have a choice of insurer and can negotiate their health plans with them. In Chile, health reforms in the early 1980s set up the *Institutos de Salud Previsional* (ISAPRE), offering health insurance on an individual or group basis, in competition with the *Fondo Nacional de Salud* (FONASA), the social health insurance fund. In Argentina, successive reforms in the 1990s have opened up the union-run *Obras Sociales* (OS), hitherto monopolistic health insurance schemes for specific groups of workers, to competition from each other and from private health insurance firms. In Colombia, reforms legislated in 1993, but implemented in 1995, established the *Entidades de Promoción de Salud* (EPS) providing health insurance plans on a competitive basis. Some EPS are newly formed for-profits private insurance providers, while others have developed out of restructured social insurance funds.

The problems inherent in health insurance markets are well documented.[1] Insurance markets generate incentives for the insured to over-demand health care, and for insurers to select groups with lower than average health risks. In Latin America, issues of governance, weak rule enforcement, and large income inequalities, present additional problems for health insurance markets. Chile, Argentina and Colombia provide contrasting experiences of health reform in the region, and demonstrate a 'learning process' in programme design.[2] The reform in Chile did not, for example, include a mechanism to curb risk-selection by health insurance firms. In Argentina, a solidarity fund will be adapted to reduce the incentives for risk-selection. Policy-makers in Colombia have sought to correct this problem by explicitly including a mechanism for 'risk adjustment'. Comparing health reform in these three countries helps to extract lessons for the region as a whole.

The chapter consists of three sections. The next section outlines the main features of health insurance reform in Chile, Argentina and Colombia. The following section considers the key problems associated with the implementation and operation of the new health insurance markets. The final section focuses on the implications of health insurance reform for risk selection, equity and the cost containment of health expenditures.

Reform of health insurance in Chile, Argentina and Colombia

There are many common elements in the development of health care financing and provision in Latin America, and in the basic features of health reforms. These are briefly noted below, before turning to the specific features of the reforms implemented in the three countries examined.

Social insurance provided the initial model of health insurance in Latin America (Mesa-Lago, 1991), developing in a piecemeal fashion, covering specific groups of workers and contingencies. Initially, schemes covered work incapacity risks, such as sickness or disability and old age, but later on insurance against health care expenditures was gradually added. In the main, social health insurance funds did not provide care themselves, but purchased it from private or public health care providers. The rich, who accessed private health care on an out-of-pocket basis, provided a further stimulus to the development of private health care. The poor and the uninsured relied on public health care services, with access to health care limited in scope, and usually of lower quality.

The financing of health care systems in Latin America shows three separate components: a public health care sector financed out of general taxation, a social insurance sector financed out of payroll contributions, and a fully private health care sector financed from out-of-pocket payments. Health insurance was therefore available only to urban formal sector workers through social insurance. The majority of the population in rural areas, and the informal sector in urban areas remained uninsured. Health care provision, on the other hand, included a public and a private sector.

The health reforms in Latin America have in common the objective of extending private provision in health insurance, by enabling for-profit health insurers to compete for affiliates with health insurance. The full package of reforms also covers the restructuring of social insurance institutions to facilitate their participation as providers in the new health insurance market. They also include a restructuring of public health care provision. The reforms aim to separate purchase from provision, to restrict the public health sector to a provider role, and to promote decentralization to health care units. These changes facilitate different combinations of financing and provision across the private and public sectors. Table 7.1 summarizes the key features of health reforms in Chile, as well as Argentina, and Colombia.

Table 7.1 Key features of health care reforms in Chile, Argentina and Colombia

	Chile	Argentina	Colombia
Date and scope of health insurance reform	1981–86 free of affiliation and private health insurers	1991–98 basic health care package, free choice of affiliation, and private health insurers	1993 (start 1995) basic health care package, free choice of affiliation, and private health insurers
Health insurers	*Institutos de Salud Previsional* (ISAPRE)	*Obras Sociales* (OS) and private health insurers	*Entidades Promotoras de Salud*
Purchaser-provider	Mainly purchaser, but some own provision	Mainly purchasers	Mainly purchasers
Financing of health insurance	7% of earnings to either ISAPREs or the public health insurer FONASA	8% of earnings (employees 3% and employers 5%)	12% of earnings (employees 4% and employers 8%)
Financing of public health care	From FONASA contributions and general taxation (35% and 65% respectively in 1996)	From general taxation	From general taxation
Health risks covered:			
Private health insurance	Basic package plus additional risks individually negotiated	Basic package plus additional risks individually negotiated	Basic package plus additional risks individually negotiated
Public health care	All subject to budget limits	All subject to budget limits	All subject to budget limits
Population covered by social insurance before reforms	73% (1980)	57% (1991)	16% (1985)

Table 7.1 (Cont.)

	Chile	Argentina	Colombia
Share of population covered by each component:	(1996)	(1991)	(1997)
Social insurance	65%	57% (17% also have private insurance)	38.5% (of which over half are subsidized)
Private	25%	5% (only private)	16.5
Other	5% (armed forces and police)		
Non-insured	5%	38%	45%
Administrative costs:			
Public	1.8% of expenditure		
Private	18% of expenditure		
Redistribution	Earnings related contributions, plus FONASA progressivity through co-payments	Earnings related contributions, plus *Fondo Solidario de Redistribución* (*Obras Sociales*)	Earnings related contributions and co-payments, plus 1% of earnings to *Fondo de Solidaridad y Garantía*
Risk adjustment	No	Partial through the *Fondo Solidario de Redistribución*	1% of earnings plus redistribution of excess of contributions over the per capita premium

Note: Compiled from various sources (CIEDESS, 1994; FEDESARROLLO, 1996; Panadeiros, 1996; Medici et al., 1997; IADB, 1996; Larrañaga, 1998; Bertranou, 1999; Yepes, 2000).

Reform of health provision and financing began to be implemented in Chile in the early 1980s, as part of a broader structural reform (Miranda, 1994; Miranda et al., 1995; Larrañaga, 1998). Its main objectives were to expand the role of the private sector in provision and financing, and to improve resource allocation and decentralization within the publicly funded sector. The first set of reforms extended the option to use private providers initially restricted to white-collar workers, to blue-collar workers. At the same time it decentralized the National Health Service (*Servicio Nacional de Salud*) into 27 areas, and transformed health care providers, hospitals and clinics, into self-managed units. This reorganization of public provision prepared the ground for the introduction of private insurers, the ISAPREs, which began operating in 1981. Affiliates were given the option of leaving the social insurance system and arranging private insurance from the ISAPREs. This created two parallel sectors for financing and provision.

Legislation implemented at the beginning of 1986 consolidated the new system. It eliminated remaining differences in provision for white- and blue-collar workers by setting up a uniform compulsory health insurance contribution of 7 per cent of earnings. FONASA was established to collect contributions from those affiliated to the public sector, and to allocate these resources to providers. Responsibility for provision for non-contributing employees and for inactives remained within the public sector (Miranda, 1989). In the absence of any 'risk-adjustment' mechanism, the ISAPREs focused their efforts on seeking out and recruiting high income workers. These are more likely to yield profits as they pay high premiums and are a better health risk. In 1990 a new *Superintendencia de ISAPRE* was created to monitor and regulate private health insurers.

In Argentina, the reform of social insurance began a decade later than in Chile, and the main goal has been to introduce competition. Health insurance in Argentina has traditionally been fragmented (Katz and Muñoz, 1988; Belmartino, 1991). First, there were over 300 OSs operating in 1990. Most of these were administered by unions and had monopolistic rights over demarcated sectors of the labour force, as entitlement to chose which OS they affiliated to was not open to workers. Secondly, there was a separate fund for elderly people: the *Programa de Atención Médica Integral* (PAMI). This fund is financed through a separate wage tax and offers a relatively generous range of services to all insured people aged 60 or over and, in theory, non-insured aged 70 or over (Lloyd-Sherlock, 1998). Thirdly, a private health insurance sector emerged in Argentina during the late 1980s consisting of for-profit and not-for-profit insurance providers (*Pre-pagas* and *Mutuales*). These offered voluntary schemes mainly for high income groups, supplementing the cover they were obliged to take with OSs. Private insurers varied in terms of size and the degree to which they relied on third party providers. *Pre-pagas* in particular were criticized for high operating costs and a lack of transparency (World Bank, 1993). An overriding characteristic of health insurance in Argentina was the virtual absence of government regulation.

The reforms have been introduced in a series of steps. They began with measures designed to liberalize and clarify contract negotiations between union insurance funds and private providers. Legislation enacted in 1991 and 1993 gave funds greater freedom to negotiate contracts with health care providers (Panadeiros, 1996; Bour, 1997; Belmartino and Bloch, 1998). In November 1996 the government defined a basic package of services, the *Programa Mínimo Obligatorio de Atención Médica*, with an estimated cost of US$40 per person per month, which all funds are obliged to provide. Workers affiliated to OSs whose health insurance contributions are below this minimum will be subsidized from the *Fondo Solidario de Redistribución*. The OSs have been registered and consolidated. A new *Superintendencia de Servicios de Salud*, was set up, entrusted with the regulation and supervision of the reformed OSs. From January 1998 insurance affiliates were given the right to select their funds.[3]

Before the reforms, health insurance in Colombia was provided by a large number of social insurance funds. The two largest were the *Caja Nacional de*

Previsión Social (CAJANAL), providing pensions and health insurance for public sector workers, and the *Instituto Colombiano de Seguros Sociales* (ICSS) for private sector workers. But smaller funds proliferated. In 1991 official estimates put the total number of public sector funds at over 1000. Despite this plethora of funds, coverage was much lower than in Chile or Argentina (Table 7.1). Neither CAJANAL nor the ICSS offered health insurance to the dependants of affiliates: these were covered through a separate scheme managed by 47 *Cajas de Compensación Familiar*.

The reforms to the Colombian health care system began in 1990 with legislation aimed at decentralizing the public health care sector, and transferring to the municipalities and departments responsibility for primary, and for secondary and tertiary health care respectively. The main reform of health insurance followed the passing of Laws 60 and 100 in 1993, and was implemented in January 1995.

The new health insurance scheme, the *Sistema de Seguridad Social en Salud* has two components: a Contributory Regime for dependent workers in formal sector employment, and for the self-employed with earnings greater than twice the minimum wage; and a Subsidized Regime for the poor. In the Contributory Regime, workers contribute 12 per cent of their earnings (8 per cent of earnings is paid by the employer and 4 per cent of earnings by the employee) to a health insurance plan with one of the EPSs. Contributors can negotiate a plan over and above the basic health care package (the *Plan Obligatorio de Salud*, POS), can choose the insurer, and have the option of transferring once a year. They are required to make a co-payment when demanding health care. In fact, the legislation provides for the level of copayment to be a prime competitive tool for EPSs. The Subsidized Regime subsidizes affiliation to a health insurance provider for low income households, who also make means-tested co-payments when they access health care. Some not-for-profit health insurance providers (the *Administradoras del Régimen Subsidiado*) focus exclusively on these groups. The subsidies are financed from a variety of government funds and taxes, and from a solidarity contribution of one per cent of earnings from those affiliated to the Contributory Regime (only Colombia has an earmarked solidarity contribution). A more limited health care package is initially offered to this group, although it is intended that it will expand to the same cover as that for the Contributory Regime. The remaining uninsured groups have access to free health care from public health care providers.

In the Contributory Regime, the EPSs are not permitted to exclude applicants on the basis of pre-existing health conditions. In addition, a 'risk adjustment' mechanism has been included in the form of a per capita premium, the *Unidad de Pago por Capitación* (UPC), which is set on an annual basis.[4] Insurers must pay any excess of workers' contributions over the per capita premium into a *Fondo de Solidaridad y Garantía*, or withdraw funds from it in the event of a shortfall. This 'risk adjustment' aims to reduce the incentives of EPSs to seek out good health risks. By the same token, it provides contributors with incentives to under-report their earnings for contribution purposes. A *Superintendencia Nacional de Salud* is in charge of regulating and monitoring the health insurance market.

The health insurance reforms in the three countries reviewed here share a common purpose in seeking to create markets by extending the role of individual insurance and the scope of private provision. Health insurance markets make strong demands upon the political process and representatives to ensure that the regulatory framework and insurance scheme design are right, and that the transition period until the new market is established goes smoothly. The next section examines these issues.

A health insurance market for Latin America?

The health insurance reforms in Latin America will need to overcome both the inherent problems of health insurance markets, and the administrative weaknesses and political conflicts present in the health sector in Latin America. These are discussed below.

Market failure and health reform

Health insurance plays an important role in reducing the adverse impact of ill health on household consumption. From the perspective of the individual household, and in the absence of tax-financed universal health care, health insurance turns unpredictable health expenditures into predictable insurance premiums (Mills, 1983; Chollet and Lewis, 1997). At the same time, the availability of insurance may produce undesirable responses from the insured and from insurers, which themselves undermine the sustainability of insurance markets. Full health insurance, which in effect eliminates the costs of health care, may result in excessive demand for care. For instance, it may result in demand for costly treatments with marginal benefits to patients. It also weakens the incentives of providers to economize in the use of resources, especially in the context of for-profit providers paid on fee-for-service terms.

Health insurance plans can incorporate design features that minimize these problems, but these design features add to the costs of insurance markets, and have themselves secondary effects. Co-payments (where the insured pays a fraction of health care costs at time of use) give the insured incentives to restrict demand for health care with marginal benefits, but they involve administration costs and may deter low income patients from seeking health care. Capitation fees (fixed payments to providers for each patient entitled to receive treatment from them) can restore providers' incentives for economizing on health interventions, but also generate incentives for under-provision. A possible mechanism for preventing under-provision is to set out a basic health care package, but such a move is likely to generate incentives among health care professionals to restrict this package as much as possible

(Medici *et al.*, 1997; Bertranou, 1999). Separating purchasers from providers helps reduce the power of health professionals, but only at the cost of creating large transaction costs and bureaucracy (as seen in pre-reform Argentina). Helping health insurance markets to work effectively involves trading off costly and imperfect solutions.

In Latin America, the need to extend provision to the uninsured, cater for the rural and urban poor, and reduce inequalities in access to health care, poses a further set of problems for the new health insurance markets. Labour market deregulation and global competition place severe restrictions on the expansion of insurance coverage in the region, as evidenced in the decline of secure formal employment (Barrientos, 1998). Rising earnings inequality pushes higher income workers towards private health care, thus further undermining the risk pooling of health insurance (FEDESARROLLO, 1996). While making health insurance payroll contributions compulsory for formal sector workers increases 'risk pooling', at the same time it raises the attraction of non-covered employment for low paid workers and their employers. Since a health insurance market is unlikely to expand coverage among vulnerable workers and the poor, public health care becomes *de facto* insurer of last resort, concentrating the bad health risks (Barrientos, 2000).

In sum, health insurance markets are unlikely to provide a solution for the problem of financing health care, and particularly so in the context of Latin America. Health insurance markets are likely to show important failures. These can be addressed with design features but only at significant administration and equity costs. The economic environment in Latin America, and health care needs, make health insurance markets less likely to be effective.

Government failure and health reform

Effective health insurance markets require a carefully designed and dynamic regulatory and supervisory framework. The experience of the three countries under examination raises a number of issues in this respect.

The design and implementation of health insurance reform in Chile took place in a context in which political checks and balances were largely absent. The ISAPREs received strong government support and subsidies, and operated largely unregulated. Numerous policy and regulatory changes in the early 1980s sought to facilitate the expansion of the ISAPREs. Initially, for example, the ISAPREs were responsible for providing maternity benefits for their affiliates, but concerns about the ISAPREs' exclusion of younger women led the government to take over responsibility for providing this benefit. The health insurance contribution rate rose from 4 to 7 per cent of earnings between 1983 and 1986.

After democracy was restored in 1990, the new government was committed instead to strengthening public health insurance and public health care provision catering for the majority of the population, and was less supportive of the ISAPREs. An official regulatory body, the *Superintendencia de ISAPRE*, was established in 1990, a decade after the reform, to supervise and regulate the ISAPREs, and there were large increases in financial resources to the public health sector. The government has removed public subsidies to lower paid workers who opted to affiliate to the ISAPREs.

In Argentina and Colombia, legislative scrutiny and the need to secure a measure of public support for the reforms, meant that more attention was paid to incorporating solidarity and private sector regulation objectives than was the case in Chile. Also, both countries had the opportunity to learn from the shortcomings of the Chilean reforms. At the same time, political instability, the influence of pressure groups, and administrative failings, have delayed and obfuscated the reform process in Argentina and Colombia, resulting in piecemeal modifications to the original design.

In Argentina the reform process can only be understood with reference to the wide range of sectional actors who had a potential stake in any change. These range from multinational lending institutions, different government departments, trade unions (not all of which took the same position), health professionals, drug companies and political parties. Since the 1940s, the *Obras Sociales* had represented a major patronage fund for many trade unions which increased potential political resistance to change. Gaining acceptance for the reform design took several years, and several different proposals were put forward by different groups. This level of debate would seem to suggest that the reform process was, at least outwardly, democratic and participatory. However, given a strong concentration of power in the executive and its alliance with a narrow range of interests (mainly from the private sector), the basic design of the reform was never in doubt. Resistance from unions was mainly countered with immediate financial incentives, rather than through substantial changes to the reform. The regulatory framework for health insurance providers is not yet fully in place; a *Superintendencia de Servicios de Salud* began operating in 1997, but so far only OSs are under its supervision. This gives private health insurers the best of both worlds as it weakens the monopolistic grip of the OSs, but leaves them outside sectoral regulation.

The reform process in Colombia was also the outcome of long debate. The implementation of the reform has continued to attract opposition from bodies representing health professionals, and from social insurance institutions, who feel they will be adversely affected by the reform. There has been strong opposition to the restructuring of the *Instituto Colombiano de Seguros Sociales*. The largest EPS, managed by the ICSS, began to participate in the 'risk-adjustment' mechanism only last year because of administrative problems with records and registration. And there has been continued opposition to the shift in the funding of public health care from its largely historic basis, to demand-side subsidies for affiliates. The expansion of coverage under the Subsidized Regime is under threat from budgetary restrictions, and from the slow shift in funding mode. The intermediation of the health insurance providers has been under intense scrutiny, and there is concern with the reduction in revenues experienced by public hospitals. In 1997 only 38 per cent of the Subsidized Regime's payments got back to public health care providers as payment for services, and the supervisory body has initiated financial checks on the relevant health insurers. There is also concern with evasion and avoidance of contributions. These issues make it unlikely that the goal of achieving universal health insurance coverage by 2002 will be met.

Regulatory and administrative structures, and durable political support, will be key factors in the evolution and success of health insurance reforms in Latin America. They are crucial to overcoming the inherent weaknesses of health insurance markets. The experience of these three countries raises concerns about whether the reforms will be successful in establishing effective health insurance markets.

The implications of health insurance reform for cost containment and equity

Health care expenditures and cost containment

An important question is whether the reform of health insurance in Chile, Argentina, and Colombia will be effective in containing costs. In Argentina health expenditures as a proportion of GDP were 7.2 per cent in 1995, as against a 7.9 per cent average for the OECD countries in 1990 (Oxley and MacFarlan, 1994). In Chile, reported health care expenditures as a proportion of GDP appear lower at 4.2 per cent in 1996, but this is mainly because over-the-counter pharmacy expenditures and co-payments are omitted. In Colombia health expenditures have been estimated at 10 per cent of GDP, although patterns of morbidity and mortality in this country have a special profile because of violence and criminality. It is not surprising therefore that concerns about containing health care costs have featured prominently in the reform of health insurance.

In Chile, where the reforms have had a longer run, private health expenditures as a proportion of GDP have risen from 0.38 per cent in 1985, to 1.27 per cent in 1990, to 1.77 per cent in 1996. By contrast, public health spending rose in the early 1990s, but has thereafter stagnated at around 2.4 per cent. Private health expenditures are driving the overall rise and the ISAPREs have not demonstrated effectiveness in containing costs (Barrientos, 2000). This is due to their marketing efforts focused on good health risk groups, and to the fact that they have not developed facilities of their own, and rely instead on a burgeoning private sector reimbursed on a fee-for-service basis. These practices ensure that cost containment incentives remain weak.

In Argentina, the impact of the reforms on cost containment is likely to be mixed. On the one hand, increased competition between the OSs would be expected to increase efficiency. The total number of OSs had fallen from 361 in 1994 to 290 in 1999, and those which disappeared tended to have smaller client bases and relatively high administration costs. However, the experiences of Chile and the USA prove that competition between insurers is not guaranteed to ensure cost containment, since price is rarely the prime consideration in consumer choice. The financial difficulties faced by many OSs have prompted them to shift away from fee-for-service to capitation payment mechanisms, which are widely viewed as more effective in controlling costs, but which may result, as noted above, in under-provision. However, most private insurers continue to use fee-for-service payments.

In Colombia, cost containment relies on the purchaser-provider roles of the EPSs and the health care providers, the *Instituciones Prestadoras de Salud*. These are at an early stage of development, and little information is as yet available. However, a number of potential obstacles can be identified. Many commentators have observed that purchasers and providers lack the administrative and managerial capacity to pursue meaningful negotiations.[5] Much of the information needed for this negotiation is missing, and the health ministry is involved in developing a sector-wide information system. This could provide the basic information in terms of affiliation, medical interventions, and cost accounting, which is needed to support the purchaser-provider roles. It will only be possible to fully evaluate the effectiveness of the new insurance market in containing costs once these structures are in place.

Preventing cream skimming

A feature of health insurance markets is that, for a given premium rate, competing insurers have incentives to select good health risk groups, that is, to 'cream skim'. This drives down their health care expenditures and increases their profits. As in Latin America health insurance contributions are earnings related, the insurers' incentives for cream skimming are even stronger. In an unregulated market, risk selection leads to rising marketing costs, the provision of lower benefit medical interventions, reduced coverage among the bad health risk groups, and rising inequality in access to health care. Health insurance design and the regulation of insurers can reduce the ability of the latter to select health risks. Creating insurance groups with a mixture of risks can prevent insurers from selecting groups ('community rating' or employer provided insurance). Alternatively, 'risk adjusting' can redistribute premiums from good risk to bad health risk groups.

In Chile, the introduction of ISAPREs was not buttressed by any design feature to preclude selection of health risks, except that insurers are not able to terminate health plans (although they are able to reassess premiums on an annual basis and raise them accordingly). As a consequence, the ISAPREs have focused their efforts on capturing good health risk groups with high earnings, and rejecting bad risk groups such as the elderly and poor. Their marketing strategy explains their high operational costs (see Table 7.1). In

1998 the ISAPREs covered 23 per cent of the population as a whole, but they covered 55.4 per cent of the top income quintile group, and only 4 per cent of the lowest income quintile group (MIDEPLAN, 1999).

In Argentina, a mechanism was established in 1970 to redistribute revenue from the richest OSs to the poorest ones, the *Fondo de Redistribución*. Ten per cent of health insurance contributions collected by the OSs were diverted to this fund, along with 50 per cent of voluntary contributions negotiated through collective bargaining. In practice, and because of shortcomings in the administration and management of the fund, the larger part of the fund has been used to cover deficits in OSs, and to support client groups (Panadeiros, 1996). It was criticized by the World Bank as operating according to a principle of 'reverse solidarity' (World Bank, 1987). As part of the recent reforms the *Fondo de Redistribución* is to be replaced by a *Fondo Solidario de Redistribución*. Instead of redistributing funds across OSs, the new fund will subsidize the health insurance contributions of low income workers to the level required to secure the basic PMO package. This is only a partial 'risk adjustment' as it applies only to the segment of workers with low contributions. Effectively, the fund reduces the incentives for OSs to discriminate against low income workers, but leaves intact the incentives to seek out the higher earnings groups. This is confirmed by the pattern of transfers across OSs allowed to date. Bertranou (1999) reports that the transfers, which occurred in 1997 and involved 5 per cent of contributors, involved mainly higher earnings workers leaving OSs with workers with below average earnings, indicating a risk selection process at work.

In Colombia, a mechanism for 'risk adjustment' involves the per capita premium and the *Fondo de Solidaridad y Garantía*. The latter redistributes one percentage point of health insurance contributions together with any excess of contributions over the per capita premium. This feature constitutes an improvement over the absence of a 'risk adjustment' mechanism in Chile, and the presence of a partial one in Argentina. The implementation of this 'risk adjustment' mechanism was initially delayed by the non-participation of the ICSS's EPS, but in 1998 the mechanism operated in full. The net balance of transfers of 'excess' contributions to the fund, and subsidies from the fund to those EPSs with a deficit of contributions relative to the per capita premium, was positive (Salud Colombia, 1999). It will be interesting to see whether the 'risk adjustment' mechanism is effective in reducing incentives for risk selection in the medium run.

Equity and health insurance

Health reforms in Chile have resulted in parallel health care financing and provision (Miranda 1989; Larrañaga 1998). The ISAPREs have concentrated on medium to high income affiliates, while FONASA has retained the low to middle income groups in the formal sector and informal sectors, as well as the uninsured and inactive groups such as the elderly (Barrientos, 2000).

This worsens inequalities in access to health care. It also precludes any complementarity between the public and private sectors. The failure by the private sector to provide health insurance cover for low income groups, and for old age related and catastrophic illnesses, concentrates bad health risk groups within FONASA, reinforcing service demand pressures on the publicly funded sector. Improved provision in the public sector directly undermines the ability of the ISAPREs to attract and retain affiliates. It is therefore unlikely that, under the current framework for providing and financing health care in Chile, the two parallel sectors could be successful at the same time. It is also unlikely that the ISAPREs could exist without FONASA.[6]

Argentina's pre-reform health care system showed large inequalities in access to health care both across the insurance and non-insurance sectors, as well as within them. As health insurance contributions are earnings related, the revenues of the OSs mirrored the earnings capacities of their respective occupational groups. In 1994, average revenue per beneficiary ranged from under US$5 a month in the poorest fund to over US$80 in the richest. Not surprisingly, those OSs with poorer affiliates provided markedly inferior benefits than richer ones, both in terms of quality and quantity. Also, poorer funds were forced to levy higher rates of co-payment.

The current reforms do little to reduce inequalities in health insurance and provision in Argentina. The transfers of workers across OSs will inevitably respond to cream-skimming marketing strategy, as well as to increased differentiation of health insurance packages and premia within OSs. The unpaid use of public sector services by insured groups is still widespread, although as hospitals became financially autonomous there will be a stronger incentive to recoup costs from insurance funds. As a result, public hospitals may seek to treat as many insured individuals as possible (to the detriment of the uninsured groups), since recovered costs are not usually deducted from their core budgets.

In Colombia, the reform of health insurance aimed to achieve universal population coverage. After the implementation of the reform, coverage increased from around 22 per cent of the population in 1994 to close to 53 per cent at the end of 1997, including 14.5 million (35.6 per cent) in the Contributory Regime, and 7 million (17.2 per cent) in the Subsidized Regime. The large rise in coverage after the reform is explained by the extension of coverage to affiliates' dependants, who were not covered in the old scheme, and the introduction of the Subsidized Regime extending coverage to previously uninsured low income groups. Further rise in coverage will depend on the expansion of the Subsidized Regime but, as noted above, there are indications that this is unlikely. Over one half of the labour force works in the informal sector, and there is also concern that coverage of the population living in low density areas of the country may be difficult to secure, given that the costs of providing health care there are much higher. Inequalities in access to health care associated with employment and region will continue. As regards the contingencies covered, the basic health insurance package, at present differentiated across scheme, is expected to have become uniform by 2001.

Conclusion

Remodelling the financing of health services is one of the major challenges for welfare reform in Latin America. The reforms adopted in Latin America pursue similar strategies, especially as regards the role allotted to private health insurers and the establishment of health insurance markets. The focus of this chapter has been to examine the experiences of health insurance reform in Chile, Argentina and Colombia, in terms of their key features, and of the difficulties inherent in creating markets in health insurance. The evolution of the health insurance reforms were evaluated, along with their impacts on cream-skimming, cost containment, and equity.

The principal conclusion is that the health insurance reforms in the three countries reviewed are unlikely to provide a satisfactory solution to the region's problem of financing health care. In particular, the reforms are unlikely to provide effective mechanisms for containing health care costs, to stem back rising inequality in access to health care, or to overcome the dysfunctional incentives present in health insurance markets. Moreover, health insurance markets will require effective and careful regulation to be sustainable in the medium to long run, as well as considerable resources to subsidize the poor and the uninsured, all of which will place demands on governments and policy-makers.

The reforms create opportunities for beneficial interactions across the public and private sectors. A three-sector health care system preceded the reform: a public health sector financed out of taxation, a private sector financed from out-of-pocket payments, and a social insurance sector financed from payroll contributions. In the reformed health care systems, there will be greater fluidity in combining private and public financing and provision. To the extent that private and public health insurers and providers complement each other, the reforms will have beneficial results. On the other hand, if public and private insurers and providers mutually undermine each other, the results will be deleterious. Securing a beneficial outcome will require effective regulation.

In Chile regulatory failures have encouraged cream skimming by the ISAPREs, leading to predictable concentrations of high income groups in the private insurance sector and vulnerable groups in the publicly funded one. The ISAPREs have few incentives to contain costs and have contributed disproportionately to rising health care spending in Chile. The reforms have led to a dualistic health care system, where the different sectors undermine rather than complement each other. In Argentina a partial risk adjustment mechanism has been introduced in the OSs sector, but private insurers remain entirely unregulated. As in Chile, the reforms have not sought to reduce segmentation, and are likely to lead to similar problems of cost containment and inter-sectoral conflict. The Colombian reform is, on paper at least, of a very different nature. It aspires to a new unitary health care system, where non-contributors can have access to the same providers as insured groups. This is made possible through extensive subsidies securing health insurance for poor and vulnerable groups, and the inclusion of a 'risk adjustment' mechanism precluding risk selection. The early signs are that these mechanisms are working as planned, although a further expansion of demand-side subsidies is doubtful, as is the managerial capacity of health insurance providers to act as effective buyers.

Hence, although the general contents of reforms in each country display many similarities, there are significant differences in basic principles. The paradox that Colombia, a country with low levels of insurance coverage and a weak tradition of redistributive policies, should be alone in adopting principles of universality and solidarity, requires some comment. The task of securing a universal unitary health insurance scheme would have been less costly (both politically and economically) in Argentina and Chile, where the majority of the population is already covered and where state institutions are relatively strong. It would seem therefore that both these countries have missed important opportunities for developing more progressive, unified systems, particularly during the first years of the Menem government in Argentina, and after the democratic restoration in Chile.

Notes

1. See (Abel-Smith, 1992; WHO, 1993; Besley and Gouveia, 1994). In fact, social insurance developed as a response to the deficiencies of private insurance markets (Beveridge, 1942).
2. Other studies comparing health reforms in these three countries include Bertranou (1999); and Medici et al. (1997).
3. From January 1998 private insurers were to be permitted to compete for these affiliates on an even footing, but implementation of this change has been postponed. This is in part because private insurers were not prepared to accept the new regulatory framework. The reluctance of private insurers was surprising, given the opportunities that the reform offered them. However, private insurers have been able to penetrate the protected social insurance sector without submitting to regulatory constraints. In a Trojan horse strategy known as 'triangulation', OSs started to contract out their administrative functions, and, in some cases, effectively served as fronts for private health insurers. A further incentive for private insurers to operate through OSs is the possibility of escaping a 22 per cent VAT levy on *Prepagas* introduced in early 1999. More recently, in November 2000, the Argentine government decreed that affiliates to *Obras Sociales* will be free to choose their health insurance provider from January 2001.
4. Different UPCs are set according to age, sex, and region. In 1995, the average UPC was set at around US$143 a year; this is larger than the estimated value of the POS

estimated at around US$120 in 1994 (La Forgia, 1998). The level of the UPC is a key regulatory variable and has been uprated in line with inflation in recent years.
5. Chile and Argentina are also engaged in developing appropriate information systems to support health reforms.
6. There is evidence that affiliates to the ISAPREs make use of public sector facilities to avoid insurance claims resulting in premium increases, or to seek treatment not covered by their insurance plan. A new computerized registration system has been introduced in the public sector to limit these practices (Economist Intelligence Unit, 1998).

Bibliography

Abel-Smith, B., 'Health insurance in developing countries: lessons from experience', in *Health Policy and Planning*, 7(3), 1992.
Barrientos, A., *Pension Reform in Latin America*, Ashgate, Aldershot, 1998.
Barrientos, A., 'Getting better after neo-liberalism: shifts and challenges of health policy in Chile', in P. Lloyd-Sherlock (ed.) *Healthcare Reform and Poverty in Latin America*, ILAS, London, 2000.
Belmartino, S., 'Fundamentos históricos de la construcción de relaciones de poder en el sector salud. Argentina 1940–1960', Pan American Health Organization, Washington D.C., 1991.
Belmartino, S. and Bloch, C., 'Desregulación/Privatización: la relación entre financiación y provisión de servicios de la reforma de la seguridad social médica en Argentina', in *Cuadernos Médicos Sociales*, 73, 61–79, 1998.
Bertranou, F., 'Are market-oriented health insurance reforms possible in Latin America? The cases of Argentina, Chile and Colombia', in *Health Policy*, 47, 19–36, 1999.
Besley, T. and Gouveia, M., 'Alternative systems of health care provision', in *Economic Policy*, 19, October, 200–58, 1994.
Beveridge, W., 'Social Insurance and Allied Services', Cmd. 5404, HMSO, London, 1942.
Bour, J.L., 'Reformas del Mercado de Trabajo en la Argentina en los '90', in CIEDLA (ed.) *Mercados Laborales en los '90*, CIEDLA, Buenos Aires, 1997.
Chollet, D.J. and Lewis, M., 'Private Insurance: Principles and Practice', in G.J. Schieber (ed.) *Innovations in Health Care Financing*, pp. 77–114, World Bank, Washington D.C., 1997.
CIEDESS, *Modernización de la Seguridad Social en Chile 1980–1993: Resultados y Tendencias*, Santiago, 1994.
Economist Intelligence Unit, 'Profile – state and private healthcare coverage in Chile', in *EIU Healthcare International*, 2nd quarter, 37–53, 1998.
FEDESARROLLO, *Las Formas de Contratación entre Prestadoras y Administradoras de Salud*, Fundación Social, Bogotá, 1996.
IADB, *Argentina: programa de modernización y reforma del sector salud*, Inter-American Development Bank, Washington D.C., 1998.
Katz, J. and Muñoz, A., *Organización del sector salud: puja distributiva y equidad*, Centro Editor de América Latina, Buenos Aires, 1988.
La Forgia, Gerard M., 'Health Sector Reform. A Financial Service Flow Model and the Colombian Case', in Cruz-Saco, M.A. and Mesa-Lago, C. (eds) *Do Options Exist? The Reform of Pension and Health Care Systems in Latin America*, University of Pittsburgh Press, Pittsburgh, 1998.
Larrañaga, O., 'Reforms of the Health Sector in Chile', mimeo, London, 1998.

Lloyd-Sherlock, P., 'Health care financing, reform and equity in Argentina: past and present', in P. Lloyd-Sherlock (ed.) *Sickening for change: health policy and equity in Latin America*, Institute of Latin American Studies, London, 1998.
Medici, A.C., Londoño, J.L., Coelho, O. and Saxenian, H., 'Managed Care and Managed Competition in Latin America and the Caribbean', in G.J. Schieber (ed.) *Innovations in Health Care Financing*, pp. 215–31, World Bank, Washington D.C., 1997.
Mesa-Lago, C., 'Social Security in Latin America and the Caribbean: A Comparative Assessment', in E. Ahmad, J. Dreze, J. Hills and A. Sen (eds), *Social Security in Developing Countries*, pp. 357–94, Clarendon Press, Oxford, 1991.
MIDEPLAN, 'Situación de la Salud en Chile', Documento 4, Ministerio de Planificación y Cooperación, Santiago, 1999.
Mills, A., 'Economic Aspects of Health Insurance', in K. Lee and A. Mills (eds), *The Economics of Health in Developing Countries*, Oxford University Press, Oxford, 1983.
Miranda, E., 'Desarrollo y Perspectivas del Sistema de ISAPRES', Documento Serie Investigación 94, Departamento de Economía, Universidad de Chile, Santiago, 1989.
Miranda, E., (ed.), *La Salud en Chile: Evolución y Perspectivas*, Centro de Estudios Públicos, Santiago, 1994.
Miranda, E., Scarpaci, J.L. and Irarrázaval, I. 'A decade of HMOs in Chile: market behaviour, consumer choice and the state', in *Health and Place*, 1(1), 51–9, 1995.
Oxley, H. and MacFarlan, M., 'Health Care Reform. Controlling Spending and Increasing Efficiency', Economics Department Working Paper 149, OECD, Paris, 1994.
Panadeiros, M. 'Organización del Seguro de Salud en la Argentina. Análisis y propuesta de reforma', in *Desarrollo Económico*, 36, Special Issue, 267–302, 1996.
Salud Colombia (1999), *Noticias. Salud Colombia*, Bogotá.
WHO, *Evaluation of recent changes in the financing of health services*, World Health Organization, Geneva, 1993.
World Bank, 'Argentina. Population, health and nutrition review', World Bank, Washington D.C., 1993.
Yepes, F., 'Health Reform and Equity in Colombia', in P. Lloyd-Sherlock (ed.) *Healthcare Reform and Poverty in Latin America*, ILAS, London, 2000.

8
Decentralization, Participation and Inclusion? Reassessing Primary Health Care Delivery in Chile

Jasmine Gideon[1]

Introduction

Since the early 1980s Chile has pursued a series of health sector reforms under a broadly neo-liberal framework. One of the principal claims made is that the introduction of decentralization and participation as part of the replacement of state activity by market arrangements has enhanced choice and the responsiveness of the system to individual and local needs. This chapter examines the mechanisms of decentralization and participation introduced within the neo-liberal approach in order to overcome social exclusion, focusing on the new model of primary health care delivery. Social exclusion can be understood in this context as the processes by which powerful groups restrict the access of outsiders to valued resources through a process of 'social closure'. Consequently, less powerful groups become polarized and are denied access to citizenship understood as full participation in the community.[2] This process raises new questions regarding the role of the state and the community and highlights the importance of understanding the nature of participation.

The analysis here identifies some general and local level consequences of decentralization and participatory mechanisms, and argues that at times they can work against inclusion in unexpected ways. The study suggests that many of the shortcomings result from the fact that participation was 'added on' to the Chilean model as a self-help mechanism to alleviate shortfalls in the public system, rather than being present from the start as a goal of political inclusion. Understanding the type of participation that is currently promoted by the Ministry of Health (MINSAL) helps explain why this is the case. The chapter argues that the ministry employed a narrow, technical definition of participation, derived from the broader neo-liberal framework. Within this context, participation is linked to economic development and citizens are urged to mobilize around social issues such as service delivery. In Chile this is an important contrast to the earlier forms of participation in the 1970s and 1980s which developed as opposition movements to the military government and had a particular ideological focus.

The study starts from the premise that a broader definition of participation is needed. In this context participation is understood as a process that incorporates citizens into decision-making arenas and is one aspect of a broader process of empowerment. If the health system is to be made more accountable, users must be incorporated into the decision-making process to ensure that the agenda and content of health service delivery is shaped by their needs. The analysis highlights some of the conflicts that have arisen as local level health groups try to access these arenas. Since the coalition governments made a commitment to improve participation, the expectations of grass-roots groups was raised. However, as illustrated by the discussion of provision of health care in El Bosque, this has not been the case. In addition, this has gendered implications since the majority of community health groups consist of women who are being denied a voice.

Under the neo-liberal package of reforms, participation has been closely linked to decentralization. Decentralization has been promoted by the World Bank as a means of improving the efficiency, management and responsiveness of public health services and it has been given considerable emphasis in the Chilean case. This discussion highlights some of the problems that have resulted in primary health care delivery because administrative decentralization has not been accompanied by fiscal decentralization, or effective political decentralization. The successful decentralization of service delivery is highly sensitive to the economic and political context. Without sufficient checks or appropriate formulae for redistribution, different regions or localities may be able to expend more resources than others resulting in increased inter-area inequality.[3]

The first part of the chapter provides a brief overview of the health system. This is followed by a discussion of selected elements of the reform: decentralization; the introduction of a new model of primary health care; and the participation programme, 'Health with the People'. Using evidence from a case study carried out in 1998 of El Bosque, a low income neighbourhood in the south of the Chilean capital, Santiago, in which five health centres serve a population of 170 000, the chapter examines the impact of these features at the local level.

Overview of the health system

Chile has a mixed health insurance system with active participation by both public and private sectors in the financing as well as supply of services. The principal financing institution in the public system is the National Health Fund (FONASA), the body responsible for the collection, administration and distribution of financial resources. FONASA resources are derived from a number of different origins – contributions, co-payments[4] and taxation. In the public system, services are provided via the 27 regional health services. These are autonomous bodies, with their own legal status and assets. Secondary and tertiary care is offered to users through a network of 188 public hospitals. Primary care is delivered through the primary care centres (329 clinics and 996 health posts); the majority of these are administered by the municipalities. The private system is made up of private health insurance companies (ISAPREs) and private providers. The *Superintendencia de ISAPREs*, a decentralized, public institution, is responsible for the registration and regulation of the ISAPREs.[5]

Chilean workers can choose between these public and private insurance institutions to contract their mandatory health insurance (a deduction of seven per cent of their salary – the *cotización*), and within FONASA users can opt between public or private providers. The seven per cent gives users a basic health plan, and they must make additional payments for other services. Workers' coverage includes health care for their dependants, but definitions of this vary between the state scheme, FONASA, and the private sector scheme, ISAPREs. Indigents (the destitute) are entitled to free care via FONASA, but are only eligible for a basic package of services. Around 65 per cent of the population are registered with FONASA; 25 per cent are registered in an ISAPRE and the remaining ten per cent are covered by other systems such as the armed forces' own health service.

Decentralization

The decentralization process was central to the Pinochet reforms in the health sector. Prior to 1974 the municipalities had only limited responsibilities and incomes and were primarily political and administrative institutions rather than providers of services.[6] In 1974–75 legislation was introduced which assigned the municipalities new responsibilities, including some of a financial and administrative nature. Municipalities were in future bound to provide a variety of services, including primary education and health care, transport and public highways, sanitation, local planning and development. These responsibilities were ratified in 1988 with the passing of the Municipal Government Law. In order to carry out these functions, the municipality had to produce an annual development plan and budget proposal; the available budget was then to be allocated to different sectors.

Municipal funds are derived from three principal sources: regional government funding, participation in the Common Municipal Fund (FCM) and self-generated funds (Article 11). Regional government funding comes from a regional development fund – the National Regional Development Fund, and is distributed for specific projects and programmes which have been prioritized according to regional sectoral investment priorities. The Common Municipal Fund is a mechanism used to distribute funding more evenly across the country, transferring funds from richer municipalities to poorer ones. However, municipalities must specifically apply for funds and eligibility is determined according to criteria set up by the Interior Ministry.[7] Funds in the FCM are collected from each municipality and are composed of money collected from a number of sources: 60 per cent of the property taxes imposed in all municipalities (this tax is applied to businesses in the neighbourhood); 50 per cent of the sale of traffic licences; and, finally, a special contribution is made by the three wealthiest municipalities in the country. In addition, municipalities can generate their own funds in a number of ways: these include land and business taxes; traffic licences; fines; municipal patents; advertising, and duties for rubbish collection and other local services. It is therefore clear that municipalities with large numbers of shops and businesses are able to generate more funds than smaller municipalities with fewer businesses and cars.

In 1980 legislation was passed (Decree Law 1–3) which implemented the transfer of primary level care to the municipalities, and in 1981 local level delivery began. The transfer of resources was to be set by and administered via a new financial system, the FAPEM,[8] with unit prices of specific treatment set by the Ministry of Health. The stated aim of the changes was to improve the control and regulation of local level facilities and to ensure that any specific character of health needs in the locality were reflected in health provision, as well as channelling municipal funds rather than national funds into the improvement of local facilities and infrastructure. It was also argued that municipalization would improve local participation and allow more inter-sectoral integration to take place, especially with other key sectors such as housing, education and sanitation.[9]

Financing mechanisms

In 1994 a new financing mechanism was introduced at the primary level. Within it, a basic package of services, the Family Health Plan, is provided by the state to FONASA users. The cost of providing these services is calculated in order to determine the per capita payment that will be contributed by the state. The per capita system is based on the idea of a pre-payment per beneficiary population assigned to each municipal health clinic. Providers are then paid a negotiated sum per month for each person who chooses to register with them for primary care, whether that person uses the service or not.

The transfer per beneficiary varies according to each municipality's urban/rural and poor/non-poor status. Municipalities are classified from low to high levels of poverty, based on their dependency on the Common Municipal Fund and capacity to generate their own resources. The classification of municipalities according to rural or urban status began in July 1994, accompanied by announcements of the amount of transfers to each neighbourhood and the calculation of the beneficiary population according to figures from the latest census and CASEN survey (national household survey). There are two characteristics of the per capita system that affect its operation. First, the effective registration of all FONASA beneficiaries, but potential beneficiaries who are not registered are generally treated if they present themselves. Secondly, the definition of management contracts between the state and municipalities since they provide a form of monitoring the quality of services delivered at the local level.[10]

Primary health care within the new model

Since the early 1990s attempts have been made to reformulate health programmes and to develop a new model of primary care delivery. This has a number of objectives: to ensure that the supply side of the programme meets the needs of the population; to incorporate increased levels of quality in the services; to reorient actions towards priority areas; to prioritize the most cost-effective actions; to develop promotional and preventative actions; and to increase the amount of social participation in the health sector.[11] These objectives have led to the definition of a new model of care, which aims to meet the needs of communities and families through a more holistic and humanized approach to health care, based on a number of basic principles which include user-centredness, equity, quality, accessibility, and social participation, that will enable people to feel protected and reassured in terms of meeting their health needs.[12]

From health centre to family centre

Attempts have been made to improve the service provided at the local level via the health centres (*consultorios*). An important recent initiative has been the introduction of new-style family health centres (*centros de salud familiar*) staffed by teams of health professionals and non-professionals who have been given specific training in the new holistic approach – the Family Health Focus (*el Enfoque Familiar en Salud*). The central idea of the approach is that staff will not just treat the medical symptoms in a patient, but will also consider ways in which the family situation may help or hinder the patient's recovery and may be a contributory cause of the symptoms.

This process was first initiated in 1990 with the return to democracy. The Ministry of Health argued that the health centres had been developed to respond to a restricted notion of intervention, one based on a bio-medical model primarily oriented towards illness prevention and cure. In contrast, the health centres were intended to work with a bio-physico-social model which incorporates other factors into the notion of health – social, cultural, environmental and psychological and thus provides a much broader approach. This uses a more integrated approach to people, considering as well their own environment and the changes which affect them through their life cycle.

In order to work with this new approach, the MINSAL argues that it is necessary to move from a health centre to a family health centre.[13]

According to the MINSAL the creation of family health centres is the last phase of this transformation.[14] This final stage was initiated in 1997, and in 1998 there are around 40 family health centres. El Bosque has four public health centres: Laurita Vicuña, Cisterna Sur, Condores de Chile and Santa Laura; in addition there is a new public health facility, designed as a family health centre, the Orlando Letelier. Each health centre works within a clearly defined geographical area of the neighbourhood.[15] By definition all FONASA registered inhabitants of El Bosque have access to a public health centre in the neighbourhood. In addition there is a mental health centre and two emergency service posts. However, any inhabitant of El Bosque who is registered in an ISAPRE is not entitled to use any of the public health facilities.

Participation

In the 1990s a central element of the reform process has been an emphasis on social participation. A Social Participation Unit was established within the Ministry of Health in the early 1990s with the objective of improving primary health care within a framework of social participation, inter-sectoral work and decentralization. In 1995 a new programme, Health with the People, was initiated. According to the Minister of Health at the time, Carlos Massad, the fundamental objective of the programme was to 'recognize and support social organizations in health ... with the idea of strengthening their roles as representatives of civil society'.[16]

The objective of the programme was to provide financial support to a number of selected groups. Selection was based on a number of criteria, fundamentally the extent to which the aims of the group reflected the needs and priorities of the Ministry. More importantly, funds for the programme did not come from the central health budget, but instead from funds raised through the national lottery (*Polla Chilena de Beneficencia*). Initially the programme was restricted to the Santiago metropolitan area and 59 groups were selected. Table 8.1 shows the area of work of those groups selected.

Once selected, groups had to sign 'Action Agreements', which laid out targets that they would work towards. These were developed in conjunction with the Ministry of Health and groups were expected to tailor their activities to fit the criteria supplied by the ministry. In this way the groups all operated according to the same agenda, which limited their capacity to pursue local needs as they perceived them, although the nature of the individual Agreement varied according to the work of the group. Funds were not intended for specific projects, but to allow groups to continue with their own activities and provide support for administrative and management running costs.

The initial phase of the programme was considered a success and subsequently extended across the country, providing funding for around two

Table 8.1 Groups selected for 'Health with the People' programme, May 1995

Area of work	Number
Health promotion groups	
The elderly	10
Women's health	3
Children's health	3
Community health	8
Disease-related groups	
Diabetes	8
Drug and alcohol abuse	7
Psychiatric	2
Children with cancer	3
Disabled	3
Haemophilia	5
Others	7
Total	59

Source: MINSAL, 1995: 28.

thousand groups. In an interview with Judith Salinas, the director of the programme (25 November 1997), she believed that the government was still committed to promoting participation and this is reflected in the funds that were allocated for this purpose.

> Today a very small part of the health budget is allocated to primary health care, around 10 per cent, ... and within that an even smaller percentage is allocated to participation and promotion – perhaps one per cent of the 10 per cent... However, the ministry does have funds which are specifically allocated to participation and promotion activities and this is an important consideration. Although the overall funds are small when compared to funds allocated to curative care, they still reflect a political will.

However, when questioned about the nature of participation of these groups, that is, the extent to which they are able to influence policy, Salinas was less optimistic. She felt that there have been some efforts to increase the participation of these groups in the policy arena, but they have been very scattered. Salinas confirmed that participation at the local level is mainly oriented towards improving the quality of service and that grass-roots health groups have no real voice in any decision-making processes. This is not surprising, but it goes against much of the rhetoric that persistently claimed the opposite:

> The ultimate aim of participation is to develop individuals and communities as the protagonists for their own health – with the means to exercise a

degree of social control over the system of health services – that support the process of the production of health and well-being in society.[17]

Mechanisms for decentralization

Mechanisms for decentralization have been put in place and many of the administrative responsibilities for primary health care delivery have now been transferred to the local level. However, the results have not been as positive as advocates of decentralization claimed. Despite the introduction of the per capita transfer mechanism, many of the health centres continue to operate with deficits. Although the per capita payment is supposed to cover the full cost of each health action, many argue that in reality it does not even cover the cost of the necessary personnel.[18] It is the responsibility of the municipality to make up the shortfall.

Decentralization makes this problem worse by placing an additional strain on the municipal resources of the most vulnerable neighbourhoods because its impact is most acute in municipalities with higher levels of poverty where the population is more dependent on the public health system. In reality, this also means that where the health budget comes from the municipality, health must compete with other sectors. This can produce tensions since the municipality may have to choose between increasing funds in the health sector but cutting funds in other sectors, and often those sectors such as sanitation, paving, recreation which contribute to health expenditure prevention. In addition, funds may be granted to a particular sector favoured by the mayor or other key players in the financial sector of the municipality. Far from being the case, therefore, that decentralization promotes coherent patterns of local provision across sectors, it leads to increased conflict between sectoral needs.

In poorer municipalities it has been necessary to apply to other sources, such as special project funds offered by MINSAL, in order to pay for basic but vital physical improvements to the health centres, even to carry out maintenance work such as painting the walls.

There is also considerable debate, even at the local level, about the administration of the per capita payment. Although it is generally accepted that there is a lack of funds in the public sector, especially at the primary care level, some would argue that the key problem is mismanagement of resources in the health centres. In theory, the health centres are free to determine how the per capita payment is distributed. Since it is not known what the ideal value of the per capita payment should be, some argue that it is hard to claim therefore that it is insufficient. Others have suggested that the key problem is that the MINSAL did not consider sufficient variables in the calculations to determine the per capita and has also underestimated the number of users registered in each health centre, therefore providing insufficient funds to afford each user the services they require.[19] Furthermore, a preliminary study in Santiago has suggested that the inequality of resources between municipalities has a particularly gendered aspect as well.[20] Municipal health departments and health centres in better-off neighbourhoods are more likely to be controlled by men, whereas those in poorer areas are more likely to be controlled by women. In addition, the health centre directors in the wealthier areas are also more likely to be doctors, while female health centre directors in the less well-off areas are generally midwives, physiotherapists and dentists. This suggests that not only are poorer municipalities becoming increasingly marginalized following decentralization, at least in this respect, but that women working in the health sector are less likely to have access to resources than men.

Registration of users

The introduction of the per capita payment has raised an important contradiction at the local level. On the one hand the per capita payment implies that the municipality has a fixed amount of expenditure per user; on the other hand, it also implies that each registered user can demand full use of all the services offered in the health centres. This has made it difficult for the municipal administration to find a point of equilibrium between the demand for services, and the available supply.[21] This creates problems for both users and primary health care providers. While the health centres must meet targets of registered users in order to maintain current levels of per capita funding, they do not have the funds to meet the demand placed upon the services by a greater number of users.

One factor contributing to the problem is the use of the public system by non-registered users, most notably those registered in the ISAPREs. This has been a major problem in the public sector and efforts have been made to eradicate it. Software is now in place in parts of the public health system that can identify beneficiaries by their identification number (RUT) and therefore people in an ISAPRE will be stopped from using the public system or can not pass themselves off as indigents. The system links all different databases, including those concerned with the pension system (AFP and INP), FONASA and ISAPREs as well as different credit databases, so that if someone applies for indigent status or tries to use the public health facilities all personal data can be cross-checked. In addition, when entering a public hospital or health centre, the identification number of the user is cross-checked to confirm the level of their FONASA plan.

The data in Table 8.2 illustrates the difference in the number of potential users (i.e. the number of people in El Bosque who are covered by FONASA) and the number of actual registered users in the five health centres in El Bosque. Since the Orlando Letelier family health centre only opened in 1997, data regarding the actual number of users was not available. Despite the number of registered users being considerably lower than the number of potential users, all five clinics experience a lack of resources and it was felt

Table 8.2 Potential users and registered users in El Bosque municipal health services

Facility	Number of users assigned	Number of users registered
Laurita Vicuña	59 945	39 521
Cisterna Sur	47 937	22 780
Condores de Chile	23 196	11 635
Santa Laura	31 392	13 542
Orlando Letelier	28 137	n.a.

Source: Programa Anual de Salud Comunal, El Bosque, 1998.

that the methodology employed by MINSAL to reach these figures was problematic, and that it failed to consider a sufficient number of variables in the calculations.[22]

Family health centres

As demonstrated above, one of the underlying objectives of the new holistic approach to primary health care is to ensure that users feel more included in the system. The introduction of family health centres can be considered as a particularly progressive aspect of the reform and, although it is too early to make a final judgement, a preliminary assessment of the cumulative impact of reform is possible.

Users' needs have clearly been considered in the design and organization of the family health centre in El Bosque, and this is an important step in ensuring that people access the system. In household interviews conducted in El Bosque, many people cited the physical appearance of the other health centres as reasons for non-attendance.[23] In contrast, the new clinic was purpose-built to serve as a family health centre clinic and the objectives are echoed in the design of the building. In terms of its physical attributes, in comparison with other health centres in El Bosque, it is much more welcoming, clean, light and user-friendly. As well as improving the situation for users, the physical working environment for the staff is also considerably better than those in other clinics in the area.

However, a number of constraints have limited the ability of the staff to implement the new approach with success. A primary factor has been a lack of resources. One consequence of this is that staff are not always able to carry out home visits. A home visit and family advice service are an integral part of the Family Health Plan, which outlines the services that must be included in the basic package provided by the family health centre. This is intended for families who are at greatest risk in terms of the bio-physico-social factors recognized in the holistic approach of the family health centre model. According to the Ministry of Health the home visit is to be carried out by the appropriate health team and the contents and objectives of the visits are decided by the team, according to the needs of the family concerned, within the holistic framework. The home visits help the health team determine the extent to which the family situation may contribute to the causes of a particular illness suffered by a patient.

Although the family health centres receive a 25 per cent increase in terms of the per capita payment per user compared to the other health centres, in real terms this is only a limited increase of resources. Nevertheless, since the Orlando Letelier receives a bigger per capita transfer payment than other health centres to cover its greater running costs, the municipality in El Bosque has refused to top up its funds, as it is obliged to do for other health centres. In addition, the family health centre approach requires a higher number of professional staff than in other health centres, meaning that running costs are higher as more money is spent on salaries. According to the director of the Orlando Letelier,[24] this is not taken into account in the resources that go to the family health centre. Therefore, in overall terms, the Orlando Letelier does not receive more funds than the other health centres, and this severely limits its ability to implement the new model of attention.

Interviews with the director and sub-director of the Orlando Letelier highlighted some of the problems in carrying out home visits. One of the main problems is, as noted above, that despite the increased role medical staff are expected to play in this model of attention, the family health centre does not have the money to employ additional staff. Moreover, both respondents felt that the assignation of resources did not take into account the cost of the home visits, fieldwork and other non-health centre based activities. For lack of funds the health centre was able only to provide curative health care, yet the family health centre model is expected to promote prevention and health promotion as well. The sub-director suggested that this limitation in turn affected the quality of human resources. She felt that added strains are being placed upon staff who were obliged to work extra hours to meet the needs of patients without being paid.

Limitations to participation

While the emphasis placed on participation by the Ministry of Health may initially appear to be a positive step aimed at overcoming exclusion, it is necessary to critically re-examine the programme. Here, drawing on the experience of a grass-roots health group, the El Bosque Health Committee (*El Comité de Salud el Bosque*), this section will highlight some of the limitations.

The El Bosque Health Committee was started in the mid-1980s when a group of women began to organize themselves and linked up with existing social organizations in the neighbourhood such as other health groups, mothers' groups and neighbourhood associations. A number of social workers and other health professionals from the local health centres also participated, but without the authorization of the municipality. Their participation was more a personal commitment to the group's aims than an institutional one. The aims of the group were to ensure that the public health sector met the needs of the local population. Lucia Palmer, one of the founding members, states that the objective of the group was 'the defence of public health ... a political statement to claim our right to health care'.[25] In the early 1990s the group was part of a local campaign to build a new health centre in El Bosque and an emergency primary health care unit (SAPU), organizing sit-ins at the Ministry of Health. The campaign was successful, and both the SAPU and the new health centre – the Orlando Letelier – were built.

Today the group continues to protest about the lack of government commitment to the public health sector. In June 1998 they participated in a day of protest organized by public health workers in the centre of Santiago against a proposed budget cut to the health sector. In addition, it focuses on health education and currently much of its work is aimed towards improving the rate of screening for cervical cancer among the local population. It is this aspect of the group's work that has received most support from the local health centres, who provide it with materials and some midwives supplied their services to a walk-in clinic that the group set up to encourage women to be screened.

One of the underlying limitations of the participation programme emphasized by the experience of the Committee is its reliance on the unpaid work of community members, who are predominantly female. There is an in-built assumption in the programme that women are free to dedicate the necessary time to projects of this type and are also willing to do so. However, many of the members of the Committee were in full-time paid employment as well as having full-time domestic responsibilities – many still had older children living at home. At times this has meant that some of the women are prevented from taking part in activities and the meetings and activities have to be organized to fit in with the domestic responsibilities and work commitments of all the group members. Furthermore, this means that they often need to arrange activities in the evenings. In contrast, this is difficult for health centre staff, who already feel overworked and are often not willing or able to commit even more hours of their day and so do not attend functions. Indeed, the majority of those working in the primary health care centres are women who have their own domestic responsibilities and therefore cannot take on further commitments. This produces friction between the health groups and health workers as the groups often feel they are left to function without the support of the health centres; and it is often only particularly dedicated individuals who participate in the group's activities.

The most important limitation of the programme is the nature of participation that is being promoted. While the Ministry of Health stresses the importance of 'strengthening the role of the family in the organization of health care', in practice it seems unlikely that this will be accomplished through the programme. Indeed, increasing women's workload through reliance on their unpaid work could in fact have the opposite effect as women's time is not infinitely elastic. Furthermore, the majority of groups selected by the ministry to receive funding are self-help and disease-specific or cluster round bio-medical issues.[26]

One of the members of the Committee, Jenny Ortiz, explained what they consider as the difference between their group and self-help groups,

> To a great extent these groups are now carrying out functions previously the responsibility of the health centres. It is now up to voluntary organizations to make up this shortfall, and in this case the majority of voluntary workers are female. Although some of the groups have been set up at the initiative of the users rather than the health centres, they still perform a limited and specific function and do not really represent 'participation' of users in a political sense. Often these groups are just carrying out unpaid work for the health centres and they are not autonomous. In the Committee we are one of the few health groups in El Bosque that has a political orientation, we are not a self-help style health group. We are more concerned with educating people about their rights in health care and educating people, who are mainly women, to participate in the public health system as well as encouraging more promotional and preventative activities. Our work should support and help the health centre, but we must not take on the responsibilities of the health centre, although of course in practice this is more complicated.[27]

Although the Committee has a clear critique of the health system and a history of politically motivated participation, this is not being encouraged by the Ministry of Health. Groups with more radical agendas have to ensure that their aims conform to those of the ministry in order to receive any funding. This is something that was very clear to the Committee when they received funds from the Health with the People programme. It was necessary for the group to bid for funding and when it was granted to them they had to sign an agreement binding them to carry out certain activities with the funds. When questioned about whether they felt compromised by this, the group answered:

> Although we had to sign an agreement, once we received the funds we could develop projects according to our own aims and methods. If someone was to come here from the ministry and tell us how to spend the money, we would not have accepted it as this is not how we function – we would look for other sources of funding, although we are not sure where from. We know what we want to do and we know what people in

the ministry want. We have always made our intentions and views clear to the Ministry. The Ministry know who we are and what are objectives are – we have worked with them before and participated in events with them over the years. To an extent we have built up a relationship with them. We are not afraid to criticize the Ministry of Health, or to make our views known.[28]

Conclusions

While caution must be expressed at the extent to which broad conclusions can be drawn from a limited case study, the analysis does raise a number of issues of potential comparative interest. The reforms of the Chilean health sector have included processes of decentralization and mechanisms for participation. Because the health reform developed out of a broadly neo-liberal perspective and issues around participation were 'added-on', a number of deficiencies in the system arose. Certain factors limit the effectiveness of the reforms and obstruct inclusion in unexpected ways. For example:

- resources remain centrally determined and local level health centres do not participate in allocation processes;
- the current organization of municipal funding means that some municipalities are less able to generate resources for primary health care than others; poorer municipalities are unable to invest sufficient resources into primary health care and in addition the health sector must compete with other sectors for resources;
- the per capita funding system is set up in such a way that it produces insufficient resources for the demand on services;
- lack of funds at the local level has meant that some health centres are not able to implement the new model of primary health care;
- while participation is encouraged at the grass roots, rather than incorporating civil society actors into key decision making arenas, it has focused around improving the quality of service for users. In doing so, it relies on unpaid work, which is predominantly carried out by women, who are already facing onerous demands on their time.

In sum, the public health sector remains a hierarchical structure with the local level health centres at the bottom, far removed from decisions. The reforms have not addressed this issue. As a consequence they do not overcome social exclusion, but rather 'include' people in ways consistent with pre-existing hierarchies and the overall neo-liberal project. The elements of the health reform focused on decentralization and participation 'include' citizens in an unequal pattern, which tends to reinforce existing regional and local inequality, and channel and limit forms of participation to those that neutralize, rather than empower opposition. It could be argued therefore that the reforms have not fundamentally altered the underlying neo-liberal orientation of policy under Pinochet, although they have clearly added a 'participatory' dimension to the initial model. The logic of the model remains that primary health care should be delivered in ways that are consistent with expanding the space within which private markets can operate and engaging the energies of users in the delivery of services where private markets alone will not meet identified health needs.

Notes

1. The author would like to thank Paul Cammack and the editors for their helpful comments.
2. Silver (1994: 570).
3. Collins (1996: 151).
4. FONASA users must pay an additional sum for services they use. These co-payments vary according to income level and type of service.
5. Aedo (1995: 9).
6. Casteñada (1992: 198).
7. Rosenfeld (1993:6).
8. See Viveros-Long (1986) and Larrañaga (1997).
9. Miranda (1988: 91).
10. Aedo (1995: 113).
11. MINSAL (1997: 143).
12. MINSAL (1997:144).
13. MINSAL (1993:40–45).
14. MINSAL (1997: 145).
15. Dirección de Salud de el Bosque (1997: 21).
16. MINSAL (1995: 12).
17. MINSAL (1995: 5).
18. Molina (1997: 6).
19. Interviews with key informants (June–July 1998).
20. De Madrid et al. (undated).
21. Chilean Association of Municipalities (undated: 3).
22. Interviews with key informants (June–July, 1998).
23. Interviews with key informants (June–July, 1998).
24. Interview (May 1998).
25. Interview (9 July 1998).
26. MINSAL (1995: 28).
27. Interview (11 May 1998).
28. Interview with Lucia Palmer (9 July 1998).

Bibliography

Aedo. I.C., 'Financiamiento de la Salud: Proposiciones de Reforma', in (ed.) Juan Giaconi, *La Salud en el Siglo XXI: Cambios Necesarios*, Centro de Estudios Publicos, Santiago, 1995.
Asociación Chilena de Municipalidades, 'Comisión Temática: Salud', mimeo, Asociación Chilena de Municipalidades, Santiago, undated.

Castañeda, T., *Combating Poverty: Innovative Social Reforms in Chile during the 1980s*, International Centre for Economic Growth/ICS Press, San Francisco, 1992.
Collins, C. 'Decentralisation', in (ed.) K. Janovsky, *Health Policy and Systems Development*, WHO, Geneva, 1996.
De Madrid, S., Draft mimeo from author on the impact of municipalization, undated.
Direccion de Salud de el Bosque, 'Programa Anual de Salud Comunal, El Bosque', Municipalidad de el Bosque, 1998.
Direccion de Salud de el Bosque, 'Plan Comunal de Salud, Municipalidad de El Bosque', 1997.
Fuenzalida, R.A., 'El Neuvo Modelo de Financiamiento del Nivel Primaria de Atención de Salud Municipal: Pago per Capita', in *Cuadernos de Economía*, 32(95), 125–8, 1995.
Larrañaga, O., 'Eficiencia y Equidad en el Sistema de Salud Chileno', *Serie Financimiento del Desarrollo, no. 49*, CEPAL, Santiago, 1997.
Ministerio de Salud (MINSAL), 'Diseño e Implementación de las Prioridades de Salud. La Reforma Programática Chilena', Division de Salud de las Personas, Ministry of Health, Santiago, 1997.
Ministerio de Salud, 'Salud con la Gente', Ministry of Health: Santiago, 1995.
Ministerio de Salud,'De Consultorio a Centro de Salud: Marco Conceptual', Ministry of Health: Santiago, 1993.
Miranda, E., 'Decentralización y Privatización del Sistema de Salud Chileno', in Miranda, E. (ed.) *La Salud en Chile: Evolución y Perspectivas*, Centro de Estudios Públicos, Santiago, 1998.
Molina, G., Draft mimeo produced for Asociación Chilena de Municipalidades. Santiago, 1997.
Rosenfeld, A.A., 'Estado, Decentralización Municipal y Gestión Economica'. Documento de Trabajo, Centro de Estudios Sociales y Educación, SUR. Santiago, 1993.
Silver, H., 'Social Exclusion and Social Solidarity: Three Paradigms', in *International Labour Review*, 133(5–6), 531–78, 1994.
Viveros-Long, A., 'Changes in Health Financing: The Chilean Experience', in *Social Science and Medicine*, 22(3), 379–83, 1986.

Part 4
Social Development Policies

9
The PROGRESA Programme and Social Change in Rural Mexico

Agustín Escobar Latapí

This chapter deals with the impact of the PROGRESA programme (*Programa Educación, Salud y Alimentación*, or Programme for Education, Health and Nutrition) on communities experiencing substantial change derived from rural economic restructuring. At the time of writing, this programme delivered cash and services to 2.6 million families in 56 000 isolated Mexican rural communities, for an approximate total of 16 million persons. My findings derive from field research and from a concern with the significance of this programme for the well-being of families and communities.[1] Other analyses focus on PROGRESA from the perspective of its design and objectives. This text provides a contrasting 'ground-level' perspective, which should serve to assess and modify its strategies concerning the beneficiary population. PROGRESA is, in budgetary terms, but one small part (approximately one-seventh) of the social programmes of the Ministry for Social Development in Mexico, and less than 1 per cent of total social expenditure.[2] It is necessary to explain why such a small programme merits special attention.

During the Zedillo presidency, the main motive for interest in the PROGRESA programme was misleading. To the public in general and many analysts, PROGRESA was simply president Zedillo's version of PRONASOL, a programme that became famous for many reasons, not all of them positive. PRONASOL (1988–94) had vast resources at its disposal for a variety of social and investment programmes within it, and it channelled the investments and spending of many other programmes in many ministries. Its operations and resources were manipulated for electoral purposes and there was an enormous regional 'variability' in its forms of operation and its political use. Thus, while in Chiapas most resources found their way into the pockets of strongmen in the state and in the PRI, in Michoacán and other states funds were channelled to the areas most clearly identified with opposition parties as elections neared (Molinar and Weldon, 1994). Among other things, these variations and biases meant that the regions that most greatly benefited were not the most marginal (Roberts and Escobar, 1997). On the other hand, access to the benefits of PRONASOL depended to a great extent on the ability to collaborate with social and political organizations, and on the mediation of officials and local and state leaders. This produced a bias, as the better-organized regions and actors received most support. As I hope to demonstrate, the design and operation of PROGRESA have made it into something substantially different from PRONASOL, in almost every respect.

Unfortunately, the manipulation of social programmes by party interests has tarnished social policy so profoundly that Congress 'froze' social spending at its 1999 levels and its 1999 modes of operation for year 2000, an election year, hoping to avoid pressure on voters by programme officers. This entailed subordinating the population's well-being to electoral priorities. But it also reveals that Congress has a probably justified deep mistrust of the Executive and very little understanding of programmes such as PROGRESA. PROGRESA is not exempt from the risk of electoral manipulation, and this chapter will show how this happens. Most other programmes, however, allow their managers far more discretion. Hence, while electoral manipulation is a valid concern, it is not an important aspect of PROGRESA. On the contrary, PROGRESA is of interest because it could have a major impact on poverty and inequality of opportunity. Here I present a preliminary evaluation and critical analysis of the interaction between the programme itself and the communities, households and public agencies of other government departments.

The programme's design and operation are original for Mexico. Reportedly, it is the most efficient of all social programmes ever implemented in Mexico (95 per cent of the programme's budget reaches beneficiaries).[3] Also, PROGRESA represents the main effort in Mexico to *free social policy programmes from political interference in order to optimize impact.* Although any governmental programme – more so one designed to eliminate poverty – is political, the design of PROGRESA subjects all of its actions to technical decisions based on levels of marginality and poverty, in which other agencies, state and local governments (practically) do not interfere. PROGRESA, then, should be free of the party biases and electoral deviations that were so heavily criticized in the *Solidarity* programme. As a consequence of this, however, the programme may turn out to be insensitive to the special conditions of each region, precisely because it does not take into account the claims and opinions of local- and state-level leaders.

There is no precedent in Mexico for targeted programmes on the scale of PROGRESA. Each beneficiary (a woman head of household) is selected on the basis of a community census, which establishes the family's level of need. Each community is selected according to its level of marginality. Also, there is an individual follow-up process of each beneficiary. Each individual in the family must comply with the conditions set in the programme, in terms of school attendance, medical check-ups and attendance to health training clinics.

Unlike earlier programmes, PROGRESA takes the initiative in the process of selection, regardless of local organizations or leaders. Potential beneficiaries only need to reply to a census. Through this action (targeting benefits precisely to the poorest people according to each family's specific needs), the programme should also avoid the distortions introduced by a process of self-selection in a country where information and the exercise of one's rights are still markedly uneven, especially in rural areas.

The programme is based on the existing staff and infrastructure of other ministries (health and education), which reduces costs significantly, although it places a large additional work-load on those agencies, and does not normally increase their pay. This is an important additional reason for cost efficiency.

The programme purports to change behaviour, and to enable the rural poor to acquire the health and human capital levels necessary for modern wage employment. But it differs from earlier programmes (or clusters of social programmes) because it is entirely devoid of any concurrent actions regarding employment in these communities. This is a huge risk: if the programme succeeds but jobs are not created, massive emigration will ensue. The programme trusts the market will reach the communities or at least nearby towns. Local development is thus beyond the scope of the programme.

As I hope to show, these features give PROGRESA definite advantages and disadvantages. After a brief appraisal of the impact of rural restructuring, this chapter provides a critique of these advantages and disadvantages as perceived by the relevant social actors in the communities themselves.

I. Rural communities at the end of the 1990s

PROGRESA is based on the following findings stressed by poverty analysts in Mexico.[4] First, poverty is more widespread in the countryside than in the cities. Second, the rural poor are poorer than the urban poor. Third, poor people in rural areas have larger families and their children have lower schooling levels, which facilitates the reproduction of extreme poverty (Hernández Laos, 1992; Boltvinik, 1994; COPLAMAR, 1983; CEPAL-INEGI, 1993; Escobar, 1995). These findings are beyond discussion, but they do not preclude a programme of PROGRESA's scale in the cities. Although rural poverty has worsened, urban workers have also undergone serious erosion of their previous level of living. From the outset this makes one question the rural bias of the programme.

Rural poverty intensified in the second half of the 1980s,[5] first as a consequence of the urban crisis – especially stagnation in employment – and later because of the restructuring of rural institutions themselves. Since the 1960s the survival of poor workers and peasants in the countryside came to rely increasingly on unskilled, seasonal and poorly paid jobs in the cities.[6] Around 1978–80 temporary labour migration to the cities ceased to be the principal means of obtaining cash for rural micro-producers because the generation of new jobs in the cities stagnated.

The second source of change in rural poverty has been the restructuring and drastic decline of financing for rural producers. Low-interest loans were not only a source of financing but also of subsidies to poor rural producers, since they were not usually paid back. This credit/subsidy system was abolished, and the new forms of credit for poor rural producers (PROCAMPO) are much smaller and received by fewer people. The third source of change has been production inputs. The privatization of seed and fertilizer-producing enterprises (pesticide and herbicide production was already in private hands), and the liberation of the markets of such inputs raised prices. The fourth factor was the liberation of grain markets and those of other agricultural products. Owing to imports and the dismantling of state distributorships, real prices for most agricultural crops have fallen.

It is estimated that, in 1980, the governmental subsidy for rural producers amounted to 20 per cent of the rural GNP. This subsidy did not spread evenly in poor rural communities. The better off and the politically connected received a larger share. But it is no longer available, and that is one less source of income for these communities. As a result, in spite of other countervailing tendencies, such as rapidly falling fertility, rural poverty has worsened, both in terms of lower incomes and greater debt levels, and in terms of the greater vulnerability of poor peasants to social, economic and 'natural' hazards. Heavy rainstorms, drought or illness can plunge the rural poor into debt and hunger.

Partly as a response to the stagnation of casual urban labour markets, there has been an increase in labour migration to the United States. However, seasonal labour migration is increasingly dangerous and costly. Increasing costs means benefits are lower. One similar 'response' takes the form of internal migration for agricultural work, but this phenomenon is also subject to cycles and instability.

Money-lending has become extremely important as a means of compensating the chronic problems in terms of income, international migration and survival. Unlike traditional money-lending, which sought control of the harvest, 'new' money-lending is after 'migradollars'. However, it is no less perverse than before. In order to pay for inputs, agricultural work or emergencies, people borrow money. To pay back the loan they ask for more money to finance a trip to the US and pay the *pollero* (*pollero* is the name commonly used for migrant smugglers) or 'coyote'. The end result is that in order to pay off one expense people frequently ask for two loans that – at a 9 to 12 per cent monthly interest rate – represent a sizeable drain on migrant earnings. Migrants usually return.

In sum, poor rural communities have suffered as a consequence of the urban employment crisis, market restructuring and the disappearance of subsidies. What can a social programme do about all of this?

II. The operation of the programme

PROGRESA provides direct subsidies in cash and kind to selected families, provided that they comply with conditions set by the programme in terms of health check-ups, health training and school attendance. Cash assistance comprises a 'basic' amount plus an additional amount for each child in grades 4–9 (more for a girl). Support in kind consists of special enriched powdered milk, produced in two different compositions, one for pregnant and breast-feeding women and another for children. Other smaller forms of support have to do with school supplies and other services. The programme's current size was reached gradually after the programme had been operating for 30 months. This growth occurred gradually. Highly marginal regions tended to be incorporated first (these criteria were generally respected, but there were exceptions).[7]

Each region, community and family is incorporated into the programme through a process that is precisely defined by coordinators at the national level. This process starts with the priority given to a region according to the index of marginality of Mexican communities, compiled and updated by CONAPO (the National Population Council). PROGRESA selects marginal and highly marginal communities from a state or region (less-marginal communities and regions were incorporated in 1999). Once this is done, PROGRESA subcontracts a census of the socio-economic characteristics of the households in the communities, and a questionnaire designed to update and amplify the information concerning the community. During this phase of the process the entire locality may be eliminated, if it turns out that the information collected through the questionnaire reveals either that families there do not have access to the health and education infrastructure required by the programme, or that the community is less marginal than expected.

There are two biases in this process. The first militates against highly marginal communities without access to health or education. Most of these communities were excluded because they lacked access to health services, and a special programme for the training of community health promoters has alleviated this problem. It was estimated that 127 000 families remained out of the programme for this reason at the end of 1999. The second is against communities inaccurately reported as less marginal. The census procedure was enlarged to include less-marginal communities in 1998, and a large number were incorporated into the programme.

It must be remembered that although the intention is to identify the poorest households, there is no nationally- or regionally-established poverty line; rather, each household is selected or rejected on the basis of a certain set of factors pertaining to all households under consideration in a given region. Thus, a particular household may be included in one region while another – equal in every way – may be rejected elsewhere.

In my opinion the fact that PROGRESA actively looks for and finds the poorest people is correct in the Mexican context. The alternative, that is, a process of self-selection confirmed by a social worker, would markedly favour the better organized and informed. Such an approach would not reach the poorest of the poor precisely because at that social level there is little organization and poor information. However, it does give rise to the problems that derive from maintaining and updating the census. It is the responsibility of the programme itself to keep track of those who enter and leave the category of *beneficiary*.

Once the census of beneficiaries in the community has been elaborated, the community is 'incorporated'. A call is issued to attend an assembly. In it, the list of beneficiaries is made public,[8] and the women beneficiaries receive training in the handling of the three basic documents of the programme: one for education, one for health care and a third that they must present in order to receive their cash benefits. The officials insist on the importance of fulfilling one's commitments and the women are then asked to elect a *promoter*. This promoter serves as the link between SEDESOL and PROGRESA, on the one hand, and the beneficiaries themselves. This person must be a woman and a beneficiary. She receives no remuneration. The absence of any compensation for promoters is an additional reason explaining the high efficiency of the programme.

From that moment forward, the programme operates with a minimum of intervention on the part of the PROGRESA staff itself. The medical and educational personnel certify that the beneficiaries and their families are fulfilling their obligations (attending school, health check ups and talks) and this information is sent to PROGRESA's national headquarters. When the information from a given region is complete, the census is updated (payment is made only to those who comply) and wire transfers are sent in the name of individual beneficiaries. Payments may be sent either to a town with a TELECOM (telegraph) office or to a larger urban centre where SEDESOL personnel pay the beneficiaries personally and in cash. Payments, because of the marginal nature of the communities, are almost never made directly there. The beneficiaries know the amount they are to receive and this is updated every six months according to the official price index. The basic or family subsidy is equivalent to £7 per month, and scholarships range from £5 per third grader to £15 for a girl in ninth grade. The average amount of cash support per household hovered around 350 pesos (£23) per month at the time of writing, and the maximum was set at 700 pesos, or £46.[9] Total household *cash* expenditure without PROGRESA was typically 500 pesos per month, although a considerable amount of food was produced directly. The impact of the programme on family spending is thus very significant.

The women must receive the money personally, in order to prevent any interference by men. In some cases, ill or disabled persons may name a representative, although PROGRESA personnel discourage this practice and we heard complaints of their refusal to pay benefits to relatives of the elderly and the ill. The women also attend talks concerning the appropriate use of the money. They are told to spend it to improve the family's nutrition, on clothing for the children and on school materials. They are also advised to purchase inexpensive foods with high nutritional content that are typically absent from their diets, especially proteins. Using the money for other purposes – such as paying off debts or making contributions to the communities' ceremonial funds – is prohibited (though not sanctioned).

Support in kind (food supplements) is granted to pregnant and breastfeeding women, to all children between six months and two years of age and to older children who are under or malnourished. These are normally handed out in the health clinic where the families must comply with medical check-ups and attendance at talks. Alternatively, visitors or health promoters who are steadily acquiring greater responsibility as PROGRESA's coverage widens may deliver them. The programme of medical check-ups and talks is very detailed and requires a great deal of attention. The frequency of check-ups varies from once a month for newborns and pregnant women to once a year for healthy adults. It must be understood that the existence of a clinic at a distance of only 10 kilometres does not necessarily mean that it is easy to reach.

The promoter

The promoters deserve special attention in this evaluation, as they are key intermediaries. The compliance of women beneficiaries depends on them and they are responsible for letting PROGRESA know who has fulfilled their obligations.

Although they apparently do not have much to do, during the programme's first year the promoters were convened about once a month to larger towns and cities to receive instructions and training. This training concerned the matters that they would broach with teachers and doctors, as well as the orientation that they themselves should offer to the beneficiaries concerning the use of money, the certification of school attendance and visits to the clinic. Furthermore, they are responsible for arranging dates and places for the delivery of PROGRESA resources and many other details necessary for the progress of the programme. Finally, they implemented changes in the details of programme operations that were put into practice as the project grew.

In general, the beneficiaries selected the promoters because they were women with a higher-than-average level of education who knew how to deal with government officials. In one indigenous community that was already burdened with an excess of committees involved in multiple government programmes, the promoter was chosen because she was one of only a few women who had no such responsibility. She accepted the nomination because she considered it to be her *'cargo'*. Everyone, sooner or later, had to accept one of these positions. On our second visit all of the promoters were still in their posts.

We saw the promoters had a great deal of work. They travelled frequently and were called to account by the beneficiaries whenever a problem came up, despite the fact that they receive no remuneration for their activities, not even bus money. Several communities supported the promoter by taking collections when she had to travel. When the promoters had small children the beneficiaries themselves recognized a certain obligation to help look after them. The general perception is that the promoters do not benefit personally from this work. In addition to the fact that the census was out of their control (they only made modifications to the original list of beneficiaries when names of people who did not live in the community were included), influence peddling was not observed. What is more, in one case this position cost the promoter her job as a domestic worker in a nearby town, a problem that was not resolved until she was named and trained as a community health care promoter.[10]

In conclusion, the promoters have done a good job in general and have not benefited unduly from their positions. They are overworked and should receive some form of remuneration, compensation for travel costs and for opportunity employment. It is paradoxical that a programme that targets individuals so carefully, and fosters self-interest to such a large extent (i.e. in individualized payments for school attendance), should force one woman in every community to perform unpaid community service for an indefinite length of time, while actually granting her no real decision-making power.

As time has passed, additional benefits and services have been added. The majority of the children who receive bursaries also get support for the purchase of school materials, either in kind or in cash. The packages of medicine for the programme's beneficiaries have grown larger and new types of care not previously provided are now included, such as *pap* tests and periodic treatments for the elimination of parasites.

III. Social changes and responses

Our evaluations sought to understand the impact of PROGRESA on the communities and households that received benefits. We performed two evaluations. The first comprised six communities in three states: Michoacán, Guanajuato and San Luis Potosí. These states in Western Mexico were involved in the first phase of PROGRESA (August 1997) and we expected to see the impact more clearly there than in areas where the programme began later. The second involved 12 communities in 12 states (Chiapas, Oaxaca, Guerrero, Yucatán, Campeche, Tabasco, Sinaloa, Sonora, Chihuahua, Veracruz, San Luis Potosí and Zacatecas). This latter study included communities more recently incorporated in the programme.

We were careful to select as great a variety of communities as possible. The sample was diverse in terms of language and ethnicity, degree of isolation, size, dominant political party and economic structure.[11] In all, our fieldwork extended from September 1998 to June 2000. We expected to detect any major changes.

The first evaluation included a survey of approximately 10 questionnaires for households that received benefits and another five for households that did not in each community. There were special questionnaires for the schoolteacher, students with and without benefits, the physician and the promoter, and a thematic guide for writing a report for each community. The second evaluation relied on longer stays in each community and only ethnographic work. Here I shall present my analysis of the impact of the programme in general terms. Community reports are available.

The impact is described from two perspectives. In the first, I refer to the operation of the programme (a process evaluation). In the second, I deal with the effects of the programme on households, communities and the public agencies (outcome evaluation).

Selection

In the first evaluation we found PROGRESA was the first federal social programme to be carried out in half of the communities (not counting schools and clinics). In other words, the formal, technical procedures for selecting the communities and households allowed the programme to contact households that before were beyond the reach of the state. On the other hand, it indicates that support programmes – such as PROCAMPO – are not reaching farmers in the more marginal communities.

Opinions concerning the precision and correction of the census of beneficiaries are highly variable. In general, the inhabitants of the communities did not know why the first census was being carried out. Although it is clear that the majority of the poorest households were selected, some very poor ones were excluded and other reasonably prosperous ones included.[12] This was to be expected, but in some cases it was serious because the reasons for exclusion had to do precisely with extreme poverty. We learned of cases of widowed or abandoned mothers who were not present in the community because their extreme poverty forced them to work in another town: their questionnaires went unanswered. The existence of members of the household in the United States was also a source of inaccurate information. If it was reported that the migrants had abandoned the home, then it was quite probable that the particular household would be named as a beneficiary. If it was reported, however, that such migrants were sending back remittances, the household was practically always excluded from the programme. Distant households were not interviewed in some cases, partly because of disagreements over their community affiliation. Owing to community disputes, on two occasions some of the poorest households were excluded. In one case PROGRESA responded by 'making' two communities out of one. In another case, a group of four households that had been expelled from the community was not included. During the initial evaluation, very poor households with only one or two elderly persons had been interviewed, but their low dependency ratios excluded them from the programme. During the second evaluation this problem was corrected. Non-interviews, however, were not corrected, simply because the programme headquarters had no information about them, and a special census of these households would have increased census costs considerably. According to the national coordinator, however, when community promoters drew a list stating 10 per cent or more of the households had not been interviewed a new census was carried out.

When the locality is incorporated, the brigade in charge of the process presents a variety of explanations for having included or excluded certain households. When they stated that the poorest households were chosen, the community responded by drawing a list of households that, in their opinion, should be included. In order to avoid conflict, incorporation staff tended to say that the process was 'like a raffle' and that other people would be included later, thus avoiding complaints. When nearly all the families from a certain town were included and the question was asked why a handful of others were left out, the head of the brigade replied that it was impossible to incorporate all.

The varying forms in which the selection process was presented had repercussions on folk explanations of the process. When this was the first occasion in which such a programme arrived in a particular locality, the level of gratitude was remarkable. A letter signed by president Zedillo himself and addressed personally to each beneficiary reinforced this. People's hopes were expressed in more or less the following terms: 'it isn't much help, but the government has finally arrived and that means they're finally going to take us into account.' In other cases, when the random nature of the selection process was emphasized, God was thought to be responsible.

There were differences in the follow-up given to complaints arising from the selection process. In one community, a second census was carried out. In other cases – despite petitions to this effect – there was no repetition of the census.

We asked each beneficiary interviewed if anyone had conditioned her enrolment in the programme on political support or adoption of family planning. We also asked if at any later date an individual had demanded that they perform some service (besides the duties indicated by the programme) in order to conserve their benefits. Answers were always negative.[13]

In our assessment, more than 90 per cent of the households receiving assistance needed it. A few did not, and in one or two communities these erroneously included households were so obvious (the owners of several shrimp farms, for example) that complaints were inevitable. In addition, however, we detected between 5 and 10 per cent of village households that were erroneously included.[14] These mistakes clearly call for a more careful census process. Increasing the length of time interviewers are in the communities by one or two days should improve selection markedly. It is also necessary to allow them to verify information (often, by simply crossing the gate was it possible to see a pick-up, a thresher or a tractor in a household reportedly owning nothing in the official census).

In all, we studied 17 communities (one in San Luis Potosí was visited for both evaluations). In all but one the census was carried out directly with potential beneficiaries. In Chihuahua, however, in a Tarahumara village, the interviewer collected all his information from the village store tender. There were a number of mistakes. Although most of the village was initially selected, all the families but one were dropped from the programme soon after because they were not trained in their obligations, and also because the radio was down and no one in the municipal presidency cared to let them know through other means that they had to attend a meeting there.

Health care

Both doctors and mothers recognized the relatively rapid effect (only a few months) of the nutritional supplement given to undernourished children. Those children overcame their lack of nutrition and began to grow and develop more rapidly thanks to the supplement. In one locality a female doctor showed us the height/weight charts and it was clear that the children who were taking the treatment were growing and gaining weight more quickly. The principal problem here was that mothers, at times, succumbed to the temptation of sharing the supplement among more people (including their husbands), against the doctors' instructions. The supplement is delivered in rations that suffice for one person (a child or the pregnant or lactating mother). If it is shared among more people, however, it will obviously not have any effect on the undernourished child. This is, first, a problem of solidarity and unity within the family itself, but it can also be a technical problem. As the diagnosis of malnourishment is based only on basic measurements, the mother may correctly perceive that another child also requires the supplement, despite having been diagnosed as healthy.

In other words, the programme's emphasis on discriminating and individualizing even within the family – though understandable – is not necessarily effective, on the one hand and, on the other, not always accurate. Extreme individualization of targeted policies is at odds with family dynamics.

The health care indicated by the PROGRESA programme was offered almost exclusively in the health clinics of the SSA (the Health Ministry) or IMSS COPLAMAR. With one exception (a town near Irapuato where medical attention was available in an urban clinic), all of the health centres were 'first-level' clinics, providing basic care and birth assistance. In the majority of the communities access to such clinics was made possible for the first time through PROGRESA or was improved through involvement in the programme. This confirms the reports of many fieldworkers in Mexico to the effect that the 'open coverage' health system in reality does not serve the majority of the population that it is supposed to aid.

In five of the six towns transportation to the health clinic was expensive and time-consuming (more than one hour). In some places people had to walk perhaps half an hour and then take a bus. Complaints abounded because, on some occasions, mothers with two small children (less than four years old) could easily spend more than half their 'basic support' on trips to the health clinic. This was especially true if, in addition to the cost of transportation, they had to spend money on food or drinks along the way. In other words, although the service itself is free, other costs involved can greatly reduce the effective support received. Cash payments are important in light of the 'subsistence' economy of highly marginal communities, but when the requirements of the programme force the beneficiaries into greater contact with the *cash* economy, this support vanishes. To this we can add the fact that most of the clinics require the mothers to perform some sort of 'voluntary labor' when they take their children for check-ups or to attend talks. This may vary from mopping the offices to weeding a vegetable or flower garden. Although such work does not imply a cash outlay, it does mean additional trips, or turning a doctor's appointment into an all-day absence from home and/or work.

In spite of the foregoing, access to health care provided by the programme was often more significant than the monetary support, especially in the case of older couples. People with long-term treatments who began to receive benefits upon entering the programme and gained access to free medicines and to second- or third-level medical attention, underwent a favourable change in their economy and their lives.

On our first visit, however, we observed that the workers in the clinics were overloaded. The waiting time for emergency attention was variable, but normally quite long. This saturation was related to the increase in the amount of work resulting from follow-up appointments for beneficiaries of the PROGRESA programme (a follow-up programme for healthy people had never before been instituted). The emergencies that gave rise to such long waits were usually due to gastrointestinal or respiratory ailments among small children who had diarrhoea or high fevers. In addition to long waits, mothers did not always receive the treatment they expected, either because medicines often ran short or else because the expected treatment was not indicated. It must be noted that private doctors freely and commonly use strong medicines that should only be prescribed after a clinical diagnosis or the failure of home remedies.

During the second round of visits to the communities, however, we observed two important changes. First, saturation at the clinics was even worse. With the passing of time more communities and households within the territory of the clinics had been included, but in only one clinic had additional personnel been hired to attend to the needs of the PROGRESA families. In the other clinics doctors had implemented one or more of the following strategies:

- intensifying the training of the mothers so they could treat basic ailments at home;
- rationing the emergency appointments allowed to the people of each village;
- setting up appointment systems for patients with non-urgent problems.

Secondly, by that time the health promoters (visitors) had begun to work in various communities. These women (in one case the promoter of PROGRESA herself) received training to carry out the basic evaluation of the state of health of children and adults and thus freed the clinics of this chore. They managed a small package of basic medicines that included 10 articles (those prescribed in more than 90 per cent of the visits to the clinics). These health promoters received a small remuneration (very small in net terms, as it was often absorbed by travel costs to the nearest town for supplies and the shipping costs for the boxes of nutritional supplement which may weigh more than 100 kilos). The PROGRESA promoter who was also trained as a health promoter was very pleased, however, because she had a small income and felt that she did indeed have some modest 'tools' with which to treat the most common complaints of her beneficiaries. Moreover, this obliged her to spend more time in her own community and so she was able to do (or supervise) her housework. The duties of the visitors include: certifying that the families show up for their medical appointments; diagnosing cases of under-nourishment through the use of measuring devices (*nutricintas*) and deciding whether or not a child needs the supplement, although all children diagnosed with malnourishment must be referred to the clinic. They also treat the most common health problems.

Obviously, after their two-month training course the capacity of the visitors cannot be compared to that of the doctors: there is a very real possibility that they might not perceive many problems. Their work, however, has allowed the system to handle the growing number of families in the programmes of systematic health care. Whatever PROGRESA's fate, it is imperative that these women be encouraged to perform this job, and that they be further trained, for no doctor will come and live in most of these villages. Also, they should receive better pay (we were told that their salary was 300 pesos or £20 per month), as their activities take up several hours of a day.

There are other limitations to the health care offered by the clinics, the first being their hours of service. In the poorest areas we visited, the only health care alternative is with traditional healers. In less marginal regions, private doctors and clinics treated medical emergencies that occur after 'office' hours. Also, patients are seen during only a few hours each day, much less than the official opening hours. Other cases were treated by druggists or with traditional, household remedies. Still, a high level of variation subsisted in the quality of attention, the saturation, and the opening hours in the different clinics. Some clinics were only opened when the nurse or the doctor heard our researchers were asking about PROGRESA; others unduly restricted their patient hours. Less than half provided attention during the length of the working day.

Secondly, there is the problem (currently being confronted) of the planning and coordination of first- and second-level services. By the end of 1998, all women above a certain age had been given pap tests as part of the programme of medical check-ups. According to information from the national coordination of the programme, this included some 800 000 women who, generally, had never before undergone that particular test. Because of the ensuing saturation in regional hospitals, attention was not provided promptly to women with evidence of cancer. Many therefore hurried to small private clinics, where they sometimes paid more than in the best hospitals.

This expense plunged families further into debt. One of the women, whose husband was working in the US, notified him of the operation so that he would stay and work for a longer time in order to pay off this new debt. Only one woman in the Michoacán village waited for two months until her next appointment and sometime later had an operation in a third-level public hospital in Morelia. In July 1999 all these women were feeling well. In our second evaluation, we found most beneficiary women had undergone this test.

There are various lessons:

1. Such tests should be programmed so as to avoid the saturation of second- and third-level centres.
2. The beneficiaries tested should receive counselling as to the urgency of future treatment.
3. It would be convenient to study the system of supervision of these services and the tariffs charged at private clinics, or perhaps to implement a system of subrogation. No private clinic made any additional tests before performing surgery, and simply chose the most expensive and risky remedy. It is possible that one or more of these women did not really require surgery.

The tests, easily accepted in the community in Michoacán (except for the anxiety of those women who tested positive), sparked conflicts in the state of San Luis Potosí, where we studied T'enek communities. There, rumours circulated alleging that the pap test was not a cancer test at all, but in reality a method of contraception. In one of those two communities all women except one refused to take the test. Those who refused then had the amount of their support reduced.[5] The doctor (a woman in this case) said the change in cash support had nothing to do with her, which thereby gave rise to other rumours.

These difficulties were not exclusive to indigenous communities, however. In the state of Zacatecas, we found a few husbands had forbidden their wives to undergo the exam. Two had even forbidden them to attend health talks, and one had refused to let her travel to another village to collect her cash. These women were dropped from the roster of beneficiaries.

Dealing with the sexuality of indigenous women is especially difficult for public health agencies. Frequently it is the husband who must consent not only to the use of birth control methods (health workers normally talk with both members of the couple), but also to any gynaecological treatment. And, just as frequently, they will not. In other cases it is the mother-in-law that must be convinced, since, when the married couple is young, she is the main beneficiary of her daughter-in-law's labour. PROGRESA does not pressure its beneficiaries to join a systematic birth control programme, although this is its second objective in the area of health care. We were especially careful to ask this. The response was always negative. In the clinics, however, they are informed of this possibility. Moreover, high-risk women are informed of their condition and the use of contraceptive methods is recommended.

Finally, there were complaints concerning the unwillingness of the medical personnel at the clinics to refer the beneficiaries to second- or third-level hospitals. In general, those who accede to such services are satisfied with them, although the overall opinion is that physicians do everything in their power to avoid giving referrals to larger urban hospitals in the system.

In synthesis, health care is the most complex aspect of the programme. It was very clear that the nutritional supplements and the health follow-ups implemented through the programme have indeed had fast, beneficial effects, especially for young children. The application of certain unfamiliar medical tests, such as that of cervical-uterine cancer, had positive effects, in the end. But, on the first occasion at least, they had consequences that were not entirely desirable, including the fact that some women took recourse to private health care services, at an extremely high cost. The availability of health care services for emergencies and for second- and third-level medical attention should be improved. In the cases where this has been authorized, the benefits for the patients have been great indeed, both in terms of the medical attention they receive and the savings they can attain, compared with the use of private services, where and when they exist. (In Michoacán such services were relatively accessible, but very expensive; while in the T'enek communities there was simply no such alternative.) The conflicts arising from rumours, a justified historical mistrust of government and lack of familiarity with medical practice within the T'enek communities should all be taken as learning experiences for the programme and its beneficiaries.

Nutrition

The final aspect of this evaluation concerns nutrition. The general opinion among the households that benefited from the programme is that nutrition has improved since the arrival of PROGRESA, although the bursaries and other cash supports are insufficient to change the alimentation for the whole of the two-month period between deliveries of programme materials.

The promoters, the staff at the clinics and the personnel that make up the 'assembly of incorporation' recommend that the women spend PROGRESA funds on high-protein foods and long-lasting foodstuffs (such as sardines and tuna), in order to maximize consumption time, since monies arrive only once in two months. The women are also urged to make their purchases as soon as they receive the money, because if these funds find their way into the home they can easily be turned to other uses; especially male vices (alcohol).

For this reason, the women arrive home carrying several bags of groceries on the day they receive their PROGRESA payments.[16] If the women do this, these groceries last an average of perhaps two weeks, or a little more; while PROGRESA payments are made approximately every eight weeks.[17] A medical evaluation is required to judge whether or not this change of diet for two weeks out of every eight actually achieves a significant improvement in the physical well-being of the beneficiaries. We were often told 'it's very little, but we do feel [the difference]', as if it was very important and the family did indeed eat better.

Once again, in the case of nutrition there arises a similar problem to that of the medical examinations. It was in the T'enek communities (visibly the poorest and most marginal ones in the study), where the doctor told us that PROGRESA resources were diverted to the purchase of alcohol, because the men demanded the money and the women were unable to put up any resistance. The second time we went to one of those communities, when programme resources had just been delivered, we found that the stores in the town had run out of liquor and that one case of domestic violence had taken place. According to the doctor, violence erupted because the husband had demanded the PROGRESA money, but the beneficiary had refused to give it to him. It would be irresponsible on our part, however, to say that we found many cases of violence or of programme funds being systematically diverted. In five of the six communities in the first evaluation it was reported that the funds were being put to good use and only in one community were there two cases of domestic violence (the aforementioned case and one earlier). It would be worthwhile strengthening the monitoring in these communities, which, curiously enough, are the ones with the greatest need of PROGRESA support. In the Zacatecas community mentioned above, we found health teams had organized youth clubs. These clubs included a variety of activities, and prepared teenagers for a more balanced division of power at marriage, as well as general hygiene and family planning. The clubs thrived in spite of extreme male authoritarianism. It seems important to organize such clubs elsewhere.

Education

The complexity of the interaction among beneficiaries and public and private health systems bear no comparison with what occurs in the case of education. Above all, there can be no doubt that attendance has improved markedly in the localities studied since PROGRESA began and that boys and girls are reaching higher grades and educational levels. At the beginning of the school year PROGRESA gives each family a school calendar and a programme that tells parents how many days the children must attend school during each month of the year, so as not to lose the educational bursary.

Mexican public schools are free, but expenses always arise. In addition to school supplies, parents have to cooperate with cash and work for various school activities. Since PROGRESA increasingly provides school supplies, the scholarships should mostly be spent on better food and clothing for the children. Although the amount of the scholarship for grade three is quite low (roughly £8), opportunity income is also low. Opportunity incomes, however, rise faster than the scholarships, although earnings from work in the fields are insecure and not net (some expenses are unavoidable). So far, there are no estimations of the optimal size of the bursary in terms of maximization of school attendance. However, it is a fact that the children who receive this support are staying in school longer.

There are many elements of judgement in the decision to keep children in school, take them out, or make them return, especially after sixth grade. Key elements are the cost of transportation in terms of money and time (which are much higher for these grades, since there are fewer schools), teachers' absenteeism and the problem of how teachers should certify attendance. In one case we were told that a *telesecundaria* (a rural secondary school with classes via satellite television), had been installed in a neighbouring town some time before, but soon abandoned. In general, however, we did not find any opposition to maintaining children in primary school.

The matter of school performance was examined only through the opinions of teachers and parents, since a separate evaluation is assessing increased enrolment on the basis of a much larger sample. Teachers in the first evaluation reported that improvements in performance, in their opinion, related to better food and increased attendance; teachers in the second evaluation were less positive. We did not, however, see systematic academic evaluations, comparisons between groups of beneficiaries and non-beneficiaries or comparisons between report cards before and after the introduction of the programme. Parents expressed the opinion that children took more interest in school and had better attendance, but that frequent teacher absences caused problems; among others, the fact that the children could not fulfil the minimum number of school days required by PROGRESA.

In the first community, the teacher (who also functioned as principal, as it was only a two-room schoolhouse) did not collaborate by certifying attendance. The opinion in town was that the SEP zone inspector did not want to overload his teachers. In place of this teacher PROGRESA had appointed an educational supervisor whose responsibility was to record daily attendance. In reality, however, it was this individual's daughter who took attendance, with all the risks that this implies. During our last visit to that community, a new teacher had taken responsibility for the PROGRESA papers. Finally, only four communities in the first evaluation responded positively as to the support for school materials. In the other towns, people did not know that this support was also coordinated by PROGRESA.

In summary, the increase in both registrations for higher grades and attendance was very clear, and we received positive opinions concerning school performance. The most important gap was found between the end of primary school and the beginning of secondary school, because of higher costs, greater investment in transportation time and the fact that such young people sometimes take on adult jobs, mostly in the fields.

PROGRESA, micropolitics and national politics

In our second evaluation we observed a significant change in the work-load of promoters. In response to complaints (and our initial evaluation) in the sense that these agents were overburdened and investing in their honorary jobs as much or more than their benefits, PROGRESA decided to shift a part of their responsibilities onto 'municipal link agents'. These persons were appointed by municipal presidents to ensure that PROGRESA functioned smoothly in their jurisdictions. Municipal presidents accepted this responsibility, and their performance in making the programme deliver goods and services became a political issue. In some municipalities, doctors came to the communities with their nurses, while in others beneficiaries had to walk for hours; in some, payments were brought to the community while in others contingents had to spend a full day in transport to, and waiting in line at, payment centres. Transport of certificates was crucial, since payments could otherwise be delayed for months. The 'links', or *enlaces*, transport school and health certificates, are in charge of organizing and communicating meetings, and also use municipal transport to deliver food supplements and cash payments to distant communities. The federal government has increased the share of the total government budget in charge of municipalities, and their ability to decide how to use it. Municipalities can hire more personnel and buy vehicles, so they are better able to carry out this task than federal agencies, which are stretched thin in Mexico's 100 000 plus marginal communities.

The *enlaces* were responsible both for an improvement in the operation in the programme (and a lightening of the load of promoters) and for the intrusion of local politics into it. Most of them performed their tasks well. A number of them realized PROGRESA was a ticket to popularity, and made an effort to do their job, communicate errors to authorities, and generally to become known to rural inhabitants. A number of them, therefore, have since been elected to office (mostly with the PRI, but also to some extent with the PRD). This is not necessarily a problem, except when significant opposition movements are marginalized as a result, or when municipal governments feel threatened by the opposition and they threaten voters or buy votes through PROGRESA. There is no way PROGRESA headquarters can verify in every case reports that a number of families have moved from a certain community, for example. *Enlaces* could therefore effectively carry out some threats, and use PROGRESA in a partisan manner (a major magazine showed food supplements stamped with official propaganda). Some of these agents were replaced when news of their activities reached the media or PROGRESA headquarters.

Increasing political diversity and a new political culture should reduce the scope for these manipulations, but this change is likely to be slow among Mexico's most marginalized inhabitants. It is clear the programme must make an effort to incorporate municipal collaboration while reducing these practices.

On the other hand, PROGRESA was clearly identified by many beneficiaries with President Zedillo. This was partly blamed on Congress, which resisted endorsing PROGRESA for several years. As a result, it was expected that PROGRESA would swell voting for the president's party, the PRI. This did not happen. PROGRESA may have enabled the PRI to retain the votes of marginal communities, but it did not earn new sympathizers. In the 2000 elections, the PRI won Mexico's most marginal electoral districts, just as it did in 1994. Major PRI figures waited, until the last minute, for the voting tide to turn in their favour thanks to an increase in PRI voting from rural areas. That increase never arrived, and the opposition triumph, defined by urban votes, was reaffirmed. Rural areas are still more pro-PRI than urban areas, but PROGRESA did not produce a significant change.

Conclusions

PROGRESA is making progress towards its basic objectives, although in some aspects of each of these fundamental goals problems have surfaced. In terms of health care we mentioned that the medical staff is overworked and that in some cases there are problems with access. Also, the bursary is insufficient to modify nutrition during the entire period between deliveries of funds. In education, the jump from primary to secondary school is being made with greater frequency than before, but there is still an important gap. There are few examples of earlier programmes that have achieved such great advances in such a coordinated manner. The 'school breakfast' and LICONSA (milk) programs have had an important impact, but not over as wide a range of activities as those covered by PROGRESA.

Owing to its contrasting biases and strategies, PROGRESA does not substitute previous generalized subsidies. We did not find that it substituted in any way for the productive financing nor for the relatively lower prices for fertilizers available in other periods. On the other hand, the principal beneficiaries of the general price subsidies for corn and tortillas prevalent in the 1980s and early 1990s were not the poorer peasants, who could only enjoy these supports if they lacked corn and bought such products in establishments where the supports were in effect. In other words, it is likely that for the peasants in general in these communities, and for their household economies, the PROGRESA programme represents an effort that has no precedents and which seems to be having a greater impact than earlier programmes.

One area of concern is the lack of a related programme for productive improvements. The national coordinator of the programme told us that there were spontaneous local initiatives to organize productive projects and that efforts were being made within PROGRESA to encourage them. We do not know if anything has been done since our second visit, but it is extremely important that sources of wealth and employment are created in these communities.

The paramount responsibility of the state in terms of its polices is to achieve greater well-being for the population in general, not only through social policies, but mainly through economic and political ones. It is not my intention here, however, to criticize neo-liberalism. I am convinced, and have attempted to show in various other texts, that new economic policies have increased poverty and inequality, but this is beyond the scope of this evaluation (Escobar 1995). It is a fact, however, that both rural and urban poverty have increased. PROGRESA should be a 'residual' programme; meaning one that deals with the most highly marginalized sectors as part of state policy. In reality, however, it is a 'central' programme, or one that provides basic attention within the state and its public policies for the countryside. It benefits the extremely – and permanently – poor rural population and those affected by change (whether necessary or not is another question). In my opinion, the government's statement to the effect that it is a 'minor' programme is not correct, because it does in fact constitute the government's major support programme for millions of poor families. It should be expanded until it can cover the entire target population – the extreme rural poor, some 19 million people – and attention to equivalent urban poor families also needs to be given.

Santiago Levy, the intellectual father of this programme, affirms that PROGRESA cannot achieve fundamental change in the well-being of the population, as that could only be attained through a sustained period of economic growth that would generate employment opportunities for all, including the inhabitants of such marginal communities. Economic growth is necessary, of course, especially after 20 years of crisis and instability, but such growth would only have an impact if it were to include the creation of real jobs and better working conditions. During the past 20 years the quantity and quality of new jobs have deteriorated. Much of this has been due to the intervention of the state apparatus, by not compensating inflation in wage increases, abolishing price controls, implementing generalized hostility towards unions, and other means.

Although the rhythm of job creation from 1996–99 seems to have changed the tendencies of the 1982–95 period in the sense that an average of almost one million formal jobs are now being created per year (an important development in itself), these jobs are created at lower than average wage levels. The minimum wage has continued to fall and most jobs are created in large and medium-sized cities. Under these conditions not even job creation will impede the continuing generation of poverty in the cities as well.

Although its objectives can only be reached in the long term, PROGRESA should be recognized for significant progress. But the government should be responsible for covering the entire needy population and to fulfil all of the programme's objectives. It should also strive to learn from the programme and modify its actions as it grows and becomes more complex (and to remain faithful to its design, without falling into the temptation of lending itself to electoral use). Aside from specific recommendations, and assuming that market forces will remain above all others in government policy, it is necessary to conclude that (1) a programme such as this should be the responsibility of the state as a whole, not just the president's. In this sense, it should rise above party politics. (2) Full coverage needs to be implemented. This includes the cities, the most marginal rural communities, and implementation of real coverage in those agencies that, particularly in the health sector, are overcrowded and unable to provide adequate services. (3) Adequate maintenance and follow-ups of the beneficiary population are necessary, even if this reduces cost efficiency, but it would also be wise to provide coverage for entire communities in some very poor areas, and do without the census. (4) Dealing with the poorest among the rural poor – the many indigenous peoples encountered by the programme – should become a priority. Although some actions have been coordinated with the National Indigenous Institute, it would seem that the programme has encountered its most severe difficulties among indigenous groups. There is a learning process ahead for the Mexican state in this regard, but it would be worth asking whether the programme can overcome its centralized, individualized focus in order to achieve the changes it is seeking.

State responsibility does not end with the implementation of continuous learning in social policy-making. The government must now be urged to intervene in a positive way in areas such as remuneration, production and employment, so that these efforts to break the cycle of poverty through targeted programmes can be complemented by changes in employment structures and opportunities.

Notes

1. The study was co-directed by Mercedes González de la Rocha. Researchers included Eric Cach, Cipactli Mercado, Corina Preciado and Irene Rojas. Santiago Bastos coordinated the application of the questionnaire.
2. Out of the total budget for programmes of subsidies and transfers, PROGRESA absorbs no more than 15 per cent (7.7 million out of 48 billion pesos).
3. The author's estimate indicates an efficiency level of around 90 per cent. The official figure is 95 per cent for 1999. The rest is divided among the application of the *ENCASEH* (*Encuesta sobre las Características Socioeconómicas de los Hogares*), or 'Survey of Socioeconomic Characteristics of Households' (that absorbed approximately 3 per cent of the budget), administration and coordination.

4. Escobar (1995) undertakes an analysis of the state of poverty studies in Mexico and relates this to discussions that have emerged among anthropologists and other social scientists.
5. It is not possible to assign a date to this deterioration. However, the analysis of income distribution and economic restructuring in general shows that in Mexico the crisis in employment and urban salaries came first and that it was later propagated to the countryside, especially after the institutional reforms that resulted.
6. In a minority of cases, in the US.
7. Chihuahua and Oaxaca were incorporated early owing to natural catastrophes. Sonora is the one clear example of irregular incorporation due to electoral priorities. It joined PROGRESA six months before local elections, and the PRI succeeded in overcoming initially adverse voting preferences. Chiapas, although highly marginal, was incorporated later, because of the conflict there.
8. Regulations state that community members should be asked to state whether the list of beneficiaries is correct or not, and whether or not they suggest adding or deleting beneficiaries. We found this was not the case. Programme authorities stated that this had invariably led to conflict when tried.
9. Cash supports are delivered bi-monthly, but only five times per year, because of the impossibility of certifying school attendance during the summer months.
10. López Pérez and Raesfeld (2000) report, however, that a promoter in the state of Hidalgo did pressure women saying she would not certify their compliance with the programme if they did not vote for the PRI. This triggered protests and she was replaced.
11. With which I recognize that we share the same suspicions as the senators that were criticized at the beginning of the text.
12. We cannot affirm with certainty that the process failed, as we cannot replicate the process through our methods (more qualitative than quantitative). However, we believe in our appreciation and those of our researchers, that after one week in the community it was possible to identify the poor and the very poor. This was frequently accomplished through obvious indicators, such as the possession of vehicles, electronic apparatuses or cattle (although this last form was rarely reported to PROGRESA), or, on the contrary, through the total lack of land and other property. Daily interaction with the families in the communities was also useful, because we were able to find out with certainty what they ate, how much and when.
13. But a reliable weekly, *Proceso*, reported that state government officials in Guerrero did tell women they had to adopt family planning to join the programme.
14. During the second evaluation we did not carry out a quantitative assessment of income or property. My assessment is derived from the field researchers' lengthy stays, which allowed them to visit families in their homes. PROGRESA interviewers, on the other hand, were not allowed to verify the information provided by respondents, and typically spent only one or two days in each community.
15. I suppose they were re-established later, but we didn't find out.
16. One consequence of this is that the majority of the spending takes place in the communities where PROGRESA funds are distributed and not in the marginal communities themselves. Another is that there have been complaints that on those days buses and store-keepers increase prices.
17. There are almost always delays in the delivery of these resources. In general, the communities blame the programme, while programme personnel affirm that the documentation for school attendance and visits to the clinics arrives late at the national offices.

Bibliography

Boltvinik, Julio, 'La satisfacción de las necesidades esenciales en México en los setenta y ochenta', in P.P. Moncayo and José Woldenberg (comps), *Desarrollo, desigualdad y medio ambiente en México*, Mexico D.F., Cal y Arena, 1994.

CEPAL-INEGI, *La pobreza en México*, Aguascalientes, Mexico: INEGI, 1993.

CONAPO (Consejo Nacional de Población), *La situación demográfica de México 1998*, Mexico D.F.: CONAPO, 1998.

CONAPO, *La situación demográfica de México 1999*, Mexico D.F.: CONAPO, 1999.

Escobar, Agustín, 'Politics and academic disciplines: Poverty research in Mexico', in El Oyen et al., *Poverty: A Global Perspective*, Copenhagen, Scandinavian University Press, 1995.

Escobar, Agustín, Frank D. Bean and Sidney Weintraub, *La dinámica de la emigración mexicana*, Mexico D.F.: Miguel Angel Porrúa-CIESAS, 1999.

Hernández Laos, Enrique, 'La pobreza en México', in *Comercio Exterior* 42(4), 1992.

López Pérez, Sócrates and Lydia Raesfeld, 'Evaluación del Programa Educación, Salud y Alimentación (PROGRESA) bajo el diseño de políticas sociales. El caso de zonas indígenas de Hidalgo', Paper delivered at Primer Congreso sobre Pobreza y Políticas de Bienestar, U.A.T. December 2000.

Molinar Horcasitas, Juan and Jeffrey Weldon, 'Programa Nacional de Solidaridad: determinantes partidistas y consecuencias electorales', *Estudios Sociológicos* 12(34), 1994.

PROGRESA (ed.), *PROGRESA. Más oportunidades para las familias pobres*. Eight Volumes. Mexico City: PROGRESA.

Roberts, Bryan and Agustín Escobar, 'Mexican Social and Economic Policy and Emigration' in F.D. Bean, R. de la Garza, B. Roberts and S. Weintraub (eds), *At the Crossroads: Mexico and U.S. Immigration Policy*, Lenham, MD: Rowman and Littlefield Publishers, 1997.

10
Stakeholder Politics in Bolivia: Revisiting Second Generation Reforms

George Gray-Molina

Some of the most ambitious and innovative public policy reforms adopted in Latin America in recent years have made stakeholder appeals to citizen participation, self-help and ownership.[1] By involving and mobilizing potential beneficiaries during reform adoption and forwarding the long-term benefits of reform to the present, politicians have hoped to make contentious reforms self-sustaining. However, five years into reform implementation, questions of long-term institutional survival are more than ever on the minds of reformers. Poor institutional performance, public disenchantment and policy reversals have started to unravel some of the more political and volatile aspects of privatization, pension and decentralization reforms throughout the region. How to make complex and divisive policy reforms succeed? How to move from policy adoption to implementation, from short-term feasibility to long-term viability? Where do the so-called second generation reforms fit in the larger scheme of political and economic development?[2]

To a large extent, stakeholder appeals have been quite successful, as illustrated by the experiences of a number of Latin American and Eastern European countries undertaking institutional reforms in the early and mid-1990s.[3] A key feature of the stakeholder approach has been to invoke citizen ownership during reform adoption, while shielding reform stakes from state, party or clientelistic capture. The Bolivian case is perhaps paradigmatic of this approach, as a stream of reforms initiated in the mid-1990s led to a period of rapid reform and to heightened optimism concerning longer-term prospects for development.[4] The Bolivian capitalization and pension reforms created new social entitlements for senior citizens (a lump-sum grant per person of US$248). The Popular Participation reform created public investment entitlements for organized community organizations (a fiscal transfer per person of US$22). Five years into the implementation of these reforms, however, policy reversals have stirred a debate on the resilience of second generation reforms and the importance of a long-term political perspective. This chapter addresses the scope and limits to the stakeholder approach as developed in Bolivia over the past five years. Three questions are considered. First, stakeholder politics are described and contrasted to other political approaches to policy reform. Second, the Bolivian capitalization/pension and Popular Participation reforms are discussed and used to illustrate the scope and limits of stakeholder politics in a context of fragile institutional development. Third, stakeholder politics are considered in the context of longer-term challenges to state-building, political institutionalization and inclusive citizenship.

I. The stakeholder approach

The stakeholder approach to policy reform represents a departure from both the stylized 'neo-liberal' approaches discussed by Nelson (1994), Haggard and Kaufman (1995) and the alternative 'populist neo-liberal' approaches discussed by Roberts (1995), Weyland (1999), and Stokes (1998). Substantively, the stakeholder approach can be characterized by a political appeal to 'citizen ownership', motivated by self-interest, insulated from state, party or clientelistic capture, and delivered through newly created institutional channels (see Graham, 1998). The stakeholder approach articulates a thicker political appeal than that made by neo-liberal reformers, but thinner than most populist neo-liberals or other more idealized consensual or deliberative approaches advanced by reformers. Social and political entitlements are at the centre of the new approach. Stakeholder politics aim at both facilitating reform adoption and mobilizing potential stakeholders during implementation. Unlike some neo-liberal reformers, the stakeholder approach does not eschew politics nor play down state activism; unlike populist neo-liberals, however, public appeals are not intended to cater to more politically charged nationalist, ethnic or corporatist political discourses. Ideas of inclusive citizenship are taken to be the political link between short-term reforms and broader development objectives.

In the Bolivian case, the stakeholder approach has depended on a relatively unique set of institutional and political conditions. Strong executive power authority and technocratic space delivered by coalition politics were coupled by proactive presidential leadership. Three aspects of the political framework stand out in the Bolivian experience. First, the practice of coalition politics allowed both the legislative and executive leeway needed to elect and empower reformist presidents. As noted by Eduardo Gamarra (1997), the relatively strong degree of political authority vested in the Bolivian presidency results from the assembly of governing coalitions based on party discipline and reinforced by the use of state patronage. In 1993, Gonzalo Sánchez de Lozada's *Movimiento Nacionalista Revolucionario* (MNR) won 34 per cent of the popular vote, enough to assemble an MNR-led coalition with the *Unión Cívica Solidaridad* (UCS) and the *Movimiento Bolivia Libre* (MBL), delivering a 61 per cent legislative majority. An outstanding characteristic of the 1993 electoral race was that most of the policy initiatives sketched in Sánchez de Lozada's electoral manifesto, the *Plan de Todos*, were eventually adopted and implemented. Sánchez de Lozada's administration was the third of five successive coalitions that would maintain legislative majorities, thus ensuring effective executive policy space.

Second, presidential leadership and technocratic decision-making became the backbone of reformist policy-making during the Sánchez de Lozada administration. The emergence of a cadre of economists, lawyers and businessmen, under direct leadership of a reformist president, insulated technical design from outside party and public opinion. Law drafting was almost exclusively made outside the legislature, in small groups presided over by the president. The Popular Participation reform, in particular, took up nearly half of the presidential working days between August 1993 and April 1994 (see Archondo, 1997; Molina, 1997). Sánchez de Lozada's overwhelming involvement in policy design was eventually to attract criticism from within the governing party and coalition. Sánchez de Lozada's public approval ratings also declined, as reform benefits trickled and failed to meet public expectations regarding change.

Third, achievements notwithstanding, the very success of stakeholder reforms was to have significant boomerang effects. Public expenditure and employment shifted from the central to local governments, and from government to the private sector. By 1997, nearly 60 per cent of the annual national public investment plan had been transferred to prefectural and municipal governments, and the equivalent of 12 per cent of annual GDP was capitalized and transferred to privately owned and managed pension funds. The new governing coalition led by Hugo Banzer Suarez' *Acción Democrática Nacionalista* (ADN) faced difficult political conditions after 1997. A grand alliance that included the centre-left *Movimiento de Izquierda Revolucionario* (MIR), the populist *Unión Cívica Solidaridad* (UCS) and *Conciencia de Patria* (CONDEPA), *Nueva Fuerza Republicana* (NFR) and other smaller parties, delivered a two-thirds legislative majority. New political actors playing by old coalition rules, however, found it hard to negotiate acceptable terms of political inclusion, leading, in 2000, to a sharp political reversal. With the expulsion of CONDEPA and the NFR from the governing coalition, the president lost a majority in congress; the first such loss in fifteen years of democratic rule. An additional factor affecting coalition politics was a wave of succession battles that threatened caudillo leadership in most of the major parties. Public disenchantment with the established political parties had also led to the appearance of two major 'anti-party' movements, set to capitalize on public discontent in the 1999 local elections.

The political conditions that promoted stakeholder politics in 1993 had largely collapsed by 1999. Political inertia and policy reversals ensured that the policy optimism which had marked the Sánchez de Lozada period, dissipated and delivered a new governing style based on more visible policy targets, including IMF/World Bank-funded Highly Indebted Poor Country (HIPC) debt-relief completion points and US-funded coca-crop eradication targets.

II. Capitalization/pension reform

Capitalization and pension reform in Bolivia have been characterized by equal measures of innovation during policy design and political reversal. The feature that caught the attention of many policy analysts during reform design – tying the privatization of public enterprises to comprehensive pension reform – also caught the attention of opposition politicians intent on reforming the system in 1998 (see von Gersdorff, 1997; Qeisser, 1998). Today, the capitalization of public enterprises is deemed a relative success; the overhaul of the pension system, however, is perceived as still pending. Although the interaction between technical and political problems is ubiquitous to policy reform, this section considers each separately to address the process of policy adoption, implementation and reversal over the past five years.

The reforms

One of the key ideas included in Sánchez de Lozada's 1993 electoral plan was a strategy to capitalize and redistribute public enterprise shares among the public. Under the 'capitalization' scheme, strategic investors were invited to double the equity capital of the major public enterprises, in exchange for direct management of the new private/public companies. Fifty per cent of the shares of these new enterprises were then transferred to a pension trust fund benefiting Bolivian citizens born by 31 December 1995, known as the Collective Capitalization Fund (FCC). Besides creating a collective fund, the reform also created individual pension accounts, under an Individual Capitalization Fund (FCI). The new mixed pension system, made up of both the FCC and FCI, replaced the old pay-as-you-go system.

The adoption of the capitalization and pension reforms faced sustained opposition. Between August 1993 and May of 1994, a small group of advisers, ministers and the president drew up the Capitalization Law. The governing coalition passed the law in June 1994 and braced itself for critical public reaction. Between 1994 and 1997 five public enterprises were successfully capitalized: the national electrification enterprise (ENDE), railroads (ENFE), telecommunications (ENTEL), airlines (LAB), and the gas and oil company (YPFB). Together, they attracted investment commitments of US$1.6 billion, equivalent to 22 per cent of Bolivian GDP. Each public offering was met with organized and mobilized worker opposition; the railways and airline company offerings led to violent conflict in 1996. By the end of the capitalization process, opposition shifted swiftly to pension reform. The second stage focused on tying the benefits from capitalization to a comprehensive reform of the existing social security system. By 1996, a new pension reform law was drafted and passed in congress. The law outlined the transformation of a defined-benefit and publicly managed pension system into a defined-contribution and privately managed system. An individual capitalization scheme, based on the Chilean model, was complemented by a collective capitalization scheme, paid as an annuity to citizens over the age of 65. The BONOSOL, as the annuity was called, was marketed as an immediate and tangible benefit of the politically conflictive capitalization process. In 1997, pensioners thus received the BONOSOL annuity of US$248 plus at least 70 per cent of the minimum monthly wage of US$48 until their savings were exhausted. While pensioners drew on savings they could expect to earn more than the minimum wage, and maintain the value of earnings as all pensions, including those transferred from the old system, were indexed to the US dollar. The law also provided for death, survivorship and disability pensions financed by insurance contracts.

Technical problems

In retrospect, two questions of institutional design stood out during reform adoption. The first involved the criteria for defining beneficiaries/stakeholders. The initial proposal discussed by Sánchez de Lozada in 1993 would have granted 'capitalization shares' to every adult citizen; the final proposal restricted benefits to senior citizens. The appeal of widespread

Table 10.1 Capitalization programme 1993–97

Mixed enterprise	Capital investor	Book value (before)	Capitalization value (after)
ENDE (Electricity)			
Corani	Dominion Energy	33.0	58.7
Garachi	Energy Initiatives	35.0	47.1
Valle Hermoso	Constellation Energy	30.7	33.9
ENTEL (Telecom)	Stet	130.0	610.0
LAB (Airlines)	Vasp	24.0	47.4
ENFE (Trains)			
FCCC Andina	Cruz Blanca Andina	29.0	13.2
FCCC Oriente	Cruz Blanca Oriente	24.0	25.8
YPFB (Oil & Gas)			
Petrolera Andina	YPF-Pluspetrol	102.3	264.7
Petrolera Chaco	Amoco	104.8	306.6
Transredes	Enron-Shell	134.8	263.5
Total (US$)		647.6	1670.9

Source: Ministry of Capitalization (1997).

stake-ownership was offset by both the arithmetic of massive redistribution (totalling a US$450 dollar lump-sum grant) and the logistics of identifying beneficiaries (a new identification registry would take two to three years to reach the entire adult population) (see Mercado, 1998). The final proposal adopted by the Sánchez de Lozada administration reduced logistical outreach problems by making the annuity payable to a self-reported cohort of senior citizens. While falsification and double claims were reported in 1997, what most surprised pension providers was the surge in identification card registration for poor and rural senior citizens, who were previously excluded from an array of other benefits, including old-age health care benefits, transportation discounts and voting. Recipients, numbering over 350 000 surpassed pension actuarial estimates by 21 per cent (original estimates predicted approximately 290 000 beneficiaries).

The second question involved the fiscal and economic effects of tying capitalization to pension reform. The fiscal cost of reforming the pension system was equivalent to 2.6 per cent of GDP in 1998, 2 per cent in 1999 and is only expected to decrease to 1 per cent by 2008. The fiscal hole is being repaid through pension fund purchases of government bonds (at 8 per cent interest, and 10 to 15 year maturity) and the liquidation of assets from the old pension system roughly equivalent to 140 million dollars. While the transition from the old to new system is estimated to have saved the Bolivian state approximately 1.2 billion dollars over 40 years, the present-day impact of the deficit is high. A second concern focused on linking annuity payments to the performance of pension administrators. The government placed a series of stringent investment criteria on administrators, with regards to the types of instruments, risk ratings, liquidity levels and others. The expectation that administrators might dynamize the local stock market have, three years into reform, gone unfulfilled.

Political problems

Two distinct problems clouded the adoption of the capitalization/pension reforms. The first concerned political timing. The BONOSOL annuity came under fire during the 1997 presidential elections. Annuities were still being paid weeks before the national elections in June, reaching over 350 000 citizens by election time. Rather than defer on redistribution, the government attempted to capitalize on the political appeal of the BONOSOL. The annuity was justified as a tangible and visible benefit from the controversial and contested capitalization and pension reform processes. The focus on senior citizens struck an additional redistributive appeal during the campaign. By election time the BONOSOL is thought to have increased the MNR vote by a sizeable margin.

The second problem concerned the politics of policy reversal. Although opposition parties had pledged not to overturn the BONOSOL payments if elected, they did favour a review of the fiscal impact of pension reform. Both the equity of an untargeted benefit for the elderly and the fiscal sustainability of a massive reform were seriously questioned. If a portion or all of the dividends of capitalization were used for other purposes, including targeted investments in basic education and sanitation services, it was argued, the overall social return on the reforms could be made significantly higher. By the time the Banzer administration was inaugurated in August, a major review of the individual and collective capitalization pension accounts was to make the first order of business. By June 1998, a new Law on Popular Property and Credit was drafted and passed by the new administration, amending the capitalization and pension reform laws. The new law suspended payments on the BONOSOL, and called for a reorganization of the collective capitalization scheme. Rather than pay dividends to citizens over 65, the new law divides the collective account into two: a popular share account, for citizens under the age of 50 in December 1995, and a solidarity account, for citizens over the age of 50, in December 1995. The first account is planned to hold 70 per cent of the shares of the collective capitalization scheme; the second will hold 30 per cent, to be paid out as an annuity, termed the BOLIVIDA, to citizens over the age of 65.

The amount of the BOLIVIDA annuity is expected to be established by executive decree, and paid out annually starting in 2001. Beneficiaries of the BOLIVIDA annuity will be able to donate their shares to a social foundation managed by the Catholic Church or transfer them to the Treasury for monetization and expenditure on public infrastructure. Recipients of the BOLIVIDA will receive approximately 30 per cent of the BONOSOL. Holders of the 'popular shares', on the other hand, will also be able to transfer their shares, cash them in or use them as collateral, either individually or collectively, for housing mortgages. By making benefits transferable, the new law effectively severs the stakeholder linkage between capitalization and pension reform. Fortunately for the current government, public opinion has shifted from opposition to capitalization in 1994 to support for the pension reform in 1997, to indifference in the present. The political battle over capitalization and pension reform, however, is not likely to whither. The stakeholder approach that sought to make every citizen a shareholder of privatization is currently on hold; it is however expected to reappear when the BOLIVIDA reappears, in 2001.

III. Popular participation/decentralization reform

Public appeals to citizen participation have characterized policy-making in Bolivia at least since the emergence of the Social Emergency Fund in 1986, and have played an important role throughout the late 1980s and early 1990s. (see Graham, 1994; Jorgensen et al., 1992) In the case of Popular Participation, however, the stakeholder approach took on a distinct form. President Sánchez de Lozada stressed the idea that the new reform linked citizen participation to social responsibility, beyond particularistic claims based on ethnicity, class or region, and despite past inequities, prejudices or biases. Popular Participation was justified and advocated not merely on the basis of expected policy outcomes, but also by virtue of the new policy process it set out to construct – open, transparent, inclusive and pluralistic concerning ethnic and regional claims to political power (see Sánchez de Lozada, 1997a,b; Gray-Molina et al., 1999).

The reform

As with most other reforms implemented during the Sánchez de Lozada administration, the Popular Participation reform was drafted by a small group of consultants and specialists under direct presidential supervision. The Popular Participation law, passed in April of 1994, outlined an ambitious fiscal and administrative decentralization reform that – unlike similar decentralization reforms in Latin America – institutionalized massive citizen participation in annual planning, budget-making, fiscal oversight and evaluation.

Territorially, the reform involved a re-division of the country into 311 municipalities, 187 of them new and covering nearly two-thirds of the country. Only 61 of the pre-existing municipalities had received central government revenue-sharing transfers. Municipalization also involved incorporating rural areas into previously urban jurisdictions, which had earlier functioned as administrative 'islands'. The reform thus aimed to incorporate the entire territory into clearly defined administrative borders.

Politically, the reform was more ambitious. Municipalities are governed by elected councilors, overseen in turn by public oversight committees composed of representatives of local grass-roots organizations. In 1999, nearly 15 000 peasant and indigenous communities and neighbourhood councils participated in annual planning. The oversight committees have veto power over annual budget decisions and provide a bridge between formal and informal channels of political participation at the local level. Public investment planning, implementation and evaluation are carried out by means of a common 'participatory planning' methodology aimed at maximizing citizen voice in the public decision-making process.

Fiscally, the reform aimed to provide municipalities with the necessary revenues for effective policy-making. Through Popular Participation, municipalities receive revenue-sharing transfers based on population size, and were granted municipal revenue-raising powers over property taxes, fees and user charges. For 200 municipalities, this meant receiving revenue-sharing transfers for the first time. On the expenditure side, municipalities were transferred responsibilities for the maintenance, equipment and investment responsibilities for urban as well as social and productive-oriented infrastructure. The fiscal effects of the reform were significant, as the first mayors of Popular Participation set out to capitalize on the redistribution of political and fiscal power. Between 1995 and 1997, the structure of public investment shifted radically from a central-to-local/departmental expenditure ratio of 75 per cent to 25 per cent before the reform, to a 25 per cent to 75 per cent ratio three years later. Municipal governments in 1996 accounted for approximately 40 per cent of national public investments. Together with a change in structure, the composition of expenditures also shifted: while in 1994, most local investments were directed towards urban development, in 1995 and 1996 there was a gradual move towards social investments in education, basic sanitation and health. In three years, aggregate social investment more than tripled from 75 million dollars in 1994 to 178 million in 1996. Smaller and more rural municipalities have invested most in the social sectors, while the capital cities have continued to invest much more in urban development.

Technical problems

Retrospectively, three problems of institutional design affected the adoption of the Popular Participation reform. The first concerns the choice of territorial unit.[5] The 311 *secciones de provincia* (provincial sections) that became 'municipalities' in April 1994, struck an odd compromise between the need to decentralize to viable administrative and territorial units while recognizing ethnic, geographic and regional diversity. Ninety-six *secciones*, almost a third of all municipalities, have populations of less than 5000, 61 of which have as the largest village a population of 250 (see Ameller, 1999). The long-term fiscal and administrative viability of municipalities such as Yunguyo (population 92), or Ixiamas in the lowlands (with a population of 3000 over a territory of 41 400 km^2, or the size of Belgium) is suspect. More difficult, however, is the case of municipalities that overlap or cut through indigenous territories, settlements or ecological parks. Most of the 80 municipalities in the eastern lowlands carve problematic boundaries for indigenous communities spanning many municipalities. The question of territorial boundaries has also exacerbated longstanding social and political fragmentation in some rural areas. Participatory planning, taxation, public service provision and other municipal services are made difficult by extreme population dispersion, distance and mismatch between customary and formal administrative boundaries.

A second problem concerns intergovernmental fiscal relations. Under the current system, expenditure transfers are systematically mismatched with responsibilities for the provision of public services. Transfers are made by expenditure outlay (brick and mortar, for example), rather than function (primary education services, for example). As outlays are the responsibility each of the central government (through dozens of ministry programmes and investment funds), prefectures and municipal government, accountability for the provision of public services frequently runs through the cracks. Education and health services, in particular, face a daunting coordination problem in order to make sure that schools and hospitals built by municipalities will be staffed by teachers and nurses appointed at the national level, but paid at the departmental level. The number of health centres that remain empty led, in 1997, to the Minister of Health calling an end to the 'building craze' brought on by the Popular Participation reform.

A third problem revolves around administrative and fiscal capacity-building. Although the government focused aggressively on institution-building both at the municipal and community level, the prospect of 'creating' new municipalities was extremely difficult. During the second semester of 1994, the Popular Participation Secretariat (SNPP) carried out nearly 400 local workshops aimed at disseminating the contents of the reform and initiating contact with municipal and local leaders.[6] The new municipal governments placed an immediate strain on the SNPP to develop administrative and fiscal operating procedures. The SNPP prepared an emergency training programme that reached hundreds of mayors and municipal agents, dozens of departmental staff and thousands of municipal staff between May and December of 1994. During that period, close to 14 000 community organizations were granted legal OTB (territorial base organisation) status, and over 200 oversight committees were also formed. Despite massive efforts at building viable administrative and fiscal units at the local level, the challenge ahead is still fairly massive. The most recent municipal census reported that only a third

Pocoata

The municipality of Pocoata has been a test case for Popular Participation under extreme social and political fragmentation. Located in the highlands of northern Potosí, Pocoata is a municipality of 16 000, with a mixed Quechua and Aymara-speaking population. Agrarian unions vie with traditional indigenous *ayllus* for territorial representation. Local and national political parties are only marginally important to local politics. Abstention is one of the highest in the country (approximating 60 per cent of eligible voters, and close to 85 per cent of potential voters), and although the centre-left *Movimiento Bolivia Libre* won by a landslide in 1995, political in-fighting led to the selection of seven different mayors between 1995 and 1999.

Despite chronic political instability, local community organizations have built close ties to non-governmental organizations to follow through with participatory planning. And while central and departmental administrations have been largely absent from Pocoata, public investment has been highly responsive to community petitioning, and social investment in education, health and water projects has quadrupled since the implementation of the reform. Participation notwithstanding, community leaders continue to regard the political arena with detachment. The process of building a viable local political arena is largely seen as pending. Stakeholder politics in Pocoata have been only marginally important in pushing the Popular Participation reform, but have opened new opportunities for community activism.

of local governments implemented computerized investment planning systems, and only two-thirds had permanent access to a telephone line. Aside from the deficit in essential physical infrastructure and equipment, perhaps the more challenging deficit concerns managerial and administrative skills. The absence of a municipal civil service or of other measures designed to promote qualified personnel tenure, has meant that political instability has frequently spilled over into administrative institution-building.

Political problems

The stakeholder approach adopted during the Popular Participation reform was not monolithic in the sense of articulating a single political message, but developed instead a number of messages throughout the reform adoption period. Three distinct political problems arose throughout the process. The first challenge was the adoption of the reform itself. The law was greeted with scepticism by political foes and faced outright opposition from the national peasant confederation (CSUTCB) and the departmental civic committee movement. The CSUTCB had already condemned Sánchez de Lozada's electoral plan during the electoral campaign months earlier, but in April focused acutely on the decision to recognize and empower community organizations at the expense of rural unions and other functional organizations (most notably producer associations). The dispute was partly terminological, as the law referred generically to 'territorial base organizations', to suggest an array of existing community organizations, including *campesino* unions, indigenous organizations (such as pre-Columbian *ayllus* in the Andes and *tentas* in the lowlands) and other forms of territorial representation. The issue of territorial versus functional group representation, however, is one that has endured and continues to confront community and producer groups in rural areas. The civic committee movement, on the other hand, opposed the new law vehemently as it bypassed the regional and departmental levels of government in favour of the municipal level. The committees had participated actively in earlier debates on decentralization and had a direct contribution in the drafting of the preceding piece of legislation introduced during the Paz Zamora administration.

The second political challenge concerned the legitimation of the reform. The 1995 municipal elections initiated a second, more political, period of reform adoption. The municipal elections of 1995 registered over a million new rural voters, who cast local ballots or ran for local office for the first time. Many groups, previously opposed to the reform, ran candidates and won races throughout the country. The case of coca producer candidates in rural Cochabamba was particularly striking as the Asamblea Soberana del Pueblo (ASP), a *campesino* political movement running under the auspices of the Izquierda Unida (IU), gained dozens of councillors in rural municipalities, winning absolute majorities in the entire Chapare region. The stakeholder approach articulated by reformers at the national level earlier was to be adopted, with important differences, by political and community leaders at the local level. While national appeals to ownership and self-help had been used to galvanize support and articulate a broad-based front favouring the reform, the stakeholder appeals made by mayors and community leaders often focused on more tangible questions related to participatory planning, emphasizing the benefits of participation and the costs of non-participation. While communities could be regarded as stakeholders for planning and budgeting purposes, for example, sub-community groups such as parent associations or irrigation groups were regarded as stakeholders during the implementation of public works. Oversight and evaluation could then be delegated to supra-community organizations, such as union hubs and sub-hubs. By defining rules of inclusion and exclusion according to different types of collective action, the local stakeholder approach multiplied the prospects of participation beyond a single social unit.

A third problem concerns the long-term viability of the reform. By 1997, the activism of the early reform period had diminished. The electoral campaign focused on some of the most visible shortcomings of the reform, including a widespread perception of local corruption, lack of transparency and weak administrative capabilities. The Banzer administration took office with a pledge to reform Popular Participation, by increasing public accountability, promoting public/private investment projects and sanctioning political corruption (see Vice-Ministry of Popular Participation 1999). A key factor that bolstered negative public opinion during this period was an extreme degree of political instability between 1997 and 1999. A provision of the Popular Participation allowed for annual censorship (or recall) votes on mayors, every year except for the last of a four-year term. In January of 1997 and 1998, close to 70 per cent of municipalities made recourse to the censorship vote, some more than twice, as in the city of La Paz which has had four mayors in five years. The worst cases of instability affected politically divided municipalities in which no party held a council majority. Divided councils, censorship votes and shifting political alliances after the presidential elections plunged a majority of municipal governments into ungovernable turmoil.

A strong slow-down in local public investment, together with a gradual reconcentration of fiscal resources, fuelled discontent in 1999. Only 75 per cent of local programmed investments were executed in that year, and 70 per cent of departmental investments. While municipal investments had accounted for 40 per cent in 1995, they slumped back to 17 per cent in 1999. Fiscal reconcentration paralysed not only public works but also local level institution-building. Three years of participatory planning and yearly local budgeting had galvanized grass-roots organizations and induced NGO cooperation along an array of municipal investments. Falling local investment resulted in faltering local participation. Departments, on the other hand, increased their share of public investments from 15 per cent in 1995 to 22 per cent in 1999.

Concerns that soft-budget rules had led to municipal over-indebtedness also affected fiscal relations between the central government and large and medium-sized cities. New provisions tightened access to credit, by limiting the threshold of local debt from current revenues. Strikes and mobilizations rocked the latter part of 1998, in anticipation of a tight fiscal picture during the 1999 electoral year. By mid-1999, the decline that had slowed the decentralization process down over the past two years gradually led to a renewed period of political mobilization in preparation for the December municipal elections. Seventeen political parties registered candidates, and over 600 000 new voters signed the electoral registry for the first time. National electoral authorities expect voter turnout to be higher than in the 1997 presidential elections.

The stakeholder appeals of the early adoption period gradually faded from public discourse during reform implementation. Local politics, marked by extreme volatility, defined the pace of fiscal and political change. Public disenchantment with the reform at the end of the Sánchez de Lozada administration, provided political space for a gradual reconcentration of fiscal power. Cycles of censorship and endless political re-negotiation had the additional effect of eroding the political credibility of the first generation of local politicians to have emerged under the Popular Participation process. Unlike the

San Javier

> In contrast to Pocoata, San Javier is characterized by long tradition of clientelistic political capture. Located in the Santa Cruz lowlands, San Javier is the outgrowth of a seventeenth century Jesuit religious mission. The current population of 12 000 includes highland migrant colonies, agricultural smallholders and large cattle ranchers. Local community organizations are highly dispersed and relatively weak. Political power has remained concentrated with a single party, the *Movimiento Nacionalista Revolucionario*, since the agrarian reform of the 1950s. The current mayor is into his sixth political term.
>
> Participatory planning has followed a sectoral rather than territorial pattern. Demands and petititons are made through peasant unions and producer associations, rather than community organizations and neighbourhood committees. This 'corporatist' rather than 'territorial' approach has strengthened the political power of traditional clientelist networks, but has also mobilized a substantial number of citizens around the participatory plannng process. The 'success' of Popular Participation in San Javier has relied neither on strong grass-roots organizational capacities, nor on an open and competitive political system. The 1999 elections, however, highlighted the political vulnerability of the current administration, with two *campesino* leaders running and winning on a 'territorial' platform.
>
> As with Pocoata, the stakeholder appeal to visible and tangible outcomes may have been intrumental in launching the reform and mobilizing local citizens. It is still early, however, to evaluate the long-term impact over such highly diverse and changing local political systems. In both cases, what counts as 'success' or 'failure' is contingent on local conditions and understandings of the reform.

more concerted political reversal of the pension reform, the decline of the Popular Participation reform fed on the inertial effects of internal and mostly local political struggles. Again, politics-as-usual played an unexpected role, allowing for massive institutional reform during the upswing of the decentralization process but providing a powerful deterrent during the downswing. By 1999, the stakeholder approach had lost its mobilization appeal, and was being substituted by more local, regional and ethnic political discourses.

IV. Stakeholders, citizens and politics

In thinking about how reforms are 'institutionalized' – and how second generation reforms become sustainable – attention turns almost by default to the political arena. Where democratic legitimacy is weak, a reputation for policy efficiency and effectiveness is likely to be important.[7] However, the construction of democratic legitimacy is itself often of major concern. Burnell and Calvert (1999) distinguish between 'performance legitimacy' (judging policy targets) and 'process legitimacy' (judging the process by which policy targets are delivered). This second-order legitimacy problem is key to an assessment of the scope and limits of the stakeholder approach. The stakeholder appeal to participation, ownership and self-help, based only on the prospects of good performance, eventually faced public opinion erosion and a political rebuttal of the reform. In the Bolivian case, the capitalization/pension and Popular Participation reforms were rocked by predictable fluctuations in performance and idiosyncratic interventions in the political distribution process. With weak process legitimacy, disenchantment about not having benefited from the reforms quickly became disenchantment with the rules by which the reforms were adopted.

Between 1993 and 1997, the Sánchez de Lozada administration advocated a 'demonstration effect' policy on reform benefits. Political capital was invested in securing legislative backing, shielding the design process from political outsiders and mobilizing new stakeholders behind tangible benefits. Critically, the reforms were sold on the basis of their appeal to entitlements – US$248 pension dollars for every citizen over the age of 65, and US$22 public investment dollars for every citizen organized into a community organization. By emphasizing the immediate benefits of the reform, but neglecting the political frailty of long-term agreements, the stakeholder approach eventually was to become an easy political target. The Banzer administration realized the winner-take-all nature of this gamble early in the new term. Pension reform was debunked for its electoralist appeal and Popular Participation was denounced for its corrupting effects over local government. The new administration's call for a 'national dialogue' to build a grand consensus on policy essentials, effectively upstaged the stakeholder approach that had relied on top-down legislative and executive activism. The pendulum thus swung back to policy process, dialogue and consensus-building.

Given the political ramifications of the stakeholder approach, the broader question of where second generation reforms fit in the longer-term scheme of democratic change has become more relevant. Bolivia shares with many other new democracies a strong degree of heterogeneity in the way the legal, bureaucratic and political scope of the state spans across places and time. A state-with-holes, where clientelistic, ethnic, NGO and other state surrogates function alongside formal institutions, often better describes the nature of institution-building, than the ideal Weberian type. One of the substantial merits of the stakeholder approach has been to frame questions of policy reform in ways that are more congenial to this fragmented and heterogeneous reality. Rather than a one-size-fits-all approach (characteristic of the stylized neo-liberal approach), or a corporate proposal based on overdrawn class, region or ethnic allegiances (as advanced by populist alternatives), the stakeholder approach articulates a broader appeal to universal entitlement in the face of social and political diversity. Less effectively, it also forwards the idea that building a common sense of citizenship is likely to begin by bringing 'rights', 'responsibilities' and 'ownership' to life through tangible reform efforts. Paradoxically, perhaps, the stakeholder approach may have suffered from 'not doing enough'. A bridging of the technical arenas of institutional design and the political arenas where designs are legitimated was never effectively achieved.

After a 15-year reign of coalition politics in Bolivia, there is evidence to suggest that the conditions that strengthened presidential powers, protected technocratic policy-making and promoted top-down activism are eroding. A recent shift toward more polarized political preferences, the resurgence of 'anti-party' politics, and the unravelling of the state patronage machine suggests that the wide net that once spanned the political centre is shrinking. Upcoming presidential elections in 2002 are likely to define a turning point in the style and contents of policy reform, as politics take centre stage.

Conclusions

Stakeholder politics, based on public appeals to ownership, self-help and citizen participation, have played an important role in promoting a period of rapid institutional change in Bolivia. Strong presidential leadership, legislative activism, technocratic policy-making and the massive mobilization of new stakeholders, have conspired in equal measures to depart from alternative neo-liberal or populist neo-liberal approaches to policy reform. However, the very features that facilitated innovative change now illustrate the limits of the stakeholder approach five years into reform. Recent political changes, public disenchantment and policy reversals suggest the self-sustaining features of the stakeholder appeal may have been exaggerated. The focus on short-term policy performance may, over the longer run, work against reform efforts in a context of adversarial politics. The added effect of rapid political change suggests that strategies that worked in the recent past are less likely to stick today. Three aspects of stakeholder politics are particularly relevant to a five-year assessment of the Bolivian reforms as they unravel in the present.

First, policy attention is shifting from the short-term politics of reform adoption, to the longer-term politics of reform implementation. The factors that account for successful legislative or executive activism, may not readily promote the broader process of public legitimation needed to ensure political survival. The decision to make annual lump-sum grants to senior citizens (BONOSOL) rather than capitalize pension accounts over the long run, for example, may have politicized the policy entitlement beyond rescue. Likewise, the decision to promote thousands of small public investment projects, over longer-term local and regional planning, has threatened to make Popular Participation a short-term patronage game rather than a long-term local development initiative. A greater focus on implementation highlights the less glamorous aspects of policy design, which deal with the day-to-day tasks of making institutions work and fit in a context of weak bureaucratic and legal capabilities, scarce resources and contested politics. Performance legitimacy thus requires complementation by process legitimacy, to persuade that the rules that produce and distribute reform benefits are as important as the benefits themselves.

Second, attention is also shifting from the technocratic arena that crafted institutional reforms to the political arena where they will ultimately float or sink. Unfortunately, the politics of contested reform are not likely to be settled by pivotal votes or once-and-for-all agreements between government and opposition. The political construction of impartial arbitration points – constitutional courts, comptroller offices, administrative justices – is hence equally important, and is itself marked by continuous political persuasion and dispute. Rather than eschew political conflict in search of institutional stability, reformers are more likely to succeed in constructing the political bases for institutional survival. This may include sacrificing first-best design for more lasting political will.

Third, as much as second generation reforms are on the international policy agenda at present, reformism is itself only a part of what democratic governments do and say over a longer period of time. Longer run concerns over how the terms of citizenship evolve, over who has the voice, resources and power to exercise existing social, political and civil rights and responsibilities, are presumably also part of a broader stakeholder agenda. Stakeholder politics that transcend instrumental appeals for public support may yet provide imaginative and creative means of legitimating progressive policy reforms. As suggested earlier, many of the challenges faced by reformers today branch out into more controversial arenas of social and political identity, conflict resolution, political sanctioning and public legitimation. Rather than abstract from these, the stakeholder approach may have helped to put them on the agenda.

Notes

1. In this chapter, the term 'stakeholder' is used to refer to the beneficiaries of social or political entitlements. In some cases, like the Bolivian pension system reform, entitlements were granted to individuals; in others, such as decentralization reform, entitlements were made to groups. In both cases, the defining characteristic of stakeholdership is the exercise of new social or political rights and obligations. 'Self-help', 'participation' and 'ownership' are discussed instrumentally, only as they relate to the political appeals used by reformers to 'sell' their policy reform ideas.
2. 'Second generation' reforms refer to institutional or state reforms that complement liberalizing and stabilizing market reforms. Some of the most prominent second-generation reforms in Latin America focus on privatization, regulatory reform, decentralization, judicial reform, pension and social service reforms. See Naim (1994) and Pastor and Wise (1999).
3. Carol Graham has forwarded the most comprehensive study of stakeholder politics in the context of second generation reforms. Her research spans cross-country research in Bolivia, Peru, Chile and Zambia and cross-sectoral research in the social and economic sectors (Graham 1998). Also see Birdsall, Graham and Sabot (1998).
4. See Mayorga (1997), Gamarra (1998), van Dijk (1998), Crabtree and Whitehead (2000) for recent analyses of the social and economic reforms implemented in Bolivia since 1993.
5. Under current territorial distributioon, *cantones* stand as the minimal political unit (1 386) followed by *secciones de provincia* (314), *provincias* (112) and *departmentos* (nine).
6. The SNPP, under the Ministry of Human Development, was the state secretariat charged with reform adoption and municipal/community strengthening. It drafted complementary legislation for the Popular Participation and Decentralization reforms and designed standard operating procedures for participatory planning.
7. Linz and Stepan (1996) have discussed this in a comparative perspective, during democratic transitions, where the imperative for policy effectiveness and efficiency is overcome by a more lasting attitudinal and behavioural commitment to democratic rule.

Bibliography

Archondo, Rafael, *Tres años de participación popular: memorias de un proceso*, La Paz, Ministerio de Desarrollo Humano, Secretaría Nacional de Participación Popular, 1997.

Ameller, Vladimir, *La problematica de los gobiernos municipales de escasa poblacion: Consideraciones socio-economicas para un tratamiento diferenciado*, La Paz, Unidad de Economia y Finanzas Municipales, Viceministerio de Participacion Popular y Fortalecimiento Municipal, 1999.

Birdsall, Nancy, Carol Graham and Richard Sabot, *Beyond Trade-Offs: Market Reform and Equitable Growth in Latin America*, Washington, D.C., Inter-American Development Bank and Brookings Institution, 1998.

Booth, David, Suzanne Clisby and Charlotta Widmark, 'Popular Participation: Democratising the State in Rural Bolivia', Report to SIDA, commissioned through the Development Studies Unit, Department of Social Anthropology, Stockholm University, 1997.

Burnell, Peter and Peter Calvert, 'The Resilience of Democracy: An Introduction', *Democratization*, 6(1), Spring, 1–32, 1999.

Calla, Ricardo y Hernando Calla, *Partidos políticos y municipios: las elecciones de 1995*, La Paz, Instituto Latinoamericano de Investigaciones Sociales (Debate Político 2), 1996.

Crabtree, John and Laurence Whitehead, *Towards Democratic Viability: The Bolivian Experience*. Basingstoke, Palgrave Macmillan, 2001.

Gamarra, Eduardo, 'Hybrid Presidentialism and Democratization: The Case of Bolivia', in *Presidentialism and Democracy in Latin America*, (eds) Scott Mainwaring and Mathew Soberg, Cambridge, Cambridge University Press, pp. 363–93, 1997.

Gamarra, Eduardo, 'Popular Participation and Political Reforms in Bolivia', in *Constructing Democratic Governance: Latin America and the Caribbean in the 1990s*, (eds) Jorge Domínguez and Abraham Lowenthal. Baltimore, Johns Hopkins University Press, 1996.

Graham, Carol, *Private Markets for Public Goods: Raising the Stakes in Economic Reform*. Washington, D.C., Brookings Institution Press, 1998.

Graham, Carol, *Safety Nets, Politics, and the Poor. Transitions to Market Economies*. Washington, D.C., Brookings Institution Press, 1994.

Gray-Molina, George, Ernesto Perez and Ernesto Yañez, 'La economía política de reformas institucionales en Bolivia', Research Network Paper 350. Washington, D.C., Inter-American Development Bank, 1999.

Gray-Molina, George (ed.), *Participación popular: construyendo políticas públicas locales en Bolivia*, La Paz, Unidad de Análisis de Políticas Sociales (UDAPSO), 1998.

Grindle, Merilee, 'Audacious Reforms: Institutional Invention and Democracy in Latin America'. Cambridge, Harvard Institute for International Development. Manuscript, 1999.

Haggard, Stephan and Robert Kaufman, *The Political Economy of Democratic Transitions*, Princeton, Princeton University Press, 1995.

Jemio, Luis Carlos, 'Providing a Foundation of Secure Benefits for Future Generations', unpublished paper. La Paz, Unidad de Análisis de Políticas Económicas (UDAPE), 1998.

Jorgensen, Steen; Margaret Grosh and Schacter, *Bolivia's Answer to Poverty, Economic Crisis and Adjustment*, Washington, D.C., World Bank, 1992.

Linz, Juan and Alfred Stepan, 'Toward Consolidated Democracies', *Journal of Democracy*, 7(2), April, 14–33, 1996.

Mayorga, René Antonio, 'Bolivia's Silent Revolution', *Journal of Democracy*, 8(1), January, 143–63, 1997.

Mercado, Marcelo, 'La reforma del sistema de pensiones de la seguridad social en Bolivia', in *Las reformas estructurales en Bolivia*, La Paz, Fundación Milenio, 1998.

Ministry of Capitalization, *Capitalizacion: El modelo boliviano de reforma economica y social*. La Paz, Ministerio de Capitalizacion, 1997.

Molina Monasterios, Fernando, *Historia de la participación popular*. La Paz, Ministerio de Desarrollo Humano, Secretaría Nacional de Participación Popular, 1997.

Movimiento Nacionalista Revolucionario (MNR), *Plan de Todos (1993–1997)*. La Paz, MNR, 1993.

Muñoz, Jorge (ed.), *The Art of Reform in Bolivia: 1982–1997*, Cambridge, MA: Harvard Institute for International Development, Manuscript, 1998.

Naim, Moises, 'Latin America: The Second Stage of Reform', *Journal of Democracy*, 5, October, 32–48, 1994.

Nelson, Joan (ed.), *A Precarious Balance: An Overview of Democracy and Economic Reform in Eastern Europe and Latin America*, San Francisco: International Centre for Economic Growth and Overseas Development Council, 1994.

O'Donnell, Guillermo, 'Illusions about Consolidation', *Journal of Democracy*, 7(2), April, 34–51, 1996.

O'Donnell, Guillermo, 'On the State, Democratization and Some Conceptual Problems: A Latin American View with Glances at some Post-Communist Countries', *World Development*, 21(8), 1355–69, 1993.

Pastor, Manuel and Carol Wise, 'The Politics of Second-Generation Reform', *Journal of Democracy*, 10(3), July, 34–48, 1999.

Queisser, Monika, *The Second Generation Pension Reforms in Latin America*, Development Centre, Organization for Economic Cooperation and Development, Paris, OECD, 1998.

Roberts, Kenneth, 'Neoliberalism and the Transformation of Populism in Latin America', *World Politics*, 48, October, 82–116, 1995.

Sánchez de Lozada, Gonzalo, 'Bolivia debe cambiar', in *El pulso de la democracia: participación ciudadana u descentralización en Bolivia*, República de Bolivia, Caracas: Nueva Sociedad, 1997a.

Sánchez de Lozada, Gonzalo, 'Problems of Change', Address at the John F. Kennedy School of Government, Harvard University, 30 April, Mimeo, 1997b.

Stokes, Susan, 'Constituency Influence and Representation', *Electoral Studies*, 17(3), 351–67, 1998.

Van Dijk, Pitou (ed.), *The Bolivian Experiment: Structural Adjustment and Poverty Alleviation*. Amsterdam, CEDLA, 1998.

Vice-Ministry of Popular Participation, 'Documento presentado por el Gobierno de Bolivia sobre Participacion Popular', Grupo Consultivo, Paris, 1999.

Von Cott, Donna Lee, 'Imposing Democracy: The Sanchez de Lozada Reforms', Dissertation Draft, Georgetown University, Mimeo, 1998.

Von Gersdorff, Hermann, 'The Bolivian Pension Reform: Innovative Solutions to Common Problems', Financial Sector Department, The World Bank, Washington, D.C., World Bank, 1997.

Weyland, Kurt, 'Neoliberal Populism in Latin America and Eastern Europe', *Comparative Politics*, July, 379–401, 1999.

Whitehead, Laurence 'Beyond Neo-Liberalism: Bolivia's Capitalization as a Route to Universal Entitlements and Substantive Citizenship Rights?' Paper presented at the North–South Center in Miami, Mimeo, April 1997.

Conclusion: New Approaches to Social Policy Reform in Latin America

Camilla T. Helgø

The chapters presented in this volume cover labour, education, health and general social policies and programmes in Chile, Mexico, Bolivia, El Salvador, Argentina and Colombia. Of particular interest is how market-enhancing reform such as demand-based provision, social policy targeting, leasing-out and privatization, and financial and administrative decentralization respond to issues of equity, social exclusion, social citizenship[1] and quality. In several of the cases presented, policies have moved beyond the stage of market-enhancing reform, to second-generation reform in which elements such as risk adjustment (in the case of health insurance in Chile, Argentina and Colombia), equality and quality-enhancing education reforms (Chile) and stakeholder approach to pension and decentralization reforms and social programmes (Bolivia) have been introduced. Also, a number of chapters analyse social programmes which have, with varying degrees of success, taken a more interactive approach. Examples are the female labour programmes PMJH and some primary health care programmes in Chile. Overall, therefore, we find evidence of responses to the market-enhancing reforms in Latin America.

In the concluding chapter of this volume we will first examine each area of social policy separately: labour, education, health and general social programmes will be discussed in the context of privatization, decentralization, targeting, participation and other features of the market-enhancing reforms. The discussion will then focus on how the chapters collectively cast light on the way social policies respond to the issue of access, either to universal or targeted social services, and incorporation of the excluded or disadvantaged into the mainstream (as discussed in the introduction to this volume).

Labour market reforms: precariousness and sporadic response

The two chapters debating the labour markets in Chile and Mexico by Haagh and Bayon *et al.*, show how changes in economic policy (liberalization, flexibilization and leasing-out) of labour markets in countries as diverse as Mexico and Chile have generalized both the problem of precariousness for those within the labour market and also social exclusion of labourers without the qualifications in demand. In Mexico the restructuring led to an expansion of informal work. Although the labour market underwent a high rate of reformalization in the period after restructuring in Chile, precariousness, defined by Haagh as the displacement of risks onto individual workers, became a permanent feature of formal work. In Mexico market deregulation also led to exclusion of the previously included, that is, full-time male employees on stable contracts in formally organized enterprises. Instead, the proportion of working women increased. The market deregulation posed an additional set of problems when the ratio of working women, also with children, rose, and social policies failed to keep up with the changes and take account of women's needs.

Louise Haagh demonstrates (in Chapter 1) how labour market deregulation had a direct impact on the decentralized (demand-based) market for labour training. The training system in Chile is an example of one of the earliest attempts to institute a pure market demand-based model of social service provision, and thus represents a good case for evaluating the success of economic decentralization in the form of a demand-based model. In Chile, the power to demand public services was transferred or leased out to the individual employer. The Chilean labour training case shows how an overemphasis on market principles without sufficient consideration of political aspects may have perverse outcomes in terms of disincentives to invest in human resources. Parallels can be drawn to the Chilean education-voucher model (discussed below) which also show how market liberalization, which may work satisfactorily when applied to products and services, typically produces unexpected outcomes in the case of human social policies. In the labour case the perverse results are linked to the reluctance of employers to invest in their workers in a situation of high turnover rates for fear of wasting their investments. Unless employers can reasonably expect to keep their workers on a long-term basis, they have no immediate incentive to invest in workers' skills. This suggests that the problem in Chile, according to Haagh, is not an economic problem in the traditional sense, but a problem of labour institutions, and specifically the under-development of labourers' property rights. In this context the labour training market cannot be left to its own devices in enhancing human resources within firms. Instead, it is proposed that institutional coordination between the providers – such as training centres, municipal offices, the employers and workers – should be enhanced.

Bayon *et al*. in their chapter (Chapter 3) highlight the consequences of market restructuring failing to complement coordinated social policies, in this case child care. In Mexico, the proportion of female workers has been increasing, yet the provision of child care has stayed virtually the same. The lack of child care harms all categories of working women, but particularly the informal sector workers without the right to social security payment.

Government-sponsored child care is scarce and limited to formal sector workers, while in the private sector unregulated child care results in large differences in facilities, quality and price. Moreover, fees range from 40 per cent to 200 per cent of the minimum wage, which inevitably excludes the poorest segment of the population. Thus, both Haagh and Bayon *et al.*, although in different ways, call for a more concerted effort in responding to the complexities produced by market liberalization. Specifically, social policies should be coordinated to ensure the needs of working women and a more efficient market for human resources.

The PMJH programme, presented by Badia (Chapter 2), seeks to tackle labour market exclusion of female heads of households in Chile. The programme was significant in being the first women-targeted public policy that focused on women as producers rather than simply as wives and mothers. PMJH is based on the assumption that the vulnerability of female heads of households is associated with their precarious position in the labour market. Similarly to PRONASOL (discussed below) the PMJH programme is based on an integrated approach and seeks to coordinate efforts from different ministries to implement labour training for women. However, while the beneficiary population is targeted, women are required to meet a series of conditions and possess levels of information unlikely to be found in the most marginal people, in order to gain access to the programme. In this way, the programme may fail to respond adequately to the very situation it is intended to resolve, that of social exclusion.

Similar arguments to those of Badia have been made in relation to social investment programmes in the region. Vivian (1995) argues that as the demand-based projects require organizational skills, writing of proposals, and often technical expertise, they tend to exclude segments of the poorest population precisely because they lack such qualities. Yet, this is not to say that the requisite for an active demand for participation on the part of the beneficieries of social programmes is always negative. It may also be argued that the demand for services and an active involvement are pertinent for certain, especially narrower, social programmes to succeed. The educational decentralization programme in El Salvador, discussed by Parandekar in Chapter 6, is an example of such a programme. Here, the initial construction and development of the programme was completely dependent on the organization and motivation of the communities involved.

Liberalizing the education sector

Chile provides an interesting case for analysis of education sector reforms as liberalization adjustments, which were intended to increase coverage, individual choice and achievements, date as far back as the late 1970s. Also, as shown by Angell in Chapter 5, in the last decade, the government has entered an interesting stage of moderating or evading the negative by-products of this reform.

Whether privatization really does produce a more effective system is one of the themes of Helgø's chapter (4). Perhaps surprisingly, Helgø shows that municipal secondary school students slightly outperform private-subsidized students in the Santiago area. Although such evidence is likely to be situation-specific and may be related to the historical evolution of the two systems, it still suggests that the link between greater privatization and efficiency[2] should not be taken as given. Helgø also strikes a sceptical note with regard to financial decentralization, as she demonstrates that the income level of the municipalities does have an impact on the quality of the schools. Angell, on the other hand, highlights the benefits of decentralization, as does Parandekar. Both these authors suggest that educational decentralization may expand the freedom of choice of the schools so that their framework may be better adapted to the specific geographical or socio-cultural situation of the students. In this context, Angell outlines how decentralized schools can be encouraged to design and implement their own programmes of educational improvement. Also Parandekar embraces decentralization and advocates that schools be free to make their own choices as he shows that, after controlling for socio-economic status and school resources, the students in decentralized EDUCO schools perform better then those in traditional rural schools.

The three case studies suggest that financial and administrative decentralization should be distinguished, particularly in the case of education. Although even administrative decentralization may have inequitable effects, the arguments in favour of such a policy, in terms of increasing effectiveness, freedom and creativity, are more convincing and the strategy less directly and visibly harmful than financial decentralization in which individuals in lower-income municipalities end up with poorer basic essential services.

Still, while positive to decentralization, both Angell and Parandekar caution against the complications associated with such as policy. In the case of the Chilean municipal decentralization process, the Pinochet government continued to appoint mayors until 1992, and thus the initial decentralization outcome cannot be labelled democratic. Also, according to Angell, for many mayors educational responsibility was a burden rather than an opportunity. In effect, the transfer of educational responsibilities to smaller geopolitical units was far from smooth and automatic. Furthermore, Parandekar points out that the typical problem of resource constraint may wipe out the positive effect associated with decentralization. Although decentralization was independently beneficial in terms of academic results in the Salvadorian case, its effect was largely counteracted by lack of resources in the decentralized schools.

Voucher systems, such as that in Chile, have been widely debated in the context of developed and developing countries.[3] The system is intended to increase the level of choice irrespective of background, economic or otherwise.

Analogies are drawn to the popularization of other commercial products, as it is typically argued that extending the range of choices within the education system will provide the greatest benefit to the poorest sector. However, the difference in the case of education is that the consumer, in this case the student, will have a direct impact on education. Thus, it is in the interest of the supplier (the schools) to select the users of their product. The 'by-product' of the system in which the selection is widened and the schools are given financial incentive to attract students, is the development of the 'waste-basket' schools which capture the least desirable students in the system. In this situation, what was supposed to bring increased levels of choice to all members of society, will benefit only the most able, while ensuring the continued poor performance of the academically disadvantaged students.

As discussed in the introduction, the development of such a liberalized system in which the outcome is inequality, in this case academic inequality, is a dangerous path for two reasons. First, much evidence, particularly based on East Asian examples, demonstrates that certain overall standards of human resources are necessary for broad-based productive economic investment. Second, and perhaps even more important for our discussion, it may be extremely costly and difficult to re-institute the mainstream once it is lost. Relevant in this context are universal programmes such as MECE-*Basica* and P-900. There is no doubt that both programmes are well organized, innovative, have had a considerable impact and may thus independently be recommended within a model to include the excluded. However, while MECE and P-900 will surely benefit the Chilean education system both in terms of quality and equality, the structural cause of the many inequality issues within the Chilean education system will, even with the introduction of these programmes, remain unchallenged.

Health insurance, decentralization and voluntary labour

Barrientos and Lloyd-Sherlock (Chapter 7) show that a feature of the typical health insurance market is that, for a given premium rate, competing insurers have incentives to select a good health risk group, or to 'cream-skim'. By doing so the health care expenditures of the insurers are minimized and profits maximized. The situation is made worse due to the effect of globalization and labour market deregulation as discussed above in relation to the chapters by Haagh and Bayon *et al.* Labour market liberalization places severe restrictions on the effective operation of the insurance system as the general decline in secure, formal employment in the region, and also the rising earning inequalities, push higher-income workers towards private health care, further undermining the risk-pooling or risk-differentiation of health insurance.

The health insurance system is analogous to that of the voucher system discussed above. In both cases the resulting polarization is the effect of increased freedom of choice on the part of both the consumer and the supplier. By introducing an element of choice in the health and education systems, the bad health-risk groups and the poorer students will lose out. The higher health-risk groups will lose because, in an unregulated market, risk selection leads to rising marketing cost, the provision of lower benefit medical intervention, reduced coverage (among this group) and rising inequality in access to health care. The 'waste-basket' students will lose out because the combination of lower teacher expectations, the peer group effect and differing school resources serve to further reduce the academic quality of their schools.

Thus, in both cases, the role of welfare policies as a mechanism of building social cohesion, or the mainstream, as discussed in the introduction of this book, is forfeited. Instead a social system which produces social segregation is fostered. Even if average educational attainment and the overall quality of health care is improved as a result of higher levels of competition and choice, as is thought to be the case in Chile, social policy within such a system might be less successful in improving standards for the most disadvantaged part of the population.

Yet, at least in the case of the health care system, attempts have been made to correct for imperfections in the system. In Colombia, risk-adjustment mechanisms have been introduced, whereby the insurer must pay any excess of workers' contributions over the per capita premium into a redistribution fund that subsidizes health insurance for low income households. However, despite such efforts, Barrientos and Lloyd-Sherlock suggest that the reforms are unlikely to stem the rising inequality in access to health care or to overcome the dysfunctional incentives present in health insurance markets.

Gideon's research (Chapter 8) sheds light on the aspect of participation within the reformed health care system in Chile. Her point of departure is that, from the outset, the military in Chile employed a narrow technical definition of participation that derived from the broader neo-liberal framework. In this context, participation was encouraged to mobilize citizens around service delivery. Her case study shows how participation in family health centres is reduced to provision of unpaid, usually female, labour with no impact on allocation of resources which are centrally determined. Participation is encouraged simply to carry out tasks that were previously the responsibility of paid personnel rather than to mobilize initiative in different segments of society. Gideon also finds that although participation is promoted, the actions of groups are to some extent restricted (particularly in the case of more radical groups) as the recipients of government funds must sign an agreement that binds them to carrying out certain activities with their resources. Thus, with the example from the decentralized Chilean health care system, Gideon shows how the all-inclusive dynamic notion of participation may be reduced to a politically restricted cost-effective measure.

The emphasis on voluntary or low-cost labour to assist in the health sector is also a feature of the health component of the integrated, targeted, rural programme PROGRESA in Mexico. Most health clinics require mothers, as the direct recipients of the social assistance, to perform some sort of voluntary labour when they take their children for check-ups. In this way a visit to the clinic can turn into an all-day absence from domestic tasks. To meet the increasing demand for health services, the programme has also created 'health promoters' or community health workers, who receive two months' training and permission to manage a small package of 10 basic, frequently prescribed medicines. In exchange for a relatively minor wage the health promoters work several hours a day. In the cases of both PROGRESA and the primary family health care service in Chile, austere financial management of the health budgets and the attempts to include larger parts of the population in the health services have required the creation of a pool of voluntary or low-paid, typically female, labour. It is evident that the practice causes additional stress for the women concerned.

Similarly to Helgø, Gideon points out that the financial decentralization in Chile has produced increasing inequalities in the resources available to municipalities of differing economic status. Since a portion of the municipal funds is self-generated, the quality of the education and health care services available varies within this highly stratified society. Grey-Molina discusses how parts of municipal revenues also in Bolivia became self-generated as municipalities were granted revenue-raising powers over property taxes. However, a crucial difference between the two countries is that in Chile attempts were made to redistribute resources through the introduction of the municipal redistribution scheme, the *Fondo Común Municipal* (FCM). Although it has been pointed out that the financial advantage of the richest 10 per cent of the municipalities is significant even after the redistribution through FCM, the negative effect of financial decentralization on the poorest municipalities might to some extent have been fended off with the operation of this scheme.[4]

Interestingly, Gideon points out that the inequality of resources has a particularly gendered aspect. Municipal health department and health centres in better-off neighbourhoods are more likely to be controlled by men, whereas those in poorer areas are more likely to be controlled by women. The effect of this gender segregation is that women working in the health sector have on the whole less access to quality resources then do men.

Together, Barrientos and Lloyd-Sherlock's and Gideon's chapters show how the increased emphasis on privatization, market effectiveness, decentralization and choice may have increased the overall quality and diversified of the health services provided, particularly for the higher-income groups. However, the reforms appear to have been less successful in mainstreaming health services and encouraging the freedom of expression and the active participation in the decision-making of different groups in the society.

New approaches to social policies

The chapters on social policies encompass Badia's discussion of the integrated approach to female poverty alleviation in Chile, the analysis of the pension and decentralization reform in Bolivia by Gray-Molina (Chapter 10), and finally Latapí's discussion of the integrated, rural poverty programme PROGRESA in Mexico (Chapter 9). The debates centre on the issues of an integrated approach to social policies, targeting of the beneficiaries and the link between political acceptance and the success of the programmes.

An interesting development in the social policy domain has been the more holistic approach to poverty alleviation. Both Badia and Latapí discuss poverty-targeted programmes, taking into account a broader social and economic context. In the case of the PMJH in Chile, the programme coordinates policies in the area of housing, health, legal support and child care, all for the purpose of facilitating the access of poorer female heads of households to the labour market. The aim of PROGRESA is to aid the transition out of poverty for families in rural, economically disadvantaged settings in Mexico through the implementation of nutrition, health and education programmes. Badia points out that while the accumulated effect of PMJH may potentially be powerful, there are important practical problems associated with this solution. Specifically, the PMJH faces institutional obstacles and difficulties in setting up networks of coordination between the different sectors. This lack of organization between the different actors tends to inhibit both local initiatives and creativity, and thus weakens the overall performance of the programme. However, the point here is not to discard the holistic approach as unfeasible, but rather to recognize its complexities and the stronger initial institutional framework required to convince the communities, the organizers and the beneficiaries, of its usefulness.

All three social policy chapters discuss the issue of targeting which became such a central concept in the social policy debate of the 1980s when welfare expenditures were cut and the remaining resources were channelled or targeted to the poorest sector of the population (Marcel and Solimano, 1994; Graham, 1993; de Kadt, 1993). In Mexico, targeting is not demand-based, or, in other words, to receive benefits is not dependent on the individual formulating a request for assistance. Instead selection is externally determined and depends on the degree of marginality of a specific area. Additionally, each household is contacted and the need, as well as potential, for accessing health and education services is assessed. Latapí notes that the programme has been relatively successful in its targeting procedures and that the formal, technical process for selecting the communities and households has allowed the PROGRESA to contact households which were previously beyond the reach of the state.

The Chilean female labour programme (PMJH), discussed above, is demand-based, on the other hand. To gain access to the programme women are required to meet a series of conditions and possess a level of information that is unlikely to be found in the most marginal people. Badia suggests that this approach to identifying beneficiaries has the effect of excluding parts of the targeted population. Gaining access to scarce social services may also depend on other criteria, such as level of participation of larger groups. Haagh points out that, in Chile, participation by unions within firms came to be an important aspect of firm-centred funding for training. Unfortunately, making the system reliant on participation meant that in firms where such activity was low, workers derived little or no benefit from training programmes. In addition, the employers have become more reluctant to train their workers because of the structure of the labour market, where 'precariousness' in the form of insecure employment and high turnover rates has become more widespread. In consequence, the training that does take place has become concentrated in firms with higher levels of union participation and in the segments of employers/owners in larger firms because of their disproportionate demand for training. In this situation the structure of the labour market, and the demand-based nature of training programmes, has helped to fuel the unequal increase in human resource capacities between different sectors of the labour market.

Another factor which may lead to exclusion of the marginalized population is the emphasis on quantitative performance indicators. Badia proposes that PMJH's great concern for labour market insertion of women will force coordinators to pre-select beneficiaries with greater potential for 'success'. Also, PROGRESA excludes portions of the marginalized population as a result of its use of beneficiary selection criteria. In this case only families that may certify their access to, and use of, health clinics and school attendance may be enrolled in the programme. However, the bias against families and communities which lack access to clinics has been reduced through the training of community health care workers and the consequently increased access to basic health care. Still, the requirement of access to primary school, even if the service is relatively widespread, continues to prevent some remote villages from benefiting from the programme.

All these factors – the emphasis on formulation of interest, participation and potential for achieving the objective of the programmes – could be advertised as measures to mobilize support, initiative and interest on the part of the beneficiaries and consequently increase the probability of success of the programmes within the context of more austere financial management and requirements to 'produce'. However, by excluding segments of the marginalized population in the initial phase of the programme, these factors might equally lead to partial failure to fulfil the mission of inclusion and may also produce greater inequalities within the targeted population it aims to assist.

As discussed in the introduction, and as shown by Angell and Latapí, targeting as a policy instrument can be effective in increasing the level of empowerment of the excluded sectors closer. However, an issue that needs to be considered is whether targeted programmes produce lasting integration into the mainstream. Latapí proposes that even if targeted programmes are effective in exposing the marginalized population to social services, this might not be enough to reduce levels of poverty. The way that PROGRESA is currently structured, it will not have the effect of radically improving the well-being of the population. To do so would also require the generation of additional employment opportunities in marginal communities. Latapí therefore concludes that to improve the well-being of the population in these communities, the state should make use not only of social policies, but also economic and political tools.

Gray-Molina's discussion of the Popular Participation law which involved both fiscal and administrative decentralization, demonstrates both the practical obstacles to decentralization and the relevance of popular support in determining the success or failure of reform. Decentralization of political power was made logistically complex because of the very small size of some municipalities, the extreme population dispersion, and fluctuating support for the reform. The participatory nature of the reform also made it more complex. The stakeholder approach multiplied citizen involvement beyond a single social unit by including sub-groups such as parent associations, irrigation groups and other community organizations which came to be instrumental in the administration and evaluation of projects. The strong emphasis on participation at all levels of decision-making made the decentralization reform initially more popular, potentially more powerful but also more volatile. Swings in the political mood allowed for massive institutional support during the initiation of the decentralization process. However, it also provided a powerful deterrent when local public investments dropped and the turnover rate of mayors began to decline.

The health reformers in Argentina and Colombia (Barrientos and Lloyd-Sherlock) and the education reformers in Chile (Angell) were aware that securing popular opinion would be a key factor in ensuring the success of the reform. The need to secure popular support could simply be viewed as an inherent aspect of the democratization process and an indication of the authentic realization of citizens' rights. In support of this view, the need in Argentina for popular support meant that more attention was paid to incorporating solidarity and private sector regulations. In Chile, P-900 brought immediate material benefit to poor schools in terms of improving buildings, books and teaching aids, and was, according to Angell, an excellent way of embodying the political mood during the transition to democracy. That the requirement of popular support may lead to prolonging the reform implementation process, as was the case in both Argentina and Colombia, may quite easily be forgiven in the name of social participation and citizenship. However, the instability it may produce, as shown in the case of Bolivia (Gray-Molina), is perhaps more critical. It is to be expected that a reform process will go through different stages, some of which may be very unsettling, before being adjusted and firmly established. However, exaggerated dependence on popular support may endanger the long-term viability of reform and may thus threaten the establishment of potentially better welfare services. Where the need for popular participation is required, the demand for institutional coordination and solid technical support for the reform effort will be even greater. As shown by Angell, and as noted in the introduction, the central coordination and the technical expertise of the reform planners were perhaps the main reasons for the success of the Chilean educational counter-reform in the period of transition to democracy.

The aim of this volume has been to highlight some central theoretical questions and present possible outcomes associated with the implementation of market-oriented social policies such as decentralization, participation, targeting and choice. Rather than provide a ready set of answers to the impact of such policies and how best to combat equality and exclusion, the purpose has been to present some of the possible outcomes of social policy experiments tested in the Latin American context, and thus to contribute to debates on the usefulness and benefits, as well as problems, associated with the different approaches. The chapters presented here have in common that they provide a balanced account and a healthy set of criticisms of the reform efforts to date. They provide an in-depth analysis of the advantages and disadvantages associated with decentralization, as they stress that bureaucratic and political decentralization, if accompanied by a strong participatory component, might render social policies more viable but also more volatile. They recognize that decentralization might not necessarily lead to a real deconcentration of power. Furthermore, they caution against financial decentralization, as they reveal that the education and health structures in the more disadvantaged communities will suffer from such policies. However, in the Chilean case, the operation of a municipal redistribution fund may have eased the impact of such reform.

The chapters are in general sceptical about liberalization without institutional coordination. The discussions of labour training and labour market restructuring show that for liberalization to benefit all sectors of the population, coordination and social policy supports structures need to be in place. The health insurance and the school voucher debates highlight how free choice on the part of suppliers and consumers, without accompanying adjustment mechanisms, may have polarizing effects. However, particularly in the Colombian, but also in the Argentinian case, the negative impact on the most disadvantaged part of the population was reduced by ensuring wider participation in the reform process. With regard to targeting, the chapters recognize that such measures may be effective in bringing the excluded into the mainstream, but caution that excessive emphasis on formulation of interest on the part of the beneficiaries, as well as their personal potential for success, may be counter-productive. An alternative would be to predetermine credentials for inclusion, as in the case of PROGRESA.

The emphasis on participation and the more holistic approach to development projection are highlighted as, on the whole, positive features of several of the programmes discussed in this volume. Participation, as Angell and

Parendekar point out, may ensure a more appropriate profile of the projects and may increase sense of ownership and therefore effectiveness of the programmes. However, when the motive for participation is to attract free labour, the measure may be reduced to a purely cost-effective one. An added danger associated with excessive emphasis on participation is the possible exclusion of individuals and communities which are lacking in such initiatives.

The programmes discussed by both Badia and Latapí go beyond addressing a specific area of need in the population they aim to assist. As noted by Badia, such cross-sectoral approaches to development aid may prove complex to administer where agencies have had little experience with cooperation and coordination in the past. Even so, if successful, holistic programmes may prove to be a superior alternative and a strategy worth strengthening in the pursuit of including the excluded and rendering the mainstream accessible for a greater proportion of the population.

Notes

1. Here defined as the right to participate in an appropriate standard of living. Citizenship involves some redistribution of resources, because rights are shared equally by all.
2. In this case 'efficiency' was measured in terms of the following four outcomes: secondary school test results, total years of education, hourly earnings and chances of obtaining non-manual employment.
3. West (1996), OECD (1994), Pring (1986).
4. Larrañaga (1995).

Bibliography

de Kadt, E., *Poverty – Focused Policies: The Experience of Chile*, Institute of Development Studies, Sussex, 1993.

Graham, C., 'From emergency employment to social investment: changing approaches to poverty alleviation in Chile', in *The Legacy of Dictatorship, Political, Economic and Social Changes in Pinochet's Chile* (eds) A. Angell and B. Pollack (Institute of Latin American Studies, University of Liverpool, Liverpool 1993).

Larrañaga, O., 'Decentralización y Equidad: El Caso de los Servicios Sociales en Chile', *Documento de Investigación* (ILADES, Georgetown University, 1–84, 1995).

Marcel, M. and Solimano, A. 'The distribution of income and economic adjustment', in *The Chilean Economy; Policy Lessons and Challenges* (eds) B. Bosworth, P. Dornbusch, R. Labán (Washington, D.C.: Brookings Institution, 1994).

OECD, *School: a Matter of Choice* (Paris: Centre for Educational Research and Innovation, OECD, 1994).

Pring, R., 'Privatization of Education' *Education and Social Class* (ed.) R. Rogers (Falmer Press, London, 1986).

Vivian, J., 'How safe are "social safety nets"?, Adjustment and restructuring in developing countries', *European Journal of Development* 7(1), 1–25, 1995.

West, E., 'Education voucher in practice and principle: a world survey', *Human Capital Development Working Papers* (World Bank, HCDWP 64, 1996).

Index

ad hoc
  contracts (see also presentialist contracts, contracts) 17
  transactions 22
administration
  administrative unity 12
  costs 20
aid 83–93
Amsden, Alice 70
Angell, Alan 38, 263
apprenticeship 61, 63
Argentina 11–12, 183–9, 191, 194–7, 261, 270, 271
ASIMET 61–2
asset specificity
  and skill investments 53
  associational practice 54
  and skills investment 54
Aylwin, Patricio 71, 78, 147, 155

basic minimum income 5, 23–5, 29
  and administrative efficiency 23, 25
  and choice 35
  and freedoms 29
  and presentialist contracts 29
  and procedural priorities of rights 25
  unconditionality 23, 25, 29, 35
Bolivia 12, 31, 242–60, 261, 269
BOLIVIDA 248
BONOSOL 246–8
Bosworth, Barry 38
bounded rationality 19
Bowles, Samuel 36
Brazil 11
Britain 25

capabilities 6
  and conversion 6
  and equity 5
  see also Sen, A.
capitalization/pension reforms 245–8
Cardoso, F. 12
child care 79, 84, 85, 89, 92, 103, 104, 107, 116, 262, 263
Chile 4, 11–12, 28–30, 263–9, 271

choice
  individual choice and welfare 9
  and individual freedom 13
  and participation 19, 33
  political 32
Colombia 28, 183–6, 188, 191–2, 194–7, 261, 266, 270, 271
Communist Party, Chile 62
community 169, 170, 175, 177, 178, 263, 269
  associations 169, 174
  participation 4, 30
Concertación 77, 157, 166
contracts 3, 103, 106
  ad hoc 17, 22
  contingency contract markets 19–20
  long-term and skills investments 17–18, 52–5, 62–70
  network 56, 70
  presentialist (see also presentialist contracts) 3, 7, 14, 17–18
corruption 10, 30
cost-containment 11
  and financial prudence 17
  and health reforms 192–4
cost effectiveness 13, 16–17
  cost efficiency and libertarianism 18
  and welfare production 20–1, 32
cost neutrality 17
Costa Rica 4
cream-skimming
  in health insurance 28, 193–4, 265
Cuba 4, 11, 30

decentralization 4, 13, 28–31, 77, 79, 84, 115, 160, 165, 170, 176
  and choice 28–9, 267
  and demand-based schemes 70–1
  of the economy 13, 55, 78
  of education; see also schooling and decentralization 3, 123
  financial 29, 264, 267, 270, 271
  of social programmes 86, 87–8, 92
  of state 9, 87, 124, 125, 126
  and training 47–9, 50, 70

273

decentred development governance
  7–9
decentred perspective 8–10
demand-based 124, 125, 261, 262
  schemes 27, 268
Denmark 25, 40, 56–7
development freedom 23–4, 53–4, 71
  see also freedom and individual
    freedom
development of human resources
  53–4
  and dynamic inefficiency 53
  investment in 52–4
  and long-term relationships
    63–8
development process
  and inclusiveness 8
dictatorship 67, 68, 70, 73, 78, 91, 97,
  115, 154, 155, 161
didactic material 171, 172

East Asia 10, 55, 72, 265
economic adjustment 110,
  123, 160
economic growth 78, 83, 97, 115, 147,
  150, 160, 238
economic inequalities 139
economic restructuring 105–6
education 78, 80, 84, 93, 123–42,
  165–78, 261
  and expenditure 150–2
  and finance 135–6, 140
  Friedman on 18
  inequalities 82, 123, 141, 149, 170,
    263, 265, 268
  performance 124, 126, 128–33,
    135, 136–7, 141, 151, 152,
    165, 171
  quality 149, 150, 151, 154, 158, 161,
    172, 174, 175, 177
  reform 3, 147–61, 165, 263, 270
  vouchers 3, 123, 124, 133, 134, 139,
    141, 261, 262, 264, 265, 271
  see also schooling
EDUCO 165–78
efficiency
  efficiency claims and welfare
    20–1
  systemic 20
  temporal dimensions 14–17, 20–1
El Salvador 30, 165–78, 261, 263, 264

employers 3
  employers' associations 58–9
entry inequalities 17, 20
EPS 183, 188, 191
equality of opportunity 14, 77, 79,
  83–4, 86, 220
equity 14, 150, 261
  equity and efficiency trade-off
    13–26, 34–5
  and health insurance 194–7
Esping-Andersen, G. 5, 37–8
Europe 12

fairness 18
  outcome fairness 18
  individualistic (impartial) concept of
    31
FCM 125–6, 132, 267, 271
female
  heads of households 80–2, 85, 263
  labour market participation 79, 80,
    81, 82, 84, 91, 92–3, 95, 101, 106,
    107, 109, 110–14, 262, 263
feminization of poverty 79, 83
Fichas CAS 31
financial prudence 17
flexibility
  of corporations (corporation-centred
    flexibility) 51
  and development of human
    resources 49
  of employers 47
FONASA 183, 185, 187, 195
foreman 62
formalization
  of work 64–5
freedom 2–3
  absolute economic freedom 25
  and choice 19, 28, 33, 265, 266
  of corporations 51
  developmental freedom 23–4,
    53–4, 71
  labour markets and distribution of 54
  and life-style 6
  of workers 51–2
  of workers' movement and choice
    51–2
  see also individual freedom
Friedman, M. 14, 18–19, 26
  and schooling 18, 25
  see also neo-liberalism

gender 93, 95
Germany 57
Gintis, H. 36
good governance 10
and market neutrality 10
governance 1
  democratic governance 10
  and financial prudence 17–18
  and health insurance 183–9
  of welfare 3
Graham, C. 37

Hayek, F. 21, 25–6, 40
Health 84, 85, 86, 89, 93, 103, 124, 261
health care 11, 78, 80, 261, 266, 267
  and Chile 11
  financing of 184–5
  private and public mix 185–6
health insurance 265, 267, 271
  and equity 194–6, 266
  and health risks 183
  and risk adjustment 184, 186–8, 194, 196, 197, 265, 266
  see also risk
health insurance markets 183–4
  and co-payments 189–90
  and income inequalities 184
  and labour market deregulation 190
  and regulation 189–94
  and solidarity contribution 188
  and sustainability of 189–95
health reform 3
  and decentralization 200–4, 207–9
  and participation 205–7
  political process of 190–2
housing 78, 84, 85, 86, 102, 124, 161
Huber, E.S. 37

ideology 11
idiosyncratic goods 70
IMF 8, 11
Import Substitution Industrialization (ISI) 11, 103, 110, 114
income distribution 5
income generation 83
income inequality 24, 34, 105, 109, 110, 114, 147, 190
  Chile 6–7

income variability 25
India (Kerala) 30
individual choice 4, 28
individual freedom
  and choice 19, 28
  and developmental freedom 23–4
  and individual autonomy 23–4
  and neo-liberalism 1
  and network efficiency 54–5
  and presentialist contracts 18
  and property right of labour 55
  and state intervention 25
inequality 5, 114, 115, 123, 127, 149, 165, 201, 208, 213, 238, 265
  and welfare 5
  of welfare outcome 20
infant mortality 6
informality 27
insecurity
  of labour 47
institutional coordination 53–4
investment
  cause of 54–5
  investment coordination 56–8
  in skills 54
ISAPRE 183, 185, 190–1, 193–6

Japan 30

Korea 30, 56–7

labour informality 4
labour management
  time-horizons of 63–5
labour market 9, 79, 101, 102, 105–6, 110, 262
  flexibility of 9
labour mobility 5, 25
  in Denmark 25
  see also turnover
labour rights
  neo-liberal framework 10
leasing out 13
Leftwich, A. 37
liberalism
  classical 13–14
libertarianism 2, 16–18
  and presentialist contracts 18
  and antecedent rights 18
  and cost efficiency 18

life-cycle 19
　life risks 19

mainstream
　and choice 28
　and cost effectiveness 18–19, 32
　and efficiency functions 6, 20
　and long-term outcome efficiency
　　20–1
　and precariousness, informality 27
　and redistribution 32
　in welfare 1–2, 20, 33
　and welfare policy 20, 35–6
　welfare service 16, 267
maquiladora 106, 107, 114
market deregulation 115
market enhancement 10, 261
market failure
　and training 57–8
market governance 1–2, 10, 13
market liberalization
market neutrality 1, 10, 14, 18–19, 26
　and Chile 11
　and political choice 10–11
　and process and outcome in welfare
　　21–2
　and welfare mainstreams 26
　and welfare production 7, 14–16
　and World Bank 10
marketization
　and ideology 11
　of welfare 1–2, 10–11
markets
　classical 11, 13
　as self-sustaining governance
　　constructs 7
Marshall, T.H.
　Marshallian balance 1–2, 9
Marx, K. 53
Maurice, M. 39
means-tests
　and health insurance 188
MECE 147, 149, 152–5, 157–60, 265
Menem, C. 12
Mexico 27, 29–31, 219–41, 261, 262,
　　267, 268
military regime 78, 125
Mill, J.S. 13–14, 37
Miller, D. 39
mobility
　individual 47

multilateral development thinking
　12
municipal school 125–6, 128–32, 137,
　　140, 141, 142, 152, 263, 264
municipality 78, 79, 96, 125, 127, 130,
　　132, 133, 135–8, 140, 148, 149,
　　157–9, 267

neoclassical
　economics 14, 19
　welfare model 16, 77
neo-liberal reform 3
　second-generation 8, 242
neo-liberal theory 18–19
　and process and outcome in welfare
　　21–2
neo-liberalism 3
　neo-liberal school 14
　and schooling 25
　see also Friedman
network efficiency 6, 18, 70
　and presentialist contracts
　　18–19
NGO 8, 78, 79, 125
Nozick, R. 18, 22–4, 26, 39
　and individuals versus groups 23
　on Rawls 22–3
　and outcome goals 21–2
　and systemic justifications for
　　redistribution 24
　and taxation and social cooperation
　　22

occupation 6
　and control over life trajectories 6
　Effective occupational chances and
　　redistribution 23
occupational life 17
　meaningful 17
　and redistribution 23
　and transitions 15–16
occupational rights 12
occupational stream 15–16
　and entry inequalities 17
Olson, M. 70
opportunism 19
OS 183, 187, 191, 194–6
OTE 57
OTIR 57
outcome fairness 14
　see also fairness

P900   147, 149, 151–4, 156–61, 256, 269
Pagano, U.   25
participation   4, 84, 125, 148, 152, 158, 160, 161, 165, 167, 173, 203, 265, 267–72
   from below   8
   and centralized management   33–4
   and choice   32
   and health reforms   205–7
   limits to and health reform   210–13
   popular participation reforms   248–50
   social and economic   13, 79, 90–2
   as stake-holding   32–3
   in territorial terms   71
Paz Estenssoro   12
peer group effect   135, 138, 140, 266
pension insurance   20
Pinochet, A.   78, 139, 147, 148, 155, 156, 158
PME   152, 155, 157
PMJH   77–96, 263, 268, 269
political elites   12
postmodernist development discourse   8, 10
poverty   27, 79–83
   two poor constituencies   27
   rural   221–2
poverty reduction   77, 93, 115
precariousness   27, 262
   and contracts   52
   and labour markets   51–2
   and mainstreams   27
   as risk, uncertainty   51
   and short-term contracts   63–4
   and turnover   52–4
   and training   52–4
presentialist contracts   3, 7, 14, 17–18, 29, 55
   definition   55
   and individual freedom   18, 29
   and libertarianism   18, 26
   and precariousness   52–5
primary goods   5
primary education   15, 126, 128–30, 140, 148, 158, 269
private subsidized schools   125, 128–32, 140–2, 152, 264
privatization   103, 115, 123, 125, 128, 140, 165, 222, 242, 245, 248, 258, 261, 264, 267

procedural priority
   and markets   11, 17–18
PROGRESA   27, 31, 34, 219–39, 266–71
   beneficiary selection   227–8
   and education   234–6
   and efficiency in delivery   220
   and health care   229
   and issues of employment   239
   and marginal communities   223
   and nutrition   233–4
   operation of   222–3
   see also targeting
PRONASOL   219–20, 115–263
property rights
   and individual freedoms   55
   of labour   54–5, 61
   liberal propriety notion of   55
provided (and purchased) services   5, 9, 31
public works programmes   13

qualification   62
   and training and occupation   62
quits   58

rationality
   bounded   19
Rawls, J.   5–6
reciprocity   19
regulation   10
repetition rates   148, 174
risk
   and gender   19
   and labour mobility   5
   and participation   33
   risk groups and welfare   28
   risk selection and health care   184–5, 187
   and social insurance   19–20, 33

safety nets   11, 115
Scandinavia   9, 25, 29
school decentralization   28
schooling   25, 28
   and efficiency and rights-based models; *see also* neo-liberalism, Friedman   25, 28
   and decentralization   28, 124–6, 130–2, 140, 141, 151, 153, 156–9, 168, 170, 173, 178, 263, 264

schooling – *continued*
  and freedom of choice 28, 133, 138, 140, 264–6
  and mainstream standards 28–9
  and selection 28, 132–5, 140, 265
  school choice 165–6
  see also education
Schultz, T. 70
secondary school 15, 123–42, 262
second-generation reforms 3, 242–5
security 29
  and freedom 52–4
  and flexibility 53
  and individual control over movement 29, 52
  in personal control over human resources 52–3
  of purchasing power *see* basic minimum income 5
Sen, A. 5–6
  capabilities 6
  capability equality 5
  and comparative importance of rights 25
SENCE 59–60
skills
  demand for in Chile 54
  and skills investments 52–4
  tradable 5
small and medium-sized firms 54
  and skill investments 54
Smith, A. 14
social contract 2, 5
  and welfare production 5, 9
social development
  holistic vision 4
social development programmes 6, 9, 101
  and employment 221
  and gender 77–96, 229–33
  and targeting 221
  see also targeting
social inequalities 96, 114
social insurance
  coverage 6–7
  crisis of 11–12
  markets 9
  price and quality 20
social justice
  multivariable theories of 24–5

social policy 2, 13, 16, 21, 27, 47–9, 60, 71, 77, 78, 84, 93, 94, 102, 105, 115, 116, 117, 124, 133, 160, 161, 220, 240, 261, 266, 268, 271
  co-ordination 87, 262
social security 102, 103, 110, 116, 124, 262
  privatization 12
  universal 12
social stratification 9
socio-economic background 89, 128, 131, 140, 175
SOFOFA 59
Solow, R. 19
stake-holding
  and citizenship 255–7
  political problems 252–4
  and social development programmes 243–5
Standing, G. 76
state
  and decentralization 9
  and development governance 7–10
state intervention 13, 25
  and individual liberty 25
structural adjustment 12
Sweden 25

Tamburi, G. 12
targeting 13, 20, 26–8, 158, 160, 261, 266, 268, 269, 271
  and *ad hoc* cost accountancy model 221, 227, 238
  and administration costs 26
  and centralization 26, 220
  geographical versus individuals 88–90, 115, 170, 221, 268
  and intermediaries 224
  and marginality and mainstreams 20–1, 26, 269, 271
  processes of beneficiary selection 88–90, 115, 170, 226, 228, 268
  and women 13, 77, 84–6, 224–6, 263
taxation 12, 25, 78, 149, 154, 267
  and social cooperation 22
  Nozick on 22
teachers 132, 138, 140, 147–9, 167–9, 172–5
temporal dimensions of efficiency 14–17, 33

Tendler, J. *38
textbooks 129, 137–8, 141, 152, 154, 160, 167, 265
see also didactic material
Titmuss, R. 36
trade liberalization 101, 106, 110
training 4, 31, 271
 and decentralization 47–9, 50
 and demand-based model 48, 268
 and tradable standards 47, 57–8
 training system 62
 youth training scheme 60–1
 turnover 65–7

unemployment
 Chile 6, 48, 55–6, 61–2, 79, 83
unemployment insurance 59–60
union–employer accords 61
unions
 age of 66–9
 local labour unions 64–70
 and participation in firms 62
United States 193
Uruguay 11–12
utilitarianism 13, 24
 cost-utilitarian arguments in welfare 18, 21
 and welfare outcome 18, 21, 23–4

voluntary labour 32, 34, 265–7, 272

wage minimum 5
'waste-basket' school 28, 133–40, 265, 266
welfare
 consumers 13, 17
 inter-dependency of different domains 5–7, 15–16
 universal 11
 welfare statistics 10
 welfare insurance 5
 welfare mainstreams 9
  and interaction effects 9
 welfare markets

 and competitive selection 28
welfare models
 decentralized 13
 holistic conception 5, 17
 neoclassical 15–16, 21
 residual 13, 17
 rights-based 6, 9, 20–1
 universal 9
welfare policy
 dual policy framework 17
 provided (and purchased) services 5, 9, 31
welfare production 2–3
welfare production 1–2, 14–18
 cyclical nature 1, 16
 and efficiency claims 20–1, 35
 equity and efficiency trade-off 13–29, 34–5
 interaction effects between process and outcome 14–15
 and libertarianism 18–26
 and measurement 2
 and positive and negative cycles 9, 29
 and process and outcome goals 21–2
 and public sphere 10
 spatial interaction effects 15–16
 systemic aspects 2, 18–19
 and temporal dimensions of efficiency 14–17, 33
 universal entitlements 10
 see also mainstream
welfare reform
 second-generation 3
welfare system
 atomized 9
 centralized 9
Williamson, O. 37, 70
women 77–96
women and poverty 79, 80
World Bank 8, 10–11, 152, 154, 155, 158, 160, 165, 167

YTS 61–2